Qt5 Python GUI Programming Cookbook

Building responsive and powerful cross-platform applications with PyQt

B.M. Harwani

BIRMINGHAM - MUMBAI

Qt5 Python GUI Programming Cookbook

Commissioning Editor: Richa Tripathi
Acquisition Editor: Alok Dhuri
Content Development Editor: Zeeyan Pinheiro
Technical Editor: Vibhuti Gawde
Copy Editor: Safis Editing
Project Coordinator: Vaidehi Sawant
Proofreader: Safis Editing
Indexer: Rekha Nair
Graphics: Jason Monteiro
Production Coordinator: Nilesh Mohite

First published: July 2018

Production reference: 1270718

Published by Packt Publishing Ltd.
Livery Place
35 Livery Street
Birmingham
B3 2PB, UK.

ISBN 978-1-78883-100-0

www.packtpub.com

I am thankful to my family—my small world: Anushka (my wife) and my two little darlings, Chirag and Naman, for allowing me to work on the book even during time that I was supposed to spend with them.

`mapt.io`

Mapt is an online digital library that gives you full access to over 5,000 books and videos, as well as industry leading tools to help you plan your personal development and advance your career. For more information, please visit our website.

Why subscribe?

- Spend less time learning and more time coding with practical eBooks and Videos from over 4,000 industry professionals

- Improve your learning with Skill Plans built especially for you

- Get a free eBook or video every month

- Mapt is fully searchable

- Copy and paste, print, and bookmark content

PacktPub.com

Did you know that Packt offers eBook versions of every book published, with PDF and ePub files available? You can upgrade to the eBook version at `www.PacktPub.com` and as a print book customer, you are entitled to a discount on the eBook copy. Get in touch with us at `service@packtpub.com` for more details.

At `www.PacktPub.com`, you can also read a collection of free technical articles, sign up for a range of free newsletters, and receive exclusive discounts and offers on Packt books and eBooks.

Contributors

About the author

B.M. Harwani is the founder and owner of Microchip Computer Education (MCE), based in Ajmer, India. He graduated with a BE in computer engineering from the University of Pune and also has a C level (masters diploma in computer technology) from DOEACC, Government of India. Having been involved in the teaching field for over 20 years, he has developed the art of explaining even the most complicated topics in a straightforward and easily understandable fashion. He is also a renowned speaker and the author of several books. To learn more, visit his blog, a site that helps programmers.

A big thank you to the entire editorial team at Packt, who worked tirelessly to produce this book. Really, I enjoyed working with each of you.

I should not forget to thank my dear students, who have been a good teacher for me as they make me understand the basic problems they face in a subject and enable me to directly hit those topics. The endless interesting queries from my students help me write books with a practical approach.

About the reviewers

Marcus Ottosson is a company director, software developer, and artist with a decade of experience in the film and visual effects industry. He has built countless user interfaces and tools with Python and Qt for projects such as *Marvel's Doctor Strange* and *Alfonso Cuaron's Gravity*. He has written several Python frameworks for use in the creation of film and games, such as Pyblish and Avalon, along with PyQt, a compatibility wrapper around all the available bindings of Qt for Python.

Sivan Grünberg has close to 20 years of multidisciplinary IT expertise and a razor-sharp eye for quality. A long-time open source devotee, his contributions can be found, literally, all over open source. He has been utilizing the Python ecosystem for R&D endeavors ever since it was pitched to him by The SABDFL and Ubuntu. Alongside Shir, a product, content, and operations expert, he runs Vitakka.co, providing infrastructure consulting and coding solutions in all-things digital.

> *My amazing family, Eric, Helena, Shir, Moshik, and the Debian/Ubuntu, Python, GNOME, and KDE communities—without you, these lines would have never been written.*

Packt is searching for authors like you

If you're interested in becoming an author for Packt, please visit `authors.packtpub.com` and apply today. We have worked with thousands of developers and tech professionals, just like you, to help them share their insight with the global tech community. You can make a general application, apply for a specific hot topic that we are recruiting an author for, or submit your own idea.

Table of Contents

Preface

PyQt is one of the best cross-platform interface toolkits currently available; it's stable, mature, and completely native. If you want control over all aspects of UI elements, PyQt is what you need. This book will guide you through every concept you need to create fully functional GUI applications using PyQT, with only a few lines of code.

As you expand your GUI using more widgets, you will cover networks, databases, and graphical libraries that greatly enhance its functionality. The book shows you how to use QT Designer to design user interfaces and implement and test dialogs, events, the clipboard, and drag and drop functionality to customize your GUI. You will learn a variety of topics, such as look and feel customization, GUI animation, graphics rendering, implementing Google Maps, and more. Lastly, the book takes you through how Qt5 can help you create cross-platform apps that are compatible with Android and iOS. You will be able to develop functional and appealing software using PyQt through interesting and fun recipes that will expand your knowledge of GUIs.

Who this book is for

This book is meant for intermediate to advanced programmers and developers who have some preliminary knowledge of Python programming. This book can be of great use for trainers, teachers, and software developers who wish to build a fully-featured GUI-based application in Python.

What this book covers

Chapter 1, *Creating a User Interface with Qt Components*, teaches readers to use certain basic widgets of Qt Designer and how to display a welcome message along with the username. You will also be learning how to choose one out of several options using radio buttons and choose more than one out of several options by making use of checkboxes.

Chapter 2, *Event Handling – Signals and Slots*, covers how to execute specific tasks on the occurrence of certain events on any widget, how to copy and paste text from one Line Edit widget to another, convert data types and make a small calculator, and use spin boxes, scrollbars, and sliders. You will also learn to perform multiple tasks using the List Widget.

Chapter 3, *Working with Date and Time*, focuses on learning how to display the system clock time using an LCD, show the date selected by the user from Calendar Widget, create a hotel reservation form, and display tabular data using Table widget.

Chapter 4, *Understanding OOP Concepts*, discusses object-oriented programming concepts such as how to use classes, single inheritance, multilevel inheritance in GUI applications, and multiple inheritance.

Chapter 5, *Understanding Dialogs*, explores the use of certain dialogs, where each dialog is meant for fetching a different kind of information. You will also learn to take input from the user using input dialog.

Chapter 6, *Understanding Layouts*, explains how to arrange widgets horizontally, vertically, and in different layouts by making use of Horizontal Layout, Vertical Layout, Grid Layout, and arranging widgets in two column layout using Form Layout.

Chapter 7, *Networking and Managing Large Documents*, demonstrates how to make a small browser, establish a connection between client and server, create a dockable and floatable sign in form, and manage more than one document using MDI. Also, you will be learn how to display information in sections using the Tab widget. You will learn how to create a custom menu bar that invokes different graphics tools when a specific menu item is chosen.

Chapter 8, *Doing Asynchronous Programming in Python*, looks at the concept of asynchronous operations using threads. To see the impact of asynchronous operations on GUIs, you will be making use of a progress bar, that is, the progress bars will be updated through threads asynchronously.

Chapter 9, *Database Handling*, outlines how to manage a SQLite database to keep information for future use. Using the knowledge gained, you will learn to make a signin form that checks whether a user's email address and password are correct or not.

Chapter 10, *Using Graphics*, explains how to display certain graphics in the application. You will also learn how to create a toolbar of your own that contains certain tools that can be used to draw different graphics.

Chapter 11, *Implementing Animation*, features how to display a 2D graphical image, make a ball move down on the click of a button, make a bouncing ball, and make a ball animate as per the specified curve.

Chapter 12, *Using Google Maps*, showcases how to use the Google API to display location and other information. You will learn to derive the distance between two locations and display location on Google Maps on the basis of longitude and latitude values that are entered.

Chapter 13, *Running Python Scripts on Android and iOS devices*, takes you through how to use QPython to run Python scripts on Android devices. You will learn how to package Kivy Python scripts on Android and iOS devices. You will be making several applications for mobile devices, such as prompting for the user's name and displaying a welcome message, understanding different buttons in a Dialog box, performing single and multiple selections from a list, selecting date using a Date Picker dialog, capturing images using a camera, making Android devices speak text, creating cross-platform Python scripts using Kivy, packaging Python scripts into the Android APK using Buildozer, and packaging Python scripts for iOS.

To get the most out of this book

You need to have some preliminary knowledge of Python programming. You need to install Python and PyQt5. The steps to install Python and PyQt are explained in the Appendix. To run Python script on Android devices, you need to install QPython on your Android device. To package Python scripts into Android's APK using the Kivy library, you need to install Kivy, a Virtual Box, and Buildozer packager. Similarly, to run Python scripts on iOS devices, you need a macOS machine and some library tools, including Cython. The steps to install these software are explained in Chapter 13, *Running Python Scripts on Android and iOS*.

Download the example code files

You can download the example code files for this book from your account at www.packtpub.com. If you purchased this book elsewhere, you can visit www.packtpub.com/support and register to have the files emailed directly to you.

You can download the code files by following these steps:

1. Log in or register at www.packtpub.com.
2. Select the **SUPPORT** tab.
3. Click on **Code Downloads & Errata**.
4. Enter the name of the book in the **Search** box and follow the onscreen instructions.

Once the file is downloaded, please make sure that you unzip or extract the folder using the latest version of:

- WinRAR/7-Zip for Windows
- Zipeg/iZip/UnRarX for Mac
- 7-Zip/PeaZip for Linux

The code bundle for the book is also hosted on GitHub at https://github.com/ PacktPublishing/Qt5-Python-GUI-Programming-Cookbook. We also have other code bundles from our rich catalog of books and videos available at https://github.com/ PacktPublishing/. Check them out!

Download the color images

We also provide a PDF file that has color images of the screenshots/diagrams used in this book. You can download it here: https://www.packtpub.com/sites/default/files/ downloads/Qt5PythonGUIProgrammingCookbook_ColorImages.pdf.

Conventions used

There are a number of text conventions used throughout this book.

CodeInText: Indicates code words in text, database table names, folder names, filenames, file extensions, pathnames, dummy URLs, user input, and Twitter handles. Here is an example: "This template creates a form whose superclass is QWidget rather than QDialog."

A block of code is set as follows:

```
import sys
from PyQt5.QtWidgets import QDialog, QApplication
from demoSignalSlot1 import *
class MyForm(QDialog):
    def __init__(self):
        super().__init__()
        self.ui = Ui_Dialog()
        self.ui.setupUi(self)
        self.show()
if __name__=="__main__":
    app = QApplication(sys.argv)
    w = MyForm()
    w.show()
    sys.exit(app.exec_())
```

When we wish to draw your attention to a particular part of a code block, the relevant lines or items are set in bold:

```
[default]
exten => s,1,Dial(Zap/1|30)
exten => s,2,Voicemail(u100)
exten => s,102,Voicemail(b100)
exten => i,1,Voicemail(s0)
```

Any command-line input or output is written as follows:

```
C:\Pythonbook\PyQt5>pyuic5 demoLineEdit.ui -o demoLineEdit.py
```

Bold: Indicates a new term, an important word, or words that you see onscreen. For example, words in menus or dialog boxes appear in the text like this. Here is an example: "The amount the slider handle moves can be specified via the **pageStep** property."

Warnings or important notes appear like this.

Tips and tricks appear like this.

Sections

In this book, you will find several headings that appear frequently (*Getting ready*, *How to do it...*, *How it works...*, *There's more...*, and *See also*).

To give clear instructions on how to complete a recipe, use these sections as follows:

Getting ready

This section tells you what to expect in the recipe and describes how to set up any software or any preliminary settings required for the recipe.

How to do it...

This section contains the steps required to follow the recipe.

How it works...

This section usually consists of a detailed explanation of what happened in the previous section.

There's more...

This section consists of additional information about the recipe in order to make you moreknowledgeable about the recipe.

See also

This section provides helpful links to other useful information for the recipe.

Get in touch

Feedback from our readers is always welcome.

General feedback: Email `feedback@packtpub.com` and mention the book title in the subject of your message. If you have questions about any aspect of this book, please email us at `questions@packtpub.com`.

Errata: Although we have taken every care to ensure the accuracy of our content, mistakes do happen. If you have found a mistake in this book, we would be grateful if you would report this to us. Please visit `www.packtpub.com/submit-errata`, selecting your book, clicking on the Errata Submission Form link, and entering the details.

Piracy: If you come across any illegal copies of our works in any form on the internet, we would be grateful if you would provide us with the location address or website name. Please contact us at `copyright@packtpub.com` with a link to the material.

If you are interested in becoming an author: If there is a topic that you have expertise in and you are interested in either writing or contributing to a book, please visit `authors.packtpub.com`.

Reviews

Please leave a review. Once you have read and used this book, why not leave a review on the site that you purchased it from? Potential readers can then see and use your unbiased opinion to make purchase decisions, we at Packt can understand what you think about our products, and our authors can see your feedback on their book. Thank you!

For more information about Packt, please visit `packtpub.com`.

Creating a User Interface with Qt Components

1

In this chapter, we will learn to use the following widgets:

- Displaying a welcome message
- Using the Radio Button widget
- Grouping radio buttons
- Displaying options in the form of checkboxes
- Displaying two groups of checkboxes

Introduction

We will be learning to create GUI applications using the Qt toolkit. The Qt toolkit, known simply as Qt, is a cross-platform application and UI framework developed by **Trolltech**, which is used for developing GUI applications. It runs on several platforms, including Windows, macOS X, Linux, and other UNIX platforms. It is also referred to as a widget toolkit because it provides widgets such as buttons, labels, textboxes, push buttons, and list boxes, which are required for designing a GUI. It includes a cross-platform collection of classes, integrated development tools, and a cross-platform IDE. To create real-time applications, we will be making use of Python bindings for the Qt toolkit called, **PyQt5**.

PyQt

PyQt is a set of Python bindings for the cross-platform application framework that combines all the advantages of Qt and Python. With PyQt, you can include Qt libraries in Python code, enabling you to write GUI applications in Python. In other words, PyQt allows you to access all the facilities provided by Qt through Python code. Since PyQt depends on the Qt libraries to run, when you install PyQt, the required version of Qt is also installed automatically on your machine.

A GUI application may consist of a main window with several dialogs or just a single dialog. A small GUI application usually consists of at least one dialog. A dialog application contains buttons. It doesn't contain a menu bar, toolbar, status bar, or central widget, whereas a main window application normally has all of those.

Dialogs are of the following two types:

- **Modal**: This dialog is one that blocks the user from interacting with other parts of the application. The dialog is the only part of the application that the user can interact with. Until the dialog is closed, no other part of the application can be accessed.
- **Modeless**: This dialog is the opposite of a modal dialog. When a modeless dialog is active, the user is free to interact with the dialog and with the rest of the application.

Ways of creating GUI applications

There are the following two ways to write a GUI application:

- From scratch, using a simple text editor
- With Qt Designer, a visual design tool with which you can create a user interface quickly using drag and drop

You will be using Qt Designer to develop GUI applications in PyQt, as it is a quick and easy way to design user interfaces without writing a single line of code. So, launch Qt Designer by double-clicking on its icon on desktop.

On opening, Qt Designer asks you to select a template for your new application, as shown in the following screenshot:

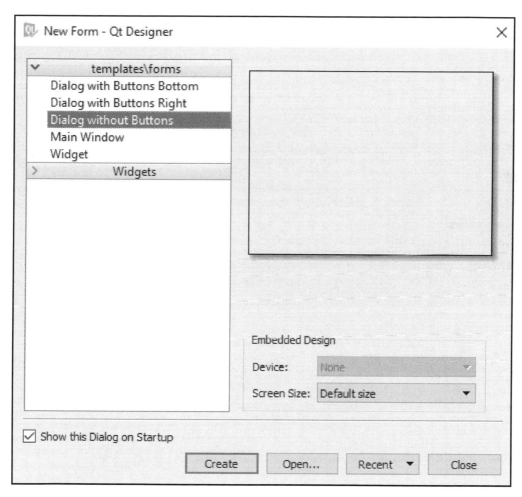

Qt Designer provides a number of templates that are suitable for different kinds of applications. You can choose any of these templates and then click the **Create** button.

Qt Designer provides the following predefined templates for a new application:

- **Dialog with Buttons Bottom**: This template creates a form with the **OK** and **Cancel** buttons in the bottom-right corner.
- **Dialog with Buttons Right**: This template creates a form with the **OK** and **Cancel** buttons in the top-right corner.

- **Dialog without Buttons**: This template creates an empty form on which you can place widgets. The superclass for dialogs is QDialog.
- **Main Window**: This template provides a main application window with a menu bar and a toolbar that can be removed if not required.
- **Widget**: This template creates a form whose superclass is QWidget rather than QDialog.

Every GUI application has a top-level widget and the rest of the widgets are called its children. The top-level widget can be QDialog, QWidget, or QMainWindow, depending on the template you require. If you want to create an application based on the dialog template, then the top-level widget or the first class that you inherit will be QDialog. Similarly, to create an application based on the **Main Window** template, the top-level widget will be QMainWindow, and to create the application based on the **Widget** template, you need to inherit the QWidget class. As mentioned previously, the rest of the widgets that are used for the user interface are called child widgets of the classes.

Qt Designer displays a menu bar and toolbar at the top. It shows a **Widget** box on the left that contains a variety of widgets used to develop applications, grouped in sections. All you have to do is drag and drop the widgets you want from the form. You can arrange widgets in layouts, set their appearance, provide initial attributes, and connect their signals to slots.

Displaying a welcome message

In this recipe, the user will be prompted to enter his/her name followed by clicking a push button. On clicking the button, a welcome message will appear, "Hello," followed by the name entered by the user. For this recipe, we need to make use of three widgets, **Label**, **Line Edit**, and **Push Button**. Let's understand these widgets one by one.

Understanding the Label widget

The **Label** widget is an instance of the QLabel class and is used for displaying messages and images. Because the **Label** widgets simply display results of computations and don't take any input, they are simply used for supplying information on the screen.

Methods

The following are the methods provided by the QLabel class:

- setText(): This method assigns text to the **Label** widget
- setPixmap(): This method assigns pixmap, an instance of the QPixmap class, to the **Label** widget
- setNum(): This method assigns an integer or double value to the **Label** widget
- clear(): This method clears text from the **Label** widget

The default text of QLabel is **TextLabel**. That is, when you add a QLabel class to a form by dragging a **Label** widget and dropping it on the form, it will display **TextLabel**. Besides using setText(), you can also assign text to a selected QLabel object by setting its **text** property in the **Property Editor** window.

Understanding the Line Edit widget

The **Line Edit** widget is that is popularly used for entering single-line data. The **Line Edit** widget is an instance of the QLineEdit class, and you can not only enter, but also edit the data too. Besides entering data, you can undo, redo, cut, and paste data in the **Line Edit** widget.

Methods

The following are the methods provided by the QLineEdit class:

- setEchoMode(): It sets the echo mode of the **Line Edit** widget. That is, it determines how the contents of the **Line Edit** widget are to be displayed. The available options are as follows:
  - Normal: This is the default mode and it displays characters the way they are entered
  - NoEcho: It switches off the **Line Edit** echo, that is, it doesn't display anything
  - Password: This option is used for password fields, no text will be displayed; instead, asterisks appear for the text entered by the user
  - PasswordEchoOnEdit: It displays the actual text while editing the password fields, otherwise it will display the asterisks for the text

- maxLength(): This method is used to specify the maximum length of text that can be entered in the **Line Edit** widget.
- setText(): This method is used for assigning text to the **Line Edit** widget.
- text(): This method accesses the text entered in the **Line Edit** widget.
- clear(): This method clears or deletes the complete content of the **Line Edit** widget.
- setReadOnly(): When the Boolean value true is passed to this method, it will make the **Line Edit** widget read-only, that is, non-editable. The user cannot make any changes to the contents displayed through the **Line Edit** widget, but can only copy.
- isReadOnly(): This method returns the Boolean value true if the **Line Edit** widget is in read-only mode, otherwise it returns false.
- setEnabled(): By default, the **Line Edit** widget is enabled, that is, the user can make changes to it. But if the Boolean value false is passed to this method, it will disable the **Line Edit** widget so the user cannot edit its content, but can only assign text via the setText() method.
- setFocus(): This method positions the cursor on the specified **Line Edit** widget.

Understanding the Push Button widget

To display a push button in an application, you need to create an instance of the QPushButton class. When assigning text to buttons, you can create shortcut keys by preceding any character in the text with an ampersand. For example, if the text assigned to a push button is Click Me, the character C will be underlined to indicate that it is a shortcut key, and the user can select the button by pressing *Alt + C*. The button emits the **clicked()** signal if it is activated. Besides text, an icon can also be displayed in the push button. The methods for displaying text and an icon in a push button are as follows:

- setText(): This method is used to assign text to the push button
- setIcon(): This method is used to assign an icon to the push button

How to do it...

Let's create a new application based on the **Dialog without Buttons** template. As said earlier, this application will prompt the user to enter a name and, on clicking the push button after entering a name, the application with display a hello message along with the entered name. Here are the steps to create this application:

1. Drag a **Label** widget from the **Display Widgets** category and drop it on the form. Set its **text** property to `Enter your name`. Set the **objectName** property of the **Label** widget to `labelResponse`.

2. Drag one more **Label** widget from the **Display Widgets** category and drop it on the form. Do not change the **text** property of this **Label** widget and leave its **text** property to its default value, **TextLabel**. This is because the **text** property of this **Label** widget will be set through code, that is, it will be used to display the hello message to the user.

3. Drag one **Line Edit** from the **Input Widgets** category and drop it on the form. Set its **objectName** property to `lineEditName`.

4. Drag one **Push Button** widget from the **Buttons** category and drop it onto the form. Set its **text** property to `Click`. You can change the **text** property of the **Push Button** widget through any of three ways: by double-clicking the **Push Button** widget and overwriting the default text, by right-clicking the **Push Button** widget and selecting the **Change text...** option from the context menu that pops up, or by selecting the **text** property from the **Property Editor** window and overwriting the default text.

5. Set the **objectName** property of the **Push Button** widget to `ButtonClickMe`.

6. Save the application with the name `demoLineEdit.ui`. Now the form will appear, as shown in the following screenshot:

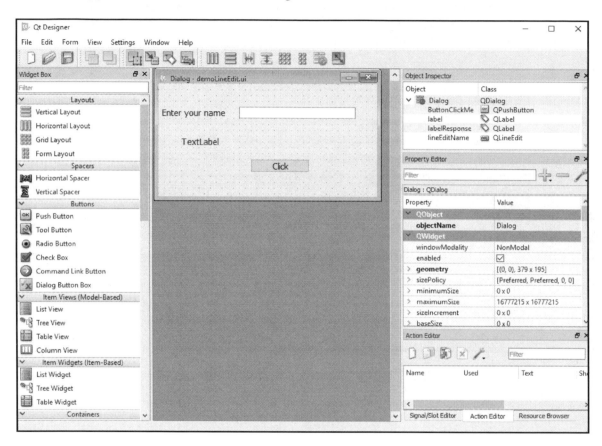

The user interface that you create with Qt Designer is stored in a `.ui` file that includes all the form's information: its widgets, layout, and so on. The `.ui` file is an XML file, and you need to convert it to Python code. That way, you can maintain a clear separation between the visual interface and the behavior implemented in code.

7. To use the `.ui` file, you first need to convert it into a Python script. The command utility that you will use for converting a `.ui` file into a Python script is `pyuic5`. In Windows, the `pyuic5` utility is bundled with PyQt. To do the conversion, you need to open a Command Prompt window and navigate to the folder where the file is saved and issue the following command:

```
C:\Pythonbook\PyQt5>pyuic5 demoLineEdit.ui -o demoLineEdit.py
```

Let's assume that we saved the form at this location: `C:\Pythonbook\PyQt5>`. The preceding command shows the conversion of the `demoLineEdit.ui` file into a Python script, `demoLineEdit.py`.

The Python code generated by this method should not be modified manually, as any changes will be overwritten the next time you run the `pyuic5` command.

The code of the generated Python script file, `demoLineEdit.py`, can be seen in the source code bundle of this book.

8. Treat the code in the `demoLineEdit.py` file as a header file, and import it to the file from which you will invoke its user interface design.

The header file is a term referred to those files which are imported into the current file. The command to import such files is usually written at the top in the script, hence named as header files.

9. Let's create another Python file with the name `callLineEdit.py` and import the `demoLineEdit.py` code into it as follows:

```python
import sys
from PyQt5.QtWidgets import QDialog, QApplication
from demoLineEdit import *
class MyForm(QDialog):
    def __init__(self):
        super().__init__()
        self.ui = Ui_Dialog()
        self.ui.setupUi(self)
        self.ui.ButtonClickMe.clicked.connect(self.dispmessage)
        self.show()
    def dispmessage(self):
        self.ui.labelResponse.setText("Hello "
        +self.ui.lineEditName.text())
if __name__=="__main__":
```

```
app = QApplication(sys.argv)
w = MyForm()
w.show()
sys.exit(app.exec_())
```

How it works...

The `demoLineEdit.py` file is very easy to understand. A class with the name of the top-level object is created, with `Ui_` prepended. Since the top-level object used in our application is `Dialog`, the `Ui_Dialog` class is created and stores the interface elements of our widget. That class has two methods, `setupUi()` and `retranslateUi()`. The `setupUi()` method sets up the widgets; it creates the widgets that you use while defining the user interface in Qt Designer. The method creates the widgets one by one and also sets their properties. The `setupUi()` method takes a single argument, which is the top-level widget in which the user interface (child widgets) is created. In our application, it is an instance of `QDialog`. The `retranslateUi()` method translates the interface.

Let's understand what `callLineEdit.py` does statement-wise:

1. It imports the necessary modules. `QWidget` is the base class of all user interface objects in PyQt5.
2. It creates a new `MyForm` class that inherits from the base class, `QDialog`.
3. It provides the default constructor for `QDialog`. The default constructor has no parent, and a widget with no parent is known as a window.
4. Event handling in PyQt5 uses signals and slots. A signal is an event, and a slot is a method that is executed on the occurrence of a signal. For example, when you click a push button, a `clicked()` event, also known as a signal, occurs. The `connect()` method connects signals with slots. In this case, the slot is a method: `dispmessage()`. That is, when the user clicks the push button, the `dispmessage()` method will be invoked. `clicked()` is an event here and an event handling loop waits for an event to occur and then dispatches it to perform some task. The event handling loop continues to work until either the `exit()` method is called or the main widget is destroyed.
5. It creates an application object with the name app through the `QApplication()` method. Every PyQt5 application must create `sys.argv` application object which contains a list of arguments from the command line, and it is passed to the method while creating the application object. The `sys.argv` parameter helps in passing and controlling the startup attributes of a script.

6. An instance of the `MyForm` class is created with the name `w`.
7. The `show()` method will display the widget on the screen.
8. The `dispmessage()` method performs event handling for the push button. It displays the **Hello** text, along with the name entered in the **Line Edit** widget.
9. The `sys.exit()` method ensures a clean exit, releasing memory resources.

 The `exec_()` method has an underscore because `exec` is a Python keyword.

On executing the preceding program, you get a window with the **Line Edit** and **Push Button** widgets, as shown in the following screenshot. When the push button is selected, the `displmessage()` method will be executed, displaying the **Hello** message along with the user's name that is entered in the **Line Edit** widget:

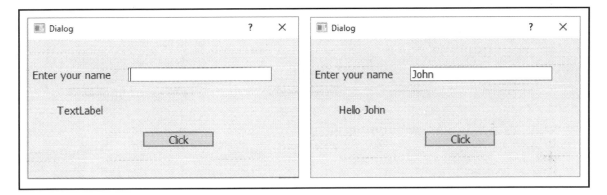

Using the Radio Button widget

This recipe displays certain flight types via **Radio Button** and when the user selects the radio button, the price associated with that flight will be displayed. We need to first understand the workings of **Radio Button**.

Understanding Radio Button

The **Radio Button** widgets are very popular when you want the user to select only one option out of the available options. Such options are known as mutually exclusive options. When the user selects an option, the previously selected option is automatically deselected. The **Radio Button** widgets are instances of the QRadioButton class. Every radio button has an associated text label. The radio button can be either in selected (checked) or unselected (unchecked) states. If you want two or more sets of radio buttons, where each set allows the exclusive selection of a radio button, put them into different button groups (instances of QButtonGroup). The methods provided by QRadioButton are shown next.

Methods

The QRadioButton class provides the following methods:

- isChecked(): This method returns the Boolean value true if the button is in the selected state.
- setIcon(): This method displays an icon with the radio button.
- setText(): This method assigns the text to the radio button. If you want to specify a shortcut key for the radio button, precede the preferred character in the text with an ampersand (&). The shortcut character will be underlined.
- setChecked(): To make any radio button appear selected by default, pass the Boolean value true to this method.

Signal description

Signals emitted by QRadioButton are as follows:

- **toggled()**: This signal is emitted whenever the button changes its state from checked to unchecked or vice versa
- **clicked()**: This signal is emitted when a button is activated (that is, pressed and released) or when its shortcut key is pressed
- **stateChanged()**: This signal is emitted when a radio button changes its state from checked to unchecked or vice versa

To understand the concept of radio buttons, let's create an application that asks the user to select the flight type and displays three options, **First Class**, **Business Class**, and **Economy Class**, in the form of radio buttons. On selecting an option through the radio button, the price for that flight will be displayed.

How to do it...

Let's create a new application based on the **Dialog without Buttons** template. This application will display different flight types along with their respective prices. When a user selects a flight type, its price will be displayed on the screen:

1. Drag and drop two **Label** widgets and three **Radio Button** widgets onto the form.

2. Set the **text** property of the first **Label** widget to `Choose the flight type` and delete the **text** property of the second **Label** widget. The **text** property of the second **Label** widget will be set through code; it will be used to display the price of the selected flight type.

3. Set the **text** property of the three **Radio Button** widgets to `First Class $150`, `Business Class $125`, and `Economy Class $100`.

4. Set the **objectName** property of the second **Label** widget to `labelFare`. The default object names of the three radio buttons are `radioButton`, `radioButton_2`, and `radioButton_3`. Change the **objectName** property of these three radio buttons to `radioButtonFirstClass`, `radioButtonBusinessClass`, and `radioButtonEconomyClass`.

5. Save the application with name `demoRadioButton1.ui`.

   Take a look at the following screenshot:

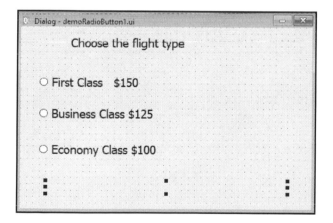

   The `demoRadioButton1.ui` application is an XML file and needs to be converted into Python code through the `pyuic5` command utility. The generated Python code, `demoRadioButton1.py`, can be seen in the source code bundle of this book.

6. Import the `demoRadioButton1.py` file as a header file in the Python script that you are going to create next to invoke the user interface design.

7. In the Python script, write the code to display the flight type on the basis of the radio button selected by the user. Name the source file `callRadioButton1.py`; its code is shown here:

```python
import sys
from PyQt5.QtWidgets import QDialog, QApplication
from demoRadioButton1 import *
class MyForm(QDialog):
    def __init__(self):
        super().__init__()
        self.ui = Ui_Dialog()
        self.ui.setupUi(self)
        self.ui.radioButtonFirstClass.toggled.connect(self.
        dispFare)
        self.ui.radioButtonBusinessClass.toggled.connect(self.
        dispFare)
        self.ui.radioButtonEconomyClass.toggled.connect(self.
        dispFare)
        self.show()
    def dispFare(self):
        fare=0
        if self.ui.radioButtonFirstClass.isChecked()==True:
            fare=150
        if self.ui.radioButtonBusinessClass.isChecked()==True:
            fare=125
        if self.ui.radioButtonEconomyClass.isChecked()==True:
            fare=100
        self.ui.labelFare.setText("Air Fare is "+str(fare))
if __name__=="__main__":
    app = QApplication(sys.argv)
    w = MyForm()
    w.show()
    sys.exit(app.exec_())
```

How it works...

The **toggled()** event of **Radio Button** is connected to the `dispFare()` function, which will display the price of the selected flight type. In the `dispFare()` function, you check the state of the radio buttons. Hence, if `radioButtonFirstClass` is selected, the value 50 is assigned to the fare variable. Similarly, if `radioButtonBusinessClass` is selected, the value 125 is assigned to the `fare` variable. Similarly, the value 100 is assigned to the `fare` variable when `radioButtonEconomyClass` is selected. Finally, the value in the `fare` variable is displayed via `labelFare`.

On executing the previous program, you get a dialog that displays three flight types and prompts the user to select the one that he/she wants to use for travel. On selecting a flight type, the price of the selected flight type is displayed, as shown in the following screenshot:

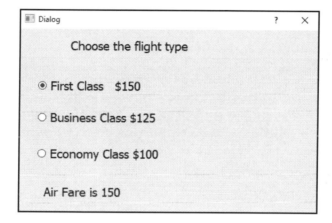

Grouping radio buttons

In this application, we will learn to create two groups of radio buttons. The user can select radio buttons from either group and accordingly the result or text will appear on the screen.

Getting ready

We will display a dialog that displays shirts of different sizes and different payment methods. On selecting a shirt size and a payment method, the selected shirt size and payment method will be displayed on the screen. We will create two groups of radio buttons, one of the shirt sizes and other payment methods. The shirt size group displays four radio buttons showing four different types of the size such as **M, L, XL,** and **XXL,** where **M** stands for medium size, **L** stands for large size, and so on. The payment method group displays three radio buttons, **Debit/Credit Card, NetBanking,** and **Cash On Delivery**. The user can select any radio button from either of the groups. When the user selects any of the shirt sizes or payment methods, the selected shirt size and payment method will be displayed.

How to do it...

Let's recreate the preceding application step by step:

1. Create a new application based on the **Dialog without Buttons** template.
2. Drag and drop three **Label** widgets and seven **Radio Button** widgets. Out of these seven radio buttons, we will arrange four radio buttons in one vertical layout and the other three radio buttons in the second vertical layout. The two layouts will help in grouping these radio buttons. Radio buttons being mutually exclusive will allow only one radio button to be selected from a layout or group.
3. Set the **text** property of the first two **Label** widgets to `Choose your Shirt Size` and `Choose your payment method` respectively.
4. Delete the **text** property of the third **Label** widget because we will display the selected shirt size and payment method through the code.
5. In the **Property Editor** window, increase the font size of all the widgets to increase their visibility in the application.
6. Set the **text** property of the first four radio buttons to `M, L, XL,` and `XXL`. Arrange these four radio buttons into one vertical layout.
7. Set the **text** property of the next three radio buttons to `Debit/Credit Card,` `NetBanking,` and `Cash On Delivery`. Arrange these three radio buttons into a second vertical layout. Remember, these vertical layouts help by grouping these radio buttons.
8. Change the object names of the first four radio buttons to `radioButtonMedium,` `radioButtonLarge, radioButtonXL,` and `radioButtonXXL`.

9. Set the **objectName** property of the first `VBoxLayout` layout to `verticalLayout`. The `VBoxLayout` layout will be used for aligning radio buttons vertically.

10. Change the object names of next three radio buttons to `radioButtonDebitCard`, `radioButtonNetBanking`, and `radioButtonCashOnDelivery`.

11. Set the **objectName** property of the second `QVBoxLayout` object to `verticalLayout_2`.

12. Set the **objectName** property of the third **Label** widget to `labelSelected`. It is through this **Label** widget that the selected shirt size and payment method will be displayed.

13. Save the application with the name `demoRadioButton2.ui`.

14. Now, the form will appear, as shown in the following screenshot:

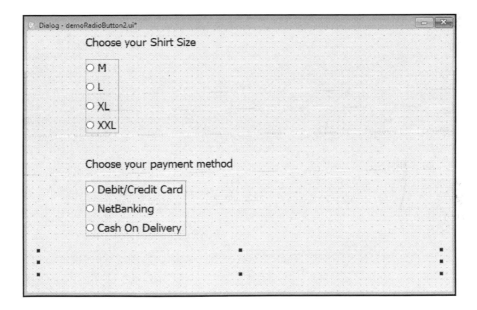

The `.ui` (XML) file is then converted into Python code through the `pyuic5` command utility. You can find the Python code, `demoRadioButton2.py`, in the source code bundle for this book.

15. Import the `demoRadioButton2.py` file, as a header file in our program to invoke the user interface design and to write code to display the selected shirt size and payment method through a **Label** widget when the user selects or unselects any of the radio buttons.

16. Let's name the program `callRadioButton2.pyw`; its code is shown here:

```python
import sys
from PyQt5.QtWidgets import QDialog, QApplication
from demoRadioButton2 import *
class MyForm(QDialog):
    def __init__(self):
        super().__init__()
        self.ui = Ui_Dialog()
        self.ui.setupUi(self)
        self.ui.radioButtonMedium.toggled.connect(self.
        dispSelected)
        self.ui.radioButtonLarge.toggled.connect(self.
        dispSelected)
        self.ui.radioButtonXL.toggled.connect(self.dispSelected)
        self.ui.radioButtonXXL.toggled.connect(self.
        dispSelected)
        self.ui.radioButtonDebitCard.toggled.connect(self.
        dispSelected)
        self.ui.radioButtonNetBanking.toggled.connect(self.
        dispSelected)
        self.ui.radioButtonCashOnDelivery.toggled.connect(self.
        dispSelected)
        self.show()
    def dispSelected(self):
        selected1="";
        selected2=""
        if self.ui.radioButtonMedium.isChecked()==True:
            selected1="Medium"
        if self.ui.radioButtonLarge.isChecked()==True:
            selected1="Large"
        if self.ui.radioButtonXL.isChecked()==True:
            selected1="Extra Large"
        if self.ui.radioButtonXXL.isChecked()==True:
            selected1="Extra Extra Large"
        if self.ui.radioButtonDebitCard.isChecked()==True:
            selected2="Debit/Credit Card"
        if self.ui.radioButtonNetBanking.isChecked()==True:
            selected2="NetBanking"
        if self.ui.radioButtonCashOnDelivery.isChecked()==True:
            selected2="Cash On Delivery"
        self.ui.labelSelected.setText("Chosen shirt size is
        "+selected1+" and payment method as " + selected2)
if __name__=="__main__":
    app = QApplication(sys.argv)
    w = MyForm()
    w.show()
    sys.exit(app.exec_())
```

How it works...

The **toggled()** event of all the radio buttons is connected to the `dispSelected()` function, which will display the selected shirt size and payment method. In the `dispSelected()` function, you check the status of the radio buttons to find out whether they are checked or unchecked. On the basis of the selected radio button in the first vertical layout, the value of the `selected1` variable will be set to `Medium`, `Large`, `Extra Large`, or `Extra Extra Large`. Similarly, from the second vertical layout, depending on the radio button selected, the value of the `selected2` variable will be initialized to **Debit/Credit Card**, **NetBanking**, or **Cash On Delivery**. Finally, the shirt size and payment method assigned to the `selected1` variable and selected variables will be displayed via the `labelSelected` widget. On running the application, you get a dialog prompting you to select the shirt size and payment method. On selecting a shirt size and payment method, the selected shirt size and payment method are displayed via the **Label** widget, as shown in the following screenshot:

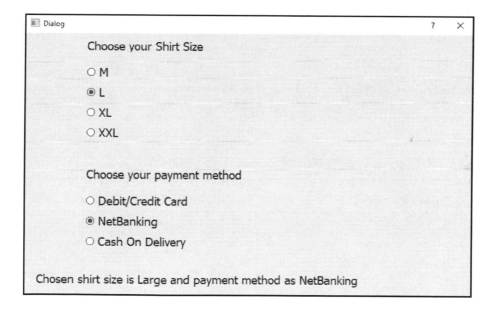

Displaying options in the form of checkboxes

While creating applications, you may come across a situation where you need to provide several options for the user to select from. That is, you want the user to select one or more than one option from a set of options. In such situations, you need to make use of checkboxes. Let's find out more about checkboxes.

Getting ready

Whereas radio buttons allow only one option to be selected in a group, checkboxes allow you to select more than one option. That is, selecting a checkbox will not affect other checkboxes in the application. Checkboxes are displayed with a text label as an instance of the QCheckBox class. A checkbox can be in any of three states: selected (checked), unselected (unchecked), or tristate (unchanged). Tristate is a no change state; the user has neither checked nor unchecked the checkbox.

Method application

The following are the methods provided by the QCheckBox class:

- isChecked(): This method returns the Boolean value true if the checkbox is checked, and otherwise returns false.
- setTristate(): If you don't want the user to change the state of the checkbox, you pass the Boolean value true to this method. The user will not be able to check or uncheck the checkbox.
- setIcon(): This method is used to display an icon with the checkbox.
- setText(): This method assigns text to the checkbox. To specify a shortcut key for the checkbox, precede the preferred character in the text with an ampersand. The shortcut character will appear as underlined.
- setChecked(): In order to make a checkbox appear as checked by default, pass the Boolean value true to this method.

Signal description

The signals emitted by QCheckBox are as follows:

- **clicked()**: This signal is emitted when a checkbox is activated (that is, pressed and released) or when its shortcut key is pressed
- **stateChanged()**: This signal is emitted whenever a checkbox changes its state from checked to unchecked or vice versa

To understand the **Check Box** widget, let's assume that you run a restaurant where several food items, such as pizzas, are sold. The pizza is sold along with different toppings, such as extra cheese, extra olives, and so on, and the price of each topping is also mentioned with it. The user can select a regular pizza with one or more toppings. What you want is that when a topping is selected, the total price of the pizza, including the selected topping, is displayed.

How to do it...

The focus of this recipe is to understand how an action is initiated when the state of a checkbox changes from checked to unchecked or vice versa. Following is the step-by-step procedure to create such an application:

1. Begin by creating a new application based on the **Dialog without Buttons** template.
2. Drag and drop three **Label** widgets and three **Check Box** widgets onto the form.
3. Set the **text** property of the first two **Label** widgets to Regular Pizza $10 and Select your extra toppings.
4. In the **Property Editor** window, increase the font size of all three labels and checkboxes to increase their visibility in the application.
5. Set the **text** property of the three checkboxes to Extra Cheese $1, Extra Olives $1, and Extra Sausages $2. The default object names of the three checkboxes are checkBox, checkBox_2, and checkBox_3.
6. Change these to checkBoxCheese, checkBoxOlives, and checkBoxSausages, respectively.
7. Set the **objectName** property of the **Label** widget to labelAmount.

8. Save the application with the name `demoCheckBox1.ui`. Now, the form will appear as shown in the following screenshot:

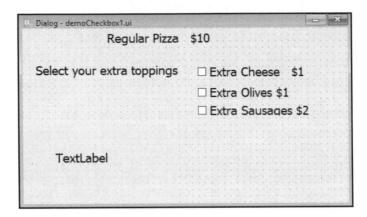

The `.ui` (XML) file is then converted into Python code through the `pyuic5` command utility. The Python code generated in the `demoCheckBox1.py` file can be seen in the source code bundle of this book.

9. Import the `demoCheckBox1.py` file, as a header file in our program to invoke the user interface design and to write code to calculate the total cost of regular pizza, along with the selected toppings, through a **Label** widget when the user selects or unselects any of the checkboxes.

10. Let's name the program `callCheckBox1.pyw`; its code is shown here:

```python
import sys
from PyQt5.QtWidgets import QDialog
from PyQt5.QtWidgets import QApplication, QWidget, QPushButton
from demoCheckBox1 import *
class MyForm(QDialog):
    def __init__(self):
        super().__init__()
        self.ui = Ui_Dialog()
        self.ui.setupUi(self)
        self.ui.checkBoxCheese.stateChanged.connect(self.
        dispAmount)
        self.ui.checkBoxOlives.stateChanged.connect(self.
        dispAmount)
        self.ui.checkBoxSausages.stateChanged.connect(self.
        dispAmount)
        self.show()
    def dispAmount(self):
        amount=10
```

```
        if self.ui.checkBoxCheese.isChecked()==True:
            amount=amount+1
        if self.ui.checkBoxOlives.isChecked()==True:
            amount=amount+1
        if self.ui.checkBoxSausages.isChecked()==True:
            amount=amount+2
        self.ui.labelAmount.setText("Total amount for pizza is
        "+str(amount))
if __name__=="__main__":
    app = QApplication(sys.argv)
    w = MyForm()
    w.show()
    sys.exit(app.exec_())
```

How it works...

The **stateChanged()** event of checkboxes is connected to the dispAmount function, which will calculate the cost of the pizza along with the toppings selected. In the dispAmount function, you check the status of the checkboxes to find out whether they are checked or unchecked. The cost of the toppings whose checkboxes are checked is added and stored in the amount variable. Finally, the addition of the amount stored in the amount variable is displayed via labelAmount. On running the application, you get a dialog prompting you to select the toppings that you want to add to your regular pizza. On selecting any toppings, the amount of the regular pizza along with the selected toppings will be displayed on the screen, as shown in the following screenshot:

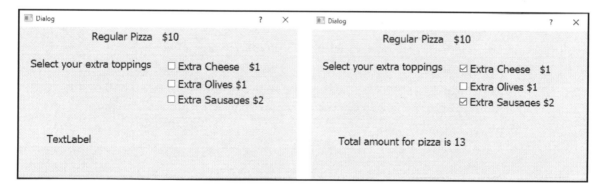

 The dispAmount function will be invoked every time the status of any checkbox changes. As a result, the total amount will be displayed via the **Label** widget, as soon as any checkbox is checked or unchecked.

Displaying two groups of checkboxes

In this application, we will learn to make two groups of checkboxes. The user can select any number of checkboxes from either group and, accordingly, the result will appear.

Getting ready

We will try displaying a menu of a restaurant where different types of ice creams and drinks are served. We will create two groups of checkboxes, one of ice creams and the other of drinks. The ice cream group displays four checkboxes showing four different types of ice cream, mint chocolate chip, cookie dough, and so on, along with their prices. The drinks group displays three checkboxes, coffee, soda, and so on, along with their prices. The user can select any number of checkboxes from either of the groups. When the user selects any of the ice creams or drinks, the total price of the selected ice creams and drinks will be displayed.

How to do it...

Here are the steps to create an application, which explain how checkboxes can be arranged into different groups and how to take respective action when the state of any checkbox from any group changes:

1. Create a new application based on the **Dialog without Buttons** template.
2. Drag and drop four **Label** widgets, seven **Check Box** widgets, and two **Group Box** widgets onto the form.
3. Set the **text** property of the first three **Label** widgets to `Menu`, `Select your IceCream`, and `Select your drink` respectively.
4. Delete the **text** property of the fourth **Label** widget because we will display the total amount of the selected ice creams and drinks through the code.
5. Through **Property Editor**, increase the font size of the all the widgets to increase their visibility in the application.
6. Set the **text** property of the first four checkboxes to `Mint Choclate Chips $4`, `Cookie Dough $2`, `Choclate Almond $3`, and `Rocky Road $5`. Put these four checkboxes into the first group box.
7. Set the **text** property of the next three checkboxes to `Coffee $2`, `Soda $3`, and `Tea $1` respectively. Put these three checkboxes into the second group box.

8. Change the object names of the first four checkboxes to `checkBoxChoclateChips`, `checkBoxCookieDough`, `checkBoxChoclateAlmond`, and `checkBoxRockyRoad`.

9. Set the **objectName** property of the first group box to `groupBoxIceCreams`.

10. Change the **objectName** property of the next three checkboxes to `checkBoxCoffee`, `checkBoxSoda`, and `checkBoxTea`.

11. Set the **objectName** property of the second group box to `groupBoxDrinks`.

12. Set the **objectName** property of the fourth **Label** widget to `labelAmount`.

13. Save the application with the name `demoCheckBox2.ui`. It is through this **Label** widget that the total amount of the selected ice creams and drinks will be displayed, as shown in the following screenshot:

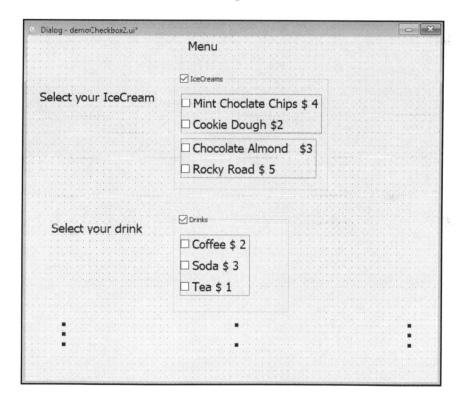

The `.ui` (XML) file is then converted into Python code through the `pyuic5` command utility. You can find the generated Python code, the `demoCheckbox2.py` file, in the source code bundle of this book.

14. Import the `demoCheckBox2.py` file as a header file in our program to invoke the user interface design, and to write code to calculate the total cost of ice creams and drinks through a **Label** widget when the user selects or unselects any of the checkboxes.

15. Let's name the program `callCheckBox2.pyw`; its code is shown here:

```
import sys
from PyQt5.QtWidgets import QDialog
from PyQt5.QtWidgets import QApplication, QWidget, QPushButton
from demoCheckBox2 import *
class MyForm(QDialog):
    def __init__(self):
        super().__init__()
        self.ui = Ui_Dialog()
        self.ui.setupUi(self)
        self.ui.checkBoxChoclateAlmond.stateChanged.connect
        (self.dispAmount)
        self.ui.checkBoxChoclateChips.stateChanged.connect(self.
        dispAmount)
        self.ui.checkBoxCookieDough.stateChanged.connect(self.
        dispAmount)
        self.ui.checkBoxRockyRoad.stateChanged.connect(self.
        dispAmount)
        self.ui.checkBoxCoffee.stateChanged.connect(self.
        dispAmount)
        self.ui.checkBoxSoda.stateChanged.connect(self.
        dispAmount)
        self.ui.checkBoxTea.stateChanged.connect(self.
        dispAmount)
        self.show()
    def dispAmount(self):
        amount=0
        if self.ui.checkBoxChoclateAlmond.isChecked()==True:
            amount=amount+3
        if self.ui.checkBoxChoclateChips.isChecked()==True:
            amount=amount+4
        if self.ui.checkBoxCookieDough.isChecked()==True:
            amount=amount+2
        if self.ui.checkBoxRockyRoad.isChecked()==True:
            amount=amount+5
        if self.ui.checkBoxCoffee.isChecked()==True:
            amount=amount+2
        if self.ui.checkBoxSoda.isChecked()==True:
            amount=amount+3
        if self.ui.checkBoxTea.isChecked()==True:
            amount=amount+1
        self.ui.labelAmount.setText("Total amount is
```

```
                 $"+str(amount))
if __name__=="__main__":
    app = QApplication(sys.argv)
    w = MyForm()
    w.show()
    sys.exit(app.exec_())
```

How it works...

The **stateChanged()** event of all the checkboxes is connected to the `dispAmount` function, which will calculate the cost of the selected ice creams and drinks. In the `dispAmount` function, you check the status of the checkboxes to find out whether they are checked or unchecked. The cost of the ice creams and drinks whose checkboxes are checked is added and stored in the `amount` variable. Finally, the addition of the amount stored in the `amount` variable is displayed via the `labelAmount` widget. On running the application, you get a dialog prompting you to select the ice creams or drinks that you want to order. On selecting the ice creams or drinks, the total amount of the chosen items will be displayed, as shown in the following screenshot:

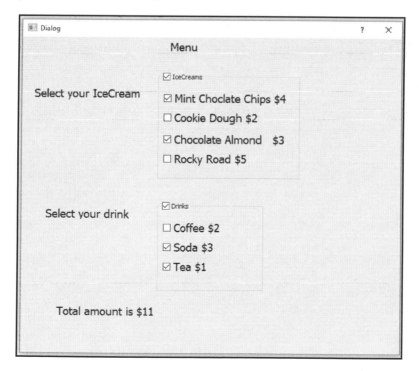

Event Handling - Signals and Slots

2

In this chapter, we will learn about the following topics:

- Using Signal/Slot Editor
- Copying and pasting text from one Line Edit widget to another
- Converting data types and making a small calculator
- Using the Spin Box widget
- Using scrollbars and sliders
- Using List Widget
- Selecting multiple list items from one List Widget and displaying them in another
- Adding items into List Widget
- Performing operations in List Widget
- Using the Combo Box widget
- Using the Font Combo Box widget
- Using the Progress Bar widget

Introduction

Event handling is an important mechanism in every application. The application should not only recognize the event, but must take the respective action to serve the event, too. The action taken on any event determines the course of the application. Each programming language has a different technique for handling or listening to events. Let's see how Python handles its events.

Using Signal/Slot Editor

In PyQt, the event handling mechanism is also known as **signals** and **slots**. An event can be in the form of clicking or double-clicking on a widget, or pressing the *Enter* key, or selecting an option from a radio button, checkbox, and so on. Every widget emits a signal when any event is applied on it and, that signal needs to be connected to a method, also known as a slot. A slot refers to the method containing the code that you want to be executed on the occurrence of a signal. Most widgets have predefined slots; you don't have to write code to connect a predefined signal to a predefined slot.

You can even edit a signal/slot by navigating to the **Edit** | **Edit Signals/Slots** tool in the toolbar.

How to do it...

To edit the signals and slots of different widgets placed on the form, you need to switch to signals and slots editing mode by performing the following steps:

1. You can press the *F4* key, navigate to the **Edit** | **Edit Signals/Slots** option, or select the **Edit Signals/Slots** icon from the toolbar. The mode displays all the signal and slot connections in the form of arrows, indicating the connection of a widget with its respective slot.

> You can also create new signal and slot connections between widgets in this mode and delete an existing signal.

2. To establish a signal and slot connection between two widgets in a form, select a widget by left-clicking the mouse on the widget, dragging the mouse towards another widget to which you want to connect, and releasing the mouse button over it.
3. To cancel the connection while dragging the mouse, simply press the *Esc* key.
4. On releasing the mouse over the destination widget, a **Connection Dialog** box appears, prompting you to select a signal from the source widget and a slot from the destination widget.
5. After selecting the respective signal and slot, select **OK** to establish the signal and slot connection.

The following screenshot shows dragging a **Push Button** over a **Line Edit** widget:

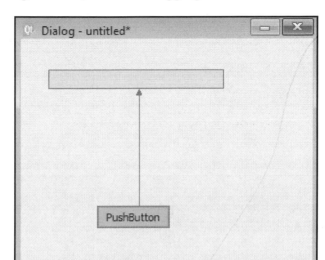

6. On releasing the mouse button on the **Line Edit** widget, you get the list of predefined signals and slots, as shown in the following screenshot:

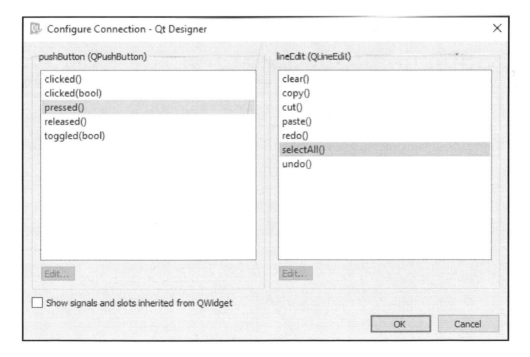

You can also select **Cancel** in the **Configure Connection** dialog box to cancel the signal and slot connection.

7. When connected, the selected signal and slot will appear as labels in the arrow, connecting the two widgets.
8. To modify a signal and slot connection, double-click the connection path or one of its labels to display the **Configure Connection** dialog box.
9. From the **Configure Connection** dialog, you can edit a signal or a slot as desired.
10. To delete a signal and slot connection, select its arrow on the form and press the *Delete* key.

The signal and slot connection can also be established between any widget and the form. To do so, you can perform the following steps:

1. Select the widget, drag the mouse, and release the mouse button over the form. The end point of the connection changes to the electrical ground symbol, representing that a connection has been established with the form.
2. To come out of signal and slot editing mode, navigate to **Edit | Edit Widgets** or press the *F3* key.

Copying and pasting text from one Line Edit widget to another

This recipe will make you understand how an event performed on one widget invokes a predefined action on the associated widget. Because we want to copy content from one **Line Edit** widget on clicking the push button, we need to invoke the `selectAll()` method on the occurrence of the **pressed()** event on push button. Also, we need to invoke the `copy()` method on occurrence of the **released()** event on the push button. To paste the content in the clipboard into another **Line Edit** widget on clicking of another push button, we need to invoke the `paste()` method on the occurrence of the **clicked()** event on another push button.

Getting ready

Let's create an application that consists of two **Line Edit** and two **Push Button** widgets. On clicking the first push button, the text in the first **Line Edit** widget will be copied and on clicking the second push button, the text copied from the first **Line Edit** widget will be pasted onto the second **Line Edit** widget.

Let's create a new application based on the **Dialog without Buttons** template by performing the following steps:

1. Begin by adding `QLineEdit` and `QPushButton` to the form by dragging and dropping the **Line Edit** and **Push Button** widgets from the **Widget** box on the form.

     To preview a form while editing, select either **Form**, **Preview**, or use *Ctrl + R* .

2. To copy the text of the **Line Edit** widget when the user selects the push button on the form, you need to connect the push button's signal to the slot of **Line Edit**. Let's learn how to do it.

How to do it...

Initially, the form is in widget editing mode, and to apply signal and slot connections, you need to first switch to signals and slots editing mode:

1. Select the **Edit Signals/Slots** icon from the toolbar to switch to signals and slots editing mode.

2. On the form, select the push button, drag the mouse to the **Line Edit** widget, and release the mouse button. The **Configure Connection** dialog will pop up, allowing you to establish a signal and slot connection between the **Push Button** and the **Line Edit** widgets, as shown in the following screenshot:

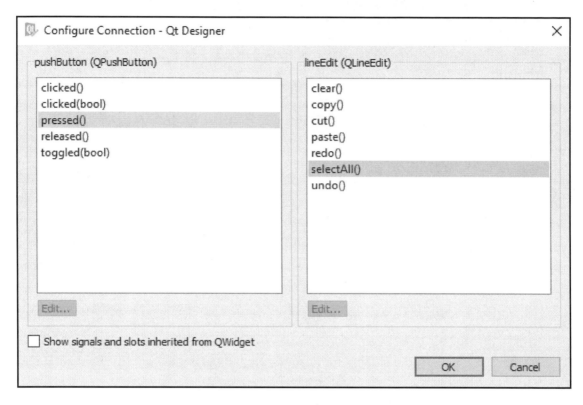

3. Select the **pressed()** event or signal from the **pushButton (QPushButton)** tab and the **selectAll()** slot for the **lineEdit (QLineEdit)** tab.

The connected signal of the **Push Button** widget with the slot of **Line Edit** will appear in the form of an arrow, representing the signal and slot connection between the two widgets, as shown in the following screenshot:

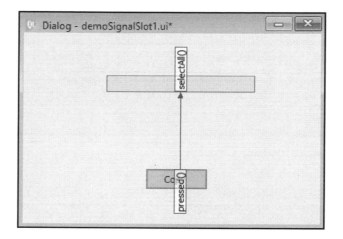

4. Set the **text** property of the **Push Button** widget to Copy to represent the fact that it will copy the text entered in the **Line Edit** widget.

5. Next, we will repeat the procedure of clicking the push button and dragging it to the **Line Edit** widget to connect the **released()** signal of the push button with the **copy()** slot of the **Line Edit** widget. On the form, you will see another arrow, representing the second signal and slot connection established between the two widgets, as is shown in the following screenshot:

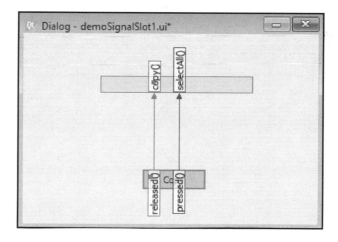

6. In order to paste the copied content, drag and drop one push button and one **Line Edit** widget on the form.

7. Set the **text** property of the **Push Button** widget to `Paste`.

8. Click the push button and, keeping the mouse button pressed, drag it and release it on the **Line Edit** widget.

9. From the **Configure Connection** dialog, select the **clicked()** event from the **pushButton (QPushButton)** column and the **paste()** slot from the **lineEdit (QLineEdit)** column.

10. Save the form with the name `demoSignal1.ui`. The form will now appear as shown in the following screenshot:

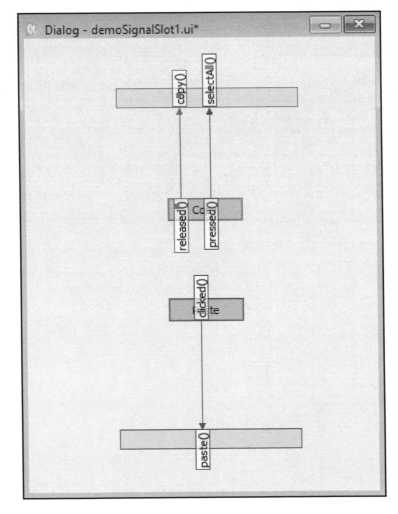

The form will be saved in a file with the `.ui` extension. The `demoSignal1.ui` file will contain all the information of the form, its widgets, layout, and so on. The .ui file is an XML file, and it needs to be converted into Python code by making use of the `pyuic5` utility. The generated Python code file, `demoSignal1.py`, can be seen in the source code bundle of this book. In the `demoSignal1.py` file, you will find that it imports everything from both modules, `QtCore` and `QtGui`, as you will be needing them for developing GUI applications:

- `QtCore`: The `QtCore` module forms the foundation of all Qt-based applications. It contains the most fundamental classes, such as `QCoreApplication`, `QObject`, and so on. These classes do important tasks, such as event handling, implementing the signal and slot mechanism, I/O operations, handling strings, and so on. The module includes several classes, including `QFile`, `QDir`, `QIODevice`, `QTimer`, `QString`, `QDate`, and `QTime`.

- `QtGui`: As the name suggests, the `QtGUI` module contains the classes required in developing cross-platform GUI applications. The module contains the GUI classes, such as `QCheckBox`, `QComboBox`, `QDateTimeEdit`, `QLineEdit`, `QPushButton`, `QPainter`, `QPaintDevice`, `QApplication`, `QTextEdit`, and `QTextDocument`.

11. Treat the `demoSignalSlot1.py` file, as a header file and import it to the file from which you will invoke its user interface design.

12. Create another Python file with the name `calldemoSignal1.py` and import the `demoSignal1.py` code into it:

```
import sys
from PyQL5.QtWidgets import QDialog, QApplication
from demoSignalSlot1 import *
class MyForm(QDialog):
    def __init__(self):
        super().__init__()
        self.ui = Ui_Dialog()
        self.ui.setupUi(self)
        self.show()
if __name__=="__main__":
    app = QApplication(sys.argv)
    w = MyForm()
    w.show()
    sys.exit(app.exec_())
```

How it works...

The sys module is imported as it supplies access to the command-line arguments stored in the sys.argv list. This is because every PyQt GUI application must have a QApplication object to provide access to information such as the application's directory, screen size, and so on, so that you create an QApplication object. To enable PyQt to use and apply command-line arguments (if any), you pass the command-line arguments while creating a QApplication object. You create an instance of MyForm and call its show() method, which adds a new event to the QApplication object's event queue. This new event is used to display all the widgets specified in the MyForm class. The app.exec_ method is called to start the QApplication object's event loop. Once the event loop begins, the top-level widget used in the class, MyForm, is displayed, along with its child widgets. All the system-generated events, as well as user interaction events, are added to the event queue. The application's event loop continuously checks to see whether an event has occurred. On the occurrence of an event, the event loop processes it and invokes the associated slot or method. On closing the top-level widget of the application, PyQt deletes the widget and performs a clean termination of the application.

In PyQt, any widget can be used as a top-level window. The super().__init__() method invokes the base class constructor from the MyForm class, that is, the constructor of the QDialog class is invoked from MyForm class to indicate that QDialog is displayed through this class is a top-level window.

The user interface design is instantiated by calling the setupUI() method of the class that was created in the Python code (Ui_Dialog). We create an instance of the Ui_Dialog class, the class that was created in the Python code, and invoke its setupUi() method. The **Dialog** widget will be created as the parent of all the user interface widgets and displayed on the screen. Remember, QDialog, QMainWindow, and all of the PyQt's widgets are derived from QWidget.

On running the application, you get two pairs of the **Line Edit** and **Push Button** widgets. On typing text into one **Line Edit** widget, when you click the **Copy** push button, the text will be copied.

Now, on clicking the **Paste** push button, the copied text will be pasted in the second **Line Edit** widget, as shown in the following screenshot:

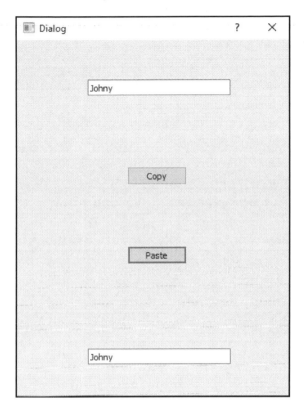

Converting data types and making a small calculator

The most commonly used widget for accepting one-line data is the **Line Edit** widget, and the default data type in a **Line Edit** widget is string. In order to do any computation on two integer values, you need to convert the string data entered in the **Line Edit** widget to the integer data type and then convert the result of computation, which will be a numeric data type, back to string type before being displaying through a **Label** widget. This recipe does exactly that.

How to do it...

To understand how data is accepted by the user and how type casting is done, let's create an application based on the **Dialog without Buttons** template by performing the following steps:

1. Add three QLabel, two QLineEdit, and one QPushButton widget to the form by dragging and dropping three **Label**, two **Line Edit**, and four **Push Button** widgets on the form.

2. Set the **text** property of the two **Label** widgets to Enter First Number and Enter Second Number.

3. Set the **objectName** property of the three Labels to labelFirstNumber, labelSecondNumber, and labelResult.

4. Set the **objectName** property of the two **Line Edit** widgets to lineEditFirstNumber and lineEditSecondNumber.

5. Set the **objectName** property of the four **Push Button** widgets to pushButtonPlus, pushButtonSubtract, pushButtonMultiply, and pushButtonDivide, respectively.

6. Set the push button's **text** property to +, −, x, and /, respectively.

7. Delete the default **text** property of the third label, because the Python script will set the value and then display it when the two numerical values are added.

8. Don't forget to drag the **Label** widget in the designer in order to ensure it is long enough to display the text that will be assigned to it through the Python script.

9. Save the UI file as demoCalculator.ui.

10. You can also increase the width of the **Label** widget by setting the **width** property under **geometry** from the **Property Editor** window:

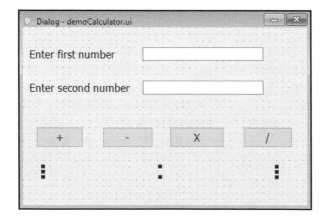

The .ui file, which is in XML format, needs to be converted into Python code.
The generated Python code, demoCalculator.py, can be seen in the source code
bundle of this book.

11. Create a Python script named callCalculator.pyw that imports the Python
code demoCalculator.py to invoke a user interface design, and that fetches the
values entered in the **Line Edit** widgets and displays their addition. The code in
the Python script callCalculator.pyw is shown here:

```
import sys
from PyQt5.QtWidgets import QDialog, QApplication
from demoCalculator import *
class MyForm(QDialog):
    def __init__(self):
        super().__init__()
        self.ui = Ui_Dialog()
        self.ui.setupUi(self)
        self.ui.pushButtonPlus.clicked.connect(self.addtwonum)
        self.ui.pushButtonSubtract.clicked.connect
        (self.subtracttwonum)
        self.ui.pushButtonMultiply.clicked.connect
        (self.multiplytwonum)
        self.ui.pushButtonDivide.clicked.connect(self.dividetwonum)
        self.show()
    def addtwonum(self):
        if len(self.ui.lineEditFirstNumber.text())!=0:
                a=int(self.ui.lineEditFirstNumber.text())
        else:
                a=0
        if len(self.ui.lineEditSecondNumber.text())!=0:
                b=int(self.ui.lineEditSecondNumber.text())
        else:
                b=0
                sum=a+b
        self.ui.labelResult.setText("Addition: " +str(sum))
    def subtracttwonum(self):
        if len(self.ui.lineEditFirstNumber.text())!=0:
                a=int(self.ui.lineEditFirstNumber.text())
        else:
                a=0
        if len(self.ui.lineEditSecondNumber.text())!=0:
                b=int(self.ui.lineEditSecondNumber.text())
        else:
                b=0
                diff=a-b
        self.ui.labelResult.setText("Substraction: " +str(diff))
    def multiplytwonum(self):
```

```
                    if len(self.ui.lineEditFirstNumber.text())!=0:
                            a=int(self.ui.lineEditFirstNumber.text())
                    else:
                            a=0
                    if len(self.ui.lineEditSecondNumber.text())!=0:
                            b=int(self.ui.lineEditSecondNumber.text())
                    else:
                            b=0
                            mult=a*b
                    self.ui.labelResult.setText("Multiplication: " +str(mult))
            def dividetwonum(self):
                    if len(self.ui.lineEditFirstNumber.text())!=0:
                            a=int(self.ui.lineEditFirstNumber.text())
                    else:
                            a=0
                    if len(self.ui.lineEditSecondNumber.text())!=0:
                            b=int(self.ui.lineEditSecondNumber.text())
                    else:
                            b=0
                            division=a/b
                    self.ui.labelResult.setText("Division: "+str(round
                    (division,2)))
        if __name__=="__main__":
            app = QApplication(sys.argv)
            w = MyForm()
            w.show()
            sys.exit(app.exec_())
```

How it works...

There are the following four functions used in this code:

- `len()`: This function returns the number of characters in the string
- `str()`: This function converts the argument passed into the string data type
- `int()`: This function converts the argument passed into the integer data type
- `round()`: This function rounds the number passed to the specified decimal digits

The `clicked()` event of `pushButtonPlus` is connected to the `addtwonum()` method to display the sum of the numbers entered in the two **Line Edit** widgets. In the `addtwonum()` method, you first validate `lineEditFirstNumber` and `lineEditSecondNumber` to ensure that if either **Line Edit** is left blank by the user, the value of that **Line Edit** is zero.

The values entered in the two **Line Edit** widgets are retrieved, converted into integers through int (), and assigned to the two variables a and b. The sum of the values in the a and b variables is computed and stored in the sum variable. The result in the variable sum is converted into string format through str method and displayed via labelResult, as shown in the following screenshot:

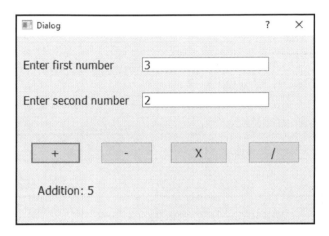

Similarly, the clicked() event of pushButtonSubtract is connected to the subtracttwonum() method to display the subtraction of the numbers entered in the two **Line Edit** widgets. Again, after validation of the two **Line Edit** widgets, the values entered in them are retrieved and converted into integers. Subtraction is applied on the two numbers and the result is assigned to the diff variable. Finally, the result in the diff variable is converted into string format through the str() method and displayed via labelResult, as shown in the following screenshot:

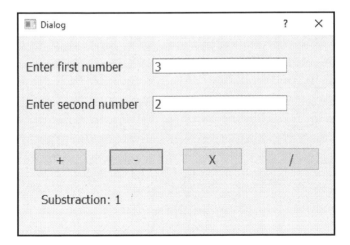

Similarly, the **clicked()** event of `pushButtonMultiply` and `pushButtonDivide` are connected to the `multiplytwonum()` and `dividetwonum()` methods, respectively. These methods multiply and divide the values entered in the two **Line Edit** widgets and display them through the `labelResult` widget.

The result of the multiplication is shown in the following screenshot:

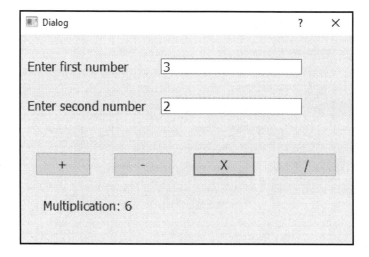

The result of the division is shown in the following screenshot:

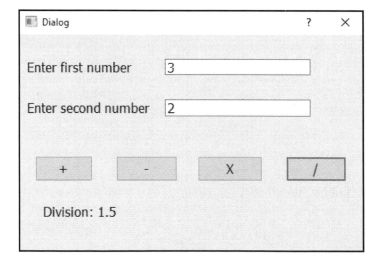

Using the Spin Box widget

The **Spin Box** widget is used for displaying integer values, floating-point values, and text. It applies a constraint on the user: the user cannot enter any random data, but can select only from the available options displayed through **Spin Box**. A **Spin Box** widget displays an initial value by default that can be increased or decreased by selecting the up/down button or up/down arrow key on the keyboard. You can choose a value that is displayed by either clicking on it or typing it in manually.

Getting ready

A **Spin Box** widget can be created using two classes, `QSpinBox` and `QDoubleSpinBox`, where `QSpinBox` displays only integer values, and the `QDoubleSpinBox` class displays floating-point values. Methods provided by `QSpinBox` are shown in the following list:

- `value()`: This method returns the current integer value selected from the spin box.
- `text()`: This method returns the text displayed by the spin box.
- `setPrefix()`: This method assigns the prefix text that is prepended to the value returned by the spin box.
- `setSuffix()`: This method assigns the suffix text that is to be appended to the value returned by the spin box.
- `cleanText()`: This method returns the value of the spin box without a suffix, a prefix, or leading or trailing whitespaces.
- `setValue()`: This method assigns the value to the spin box.
- `setSingleStep()`: This method sets the step size of the spin box. Step size is the increment/decrement value of the spin box, that is, it is the value by which the spin box's value will increase or decrease on selecting the up or down buttons.
- `setMinimum()`: This method sets the minimum value of the spin box.
- `setMaximum()`: This method sets the maximum value of the spin box.
- `setWrapping()`: This method passes the Boolean value true to this method to enable wrapping in the spin box. Wrapping means the spin box returns to the first value (minimum value) when the up button is pressed while displaying the maximum value.

Signals emitted by the `QSpinBox` class are as follows:

- **valueChanged()**: This signal is emitted when the value of the spin box is changed either by selecting the up/down button or using the `setValue()` method
- **editingFinished()**: This signal is emitted when focus is lost on the spin box

The class used for dealing with float values in spin boxes is `QDoubleSpinBox`. All the preceding methods are supported by the `QDoubleSpinBox` class too. It displays values up to two decimal places by default. To change the precision, use `round()`, which displays the values up to the specified number of decimal places; the value will be rounded to the specified number of decimals.

 The default **minimum**, **maximum**, **singleStep**, and **value** properties of a spin box are **0**, **99**, **1**, and **0**, and of a double spin box are **0.000000**, **99.990000**, **1.000000**, and **0.000000**, respectively.

Let's create an application that will ask the user to enter a price for a book, followed by the quantity of the books purchased by the customer, and will display the total amount of books. Also, the application will prompt you to enter a price for 1 kg of sugar, followed by the quantity of sugar bought by the user. On entering the quantity of sugar, the app will display the total amount of sugar. The quantity of the books and the sugar will be entered through a spin box and double spin box, respectively.

How to do it...

To understand how integer and float values can be accepted through spin boxes and used in further computation, let's create a new application based on the **Dialog without Buttons** template and follow these steps:

1. Let's begin by dragging and dropping three **Label**, a **Spin Box**, a **Double Spin Box**, and four **Line Edit** widgets.
2. The **text** property of two Label widgets is set to `Book Price value` and `Sugar Price`, and the **objectName** property of the third **Label** widget is set to `labelTotalAmount`.
3. Set the **objectName** property of the four **Line Edit** widgets to `lineEditBookPrice`, `lineEditBookAmount`, `lineEditSugarPrice`, and `lineEditSugarAmount`, respectively.

4. Set the **objectName** property of the **Spin Box** widget to `spinBoxBookQty` and that of the **Double Spin Box** widget to `doubleSpinBoxSugarWeight`.

5. Delete the default **text** property of the third **Label** widget, **TextLabel**, as you will be setting its text in the program to display the total amount.

6. The third **Label** widget will become invisible on deleting its **text** property.

7. Disable the two **Line Edit** widgets, `lineEditBookAmount` and `lineEditSugarAmount`, by unchecking their enabled property from the **Property Editor** window as you want them to display non-editable values.

8. Save the application with the name `demoSpinner.ui`:

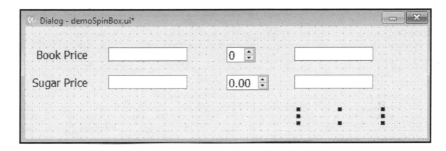

9. On using the `pyuic5` command utility, the `.ui` (XML) file will be converted into Python code. The generated Python code file, `demoSpinner.py`, can be seen in the source code of this book.

10. Create a Python script file named `calldemoSpinner.pyw` that imports the code, `demoSpinner.py`, enabling you to invoke the user interface design that displays the numbers selected through spin boxes and also compute the total book amount and total sugar amount. The `calldemoSpinner.pyw` file will appear as shown here:

```
import sys
from PyQt5.QtWidgets import QDialog, QApplication
from demoSpinBox import *
class MyForm(QDialog):
    def __init__(self):
        super().__init__()
        self.ui = Ui_Dialog()
        self.ui.setupUi(self)
        self.ui.spinBoxBookQty.editingFinished.connect(self.
        result1)
        self.ui.doubleSpinBoxSugarWeight.editingFinished.connect
        (self.result2)
        self.show()
```

```
def result1(self):
    if len(self.ui.lineEditBookPrice.text())!=0:
        bookPrice=int(self.ui.lineEditBookPrice.text())
    else:
        bookPrice=0
        totalBookAmount=self.ui.spinBoxBookQty.value() *
        bookPrice
        self.ui.lineEditBookAmount.setText(str
        (totalBookAmount))
def result2(self):
    if len(self.ui.lineEditSugarPrice.text())!=0:
        sugarPrice=float(self.ui.lineEditSugarPrice.
        text())
    else:
        sugarPrice=0
        totalSugarAmount=self.ui.
        doubleSpinBoxSugarWeight.value() * sugarPrice
        self.ui.lineEditSugarAmount.setText(str(round
        (totalSugarAmount,2)))
        totalBookAmount=int(self.ui.lineEditBookAmount.
        text())
        totalAmount=totalBookAmount+totalSugarAmount
        self.ui.labelTotalAmount.setText(str(round
        (totalAmount,2)))
if __name__=="__main__":
    app = QApplication(sys.argv)
    w = MyForm()
    w.show()
    sys.exit(app.exec_())
```

How it works...

In this code, you can see that the editingFinished signal of the two spin boxes is
attached to the result1 and result2 functions. It means that when focus is lost on any of
the spin boxes, the respective method will be invoked. Focus is lost on a widget when the
user moves onto other widgets with the mouse or by pressing the **Tab** key:

- In the result1 method, you retrieve the integer value for the purchased book
  quantity from the **Spin Box** widget and multiply it with the book price entered in
  the lineEditBookPrice widget to compute the total book cost. The total book
  cost is then displayed through the lineEditBookAmount widget.

- Similarly, in the `result2` method, you retrieve the floating-point value that is the weight of the sugar purchased from the double spin box and multiply it with the price of the sugar per kg entered in the `lineEditSugarPrice` widget to compute the total sugar cost, which is then displayed through the `lineEditSugarAmount` widget. The total of the book cost and sugar cost is finally displayed through the `labelTotalAmount` widget, as shown in the following screenshot:

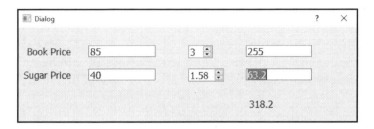

Using scrollbars and sliders

Scrollbars are useful while looking at large documents or images that cannot appear in a limited visible area. Scrollbars appear horizontally or vertically, indicating your current position in the document or image and the size of the region that is not visible. Using the slider handle provided with these bars, you can access the hidden part of the document or image.

Sliders are a way of selecting an integer value between two values. That is, a slider can represent a minimum and maximum range of values, and the user can select a value within this range by moving the slider handle to the desired location in the slider.

Getting ready

Scrollbars are used for viewing documents or images that are larger than the view area. To display horizontal or vertical scrollbars, you use the `HorizontalScrollBar` and `VerticalScrollBar` widgets, which are instances of the `QScrollBar` class. These scrollbars have a slider handle that can be moved to view the area that is not visible. The location of the slider handle indicates the location within the document or image. A scrollbar has the following controls:

- **Slider handle**: This control is used to move to any part of the document or image quickly.

- **Scroll arrows**: These are the arrows on either side of the scrollbars that are used to view the desired area of the document or image that is not currently visible. On using these scroll arrows, the position of the slider handle moves to show the current location within the document or image.
- **Page control**: The page control is the background of the scrollbar over which the slider handle is dragged. When the background is clicked, the slider handle moves towards the click by one page. The amount the slider handle moves can be specified via the **pageStep** property. The page step is the amount by which a slider moves when the user presses the *Page Up* and *Page Down* keys. You can set the amount of the **pageStep** property by using the setPageStep() method.

The method that is specifically used to set and retrieve values from scrollbars is the value() method, described here.

The value() method fetches the value of the slider handle, that is, its distance value from the start of the scrollbar. You get the minimum value of the scrollbar when the slider handle is at the top edge in a vertical scrollbar or at the left edge in a horizontal scrollbar, and you get the maximum value of the scroll bar when the slider handle is at the bottom edge in a vertical scrollbar or at the right edge in a horizontal scrollbar. You can move the slider handle to its minimum and maximum values via the keyboard too, by pressing the *Home* and *End* keys, respectively. Let's take a look at the following methods:

- setValue(): This method assigns value to the scrollbar and, as per the value assigned, the location of the slider handle is set in the scrollbar
- minimum(): This method returns the minimum value of the scrollbar
- maximum(): This method returns the maximum value of the scrollbar
- setMinimum(): This method assigns the minimum value to the scrollbar
- setMaximum(): This method assigns the maximum value to the scrollbar
- setSingleStep(): This method sets the single step value
- setPageStep(): This method sets the page step value

 QScrollBar provides only integer values.

The signals emitted through the QScrollBar class are shown in the following list:

- **valueChanged()**: This signal is emitted when the scrollbar's value is changed, that is, when its slider handle is moved

- **sliderPressed()**: This signal is emitted when the user starts to drag the slider handle
- **sliderMoved()**: This signal is emitted when the user drags the slider handle
- **sliderReleased()**: This signal is emitted when the user releases the slider handle
- **actionTriggered()**: This signal is emitted when the scrollbar is changed by user interaction

Sliders are generally used to represent some integer value. Unlike scrollbars, which are mostly used to display large documents or images, the sliders are interactive and an easier way to enter or represent integer values. That is, by moving and positioning its handle along a horizontal or vertical groove, you can make a horizontal or vertical slider to represent some integer value. To display horizontal and vertical sliders, the `HorizontalSlider` and `VerticalSlider` widgets are used, which are instances of the `QSlider` class. Similar to the methods that we saw in scrollbars, the sliders too generate signals such as **valueChanged()**, **sliderPressed()**, **sliderMoved()**, **sliderReleased()**, and many more on moving the slider handle.

The slider handle in scrollbars and sliders represents a value within the minimum and maximum range. To change the default minimum and maximum values, you can change their values by assigning values to the **minimum**, **maximum**, **singleStep**, and **pageStep** properties.

 The default values of the **minimum**, **maximum**, **singleStep**, **pageStep**, and **value** properties of sliders are **0**, **99**, **1**, **10**, and **0**, respectively.

Let's create an application consisting of horizontal and vertical scrollbars, as well as horizontal and vertical sliders. The horizontal scrollbar and slider will represent sugar level and blood pressure respectively. That is, on moving the horizontal scroll bar, the sugar level of the patient will be displayed through the **Line Edit** widget. Similarly, the horizontal slider, when moved, will represent blood pressure and will be displayed through the **Line Edit** widget.

The vertical scrollbar and slider will represent the heart rate and cholesterol level, respectively. On moving the vertical scrollbar, the heart rate will be displayed via the **Line Edit** widget and on moving the vertical slider, the cholesterol level will be displayed through the **Line Edit** widget.

How to do it...

To understand the working of the horizontal and vertical scrollbars, and the working of the horizontal and vertical sliders, to understand how scrollbars and sliders generate signals when their values are changed, and the how respective slot or method can be associated to them, perform the following steps:

1. Let's create a new application of the **Dialog without Buttons** template and drag and drop horizontal and vertical scrollbars and sliders onto the form.

2. Drop four **Label** widgets and a **Line Edit** widget to display the value of the scrollbar and slider handle.

3. Set the **text** property of the four **Label** widgets to `Sugar Level`, `Blood Pressure`, `Pulse rate`, and `Cholesterol`, respectively.

4. Set the **objectName** property of the horizontal scrollbar to `horizontalScrollBarSugarLevel`, vertical scroll bar to `verticalScrollBarPulseRate`, horizontal slider to `horizontalSliderBloodPressure`, and vertical slider to `verticalSliderCholestrolLevel`.

5. Set the **objectName** property of the **Line Edit** widget to `lineEditResult`.

6. Save the application with the name `demoSliders.ui`. The form will appear as shown in the following screenshot:

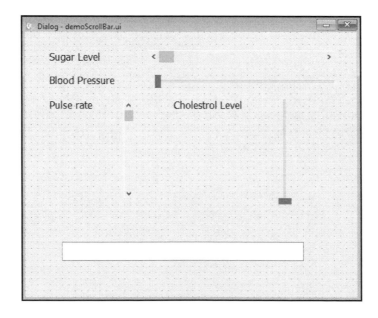

The `pyuic5` command utility will convert the `.ui` (XML) file into Python code. The generated Python file, `demoScrollBar.py`, can be seen in the source code bundle of this book.

7. Create a Python script file named `callScrollBar.pyw` that imports the code, `demoScrollBar.py`, to invoke the user interface design and synchronizes the movement of the scrollbar and slider handles. The script will also display the value of the scrollbar and slider handle with a **Label** widget. The Python script `callScrollBar.pyw` will appear, as shown here:

```python
import sys
from PyQt5.QtWidgets import QDialog, QApplication
from demoScrollBar import *
class MyForm(QDialog):
    def __init__(self):
        super().__init__()
        self.ui = Ui_Dialog()
        self.ui.setupUi(self)
        self.ui.horizontalScrollBarSugarLevel.valueChanged.connect
        (self.scrollhorizontal)
        self.ui.verticalScrollBarPulseRate.valueChanged.connect
        (self.scrollvertical)
        self.ui.horizontalSliderBloodPressure.valueChanged.connect
        (self.sliderhorizontal)
        self.ui.verticalSliderCholestrolLevel.valueChanged.connect
        (self.slidervertical)
        self.show()
    def scrollhorizontal(self,value):
        self.ui.lineEditResult.setText("Sugar Level : "+str(value))
    def scrollvertical(self, value):
        self.ui.lineEditResult.setText("Pulse Rate : "+str(value))
    def sliderhorizontal(self, value):
        self.ui.lineEditResult.setText("Blood Pressure :
        "+str(value))
    def slidervertical(self, value):
        self.ui.lineEditResult.setText("Cholestrol Level :
        "+str(value))
if __name__=="__main__":
    app = QApplication(sys.argv)
    w = MyForm()
    w.show()
    sys.exit(app.exec_())
```

How it works...

In this code, you are connecting the valueChanged() signal of each widget with the respective functions so that if the scrollbar or slider handle of the widget is moved, the corresponding function is invoked to perform the desired task. For instance, when the slider handle of the horizontal scrollbar is moved, the scrollhorizontal function is invoked. The scrollhorizontal function displays the value represented by the scrollbar, that is, **Sugar Level**, through the **Label** widget. Similarly, when the slider handle of the vertical scrollbar or slider is moved, the scrollvertical function is invoked and the heart rate, the value of the slider handle of the vertical scrollbar, is displayed through the **Label** widget, as shown in the following screenshot:

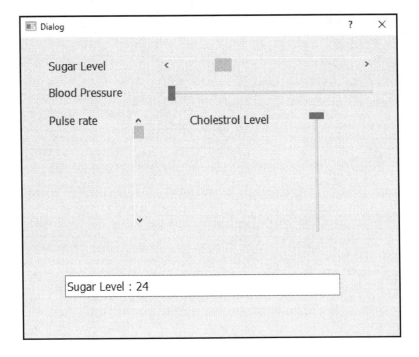

Similarly, when the horizontal and vertical sliders are moved, the blood pressure and cholesterol levels are displayed accordingly, as shown in the following screenshot:

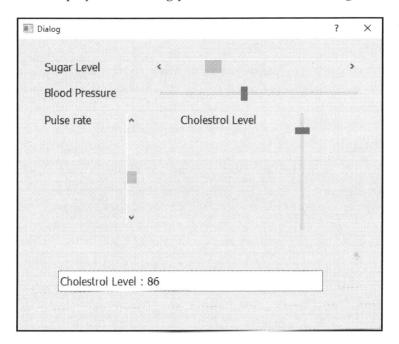

Using List Widget

To display several values in an easier and expandable format, you can use **List Widget**, which is an instance of the QListWidget class. **List Widget** displays several items that can not only be viewed, but can be edited and deleted, too. You can add or remove list items one at a time from the **List Widget** item, or collectively you can set list items by using its internal model.

Getting ready

Items in the list are instances of the QListWidgetItem class. The methods provided by QListWidget are shown in the following list:

- insertItem(): This method inserts a new item with the supplied text into **List Widget** at the specified location.

- `insertItems()`: This method inserts multiple items from the supplied list, starting at the specified location.
- `count()`: This method returns the count of the number of items in the list.
- `takeItem()`: This method removes and returns items from the specified row in **List Widget**.
- `currentItem()`: This method returns the current item in the list.
- `setCurrentItem()`: This method replaces the current item in the list with the specified item.
- `addItem()`: This method appends the item with the specified text at the end of **List Widget**.
- `addItems()`: This method appends items from the supplied list at the end of **List Widget**.
- `clear()`: This method removes all items from **List Widget**.
- `currentRow()`: This method returns the row number of the current selected list item. If no list item is selected, it returns the value −1.
- `setCurrentRow()`: This method selects the specified row in **List Widget**.
- `item()`: This method returns the list item at the specified row.

Signals emitted by the `QListWidget` class are shown in the following list:

- **currentRowChanged()**: This signal is emitted when the row of the current list item changes
- **currentTextChanged()**: This signal is emitted whenever the text in the current list item is changed
- **currentItemChanged()**: This signal is emitted when the focus of the current list item is changed

How to do it...

So, let's create an application that displays certain diagnostic tests through **List Widget**, and that when the user selects any test from **List Widget**, the selected test is displayed through a **Label** widget. Here is the step-by-step procedure to create the application:

1. Create a new application of the **Dialog without Buttons** template and drag and drop two **Label** widgets and one **List Widget** onto the form.
2. Set the **text** property of the first **Label** widget to `Choose the Diagnosis Tests`.

3. Set the **objectName** property of **List Widget** to `listWidgetDiagnosis`.

4. Set the **objectName** property of the **Label** widget to `labelTest`.

5. Delete the default **text** property of the `labelTest` widget as we will display the selected diagnosis test through this widget via code.

6. To display diagnosis tests through **List Widget**, right-click on it and from the context menu that opens up, select the **Edit Items** option.

7. Add the diagnosis tests one by one, followed by clicking on the + button at the bottom after typing every test, as shown in the following screenshot:

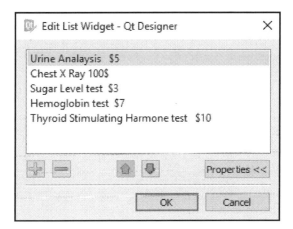

8. Save the application with the name `demoListWidget1.ui`. The form will appear as shown in the following screenshot:

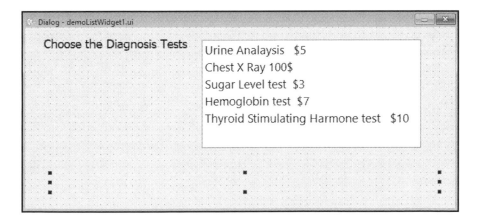

The `pyuic5` command utility will convert the `.ui` (XML) file into Python code. The generated Python code, `demoListWidget1.py`, can be seen in the source code bundle of this book.

9. Create a Python script file named `callListWidget1.pyw` that imports the code, `demoListWidget1.py`, to invoke the user interface design and the code that displays the diagnosis test selected from **List Widget.** The code in the Python script, `callListWidget1.pyw`, is as shown here:

```python
import sys
from PyQt5.QtWidgets import QDialog, QApplication
from demoListWidget1 import *
class MyForm(QDialog):
    def __init__(self):
        super().__init__()
        self.ui = Ui_Dialog()
        self.ui.setupUi(self)
        self.ui.listWidgetDiagnosis.itemClicked.connect(self.
        dispSelectedTest)
        self.show()
    def dispSelectedTest(self):
        self.ui.labelTest.setText("You have selected
        "+self.ui.listWidgetDiagnosis.currentItem().text())
if __name__=="__main__":
    app = QApplication(sys.argv)
    w = MyForm()
    w.show()
    sys.exit(app.exec_())
```

How it works...

You can see that the `itemClicked` event of **List Widget** is connected to the `dispSelectedTest()` method. That is, on clicking any of the list items from **List Widget**, the `dispSelectedTest()` method is invoked, which uses the `currentItem` method of **List Widget** to display the selected item of **List Widget** through the label called `labelTest`.

On running the application, you will see **List Widget** showing a few diagnosis tests; on selecting a test from the **List Widget**, the test will appear through the **Label** widget, as shown in the following screenshot:

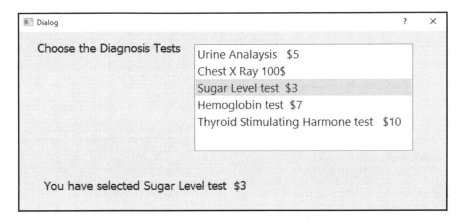

Selecting multiple list items from one List Widget and displaying them in another

In the preceding application, you were selecting only a single diagnosis test from the **List Widget** item. What if I want to do multiple selections from the **List Widget** item? In the case of multiple selections, instead of a **Line Edit** widget, you need another **List Widget** to store the selected diagnosis test.

How to do it...

Let's create an application that displays certain diagnosis tests through **List Widget** and when user selects any test from **List Widget**, the selected test will be displayed in another **List Widget**:

1. So, create a new application of the **Dialog without Buttons** template and drag and drop two **Label** widgets and two **List Widget** onto the form.
2. Set the text property of the first **Label** widget as Diagnosis Tests and that of the other to Selected tests are.
3. Set the **objectName** property of the first **List Widget** to listWidgetDiagnosis and of the second **List Widget** to listWidgetSelectedTests.

4. To display diagnosis tests through **List Widget,** right-click on it and from the context menu that opens up, select the **Edit Items** option.

5. Add the diagnosis tests one by one followed by clicking on the + button at the bottom after typing every test.

6. To enable multiple selections from **List Widget,** select the `listWidgetDiagnosis` widget and from the **Property Editor** window, change the **selectionMode** property from `SingleSelection` to `MultiSelection`.

7. Save the application with the name `demoListWidget2.ui`. The form will appear as shown in the following screenshot:

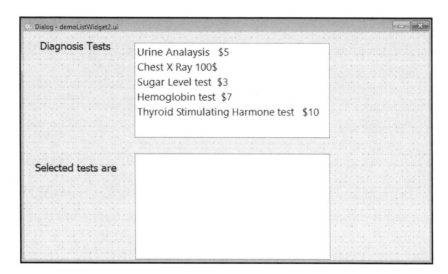

By using the `pyuic5` utility, the XML file `demoListWidget2.ui` will be converted into Python code as the `demoListWidget2.py` file. The generated Python code, from the `demoListWidget2.py` file, can be seen in the source code bundle of this book.

8. Create a Python script file named `callListWidget2.pyw` that imports the code, `demoListWidget2.py`, to invoke the user interface design and the code that displays the multiple selected diagnosis tests selected from **List Widget.** The Python script `callListWidget2.pyw` will appear as shown here:

```
import sys
from PyQt5.QtWidgets import QDialog, QApplication
from demoListWidget2 import *
class MyForm(QDialog):
    def __init__(self):
        super().__init__()
```

```
        self.ui = Ui_Dialog()
        self.ui.setupUi(self)
        self.ui.listWidgetDiagnosis.itemSelectionChanged.connect
        (self.dispSelectedTest)
        self.show()
    def dispSelectedTest(self):
        self.ui.listWidgetSelectedTests.clear()
        items = self.ui.listWidgetDiagnosis.selectedItems()
        for i in list(items):
            self.ui.listWidgetSelectedTests.addItem(i.text())
if __name__=="__main__":
    app = QApplication(sys.argv)
    w = MyForm()
    w.show()
    sys.exit(app.exec_())
```

How it works...

You can see that the `itemSelectionChanged` event of the first **List Widget** is connected to the `dispSelectedTest()` method. That is, on selecting or unselecting any of the list items from the first **List Widget** item, the `dispSelectedTest()` method is invoked. The `dispSelectedTest()` method invokes the `selectedItems()` method on **List Widget** to get the list of all the selected items. Thereafter, using the `for` loop, all the selected items are added to the second **List Widget** by invoking the `addItem()` method on it.

On running the application, you will see **List Widget** showing a few diagnosis tests; on selecting any number of tests from the first **List Widget**, all the selected tests will appear through the second **List Widget** item, as shown in the following screenshot:

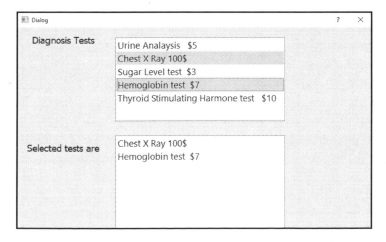

Adding items into List Widget

Although you can add items to the **List Widget** item manually through **Property Editor**, sometimes you need to add items to the **List Widget** item dynamically through code. Let's create an application that explains the process of adding items to **List Widget**.

In this application, you will use **Label**, **Line Edit**, **Push Button**, and **List Widget**. The **List Widget** item will be empty initially, and the user is asked to enter desired food items into **Line Edit** and select an **Add to List** button. The entered food item will then be added to the **List Widget** item. All subsequent food items will be added below the previous entry.

How to do it...

Perform the following steps to know how items can be added to the **List Widget** item:

1. We will begin by creating a new application based on the **Dialog without Buttons** template and dragging and dropping **Label**, **Line Edit**, **Push Button**, and **List Widget** onto the form.
2. Set the **text** property of the **Label** and **Push Button** widgets to `Your favourite food item` and `Add to List`, respectively.
3. Set the **objectName** property of the **Line Edit** widget to `lineEditFoodItem`, that of **Push Button** to `pushButtonAdd`, and that of **List Widget** to `listWidgetSelectedItems`.
4. Save the application with the name `demoListWidget3.ui`. The form will appear as shown in the following screenshot:

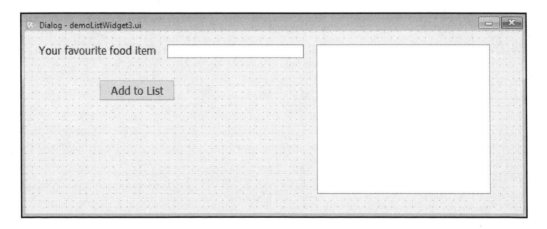

On executing the `pyuic5` utility, the XML file `demoListWidget3.ui` will be converted into Python code as `demoListWidget3.py`. The code of the generated Python file, `demoListWidget3.py`, can be seen in the source code bundle of this book.

5. Create a Python script file named `callListWidget3.pyw` that imports the Python code `demoListWidget3.py` to invoke the user interface design and adds the food items entered by the user in **Line Edit** to **List Widget**. The Python code in the `callListWidget3.pyw` file will appear as shown here:

```python
import sys
from PyQt5.QtWidgets import QDialog, QApplication
from demoListWidget3 import *
class MyForm(QDialog):
    def __init__(self):
        super().__init__()
        self.ui = Ui_Dialog()
        self.ui.setupUi(self)
        self.ui.pushButtonAdd.clicked.connect(self.addlist)
        self.show()
    def addlist(self):
        self.ui.listWidgetSelectedItems.addItem(self.ui.
        lineEditFoodItem.text())
        self.ui.lineEditFoodItem.setText('')
        self.ui.lineEditFoodItem.setFocus()
if __name__=="__main__":
    app = QApplication(sys.argv)
    w = MyForm()
    w.show()
    sys.exit(app.exec_())
```

How it works...

The **clicked()** event of the **Push Button** widget is connected to the `addlist` function. Hence, after entering the text to be added to **List Widget** in the **Line Edit** widget, when the user selects the **Add to List** button, the `addlist` function is invoked. The `addlist` function retrieves the text entered in **Line Edit** and adds it to **List Widget**. The text in the **Line Edit** widget is then removed, and the focus is set on it, enabling the user to enter different text.

In the following screenshot, you can see the text entered by the user in the **Line Edit** widget is added to **List Widget** when the user selects the **Add to List** button:

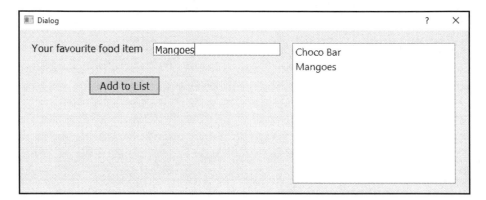

Performing operations in List Widget

In this recipe, you will learn how to perform different operations on list items in **List Widget**. **List Widget** is basically used for showing a collection of similar items, enabling the user to choose the desired items. Consequently, you need to add items to **List Widget**. Also, you might require to edit any item in **List Widget**. Sometimes, you might require to delete an item from **List Widget**. One more operation that you might want to perform on **List Widget** is deleting all items from it, clearing the entire **List Widget** item. Before learning how to add, edit, and delete items from **List Widget**, let's understand the concept of a list item.

Getting ready

List Widget consists of several list items. These list items are instances of the `QListWidgetItem` class. The list items can be inserted into **List Widget** using the `insertItem()` or `addItem()` methods. List items may be in text or icon form and can be checked or unchecked. Methods provided by `QListWidgetItem` are given next.

Methods provided by the QListWidgetItem class

Let's take a look at the following methods provided by the `QListWidgetItem` class:

- `setText()`: This method assigns the specified text to the list item

- setIcon(): This method assigns the specified icon to the list item
- checkState(): This method returns the Boolean value depending on whether the list item is in a checked or unchecked state
- setHidden(): This method passes the Boolean value true to this method to hide the list item
- isHidden(): This method returns true if the list item is hidden

We have learned to add items to **List Widget**. What if you want to edit an existing item in **List Widget**, or you want to delete an item from **List Widget**, or you want to delete all the items from **List Widget**?

Let's learn to perform different operations on **List Widget** by creating an application. This application will display **Line Edit**, **List Widget**, and a couple of **Push Button** widgets. You can add items to **List Widget** by entering the text in **Line Edit**, followed by clicking the **Add** button. Similarly, you can edit any item from **List Widget** by clicking an item from **List Widget**, followed by clicking the **Edit** button. Not only this, but you can even delete any item from **List Widget** by clicking the **Delete** button. If you want to clear the entire **List Widget**, simply click on the **Delete All** button.

How to do it....

Perform the following steps to understand how different operations can be applied on the **List Widget** item; how items can be added, edited, and deleted from the **List Widget** item; and how the entire **List Widget** item can be cleared:

1. Open Qt Designer, create a new application based on the **Dialog without Buttons** template, and drag and drop a **Label**, **Line Edit**, four **Push Button**, and **List Widget** widgets onto the form.
2. Set the **text** property of the **Label** widget to `Enter an item`.
3. Set the **text** property of the four **Push Button** widgets to `Add`, `Edit`, `Delete`, and `Delete All`.
4. Set the **objectName** property of the four **Push Button** widgets to `psuhButtonAdd`, `pushButtonEdit`, `pushButtonDelete`, and `pushButtonDeleteAll`.
5. Save the application with the name `demoListWidgetOp.ui`.

The form will appear as shown in the following screenshot:

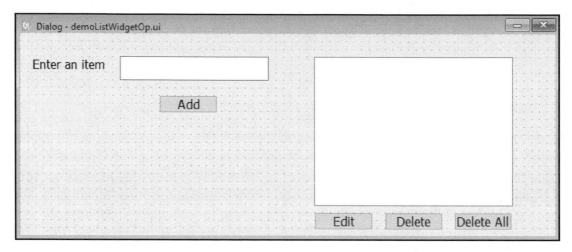

The XML file `demoListWidgetOp.ui` needs to be converted into the Python script by making use of the `pyuic5` command utility. The generated Python file `demoListWidgetOp.py` can be seen in the source code bundle of this book.

6. Create a Python script file named `callListWidgetOp.pyw` that imports the Python code, `demoListWidgetOp.py`, enabling you to invoke the user interface design and add, delete, and edit the list items in **List Widget**. The code in the Python script `callListWidgetOp.pyw` is shown here:

```python
import sys
from PyQt5.QtWidgets import QDialog, QApplication, QInputDialog,
QListWidgetItem
from demoListWidgetOp import *
class MyForm(QDialog):
    def __init__(self):
        super().__init__()
        self.ui = Ui_Dialog()
        self.ui.setupUi(self)
        self.ui.listWidget.addItem('Ice Cream')
        self.ui.listWidget.addItem('Soda')
        self.ui.listWidget.addItem('Coffee')
        self.ui.listWidget.addItem('Chocolate')
        self.ui.pushButtonAdd.clicked.connect(self.addlist)
        self.ui.pushButtonEdit.clicked.connect(self.editlist)
        self.ui.pushButtonDelete.clicked.connect(self.delitem)
        self.ui.pushButtonDeleteAll.clicked.connect
        (self.delallitems)
        self.show()
```

```
        def addlist(self):
            self.ui.listWidget.addItem(self.ui.lineEdit.text())
            self.ui.lineEdit.setText('')
            self.ui.lineEdit.setFocus()
        def editlist(self):
            row=self.ui.listWidget.currentRow()
            newtext, ok=QInputDialog.getText(self, "Enter new text",
            "Enter new text")
            if ok and (len(newtext) !=0):
                    self.ui.listWidget.takeItem(self.ui.listWidget.
                    currentRow())
                    self.ui.listWidget.insertItem(row,
                    QListWidgetItem(newtext))
        def delitem(self):
            self.ui.listWidget.takeItem(self.ui.listWidget.
            currentRow())
        def delallitems(self):
            self.ui.listWidget.clear()
    if __name__=="__main__":
        app = QApplication(sys.argv)
        w = MyForm()
        w.show()
        sys.exit(app.exec_())
```

How it works...

The **clicked()** event of `pushButtonAdd` is connected to the `addlist` function. Similarly, the **clicked()** event of the `pushButtonEdit`, `pushButtonDelete`, and `pushButtonDeleteAll` objects are connected to the `editlist`, `delitem`, and `delallitems` functions, respectively. That is, on clicking any push button, the respective function is invoked. The `addlist` function calls the `addItem` function on the **List Widget** item to add the text entered in the **Line Edit** widget. The `editlist` function uses the `currentRow` method on **List Widget** to find out the list item to be edited. The `getText` method of the `QInputDialog` class is invoked to prompt the user for the new text or edited text. On clicking the **OK** button in the dialog, the current list item will be replaced by the text entered in the dialog box. The `delitem` function invokes the `takeItem` method on **List Widget** to delete the current row, that is, the selected list item. The `delallitems` function invokes the `clear` method on the**List Widget** item to clear or delete all the list items from the **List Widget** item.

On running the application, you will find an empty **List Widget**, **Line Edit**, and **Add** push button below the **Line Edit** widget. Add any text in the **Line Edit** widget and click on the **Add** button to add that item to **List Widget**. After adding four items to **List Widget,** it might appear as shown in the following screenshot:

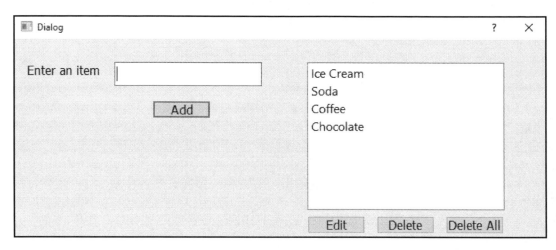

Let's add one more item, Pizza, to **List Widget**. Type `Pizza` in the **Line Edit** widget and click the **Add** button. The **Pizza** item will be added to the **List Widget** item, as shown in the following screenshot:

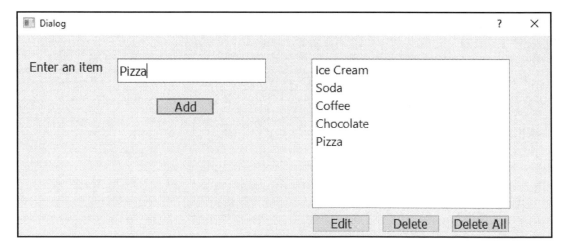

Assuming we want to edit the **Pizza** item from **List Widget**, click the **Pizza** item in **List Widget** and click on the **Edit** button. On clicking the **Edit** button, you get a dialog box prompting you to enter a new item to replace the **Pizza** item. Let's enter `Cold Drink` in the dialog box, followed by clicking the **OK** button, as shown in the following screenshot:

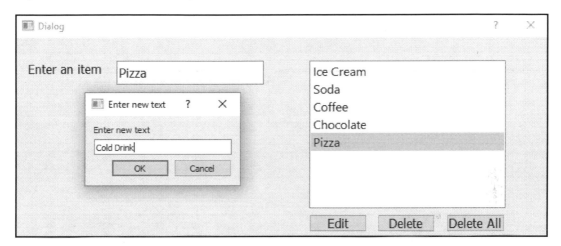

You can see in the following screenshot that the **Pizza** item in **List Widget** is replaced by the text **Cold Drink**:

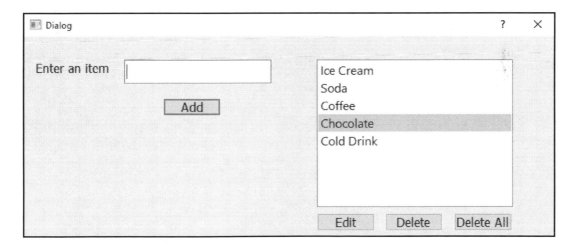

In order to delete any item from **List Widget**, simply click that item from **List Widget**, followed by clicking the **Delete** button. Let's click the **Coffee** item from **List Widget** and click on the **Delete** button; the **Coffee** item will be deleted from **List Widget**, as shown in the following screenshot:

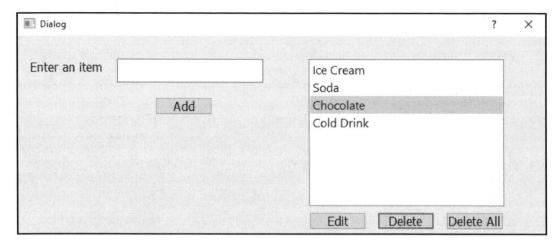

On clicking the **Delete All** button, the entire **List Widget** item will become empty, as shown in the following screenshot:

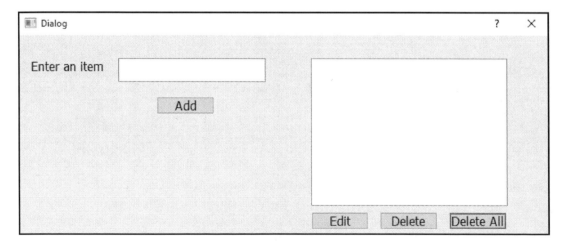

Using the Combo Box widget

Combo boxes are used for getting input from the user with an applied constraint; that is, the user will be shown certain options in the form of a popup list and he/she can only select from the available choices. A combo box takes less space when compared with **List Widget**. The QComboBox class is used for displaying combo boxes. Not only can you display text through a combo box, but pixmaps too. Here are the methods provided by the QComboBox class:

Method	Usage
setItemText()	Sets or changes the text of the item in the combo box.
removeItem()	Removes the specific item from the combo box.
clear()	Removes all items from the combo box.
currentText()	Returns the text of the current item, that is, the item that is currently chosen.
setCurrentIndex()	Sets the current index of the combo box, that is, it sets the desired item in the combo box as the currently chosen item.
count()	Returns the count of the items in the combo box.
setMaxCount()	Sets the maximum number of items that are allowed in the combo box.
setEditable()	Make the combo box editable, that is, the user can edit items in the combo box.
addItem()	Appends the specified content to the combo box.
addItems()	Appends each of the strings supplied in the text to the combo box.
itemText()	Returns the text at the specified index location in the combo box.
currentIndex()	Returns the index location of the currently chosen item in the combo box. If the combo box is empty or no item is currently chosen in the combo box, the method will return −1 as the index.

The following are the signals that are generated by QComboBox:

Signal	Description
currentIndexChanged()	Emitted when the index of the combo box is changed, that is, the user selects some new item in the combo box.
activated()	Emitted when the index is changed by the user.
highlighted()	Emitted when the user highlights an item in the combo box.
editTextChanged()	Emitted when the text of an editable combo box is changed.

To understand the workings of a combo box practically, let's create a recipe. This recipe will display certain bank account types via a combo box and will prompt the user to choose the type of bank account he/she wants to open. The selected bank account type from the combo box will be displayed on the screen through a **Label** widget.

How to do it...

The following are the steps to create an application that makes use of a combo box to show certain options and explains how the selected option from the combo box can be displayed:

1. Create a new application of the **Dialog without Buttons** template, drag two **Label** widgets and a **Combo Box** widget from the **Widget** box, and drop them onto the form.
2. Set the **text** property of the first **Label** widget to Select your account type.
3. Delete the default **text** property of the second **Label** widget, as its text will be set through code.
4. Set the **objectName** property of the **Combo Box** widget to comboBoxAccountType.
5. The second **Label** widget will be used to display the bank account type that is chosen by the user, so set the **objectName** property of the second **Label** widget to labelAccountType.
6. As we want the **Combo Box** widget to display certain bank account types, right-click on the **Combo Box** widget and from the context menu that opens up, select the **Edit Items** option.
7. Add some bank account types to the **Combo Box** widget one by one.
8. Save the application by name as demoComboBox.ui.
9. Click the **+** button displayed at the bottom of the dialog to add a bank account type to the **Combo Box** widget, as shown in the following screenshot:

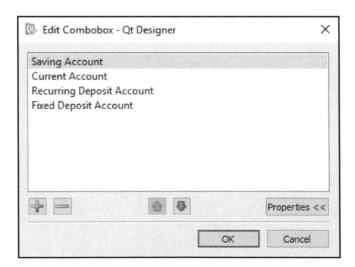

10. After adding the desired bank account types, click on the **OK** button to exit from the dialog. The form will now appear, as shown in the following screenshot:

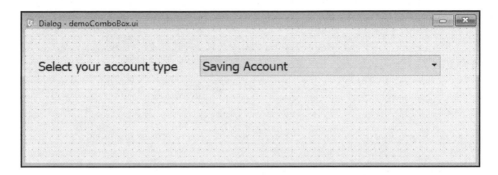

The user interface created with Qt Designer is stored in a .ui file, which is an XML file, and needs to be converted to the Python code. The pyuic5 utility can be used for generating Python code from the XML file. The generated file, demoComboBox.py, can be seen in the source code bundle of this book.

11. Treat the demoComboBox.py file as a header file, and import it to the file from which you will invoke its user interface design that is you will be able to access the combo box.

12. Create another Python file with the name callComboBox.pyw and import the demoComboBox.py code into it. The code in the Python script callComboBox.pyw is as shown here:

```python
import sys
from PyQt5.QtWidgets import QDialog, QApplication
from demoComboBox import *
class MyForm(QDialog):
    def __init__(self):
        super().__init__()
        self.ui = Ui_Dialog()
        self.ui.setupUi(self)
        self.ui.comboBoxAccountType.currentIndexChanged.connect
        (self.dispAccountType)
        self.show()

    def dispAccountType(self):
        self.ui.labelAccountType.setText("You have selected
        "+self.ui.comboBoxAccountType.itemText(self.ui.
        comboBoxAccountType.currentIndex()))

if __name__=="__main__":
```

```
app = QApplication(sys.argv)
w = MyForm()
w.show()
sys.exit(app.exec_())
```

How it works...

In the `demoComboBox.py` file, a class with the name of the top-level object is created with `Ui_` prepended. That is, for the top-level object, `Dialog`, the `Ui_Dialog` class, is created and stores the interface elements of our widget. That class includes two methods, `setupUi` and `retranslateUi`.

The `setupUi` method creates the widgets that are used in defining the user interface in Qt Designer. Also, the properties of the widgets are set in this method. The `setupUi` method takes a single argument, which is the top-level widget of the application, an instance of `QDialog`. The `retranslateUi` method translates the interface.

In the `callComboBox.pyw` file, whenever the user selects any item from the combo box, the `currentIndexChanged` signal will be emitted and the `currentIndexChanged` signal is connected to the `dispAccountType` method, so whenever any item is selected from the combo box, the `dispAccountType` method will be invoked.

In the `dispAccountType` method, you access the currently selected index number by invoking the `currentIndex` method of the `QComboBox` class and passing the fetched index location to the `itemText` method of the `QComboBox` class to get the text of the currently selected combo box item. The currently selected combo box item is then displayed through the **Label** widget.

On running the application, you will find a combo box showing four bank account types: **Saving Account**, **Current Account**, **Recurring Deposit Account**, and **Fixed Deposit Account**, as shown in the following screenshot:

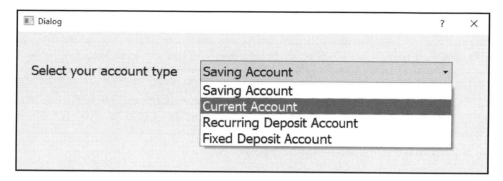

On selecting a bank account type from the combo box, the chosen bank account type will be displayed through the **Label** widget, as shown in the following screenshot:

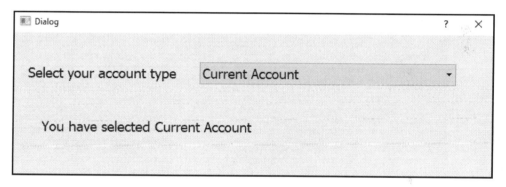

Using the Font Combo Box widget

The **Font Combo Box** widget, as the name suggests, displays a list of font styles to choose from. The chosen font style can be applied to the desired content if required.

Getting ready

To understand the workings of the **Font Combo Box** widget practically, let's create a recipe. This recipe will display a **Font Combo Box** widget and a **Text Edit** widget. The user will be able to type the desired content in the **Text Edit** widget. After typing the text in the **Text Edit** widget, when the user selects any font style from the **Font Combo Box** widget, the selected font will be applied to the content typed into the **Text Edit** widget.

How to do it...

Here are the steps to display an active **Font Combo Box** widget and to apply the selected font to the text written in the **Text Edit** widget:

1. Create a new application of the **Dialog without Buttons** template and drag two **Label** widgets, a **Font Combo Box** widget, and a **Text Edit** widget from the **Widget** box and drop them onto the form.

2. Set the text property of the first **Label** widget to Select desired font and that of the second **Label** widget to Type some text.

3. Save the application by name as demoFontComboBox.ui. The form will now appear as shown in the following screenshot:

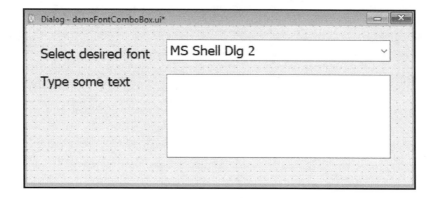

The user interface created with Qt Designer is stored in a .ui file, which is an XML file, and needs to be converted to the Python code. On converting to Python code, the generated file, demoFontComboBox.py, can be seen in the source code bundle of this book. The preceding code will be used as a header file and is imported into the file in which the GUI is desired, that is, the user interface designed can be accessed in any Python script by simply importing the preceding code.

4. Create another Python file with the name callFontFontComboBox.pyw and import the demoFontComboBox.py code into it.

The code in the Python script, `callFontComboBox.pyw`, is as shown here:

```
import sys
from PyQt5.QtWidgets import QDialog, QApplication
from demoFontComboBox import *
class MyForm(QDialog):
    def __init__(self):
        super().__init__()
        self.ui = Ui_Dialog()
        self.ui.setupUi(self)
        myFont=QtGui.QFont(self.ui.fontComboBox.itemText(self.ui.
        fontComboBox.currentIndex()),15)
        self.ui.textEdit.setFont(myFont)
        self.ui.fontComboBox.currentFontChanged.connect
        (self.changeFont)
        self.show()
    def changeFont(self):
        myFont=QtGui.QFont(self.ui.fontComboBox.itemText(self.ui.
        fontComboBox.currentIndex()),15)
        self.ui.textEdit.setFont(myFont)
if __name__=="__main__":
    app = QApplication(sys.argv)
    w = MyForm()
    w.show()
    sys.exit(app.exec_())
```

How it works...

In the `callFontComboBox.pyw` file, whenever the user selects any font style from the **Font Combo Box** widget, the `currentFontChanged` signal is emitted and this signal is connected to the `changeFont` method, so whenever any font style is chosen from the **Font Combo Box** widget, the `changeFont()` method will be invoked.

In the `changeFont()` method, you access the selected font style by invoking two methods. The first method invoked is the `currentIndex()` method of the `QFontComboBox` class, which fetches the index number of the selected font style. The second method invoked is the `itemText()` method, and the index location of the currently selected font style is passed to this method to access the chosen font style. The chosen font style is then applied to the content written in the **Text Edit** widget.

On running the application, you will find a **Font Combo Box** widget showing available font styles in the system, as shown in the following screenshot:

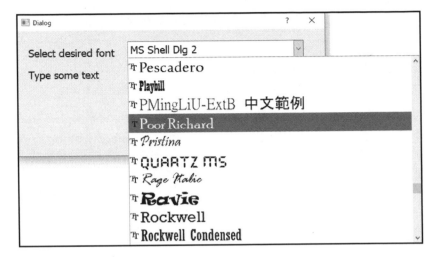

Type some text in the **Text Edit** widget and choose the desired font from the font combo box. The chosen font style will be applied to the text written in the **Text Edit** widget, as shown in the following screenshot:

Using the Progress Bar widget

The **Progress Bar** widget is very useful in representing the progress of any task. Whether it is downloading a file from a server, virus scanning on a machine, or some other critical task, the **Progress Bar** widget helps inform the user of the percentage of the task that is done and the percentage that is pending. As the task completes, the **Progress Bar** widget keeps updating, indicating progress in the task.

Getting ready

To understand how the progress bar is updated to show the progress of any task, let's create a recipe. This recipe will display a **Progress Bar** widget, indicating the total time required to download a file. When the user clicks the push button to begin downloading the file, the **Progress Bar** widget will update from **0%** to **100%** gradually; that is, the progress bar will update as the file is being downloaded. The **Progress Bar** widget will show **100%** when the file is completely downloaded.

How to do it...

Initially, the **Progress Bar** widget is at **0%** and to make it go up, we need to make use of a loop. The loop will increment its value as the task represented by the **Progress Bar** widget progresses towards completion. Every increment in the loop value will add to some progress in the **Progress Bar** widget. Here is the step-by-step procedure to show how a progress bar can be updated:

1. Create a new application from the **Dialog without Buttons** template, and drag a **Label** widget, a **Progress Bar** widget, and a **Push Button** widget from the **Widget box** and drop them onto the form.
2. Set the **text** property of the **Label** widget to Downloading the file and that of the **Push Button** widget to Start Downloading.
3. Set the **objectName** property of the **Push Button** widget to pushButtonStart.
4. Save the application by name as demoProgressBar.ui. The form will now appear, as shown in the following screenshot:

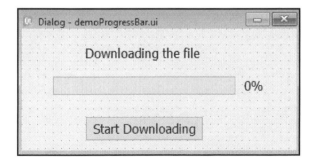

The user interface created with Qt Designer is stored in a `.ui` file, which is an XML file and needs to be converted into Python code. The generated Python code, demoProgressBar.py, can be seen in the source code bundle of this book. The preceding code will be used as a header file and is imported into the file in which the GUI is desired; that is, the user interface designed in the code can be accessed in any Python script by simply importing the preceding code.

5. Create another Python file with the name callProgressBar.pyw and import the demoProgressBar.py code into it. The code in the Python script callProgressBar.pyw is as shown here:

```python
import sys
from PyQt5.QtWidgets import QDialog, QApplication
from demoProgressBar import *
class MyForm(QDialog):
    def __init__(self):
        super().__init__()
        self.ui = Ui_Dialog()
        self.ui.setupUi(self)
        self.ui.pushButtonStart.clicked.connect(self.updateBar)
        self.show()

    def updateBar(self):
        x = 0
        while x < 100:
            x += 0.0001
            self.ui.progressBar.setValue(x)

if __name__=="__main__":
    app = QApplication(sys.argv)
    w = MyForm()
    w.show()
    sys.exit(app.exec_())
```

How it works...

In the `callProgressBar.pyw` file, because we want the progress bar to show its progress when the push button is pressed, the **clicked()** event of the progress bar is connected to the `updateBar()` method, so when the push button is clicked, the `updateBar()` method will be invoked. In the `updateBar()` method, a `while` loop is used that loops from 0 to 100. A variable, x, is initialized to the value 0. With every iteration of the while loop, the value of x is incremented by 0.0001. The value in the x variable is applied to the progress bar when updating it. That is, with every iteration of the while loop, the value of x is incremented and the value of x is used in updating the progress bar. Hence, the progress bar will begin its progress at **0%** and continue until it reaches **100%**.

On running the application, initially, you will find the **Progress Bar** widget at **0%** along with the push button at the bottom with the caption **Start Downloading** (see the following screenshot). Click the **Start Downloading** push button and you will see that the progress bar begins showing progress gradually. The progress bar keeps going up until it reaches **100%** to indicate that the file is completely downloaded:

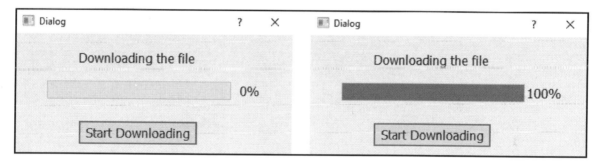

Working with Date and Time 3

In this chapter, we will cover the following topics:

- Displaying LCD digits
- Displaying system clock time in LCD-like digits
- Displaying the data selected by the user from Calendar Widget
- Creating a hotel reservation form
- Displaying tabular data using Table Widget

Displaying LCD digits

Qt Designer enables us to display LCD-like digits of any size by making use of its **LCD Number** widget. The **LCD Number** widget is an instance of the QLCDNumber class and it can be used to display decimal, hexadecimal, octal, and binary digits of any size. The methods provided by QLCDNumber are as follows:

- **setMode()**: This method is used to change the base of the numbers. Available options are as follows:
    - **Hex**: This option is used to display hexadecimal digits
    - **Dec**: This option is used to display decimal digits
    - **Oct**: This option is used to display octal digits
    - **Bin**: This option is used to display binary digits
- **display()**: This method is used to display the supplied data in LCD digit format.
- **value()**: This method returns the numerical value displayed by the **LCD Number** widget.

We want the displayed system clock time to be updated automatically. For this, we need to implement timers.

Using Timers

Timers are used for performing repetitive tasks. A timer is an instance of the QTimer class. The task to be repeated needs to be written in a method and that method, in turn, is invoked via the **timeout()** signal of the QTimer instance. The **timeout()** signal can be configured or adjusted using the following methods:

- start(n): It compels the timer to generate the **timeout()** signal at *n* millisecond intervals
- setSingleShot(true): It constrains the timer to generate the **timeout()** signal only once
- singleShot(n): It makes the timer generate a **timeout()** signal only once, and that too after *n* milliseconds

Before we go ahead and make an application, we need to understand one more class, QTime, which is used to fetch and measure system clock time.

Using the QTime class

The QTime class not only helps in reading the current time from the system clock but also provides all clock time functions. It shows time in terms of hours, minutes, seconds, and milliseconds since midnight. Also, it helps in measuring the span of elapsed time. The time returned by the QTime class is in 24-hour format. The methods provided by the QTime class are as follows:

- currentTime(): This method accesses the system clock time and returns it as a QTime object
- hour(): This method returns the number of hours
- minute(): This method returns the number of minutes
- seconds(): This method returns the number of seconds
- msec(): This method returns the number of milliseconds
- addSecs(): This method returns the time after adding the specified number of seconds
- addMSecs(): This method returns the time after adding the specified number of milliseconds
- secsTo(): This method returns the difference in the number of seconds between two QTime objects

- `msecsTo()`: This method returns the difference in the number of milliseconds between two times

Displaying system clock time in LCD-like digits

Liquid Crystal Display (LCD) digits are a seven-segment display that is commonly used in almost all electronic devices. These LCD digits are much more readable than dot matrix displays. Let's create an application that displays system clock time in LCD-like digits.

How to do it...

In this application, we will be making use of the `QTime` class to fetch the current system's time. Following are the steps to create such an application:

1. Open Qt Designer and create a new application based on the **Dialog without Buttons** template.
2. Save the application with the name `demoLCD.ui`.
3. Since we want to display LCD-like digits, drag and drop the **LCD Number** widget onto the form, as shown in the following screenshot:

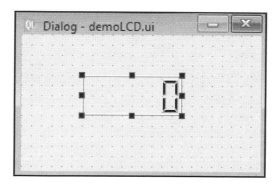

4. From the **Property Editor** window, set the **Width** and **Height** properties of the **LCD Number** widget to `100` and `40` respectively, just to make the system clock quite visible. Use the `pyuic5` command utility to convert the `.ui` (XML) file into Python code. The generated Python `demoLCD.py` file can be seen in the source code bundle of the book.

5. Create a Python script named `callLCD.pyw` which imports the code, `demoLCD.py`, to invoke the user interface design and display the current system clock time through the **LCD Number** widget.

6. The script must also include a timer to keep updating the LCD display at fixed intervals. The Python `callLCD.pyw` script appears as shown here:

```python
import sys
from PyQt5.QtWidgets import QDialog, QApplication
from demoLCD import *
class MyForm(QDialog):
    def __init__(self):
        super().__init__()
        self.ui = Ui_Dialog()
        self.ui.setupUi(self)
        timer = QtCore.QTimer(self)
        timer.timeout.connect(self.showlcd)
        timer.start(1000)
        self.showlcd()
    def showlcd(self):
        time = QtCore.QTime.currentTime()
        text = time.toString('hh:mm')
        self.ui.lcdNumber.display(text)
if __name__=="__main__":
    app = QApplication(sys.argv)
    w = MyForm()
    w.show()
    sys.exit(app.exec_())
```

How it works...

In this code, you can see that an instance of `QTimer` is created with the named timer, and its **timeout()** signal is connected to `showlcd()`. Whenever **timeout()** is generated, the `showlcd()` method will be invoked. Also, via `start()`, you set the timer to generate a **timeout()** signal after every 1,000 milliseconds.

In the showlcd() method, you fetch the current system clock time, convert it into a string data type, make it appear in the HH:MM format, and display it with the **LCD Number** widget, as shown in the following screenshot:

Displaying the date selected by the user from Calendar Widget

This application will make use of two widgets, **Calendar Widget** and **Date Edit**. The date selected by the user from **Calendar Widget** will be reflected in the **Date Edit** widget. Both widgets are commonly used when displaying current date as well as the date required by the user, with the only difference that **Calendar Widget** has a bigger and more readable visual, whereas the **Date Edit** widget consumes much less space.

Getting ready

To make this recipe, we need to understand the following things first:

- **Calendar Widget** displays the desired monthly calendar
- The QDate class accesses the date from the system clock
- The **Date Edit** widget will display the date that is selected from **Calendar Widget**

So, let's first understand the preceding widgets and class one by one.

Displaying a calendar

In order to enable the user to select a date, you need to display a monthly calendar. **Calendar Widget** in Qt Designer helps in doing so. This widget is an instance of the `QCalendarWidget` class that displays the current month and year by default and can be changed if desired. The days appear in short form (**Sun**, **Mon**, **Tue**, and so on), and Saturday and Sunday are marked in red. Also, Sunday is displayed as the first column in the calendar. You can use the following properties of **Calendar Widget** to configure its display:

- **minimumDate**: This property is used for specifying the minimum date range.
- **maximumDate**: This property is used for specifying the maximum date range.
- **selectionMode**: This property helps in enabling or disabling the user's ability to select a date from **Calendar Widget**. If this property is set to **NoSelection**, it will not allow the user to select any date.
- **verticalHeaderFormat**: You can remove the week numbers from **Calendar Widget** by setting this property to **NoVerticalHeader**.
- **gridVisible**: This property helps in making the calendar grid visible or invisible. You can set this property to the Boolean value **True** to make the calendar grid visible.
- **HorizontalHeaderFormat**: This property is used for setting the days format to be displayed. The following are the available options:
  - **SingleLetterDayNames**: A single letter for days is displayed in the header, such as **M** for Monday, **T** for Tuesday, and so on.
  - **ShortDayNames**: The short form of days are displayed in the header, such as **Mon** for Monday, **Tue** for Tuesday, and so on.
  - **LongDayNames**: The header displays days in complete forms, such as **Monday**, **Tuesday**, and so on.
  - **NoHorizontalHeader**: Using this option in **HorizontalHeaderFormat** makes the header invisible.

The methods provided by `QCalendarWidget` are given in the following list:

- `selectedDate()`: This method returns the currently selected date. The date is returned as a `QDate` object.
- `monthShown()`: This method returns the currently displayed month.
- `yearShown()`: This method returns the currently displayed year.
- `setFirstDayOfWeek()`: This method is used to set the day of the week in the first column.

- selectionChanged(): This method is invoked when the user changes the currently selected date.

Let's look at the QDate class as the system date is returned as an instance of this class only. Also, the QDate class provides methods to extract the year, month, and day from the QDate instance.

Using the QDate class

The QDate class helps in handling dates. The instance of the QDate class accesses the date from the system clock and displays the date, which includes the year, month, and day, using the Gregorian calendar. The following is the list of methods provided by the QDate class:

- currentDate(): This method returns the system date as a QDate instance.
- setDate(): This method sets the date based on the supplied year, month, and day.
- year(): This method returns the year from the specified QDate instance.
- month(): This method returns the month from the specified QDate instance.
- day(): This method returns the day from the specified QDate instance.
- dayOfWeek(): This method returns the day of the week from the specified QDate instance.
- addDays(): This method adds the specified number of days to the specified date and returns the new date.
- addMonths(): This method adds the specified number of months to the specified date and returns the new date.
- addYears(): This method adds the specified number of years to the specified date and returns the new date.
- daysTo(): This method returns the number of days between two dates.
- daysInMonth(): This method returns the number of days in the specified month.
- daysInYear(): This method returns the number of days in the specified year.
- isLeapYear(): This method returns true if the specified date is in a leap year.
- toPyDate(): This method returns the date as a string. The format parameter determines the format of the result string.

The following expressions are used for specifying the format:

- **d**: This expression displays the day as a number without a leading zero (1 to 31)
- **dd**: This expression displays the day as a number with a leading zero (01 to 31)
- **ddd**: This expression displays the day in short format (Mon, Tue, and so on)
- **dddd**: This expression displays the day in long format (Monday, Tuesday, and so on)
- **M**: This expression displays the month as a number without a leading zero (1 to 12)
- **MM**: This expression displays the month as a number with a leading zero (01 to 12)
- **MMM**: This expression displays the month in short format (Jan, Feb, and so on)
- **MMMM**: This expression displays the month in long format (January, February, and so on)
- **yy**: This expression displays the year as a two-digit number (00 to 99)
- **yyyy**: This expression displays the year as a four-digit number

Let's take a look at the following examples:

- dd.MM.yyyy will display the date as 15.01.2018
- ddd MMMM d yy will display the date as Sun January 15 18

To display the date that is selected by the user in **Calendar Widget**, you use a **Date Edit** widget.

Using the Date Edit widget

To display and edit dates, the **Date Edit** widget is used, which is an instance of the `QDateEdit` class.

The properties used to configure the **Date Edit** widget are as follows:

- **minimumDate**: A minimum date can be defined for the widget by making use of this property
- **maximumDate**: A maximum date can be defined for the widget by making use of this property

The following are the methods provided by the `QDateEdit` class:

- `setDate()`: This method is used to set the date to be displayed in the widget

- `setDisplayFormat()`: This method is used to set the date format for the date being displayed in the **Date Edit** widget

The formats, with their output, are as follows:

- dd.MM.yyyy 15.01.2018
- MMM d yy Jan 15 18
- MMM d yyyy Jan 15 2018
- MMMM d yy January 15 18

As mentioned previously, in the following application you will learn to display the date that is selected by the user in **Calendar Widget** with the **Date Edit** widget.

How to do it...

Both widgets, **Calendar Widget** and **Date Edit**, are meant for accepting dates, with the only difference that **Calendar Widget** has a bigger display and shows weekdays too, along with the dates, whereas the **Date Edit** widget provides the spin buttons to spin between days, months, and years. Here are the steps to build an application that displays the date selected through **Calendar Widget** in the **Date Edit** widget:

1. Open Qt Designer and create a new **Dialog without Buttons** template.
2. Drag and drop the **Calendar Widget** and **Date Edit** widgets onto the form,
3. Save the application with the name `demoCalendar.ui`. The application is shown in the following screenshot:

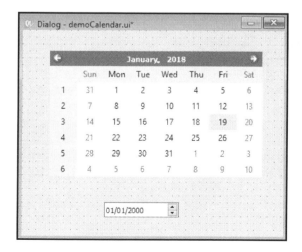

The `pyuic5` command utility will convert the `.ui` (XML) file into Python code. You can find the generated Python script, `demoCalendar.py`, in the source code bundle of the book.

4. Create a Python script named `callCalendar.pyw` that imports the code, `demoCalendar.py`, to invoke the user interface design and display the selected date from **Calendar Widget** in the **Date Edit** widget. The Python script, `callCalendar.pyw`, appears as shown here:

```python
import sys
from PyQt5.QtWidgets import QDialog, QApplication
from demoCalendar import *
class MyForm(QDialog):
    def __init__(self):
        super().__init__()
        self.ui = Ui_Dialog()
        self.ui.setupUi(self)
        self.ui.calendarWidget.selectionChanged.connect
        (self.dispdate)
        self.show()
    def dispdate(self):
        self.ui.dateEdit.setDate(self.ui.calendarWidget.
        selectedDate())
if __name__=="__main__":
    app = QApplication(sys.argv)
    w = MyForm()
    w.show()
    sys.exit(app.exec_())
```

How it works...

In the code, you can see that the `selectionChanged` signal of **Calendar Widget** is connected to the `dispdate` function. Hence, as the user selects a date, the `dispdate` function will be invoked. In the `dispdate` function, the date selected by the user is retrieved through the `selectedDate()` method and displayed in the **Date Edit** widget through `setDate`.

On running the application, **Calendar Widget** will display the current system date and the **Date Edit** widget will simply display the default date, **01/01/2000**.

The date is displayed in the default date format, mm/dd/yyyy, as shown in the following screenshot:

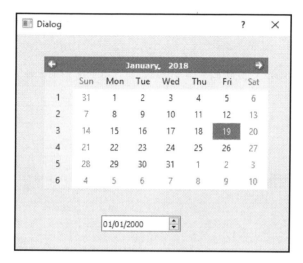

On selecting any date from **Calendar Widget**, the selected date will be displayed on the **Date Edit** widget, as shown in the following screenshot:

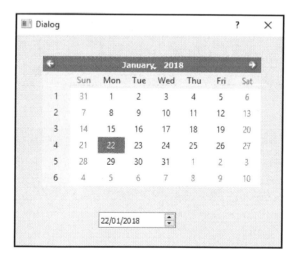

You can display the date in a different format with the `setDisplayFormat()` method. Let's modify the `dispdate()` function to display the date in MMM d yyyy format:

```
def dispdate(self):
    self.ui.dateEdit.setDisplayFormat('MMM d yyyy')
    self.ui.dateEdit.setDate(self.ui.calendarWidget.selectedDate())
```

Now, the date selected from **Calendar Widget** will appear in the desired format in the **Date Edit** widget, as shown in the following screenshot:

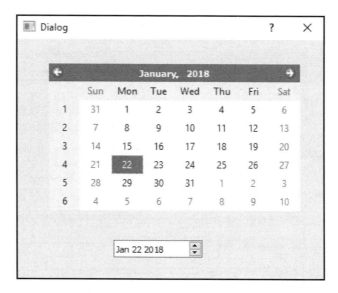

Creating a hotel reservation form

This application will display **Calendar Widget**, prompting the user to select the date for reserving a room. Also, a **Spin Box** widget will be displayed that asks the user to choose the number of days they want to stay. Besides this, a **Combo Box** widget will be displayed on the hotel reservation form that prompts the user to select the room type. The room rent will be based on the selected room type.

Getting ready

Before we begin creating a hotel reservation form, let's understand the use of the **Combo Box** widget first.

In order to display several options in minimum space, **Combo Box** is preferred. The QComboBox class is used for displaying a **Combo Box** widget. Not only text, but graphic images too can be displayed via a **Combo Box** widget. Here are the methods provided by the QComboBox class:

- setItemText(): This method is used to change the item in the **Combo Box** widget.
- removeItem(): This method is used to remove an item from the **Combo Box** widget.
- clear(): This method is used for removing all items from the **Combo Box** widget.
- currentText(): This method returns the text of the currently selected item from the **Combo Box** widget.
- setCurrentIndex(): This method is used to set the current item.
- count(): This method returns the count of the number of items in the **Combo Box** widget.
- setMaxCount(): This method is used to set the maximum count of the number of items allowed in the **Combo Box** widget. It sets the maximum capacity of the **Combo Box** widget.
- setEditable(): If the Boolean value **True** is passed to this method, it will make the **Combo Box** widget editable.
- addItem(): This method is used to append the specified text to the **Combo Box** widget.
- addItems(): This method is used to append each of the strings supplied in this method to the **Combo Box** widget. Each string is appended, one below the other.
- itemText(): This method returns the text at the specified index location in the **Combo Box** widget.
- currentIndex(): This method returns the index of the currently selected item in the **Combo Box** widget. An empty combo box or a combo box with no selected item returns −1.

The signals generated by the **Combo Box** widget are shown in the following list:

- **currentIndexChanged()**: This signal is emitted if the index of the **Combo Box** widget is changed, that is, when some text other than the currently selected text is chosen in the **Combo Box** widget
- **activated()**: This signal is emitted when the index is changed by user interaction

- **highlighted()**: This signal is emitted when the user highlights an item in the **Combo Box** widget
- **editTextChanged()**: This signal is emitted when the text of an editable **Combo Box** widget is changed

The next application is a hotel reservation form that prompts the user to specify the date of the reservation, the number of days staying, and the room type the user wants to book. Then, it computes the total room rent accordingly. The user can specify the date of his journey with **Calendar Widget**, the number of days with a **Spin Box** widget, and the room type with a **Combo Box** widget. The **Combo Box** widget will display four room class options: **Suite**, **Super Luxury**, **Super Deluxe**, and **Ordinary room**. The rate of these room types is assumed to be $40, $30, $20, and $10, respectively.

How to do it...

In this application, you will learn to make use of **Calendar Widget**, **Spin Box**, and **Combo Box**. All three widgets make the data entry easier and error-proof. The **Calendar Widget** item gives you the comfort of switching to the desired month and day. Similarly, the **Spin Box** widget enables you to select a value from the available options; the user cannot enter any invalid data and this is also the case with the **Combo Box** widget. This is the step-by-step procedure to develop this application:

1. In the application, six **Label** widgets, a **Calendar Widget** item, a **Spin Box** widget, a **Combo Box** widget, and a **Push Button** widget are used.
2. The **text** property of the first four **Label** widgets is set to `Hotel Room Reservation`, `Date of Reservation`, `Number of days`, and `Room type`.
3. Set the **objectName** property of the fifth and sixth **Label** widgets to `Enteredinfo` and `RoomRentinfo`, respectively.
4. The `Enteredinfo` widget will be used to display the options selected in the different widgets by the user, and the `RoomRentinfo` widget will be used to display the computed room rent.
5. Delete the **text** property of the two **Label** widgets, `Enteredinfo` and `RoomRentinfo`, to make them invisible in the form; their respective text will be assigned through programming.

6. The **text** property of the **Push Button** widget is set to `Calculate Room Rent`, the point size of the **Label** widget representing the **Hotel Room Reservation** text is increased, and its **Bold** property is set to make it appear as the header of the application

7. Save the application with the name `reservehotel.ui`. The application is shown in the following screenshot:

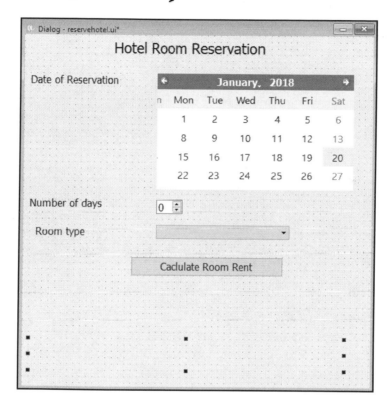

The `pyuic5` command utility converts the `.ui` (XML) file into Python code. The generated Python code, `reservehotel.py`, can be seen in the code bundle of the book.

8. Create a Python script named `computeRoomRent.pyw` that imports the code, `reservehotel.py`, to invoke the user interface design and compute and display the total room rent on the basis of the number of persons and room type selected. The script will also display the date, a number of persons, and room type options selected by the user.

The Python script `computeRoomRent.pyw` will appear as shown here:

```python
import sys
from PyQt5.QtWidgets import QDialog, QApplication
from reservehotel import *
class MyForm(QDialog):
    def __init__(self):
        super().__init__()
        self.ui = Ui_Dialog()
        self.ui.setupUi(self)
        self.roomtypes=['Suite', 'Super Luxury', 'Super Deluxe',
        'Ordinary']
        self.addcontent()
        self.ui.pushButton.clicked.connect(self.computeRoomRent)
        self.show()
    def addcontent(self):
        for i in self.roomtypes:
            self.ui.comboBox.addItem(i)
    def computeRoomRent(self):
        dateselected=self.ui.calendarWidget.selectedDate()
        dateinstring=str(dateselected.toPyDate())
        noOfDays=self.ui.spinBox.value()
        chosenRoomType=self.ui.comboBox.itemText(self.ui.comboBox.
        currentIndex())
        self.ui.Enteredinfo.setText('Date of reservation:
        '+dateinstring+ ', Number of days: '+ str(noOfDays) + '
        nand Room type selected: '+ chosenRoomType)
        roomRent=0
        if chosenRoomType=="Suite":
            roomRent=40
        if chosenRoomType=="Super Luxury":
            roomRent=30
        if chosenRoomType=="Super Deluxe":
            roomRent=20
        if chosenRoomType=="Ordinary":
            roomRent=10
            total=roomRent*noOfDays
            self.ui.RoomRentinfo.setText('Room Rent for single
            day for '+ chosenRoomType +' type is '+
            str(roomRent)+ '$. nTotal room rent is '+
            str(total)+ ')
if __name__=="__main__":
    app = QApplication(sys.argv)
    w = MyForm()
    w.show()
    sys.exit(app.exec_())
```

How it works...

In this code, you can see that a `roomtypes` list is defined with four elements: `Suite`, `Super Luxury`, `Super Deluxe`, and `Ordinary`. To make the elements of the `roomtypes` list appear as options in the **Combo Box** widget, the `addcontent` method is invoked and adds the elements of `roomtypes` to the **Combo Box** widget with the `addItem()` method. Also, the **clicked()** signal of the **Push Button** widget is connected to the `computeRoomRent()` method, which is invoked when the user selects the push button after selecting the date of the reservation, the number of persons staying, and room type. In the `computeRoomRent()` method, you fetch the date from **Calendar Widget**, the number of persons from the **Spin Box** widget, and the room type from the **Combo Box** widget, and then display them through an `Enteredinfo` widget to indicate the options that are selected by the user. Then, the room rent of an individual is determined on the basis of the room type selected and is multiplied by the number of persons to compute the total room rent. The total room rent is then displayed via `roomRent`, as shown in the following screenshot:

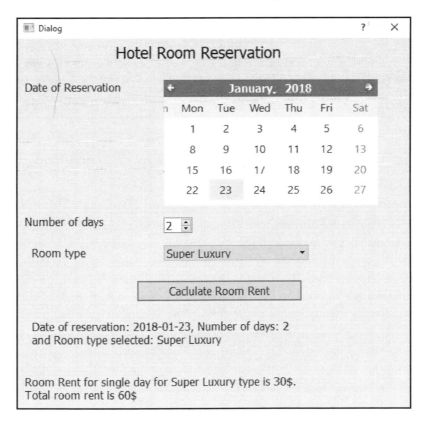

Displaying tabular data using Table Widget

In this recipe, we will learn to display data in tabular format, that is, in the row and column format. We will display the different room types of a hotel and their respective rents per day.

Getting ready

Before we begin creating this recipe, let's first understand **Table Widget**.

Table Widget

Table Widget is used for displaying data in tabular format, arranged in rows and columns. **Table Widget** is an instance of the `QTableWidget` class and the items that are displayed in the different rows and columns of a table are instances of the `QTableWidgetItem` class. Here are the methods provided by the `QTableWidget` class:

- `setRowCount()`: This method is used to define the number of rows you want in **Table Widget**
- `setColumnCount()`: This method is used to define the number of columns required in **Table Widget**
- `rowCount()`: This method returns the number of rows in the table
- `columnCount()`: This method returns the number of columns in the table
- `clear()`: This method clears the entire table
- `setItem()`: This method sets the content for a given row and column of the table

The QTableWidgetItem class

As mentioned earlier, the items displayed in **Table Widget** are instances of the `QTableWidgetItem` class. You can display text, images, or any other widgets as items in **Table Widget**. Here are the methods provided by the `QTableWidgetItem` class:

- `setFont()`: This method sets the font for the text label of the **Table Widget** item
- `setCheckState()`: This method passes the Boolean value **True** to this method to check the table item and passes the value **False** to uncheck the **Table Widget** item

- `checkState()`: This method returns the Boolean value as **True** if the **Table Widget** item is checked, or otherwise returns **False**

Let's now create an application to demonstrate how information is displayed with a **Table Widget** item.

How to do it...

Information displayed in tabular format is more organized, more readable, and more easily comparable than data that is displayed in traditional paragraphs. Here are the steps to make an application that displays data via **Table Widget**:

1. Open Qt Designer and create a new application based on the **Dialog without Buttons** template.
2. Drag and drop a **Table Widget** item onto the form.
3. To assign it the default size of three rows and two columns, from the **Property Editor** window set the value of **rowCount** and **columnCount** to 4 and 2, respectively.
4. To display the row and column headers, the **horizontalHeaderVisible** and **verticalHeaderVisible** properties are already checked by default
5. Save the application with the name `DemoTableWidget.ui`. The **Table Widget** item will appear as shown in the following screenshot:

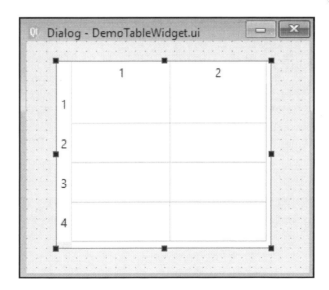

The `pyuic5` command utility is used for generating Python code. The generated Python script, `DemoTableWidget.py`, can be seen in the source code bundle of this book.

6. Create a Python script named `callTableWidget.pyw` that imports the Python code, `DemoTableWidget.py`, which enables us to invoke the user interface design and displays information in the **Table Widget** item. The code in the Python script, `callTableWidget.pyw`, is as shown here:

```python
import sys
from PyQt5.QtWidgets import QDialog, QApplication,QTableWidgetItem
from DemoTableWidget import *
class MyForm(QDialog):
    def __init__(self,data):
        super().__init__()
        self.ui = Ui_Dialog()
        self.ui.setupUi(self)
        self.data=data
        self.addcontent()
    def addcontent(self):
        row=0
        for tup in self.data:
            col=0
            for item in tup:
                oneitem=QTableWidgetItem(item)
                self.ui.tableWidget.setItem(row, col, oneitem)
                col+=1
            row+=1
data=[]
data.append(('Suite', '40'))
data.append(('Super Luxury', '30'))
data.append(('Super Deluxe', '20'))
data.append(('Ordinary', '10'))
if __name__=="__main__":
    app = QApplication(sys.argv)
    w = MyForm(data)
    w.show()
    sys.exit(app.exec_())
```

How it works...

If you want to display information in four rows and two columns of **Table Widget**, create a list named `data` that stores four tuples, each of which consists of two elements, `roomtypes` and `roomRent`. In the `addcontent` method, you fetch one tuple at a time from the `data` list and assign it temporarily to the `tup` variable. The `tup` variable contains two elements, room type and room rent. With the help of another `for` loop, you fetch each element from the `tup` variable; that is, you fetch room type and room rent and assign them to the `item` variable. The content of the `item` variable is then converted into an instance of `QTableWidgetItem` and assigned to `oneitem`, which in turn is further assigned to and displayed in **Table Widget** at a particular row and column position using the `setItem` method. With the help of nested `for` loops, you display the information of the data list in **Table Widget**, as shown in the following screenshot:

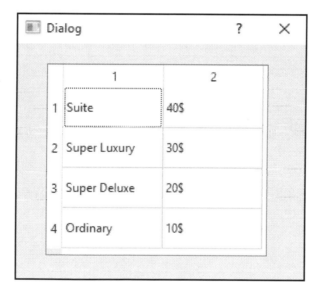

Understanding OOP Concepts

4

In this chapter, we will cover the following topics:

- Object-oriented programming
- Using classes in GUI
- Using single inheritance
- Using multilevel inheritance
- Using multiple inheritance

Object-oriented programming

Python supports **object-oriented programming (OOP)**. OOP supports reusability; that is, code that was written earlier can be reused for making large applications, instead of starting from scratch. The term object in OOP refers to a variable or instance of a class, where a class is a template or blueprint of a structure that consists of methods and variables. The variables in the class are called **data members**, and the methods are called **member functions**. When instances or objects of a class are made, the objects automatically get access to data members and methods.

Creating a class

The class statement is used for creating a class. The following is the syntax for creating a class:

```
class class_name(base_classes):
    statement(s)
```

Here, class_name is an identifier to identify the class. After the class statement comes the statements that make up the body of the class. The class body consists of different methods and variables to be defined in that class.

You can make an individual class or a class that inherits another class. The class that is being inherited is called the **base class**. The `base_classes` parameter after `class_name` in the syntax represents all the base classes that this class will be inheriting. If there is more than one base class, then they need to be separated by commas. The class that is being inherited is called the **super class** or **base class**, and the inheriting class is called a **derived class** or **subclass**. The derived class can use the methods and variables of the base class, and hence implements reusability:

```
class Student:
    name = ""
    def __init__(self, name):
        self.name = name
    def printName(self):
        return self.name
```

In this example, `Student` is a class that contains an attribute called `name` that is initialized to null.

Using the built-in class attributes

A `class` statement automatically assigns certain values to certain fixed class attributes. Those class attributes can be used to fetch information about the class. The list of class attributes are as follows:

- `__name__`: This attribute represents the class name used in the `class` statement
- `__bases__`: This attribute represents the base class names mentioned in the `class` statement
- `__dict__`: The dictionary object that represents other class attributes
- `__module__`: This attribute represents the module name in which the class is defined

A class can have any number of methods, and each method can have any number of parameters. One mandatory first parameter is always defined in a method, and that first parameter is usually named `self` (though you can give any name to this parameter). The `self` parameter refers to the instance of the class that calls the method. The syntax for defining methods in a class is as follows:

```
class class_name(base_classes):
    Syntax:
        variable(s)
    def method 1(self):
        statement(s)
```

```
[def method n(self):
    statement(s)]
```

A class can have the following two types of data member:

- **Class variable**: These are the variables that are shareable by all instances, and changes made to these variables by any one instance can be seen by other instances too. These are the data members that are defined outside of any method of the class.
- **Instance variable**: These variables, which are defined inside a method, only belong to the current instance of the object and are known as **instance variables**. Changes made to instance variables by any instance are limited to that particular instance and don't affect the instance variables of other instances.

Let's see how to create an instance method and how it can be used to access class variables.

Accessing class variables in instance methods

To access class variables, the class variables must be prefixed with the class name. For example, to access the `name` class variable of the `Student` class, you need to access it as follows:

```
Student.name
```

You can see that the `name` class variable is prefixed with the `Student` class name.

Instances

To use the variables and methods of any class, we need to create its objects or instances. An instance of a class gets its own copy of variables and methods. This means the variable of one instance will not interfere with the variable of another instance. We can create as many instances of a class as desired. To create an instance of a class, you need to write the class name followed by arguments (if any). For example, the following statement creates an instance of the `Student` class with the name `studentObj`:

```
studentObj=Student()
```

You can create any number of instances of the `Student` class. For example, the following line creates another instance of the `Student` class:

```
courseStudent=Student()
```

Now, the instance can access the class attribute and method of the class.

You need to specify `self` explicitly when defining the method. While calling the method, `self` is not mandatory because Python adds it automatically.

To define the variables of a class, we get help from the __init__() method. The __init__() method is like a constructor in traditional OOP languages and is the first method to be executed after the creation of an instance. It is used for initializing the variables of the class. Depending on how the __init__() method is defined in the class, that is, with or without parameters, the arguments may or may not be passed to the __init__() method.

As mentioned earlier, the first argument of every class method is a class instance that is called `self`. In the __init__() method, `self` refers to the newly created instance:

```
class Student:
    name = ""
    def __init__(self):
        self.name = "David"
        studentObj=Student()
```

In the preceding example, the `studentObj` instance is the instance of the `Student` class being created, and its class variable will be initialized to the `David` string.

Even arguments can be passed to the __init__() method, as shown in the following example:

```
class Student:
    name = ""
    def __init__(self, name):
        self.name = name
        studentObj=Student("David")
```

In the preceding example, the `studentObj` instance is created and the `David` string is passed to it. The string will be assigned to the `name` parameter defined in the __init__() method, which, in turn, will be used to initialize the class variable, `name`, of the instance. Remember, the __init__() method must not return a value.

Like the class variables, the methods of the class can be accessed by the instance of the class, followed by the method name, with a period (.) in between. Assuming there is a `printName()` method in the `Student` class, it can be accessed via the `studentObj` instance with the following statement:

```
studentObj.printName()
```

Using classes in GUI

The data received from the user through the GUI can be directly processed by making use of simple variables, and the processed data can be displayed through variables only. But to keep the data in a structured format and get the benefits of OOP, we will learn to keep data in the form of classes. That is, the data accessed by the user through the GUI can be assigned to the class variables, processed, and displayed through class methods.

Let's create an application that will prompt the user to enter a name and, on clicking the push button after entering a name, the application will display a hello message along with the entered name. The name entered by the user will be assigned to a class variable and the hello message will also be generated by invoking the class method of the class.

How to do it...

The focus of this recipe is to understand how the data entered by the user is assigned to the class variable, and how the message displayed can be accessed via class methods. Let's create a new application based on the **Dialog without Buttons** template and follow these steps:

1. Drag and drop two **Label** widgets, one **Line Edit**, and one **Push Button** widget onto the form.
2. Set the **text** property of the first **Label** widget to `Enter your name`.

 Let's not change the **text** property of the second **Label** widget and keep its **text** property to its default value of **TextLabel**. This is because its **text** property will be set through code to display the hello message.

3. Set the **text** property of the **Push Button** widget to `Click`.
4. Set the **objectName** property of the **Line Edit** widget to `lineEditName`.
5. Set the **objectName** property of the **Label** widget to `labelResponse`.
6. Set the **objectName** property of the **Push Button** widget to `ButtonClickMe`.
7. Save the application with the name `LineEditClass.ui`. The application will appear as shown in the following screenshot:

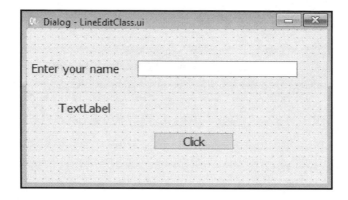

The user interface created with Qt Designer is stored in a `.ui` file, which is an XML file and needs to be converted to Python code.

8. To do the conversion, you need to open a Command Prompt window, navigate to the folder where the file is saved, and issue the following command line:

```
C:\Pythonbook\PyQt5>pyuic5 LineEdit.uiClass -o LineEditClass.py
```

The generated Python script, `LineEditClass.py`, can be seen in the source code bundle of this book.

9. Treat the preceding code as a header file, and import it into the file from which you will invoke its user interface design.
10. Create another Python file with the name `callLineEditClass.pyw` and import the `LineEditClass.py` code into it:

```
import sys
from PyQt5.QtWidgets import QDialog, QApplication
from LineEditClass import *
class Student:
    name = ""
    def __init__(self, name):
        self.name = name
    def printName(self):
```

```
            return self.name
class MyForm(QDialog):
    def __init__(self):
        super().__init__()
        self.ui = Ui_Dialog()
        self.ui.setupUi(self)
        self.ui.ButtonClickMe.clicked.connect(self.dispmessage)
        self.show()
    def dispmessage(self):
        studentObj=Student(self.ui.lineEditName.text())
        self.ui.labelResponse.setText("Hello
        "+studentObj.printName())
if __name__=="__main__":
    app = QApplication(sys.argv)
    w = MyForm()
    w.show()
    sys.exit(app.exec_())
```

How it works...

In the LineEditClass.py file, a class with the name of the top-level object is created with Ui_ prepended. That is, for the top-level object, Dialog, the Ui_Dialog class is created and stores the interface elements of our widget. That class has two methods, setupUi() and retranslateUi(). The setupUi() method creates the widgets that are used in defining the user interface in Qt Designer. Also, the properties of the widgets are set in this method. The setupUi() method takes a single argument, which is the top-level widget of the application, an instance of QDialog. The retranslateUi() method translates the interface.

In the callLineEditClass.py file, you can see that a class is defined called Student. The Student class includes a class variable called name and the following two methods:

- __init__(): It is a constructor that takes the mandatory self parameter and a name parameter, which will be used to initialize the name class variable
- printName: This method simply returns the value in the name class variable

The clicked() event of the **Push Button** widget is connected to the dispmessage() method; after entering a name in the **Line Edit** widget, when the user clicks the push button, the dispmessage() method will be invoked. The dispmessage() method defines the object of the Student class by name, studentObj, and passes the name entered by the user in the **Line Edit** widget as a parameter. Hence, the constructor of the Student class will be invoked and the name entered by the user is passed to the constructor. The name entered in the **Line Edit** widget will be assigned to the class variable, name. After that, the **Label** widget called labelResponse is set to display the string, Hello, and the printName method of the Student class is invoked, which returns the string assigned to the name variable. Hence, on clicking the push button, the **Label** widget will be set to display the string, Hello, followed by the name entered by the user in the **Line Edit** box, as shown in the following screenshot:

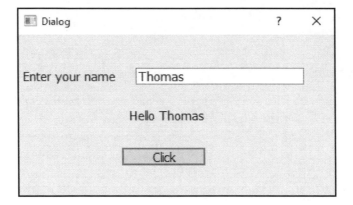

Making the application more elaborate

We can also make use of two or more class attributes in the class.

Let's assume that besides the class name Student, we want to also add student's code to the class. In that case, we need to add one more attribute, code to the class, and also a getCode() method, which will access the student code assigned. Besides the class, the GUI will also change.

We need to add one more **Label** widgets and one **Line Edit** widget to the application and let's save it by another name, demoStudentClass. After adding the **Label** and **Line Edit** widgets, the user interface will appear as shown in the following screenshot:

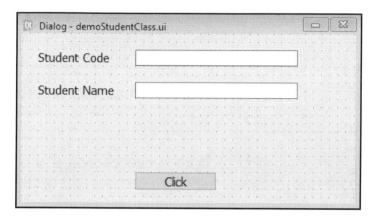

The user interface file, demoStudentClass.ui, needs to be converted into Python code. The generated Python script, demoStudentClass.py, can be seen in the source code bundle of this book.

Let's create another Python file with the name callStudentClass.pyw and import the demoStudentClass.py code to it. The code in callStudentClass.pyw is as follows:

```
import sys
from PyQt5.QtWidgets import QDialog, QApplication
from demoStudentClass import *
class Student:
    name = ""
    code = ""
    def __init__(self, code, name):
        self.code = code
        self.name = name
    def getCode(self):
        return self.code
    def getName(self):
        return self.name
class MyForm(QDialog):
    def __init__(self):
        super().__init__()
        self.ui = Ui_Dialog()
        self.ui.setupUi(self)
        self.ui.ButtonClickMe.clicked.connect(self.dispmessage)
        self.show()
    def dispmessage(self):
```

```
        studentObj=Student(self.ui.lineEditCode.text(),
        self.ui.lineEditName.text())
        self.ui.labelResponse.setText("Code:
        "+studentObj.getCode()+",  Name:"+studentObj.getName())
if __name__=="__main__":
    app = QApplication(sys.argv)
    w = MyForm()
    w.show()
    sys.exit(app.exec_())
```

In the preceding code, you see that a class is defined called `Student`. The `Student` class includes the two class variables called `name` and `code`. Besides the two class variables, the `Student` class includes the following three methods too:

- `__init__()`: It is a constructor that takes the mandatory `self` parameter and two parameters, `code` and `name`, which will be used to initialize the two class variables, `code` and `name`
- `getCode()`: This method simply returns the value in the `code` class variable
- `getName()`: This method simply returns the value in the `name` class variable

The `clicked()` event of the **Push Button** widget is connected to the `dispmessage()` method; after entering the code and name in the **Line Edit** widget, when the user clicks the Push Button, the `dispmessage()` method will be invoked. The `dispmessage()` method defines the object of the `Student` class by name, `studentObj`, and passes the code and name entered by the user in the **Line Edit** widgets as parameters. The constructor of the `Student` class, `__init__()`, will be invoked and the code and name entered by the user are passed to it. The code and name entered will be assigned to the class variables code and name, respectively. After that, the **Label** widget called `labelResponse` is set to display the code and name entered by invoking the two methods, `getCode` and `getName`, via the `studentObj` object of the `Student` class.

Hence, on clicking the push button, the **Label** widget will display the code and name entered by the user in two **Line Edit** widgets, as shown in the following screenshot:

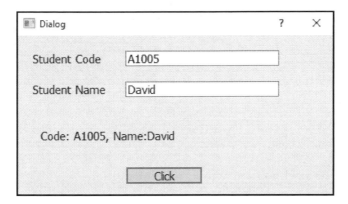

Inheritance

Inheritance is a concept by which the method and variables of an existing class can be reused by another class, without the need for re-coding them. That is, existing code that is tested and run can be reused immediately in other classes.

Types of inheritance

The following are the three types of inheritance:

- **Single inheritance**: One class inherits another class
- **Multilevel inheritance**: One class inherits another class, which in turn is inherited by some other class
- **Multiple inheritance**: One class inherits two or more classes

Using single inheritance

Single inheritance is the simplest type of inheritance, where one class is derived from another single class, as shown in the following diagram:

Class **B** inherits class **A**. Here, class **A** will be called the super class or base class, and class **B** will be called the derived class or subclass.

The following statement defines single inheritance where the Marks class inherits the Student class:

```
class Marks(Student):
```

In the preceding statement, Student is the base class and Marks is the derived class. Consequently, the instance of the Marks class can access the methods and variables of the Student class.

Getting ready

To understand the concept of single inheritance through a running example, let's create an application that will prompt the user to enter the code, name, and history and geography marks of a student, and will display them on the click of a button.

The code and name entered by the user will be assigned to the class members of a class called Student. The history and geography marks will be assigned to the class members of another class called Marks. To access code and name, along with the history and geography marks, the Marks class will inherit the Student class. Using inheritance, the instance of the Marks class will access and display the code and name of the Student class.

How to do it...

Launch Qt Designer and create a new application based on the **Dialog without Buttons** template by performing the following steps:

1. In the application, drag and drop five **Label** widgets, four **Line Edit** widgets, and one **Push Button** widget onto the form.
2. Set the **text** property of the four **Label** widgets to Student Code, Student Name, History Marks, and Geography Marks.
3. Delete the **text** property of the fifth **Label** widget, as its **text** property will be set through the code to display the code, name, and history and geography marks.
4. Set the **text** property of the **Push Button** widget to Click.
5. Set the **objectName** property of the four **Line Edit** widgets to lineEditCode, lineEditName, lineEditHistoryMarks, and lineEditGeographyMarks.
6. Set the **objectName** property of the **Label** widget to labelResponse and the **objectName** property of the **Push Button** widget to ButtonClickMe.
7. Save the application with the name demoSimpleInheritance.ui. The application will appear as shown in the following screenshot:

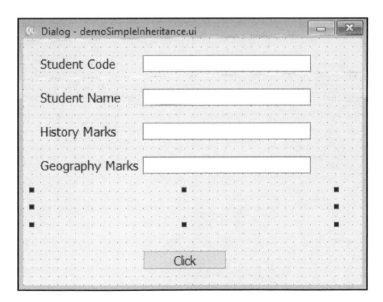

The user interface file, `demoSimpleInheritance.ui`, is an XML file and is converted into Python code using the `pyuic5` utility. You can find the generated Python script, `demoSimpleInheritance.py`, in the source code bundle of this book. The preceding code will be used as a header file, and will be imported in another Python script file, which will invoke the user interface design defined in, `demoSimpleInheritance.py` file.

8. Create another Python file with the name `callSimpleInheritance.pyw` and import the `demoSimpleInheritance.py` code into it. The code in the Python script, `callSimpleInheritance.pyw`, is as given here:

```python
import sys
from PyQt5.QtWidgets import QDialog, QApplication
from demoSimpleInheritance import *
class Student:
    name = ""
    code = ""
    def __init__(self, code, name):
        self.code = code
        self.name = name
    def getCode(self):
        return self.code
    def getName(self):
        return self.name
class Marks(Student):
    historyMarks = 0
    geographyMarks = 0
    def __init__(self, code, name, historyMarks,
    geographyMarks):
        Student.__init__(self,code,name)
        self.historyMarks = historyMarks
        self.geographyMarks = geographyMarks
    def getHistoryMarks(self):
        return self.historyMarks
    def getGeographyMarks(self):
        return self.geographyMarks
class MyForm(QDialog):
    def __init__(self):
        super().__init__()
        self.ui = Ui_Dialog()
        self.ui.setupUi(self)
        self.ui.ButtonClickMe.clicked.connect(self.dispmessage)
        self.show()
    def dispmessage(self):
        marksObj=Marks(self.ui.lineEditCode.text(),
        self.ui.lineEditName.text(),
```

```
            self.ui.lineEditHistoryMarks.text(),
            self.ui.lineEditGeographyMarks.text())
            self.ui.labelResponse.setText("Code:
            "+marksObj.getCode()+", Name:"+marksObj.getName()+"
            nHistory Marks:"+marksObj.getHistoryMarks()+", Geography
            Marks:"+marksObj.getGeographyMarks())
    if __name__=="__main__":
        app = QApplication(sys.argv)
        w = MyForm()
        w.show()
        sys.exit(app.exec_())
```

How it works...

In this code, you see that a class is defined, called Student. The Student class includes two class variables called name and code, along with the following three methods:

- __init__(): It is a constructor that takes the mandatory self parameter and two parameters, code and name, that will be used to initialize the two class variables, code and name
- getCode(): This method simply returns the value in the code class variable
- getName(): This method simply returns the value in the name class variable

The Marks class inherits the Student class. Consequently, an instance of the Marks class will not only be able to access its own members, but also that of the Student class.

The Marks class includes two class variables called historyMarks and geographyMarks, along with the following three methods:

- __init__(): It is a constructor that takes the mandatory self parameter and four parameters, code, name, historyMarks, and geographyMarks. From this constructor, the constructor of the Student class will be invoked and the code and name parameters will be passed to this constructor. The historyMarks and geographyMarks parameters will be used to initialize the class members, historyMarks, and geographyMarks.
- getHistoryMarks(): This method simply returns the value in the historyMarks class variable.
- getGeographyMarks(): This method simply returns the value in the geographyMarks class variable.

The `clicked()` event of the Push Button is connected to the `dispmessage()` method. After entering the code, name, and history and geography marks in the **Line Edit** widgets, when the user clicks the push button, the `dispmessage()` method will be invoked. The `dispmessage()` method defines the object of the `Marks` class by name, `marksObj`, and passes the code, name, and history and geography marks entered by the user in the **Line Edit** widgets as parameters. The constructor of the `Marks` class, `__init__()`, will be invoked and the code, name, history, and geography marks entered by the user are passed to it. From the constructor of the `Marks` class, the constructor of the `Student` class will be invoked and `code` and `name` will be passed to that constructor. The `code` and `name` parameters will be assigned to the `code` and `name` class variables, respectively, of the `Student` class. Similarly, the history and geography marks will be assigned to `historyMarks` and `geographyMarks` class variables, respectively, of the `Marks` class. After that, the **Label** widget called `labelResponse` is set to display the code, name, and history and geography marks entered by invoking the four methods, `getCode`, `getName`, `getHistoryMarks`, and `getGeographyMarks`, via the `marksObj` object. The `marksObj` object of the `Marks` class gets the right to access the `getCode` and `getName` methods of the `Student` class because of using inheritance. Hence, on clicking the push button, the **Label** widget will display the code, name, history marks, and geography marks entered by the user via the **Label** widget called `labelResponse`, as shown in this screenshot:

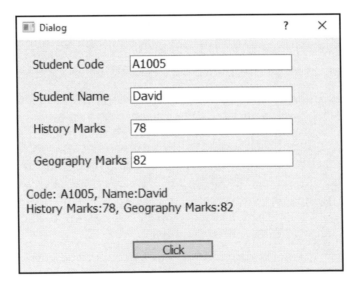

Using multilevel inheritance

Multilevel inheritance is where one class inherits another single class. The inheriting class in turn is inherited by a third class, as shown in the following diagram:

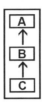

In the preceding diagram, you can see that class **B** inherits class **A** and class **C**, in turn, inherits class **B**.

The following statement defines multilevel inheritance, where the Result class inherits the Marks class and the Marks class, in turn, inherits the Student class:

```
class Student:
    class Marks(Student):
        class Result(Marks):
```

In the preceding statement, Student is the base class and the Marks class inherits the Student class. The Result class inherits the Marks class. Consequently, the instance of the Result class can access the methods and variables of the Marks class, and the instance of the Marks class can access the methods and variables of the Student class.

Getting ready

To understand the concept of multilevel inheritance, let's create an application that will prompt the user to enter the code, name, history marks, and geography marks of a student and will display the total marks and percentage on the click of a button. The total marks will be the sum of history marks and geography marks. Assuming the maximum mark is 100, the formula for computing the percentage is: total marks/200 * 100.

The code and name entered by the user will be assigned to the class members of a class called `Student`. The history and geography marks will be assigned to the class members of another class called `Marks`. To access code and name along with the history and geography marks, the `Marks` class will inherit the `Student` class. Using this multilevel inheritance, the instance of the `Marks` class will access the code and name of the `Student` class. To calculate total marks and percentage, one more class is used, called the `Result` class. The `Result` class will inherit the `Marks` class. Consequently, the instance of the `Result` class can access the class members of the `Marks` class, as well as those of the `Student` class. The `Result` class has two class members, `totalMarks` and `percentage`. The `totalMarks` class member will be assigned the sum of the `historyMarks` and `geographyMarks` members of the `Marks` class. The `percentage` member will be assigned the percentage acquired on the basis of the history and geography marks.

How to do it...

In all, there are three classes, named `Student`, `Marks`, and `Result`, where the `Result` class will inherit the `Marks` class and the `Marks` class, in turn, will inherit the `Student` class. Consequently, the members of the `Result` class can access the class members of the `Marks` class as well as those of the `Student` class. Here is the step-by-step procedure to create this application:

1. Launch Qt Designer and create a new application based on the **Dialog without Buttons** template.
2. Drag and drop six **Label** widgets, six **Line Edit** widgets, and one **Push Button** widget onto the form.
3. Set the **text** property of the six **Label** widgets to `Student Code`, `Student Name`, `History Marks`, `Geography Marks`, `Total`, and `Percentage`.
4. Set the **text** property of the **Push Button** widget to `Click`.
5. Set the **objectName** property of the six **Line Edit** widgets to `lineEditCode`, `lineEditName`, `lineEditHistoryMarks`, `lineEditGeographyMarks`, `lineEditTotal`, and `lineEditPercentage`.
6. Set the **objectName** property of the **Push Button** widget to `ButtonClickMe`.
7. Disable the `lineEditTotal` and `lineEditPercentage` boxes by unchecking the **Enable** property from the **Property Editor** window. The `lineEditTotal` and `lineEditPercentage` widgets are disabled because values in these boxes will be assigned through the code and we don't want their values to be altered by the user.

8. Save the application with the name demoMultilevelInheritance.ui. The application will appear as shown in the following screenshot:

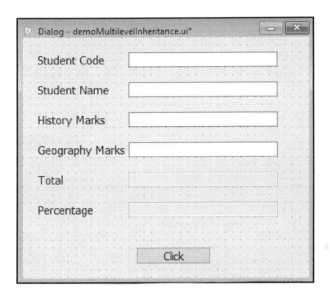

The user interface file, demoMultilevelInheritance.ui, is an XML file and is converted into Python code by making use of the pyuic5 utility. You can see the generated Python script, demoMultilevelInheritance.py, in the source code bundle of this book. The demoMultilevelInheritance.py file will be used as a header file, and will be imported in another Python script file, which will use the GUI created in demoMultilevelInheritance.py.

9. Create another Python file with the name callMultilevelInheritance.pyw and import the demoMultilevelInheritance.py code into it. The code in the Python script, callMultilevelInheritance.pyw, is as shown here:

```python
import sys
from PyQt5.QtWidgets import QDialog, QApplication
from demoMultilevelInheritance import *
class Student:
    name = ""
    code = ""
    def __init__(self, code, name):
        self.code = code
        self.name = name
    def getCode(self):
        return self.code
    def getName(self):
```

```
            return self.name
class Marks(Student):
    historyMarks = 0
    geographyMarks = 0
    def __init__(self, code, name, historyMarks,
    geographyMarks):
        Student.__init__(self,code,name)
        self.historyMarks = historyMarks
        self.geographyMarks = geographyMarks
    def getHistoryMarks(self):
        return self.historyMarks
    def getGeographyMarks(self):
        return self.geographyMarks
class Result(Marks):
    totalMarks = 0
    percentage = 0
    def __init__(self, code, name, historyMarks,
    geographyMarks):
        Marks.__init__(self, code, name, historyMarks,
        geographyMarks)
        self.totalMarks = historyMarks + geographyMarks
        self.percentage = (historyMarks +
        geographyMarks) / 200 * 100
    def getTotalMarks(self):
        return self.totalMarks
    def getPercentage(self):
        return self.percentage
class MyForm(QDialog):
    def __init__(self):
        super().__init__()
        self.ui = Ui_Dialog()
        self.ui.setupUi(self)
        self.ui.ButtonClickMe.clicked.connect(self.dispmessage)
        self.show()
    def dispmessage(self):
        resultObj=Result(self.ui.lineEditCode.text(),
        self.ui.lineEditName.text(),
        int(self.ui.lineEditHistoryMarks.text()),
        int(self.ui.lineEditGeographyMarks.text()))
        self.ui.lineEditTotal.setText(str(resultObj.
        getTotalMarks()))
        self.ui.lineEditPercentage.setText(str(resultObj.
        getPercentage()))
if __name__=="__main__":
    app = QApplication(sys.argv)
    w = MyForm()
    w.show()
    sys.exit(app.exec_())
```

How it works...

In the preceding code, in the `callMultilevelInheritance.pyw` file, you can see that a class is defined called `Student`. The `Student` class includes two class variables called `name` and `code`, along with the following three methods:

- `__init__()`: It is a constructor that takes the mandatory `self` parameter and two parameters, `code`, and `name`, that will be used to initialize the two class variables `code` and `name`
- `getCode()`: This method simply returns the value in the `code` class variable
- `getName()`: This method simply returns the value in the `name` class variable

The `Marks` class inherits the `Student` class. Consequently, an instance of the `Marks` class will not only be able to access its own members, but also those of the `Student` class.

The `Marks` class includes two class variables called `historyMarks` and `geographyMarks`, along with the following three methods:

- `__init__()`: It is a constructor that takes the mandatory `self` parameter and four parameters, `code`, `name`, `historyMarks`, and `geographyMarks`. From this constructor, the constructor of the `Student` class will be invoked and the `code` and `name` parameters will be passed to this constructor. The `historyMarks` and `geographyMarks` parameters will be used to initialize the `historyMarks` and `geographyMarks` class members.
- `getHistoryMarks()`: This method simply returns the value in the `historyMarks` class variable.
- `getGeographyMarks()`: This method simply returns the value in the `geographyMarks` class variable.

The `Result` class inherits the `Marks` class. An instance of the `Result` class will not only be able to access its own members, but also those of the `Marks` class and of the `Student` class too.

The `Result` class includes two class variables, called `totalMarks` and `percentage`, along with the following three methods:

- `__init__()`: It is a constructor that takes the mandatory `self` parameter and four parameters, `code`, `name`, `historyMarks`, and `geographyMarks`. From this constructor, the constructor of the `Marks` class will be invoked and the `code`, `name`, `historyMarks`, and `geographyMarks` parameters will be passed to that constructor. The sum of `historyMarks` and `geographyMarks` will be assigned to the `totalMarks` class variable. Assuming the maximum mark for each is 100, the percentage of the history and geography marks will be computed and assigned to the percentage class variable.
- `getTotalMarks()`: This method simply returns the sum of the `historyMarks` and `geographyMarks` class variables.
- `getPercentage()`: This method simply returns the percentage of the history and geography marks.

The `clicked()` event of the **Push Button** widget is connected to the `dispmessage()` method. After entering code, name, history marks, and geography marks in the **Line Edit** widgets, when the user clicks the push button, the `dispmessage()` method will be invoked. The `dispmessage()` method defines the object of the `Result` class by name, `resultObj`, and passes the code, name, history, and geography marks entered by the user in the **Line Edit** widgets as parameters. The constructor of the `Result` class, `__init__()`, will be invoked and the code, name, history marks, and geography marks entered by the user are passed to it. From the `Result` class's constructor, the `Marks` class's constructor will be invoked and code, name, history marks, and geography marks will be passed to that constructor. From the `Marks` class's constructor, the `Student` class constructor will be invoked and the `code` and `name` parameters are passed to it. In the `Student` class's constructor, the `code` and `name` parameters will be assigned to the class variables `code` and `name`, respectively. Similarly, the history and geography marks will be assigned to the `historyMarks` and `geographyMarks` class variables, respectively, of the `Marks` class.

The sum of `historyMarks` and `geographyMarks` will be assigned to the `totalMarks` class variable. Also, the percentage of the history and geography marks will be computed and assigned to the `percentage` class variable.

After that, the **Line Edit** widget called `lineEditTotal` is set to display the total marks, that is, the sum of history and geography marks, by invoking the `getTotalMarks` method via `resultObj`. Also, the **Line Edit** widget called `lineEditPercentage` is set to display the percentage of marks by invoking the `getPercentage` method via `resultObj`.

Hence, on clicking the push button, the **Line Edit** widgets called `lineEditTotal` and `lineEditPercentage` will display the total marks and percentage of history and geography marks entered by the user, as shown in the following screenshot:

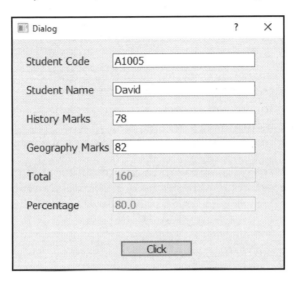

Using multiple inheritance

Multiple inheritance is where one class inherits two or more classes, as shown in the following diagram:

Class **C** inherits both classes, class **A** and class **B**.

The following statement defines multilevel inheritance where the `Result` class inherits the `Marks` class and the `Marks` class in turn inherits the `Student` class:

```
class Student:
    class Marks:
        class Result(Student, Marks):
```

In the preceding statements, `Student` and `Marks` are the base classes and the `Result` class inherits both the `Student` class and the `Marks` class. Consequently, the instance of the `Result` class can access the methods and variables of the `Marks` and `Student` classes.

Getting ready

To understand the concept of multilevel inheritance practically, let's create an application that will prompt the user to enter the code, name, history marks, and geography marks of a student, and will display the total marks and percentage on the click of a button. The total marks will be the sum of history marks and geography marks. Assuming the maximum mark for each is 100, the formula for computing the percentage is: total marks/200 * 100.

The code and name entered by the user will be assigned to the class members of a class called `Student`. The history and geography marks will be assigned to the class members of another class called `Marks`.

To access code and name, along with the history and geography marks, the `Result` class will inherit both classes, the `Student` class as well as the `Marks` class. Using this multiple inheritance, the instance of the `Result` class can access the code and name of the `Student` class, as well as the `historyMarks` and `geographyMarks` class variables of the `Marks` class. In other words, using multiple inheritance, the instance of the `Result` class can access the class members of the `Marks` class, as well as those of the `Student` class. The `Result` class has two class members, `totalMarks` and `percentage`. The `totalMarks` class member will be assigned the sum of the `historyMarks` and `geographyMarks` members of the `Marks` class. The percentage member will be assigned the percentage acquired on the basis of the history and geography marks.

How to do it...

Let's understand through a step-by-step procedure how multilevel inheritance is applied to three classes, `Student`, `Marks`, and `Result`. The `Result` class will inherit both classes, `Student` and `Marks`. These steps explain how the members of the `Result` class can access the class members of the `Student` and `Marks` classes through multilevel inheritance:

1. Launch Qt Designer and create a new application based on the **Dialog without Buttons** template.
2. In the application, drag and drop six **Label** widgets, six **Line Edit** widgets, and one **Push Button** widget onto the form.

3. Set the **text** property of the six **Label** widgets to `Student Code`, `Student Name`, `History Marks`, `Geography Marks`, `Total`, and `Percentage`.

4. Set the **text** property of the **Push Button** widget to `Click`.

5. Set the **objectName** property of the six **Line Edit** widgets to `lineEditCode`, `lineEditName`, `lineEditHistoryMarks`, `lineEditGeographyMarks`, `lineEditTotal`, and `lineEditPercentage`.

6. Set the **objectName** property of the **Push Button** widget to `ButtonClickMe`.

7. Disable the `lineEditTotal` and `lineEditPercentage` boxes by unchecking the **Enable** property from the **Property Editor** window. The `lineEditTotal` and `lineEditPercentage` boxes are disabled because values in these boxes will be assigned through the code, and we don't want their values to be altered by the user.

8. Save the application with the name `demoMultipleInheritance.ui`. The application will appear as shown in the following screenshot:

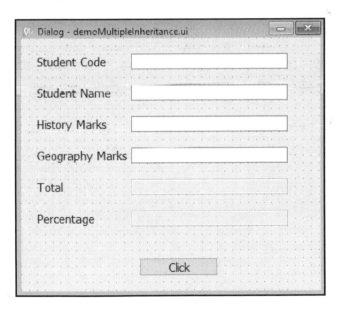

The user interface file `demoMultipleInheritance .ui` is an XML file and is converted into Python code using the `pyuic5` utility. You can find the generated Python code, `demoMultipleInheritance.py`, in the source code bundle of this book. The `demoMultipleInheritance.py` file will be used as a header file and will be imported in another Python script file, which will invoke the GUI created in the `demoMultipleInheritance.py` file.

9. Create another Python file with the name `callMultipleInheritance.pyw` and import the `demoMultipleInheritance.py` code into it:

```python
import sys
from PyQt5.QtWidgets import QDialog, QApplication
from demoMultipleInheritance import *
class Student:
    name = ""
    code = ""
    def __init__(self, code, name):
        self.code = code
        self.name = name
    def getCode(self):
        return self.code
    def getName(self):
        return self.name
class Marks:
    historyMarks = 0
    geographyMarks = 0
    def __init__(self, historyMarks, geographyMarks):
        self.historyMarks = historyMarks
        self.geographyMarks = geographyMarks
    def getHistoryMarks(self):
        return self.historyMarks
    def getGeographyMarks(self):
        return self.geographyMarks
class Result(Student, Marks):
    totalMarks = 0
    percentage = 0
    def __init__(self, code, name, historyMarks,
    geographyMarks):
        Student.__init__(self, code, name)
        Marks.__init__(self, historyMarks, geographyMarks)
        self.totalMarks = historyMarks + geographyMarks
        self.percentage = (historyMarks +
        geographyMarks) / 200 * 100
    def getTotalMarks(self):
        return self.totalMarks
    def getPercentage(self):
        return self.percentage
class MyForm(QDialog):
    def __init__(self):
        super().__init__()
        self.ui = Ui_Dialog()
        self.ui.setupUi(self)
        self.ui.ButtonClickMe.clicked.connect(self.dispmessage)
        self.show()
    def dispmessage(self):
```

```
            resultObj=Result(self.ui.lineEditCode.text(),
            self.ui.lineEditName.text(),
            int(self.ui.lineEditHistoryMarks.text()),
            int(self.ui.lineEditGeographyMarks.text()))
            self.ui.lineEditTotal.setText(str(resultObj.
            getTotalMarks()))
            self.ui.lineEditPercentage.setText(str(resultObj.
            getPercentage()))
    if __name__=="__main__":
        app = QApplication(sys.argv)
        w = MyForm()
        w.show()
        sys.exit(app.exec_())
```

How it works...

In this code, you can see that a class is defined called Student. The Student class includes two class variables called name and code, along with the following three methods:

- __init__(): It is a constructor that takes the mandatory self parameter and two parameters, code and name, that will be used to initialize the two class variables code and name
- getCode(): This method simply returns the value in the code class variable
- getName(): This method simply returns the value in the name class variable

The Marks class includes two class variables, called historyMarks and geographyMarks, along with the following three methods:

- __init__(): It is a constructor that takes the mandatory self parameter and two parameters, historyMarks and geographyMarks. The historyMarks and geographyMarks parameters will be used to initialize the historyMarks and geographyMarks class members.
- getHistoryMarks(): This method simply returns the value in the historyMarks class variable.
- getGeographyMarks(): This method simply returns the value in the geographyMarks class variable.

The Result class inherits the Student class as well as the Marks class. An instance of the Result class will not only be able to access its own members, but also those of the Marks class and of the Student class too.

The `Result` class includes two class variables called `totalMarks` and `percentage`, along with the following three methods:

- `__init__()`: It is a constructor that takes the mandatory `self` parameter and four parameters, `code`, `name`, `historyMarks`, and `geographyMarks`. From this constructor, the `Student` class constructor will be invoked and the `code` and `name` parameters will be passed to that constructor. Also, from this constructor, the `Marks` class constructor will be invoked and the `historyMarks` and `geographyMarks` parameters will be passed to that constructor. The sum of `historyMarks` and `geographyMarks` will be assigned to the `totalMarks` class variable. Assuming the maximum mark for each is 100, the percentage of the history and geography marks will be computed and assigned to the `percentage` class variable.
- `getTotalMarks()`: This method simply returns the sum of the `historyMarks` and `geography` class variables.
- `getPercentage()`: This method simply returns the percentage of history and geography marks.

The `clicked()` event of the **Push Button** widget is connected to the `dispmessage()` method. After entering code, name, history marks, and geography marks in the **Line Edit** widgets, when the user clicks the push button, the `dispmessage()` method will be invoked. The `dispmessage()` method defines the object of the `Result` class by name, `resultObj`, and passes the code, name, history marks, and geography marks entered by the user in the **Line Edit** widgets as parameters. The constructor of the `Result` class, `__init__()`, will be invoked and the code, name, history marks, and geography marks entered by the user are passed to it. From the `Result` class's constructor, the `Student` class constructor and the `Marks` class constructor will be invoked. The code and name will be passed to the `Student` class constructor, and history and geography marks will be passed to the `Marks` class constructor.

In the `Student` class constructor, the code and name will be assigned to the `code` and `name` class variables, respectively. Similarly, in the `Marks` class constructor, the history and geography marks will be assigned to the `historyMarks` and `geographyMarks` class variables, respectively, of the `Marks` class.

The sum of `historyMarks` and `geographyMarks` will be assigned to the `totalMarks` class variable. Also, the percentage of the history and geography marks will be computed and assigned to the `percentage` class variable.

After that, the **Line Edit** widget called `lineEditTotal` is set to display the total marks, that is, the sum of the history and geography marks, by invoking the `getTotalMarks` method via `resultObj`. Also, the **Line Edit** widget called `lineEditPercentage` is set to display the percentage of marks by invoking the `getPercentage` method via `resultObj`.

Hence, on clicking the push button, the **Line Edit** widgets called `lineEditTotal` and `lineEditPercentage` will display the total marks and percentage of the history and geography marks entered by the user, as shown in the following screenshot:

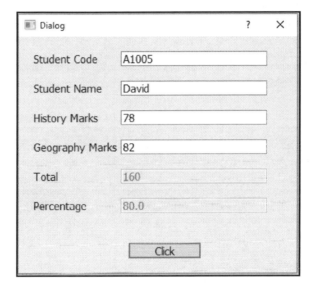

5
Understanding Dialogs

In this chapter, we will learn how to use the following types of dialog:

- The input dialog box
- Using the input dialog
- Using the color dialog
- Using the font dialog
- Using the file dialog

Introduction

Dialogs are required in all applications to get input from the user, and also to guide the user to enter the correct data. Interactive dialogs make the application quite user-friendly too. There are basically the following two types of dialog:

- **Modal dialog**: A modal dialog is a dialog that wants the user to enter mandatory information. This type of dialog doesn't allow the user to use other parts of the application until the modal dialog is closed. That is, the user needs to enter the required information in the modal dialog, and after closing the dialog, the user can access the rest of the application.
- **Non-modal or modeless dialogs**: These are dialogs that enable the user to interact with the rest of the application and dialog box too. That is, the user can continue interacting with the rest of the application while keeping the modeless dialog open. That is why modeless dialogs are usually used for getting non-essential or non-critical information from the user.

The input dialog box

An input dialog box is created with the help of the QInputDialog class. The QInputDialog class provides a dialog to get a single value from the user. The provided input dialog consists of a text field and two buttons, **OK** and **Cancel**. The text field enables us to get a single value from the user, where that single value can be a string, a number, or an item from a list. The following are the methods provided by the QInputDialog class to accept different types of input from the user:

- getInt(): This method shows a spin box for accepting an integer number. To get an integer from the user, you need to use the following syntax:

```
getInt(self, window title, label before LineEdit widget, default
value, minimum, maximum and step size)
```

Take a look at the following example:

```
quantity, ok = QInputDialog.getInt(self, "Order Quantity", "Enter
quantity:", 2, 1, 100, 1)
```

The preceding code prompts the user to enter quantity. If the user does not enter any value, the default value 2 will be assigned to the quantity variable. The user can enter any value between 1 and 100.

- getDouble(): This method shows a spin box with a floating point number to accept fractional values. To get a fractional value from the user, you need to use the following syntax:

```
getDouble(self, window title, label before LineEdit widget, default
value, minimum, maximum and number of decimal places desired)
```

Take a look at the following example:

```
price, ok = QInputDialog.getDouble(self, "Price of the product",
"Enter price:", 1.50,0, 100, 2)
```

The preceding code prompts the user to enter the price of the product. If the user does not enters any value, the default value 1.50 will be assigned to the price variable. The user can enter any value between 0 and 100.

- `getText()`: This method shows a **Line Edit** widget to accept text from the user. To get text from the user, you need to use the following syntax:

    ```
    getText(self, window title, label before LineEdit widget)
    ```

    Take a look at the following example:

    ```
    name, ok = QtGui.QInputDialog.getText(self, 'Get Customer Name',
    'Enter your name:')
    ```

    The preceding code will display an input dialog box with the title, **Get Customer Name**. The dialog box will also display a **Line Edit** widget allowing user to enter some text. A **Label** widget will also be displayed before the **Line Edit** widget showing the text, **Enter your name:**. The customer's name, entered in the dialog box will be assigned to the name variable.

- `getItem()`: This method shows a combo box displaying several items to choose from. To get an item from a drop-down box, you need to use the following syntax:

    ```
    getItem(self, window title, label before combo box, array , current
    item, Boolean Editable)
    ```

    Here, array is the list of items that need to be displayed in the combo box. The current item is the item that is treated as the current item in the combo box. Editable is the Boolean value, which, if set to True, means the user can edit the combo box and enter their own text. When Editable is set to False, it means the user can only select an item from the combo box but cannot edit items. Take a look at the following example:

    ```
    countryName, ok = QInputDialog.getItem(self, "Input Dialog", "List
    of countries", countries, 0, False)
    ```

    The preceding code will display an input dialog with the title **Input Dialog**. The dialog box shows a combo box showing a list of countries that are displayed via the elements from the countries array. The **Label** widget before the combo box shows the text, **List of countries**. The selected country name from the combo box will be assigned to the countryName variable. Users can only choose the country from the combo box but cannot edit any country name from the combo box.

Using the input dialog

The input dialog can accept data of any type, including integer, double, and text. In this recipe, we will learn to get text from the user. We will make use of an input dialog to know the name of the country in which the user lives.

The input dialog box will display a combo box showing different country names. On choosing a country by name, the chosen country name will appear in the textbox.

How to do it...

Let's create a new application based on the **Dialog without Buttons** template by performing the following steps:

1. Since the application will prompt the user to choose the country that he/she lives, via input dialog, so drag and drop one **Label** widget, one **Line Edit** widget, and one **Push Button** widget onto the form.
2. Set the **text** property of the **Label** widget to `Your Country`.
3. Set the **text** property of the **Push Button** widget to `Choose Country`.
4. Set the **objectName** property of the **Line Edit** widget to `lineEditCountry`.
5. Set the **objectName** property of the **Push Button** widget to `pushButtonCountry`.
6. Save the application with the name `demoInputDialog.ui`.

    The form will now look as follows:

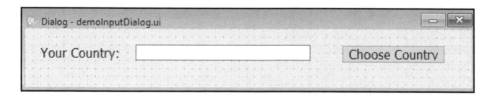

    The user interface created with Qt Designer is stored in a `.ui` file, which is an XML file and needs converting to Python code.

7. To do the conversion, you need to open a Command Prompt window, navigate to the folder where the file is saved, and issue the following command line:

```
C:\Pythonbook\PyQt5>pyuic5 demoInputDialog.ui -o demoInputDialog.py
```

You can find the generated Python script, demoInputDialog.py, in the source code bundle of this book.

8. Treat the demoInputDialog.py script as a header file, and import it to the file from which you will invoke its user interface design.
9. Create another Python file with the name callInputDialog.pyw and import the demoInputDialog.py code into it:

```
import sys
from PyQt5.QtWidgets import QDialog, QApplication, QInputDialog
from demoInputDialog import *
class MyForm(QDialog):
    def __init__(self):
        super().__init__()
        self.ui = Ui_Dialog()
        self.ui.setupUi(self)
        self.ui.pushButtonCountry.clicked.connect(self.dispmessage)
        self.show()
    def dispmessage(self):
        countries = ("Albania", "Algeria", "Andorra", "Angola",
        "Antigua and Barbuda", "Argentina", "Armenia", "Aruba",
        "Australia", "Austria", "Azerbaijan")
        countryName, ok = QInputDialog.getItem(self, "Input
        Dialog", "List of countries", countries, 0, False)
        if ok and countryName:
            self.ui.lineEditCountry.setText(countryName)
if __name__=="__main__":
    app = QApplication(sys.argv)
    w = MyForm()
    w.show()
    sys.exit(app.exec_())
```

How it works...

In the demoInputDialog.py file, a class with the name of the top-level object is created with Ui_ prepended. That is, for the top-level object, **Dialog**, the Ui_Dialog class is created and stores the interface elements of our widget. That class has two methods, setupUi() and retranslateUi().

The setupUi() method creates the widgets that are used in defining the user interface in Qt Designer. Also, the properties of the widgets are set in this method. The setupUi() method takes a single argument, which is the top-level widget of the application, an instance of QDialog. The retranslateUi() method translates the interface.

In the `callInputDialog.pyw` file, you can see that the click event of the **Push Button** widget is connected to the `dispmessage()` method that is used to select the country; when the user clicks the push button, the `dispmessage()` method will be invoked. The `dispmessage()` method defines a string array called countries that contains several country names in the form of array elements. After that, the `getItem` method of the `QInputDialog` class is invoked and opens up an input dialog box displaying a combo box. When the user clicks the combo box, it will expand, showing the country names that are assigned to the `countries` string array. When the user selects a country, followed by clicking the **OK** button in the dialog box, the selected country name will be assigned to the `countryName` variable. The selected country name will then be displayed through the **Line Edit** widget.

On running the application, you get an empty **Line Edit** widget and a push button, **Choose Country**, as shown in the following screenshot:

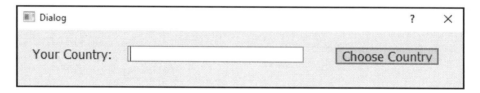

On clicking the **Choose Country** button, the input dialog box will open, as shown in the following screenshot. The input dialog shows a combo box along with two buttons, **OK** and **Cancel**. On clicking the combo box, it will expand to show all the country names, as shown in the following screenshot:

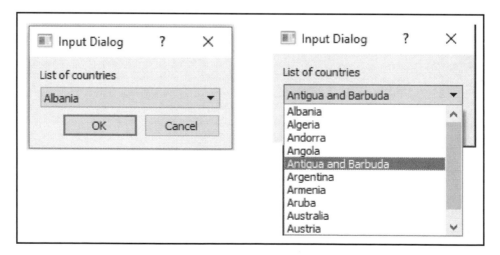

After choosing a country name from the combo box, followed by clicking the **OK** button, the chosen country name will be displayed in the **Line Edit** box, as shown in the following screenshot:

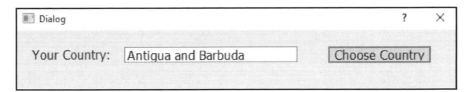

Using the color dialog

In this recipe, we will learn to use color dialog to display a color palette, allowing users to select predefined colors from the palette or create a new custom color.

The application includes a frame, and when the user selects any color from the color dialog, the chosen color will be applied to the frame. Besides this, the hex code of the selected color will also be displayed via a **Label** widget.

In this recipe, we will be making use of the `QColorDialog` class, which provides a dialog widget for selecting color values.

How to do it...

Let's create a new application based on the **Dialog without Buttons** template by performing the following steps:

1. Drag and drop a **Push Button**, a **Frame**, and a **Label** widget onto the form.
2. Set the **text** property of the **Push Button** widget to `Choose color`.
3. Set the **objectName** property of the **Push Button** widget to `pushButtonColor`.
4. Set the **objectName** property of the **Frame** widget to `frameColor`.
5. Set the **Label** widget to `labelColor`.

6. Save the application with the name `demoColorDialog.ui`.

The form will now look as follows:

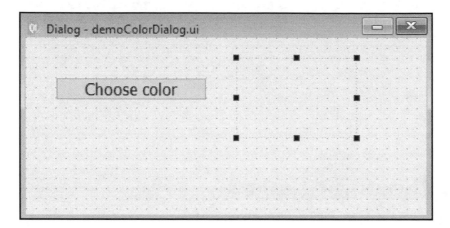

The user interface created with Qt Designer is stored in a .ui file, which is an XML file. You can use pyuic5 utility to convert the XML file into Python code. The generated Python script, demoColorDialog.py, can be seen in the source code bundle of this book. The demoColorDialog.py script will be used as a header file, and will be imported in another Python script file, which will invoke this user interface design.

7. Create another Python file with the name callColorDialog.pyw and import the demoColorDialog.py code into it:

```python
import sys
from PyQt5.QtWidgets import QDialog, QApplication, QColorDialog
from PyQt5.QtGui import QColor
from demoColorDialog import *
class MyForm(QDialog):
    def __init__(self):
        super().__init__()
        col = QColor(0, 0, 0)
        self.ui = Ui_Dialog()
        self.ui.setupUi(self)
        self.ui.frameColor.setStyleSheet("QWidget { background-
        color: %s }" % col.name())
        self.ui.pushButtonColor.clicked.connect(self.dispcolor)
        self.show()
    def dispcolor(self):
        col = QColorDialog.getColor()
        if col.isValid():
            self.ui.frameColor.setStyleSheet("QWidget { background-
            color: %s }" % col.name())
```

```
            self.ui.labelColor.setText("You have selected the color
    with
            code: " + str(col.name())))
if __name__=="__main__":
    app = QApplication(sys.argv)
    w = MyForm()
    w.show()
    sys.exit(app.exec_())
```

How it works...

In the `callColorDialog.pyw` file, you can see that the **click()** event of the push button is connected to the `dispcolor()` method; that is, when the user clicks the **Choose color** button, the `dispcolor()` method will be invoked. The `dispmessage()` method invokes the `getColor()` method of the `QColorDialog` class, which opens up a dialog showing different colors. Not only can the user choose any predefined basic color from the dialog box, but they can create a new custom color too. After choosing the desired color, when the user clicks the **OK** button from the color dialog, the chosen color will be assigned to the frame by invoking the `setStyleSheet()` method on the **Frame** widget class. Also, the hex code of the chosen color is displayed via the **Label** widget.

On running the application, initially you see a push button, **Choose color**, and a frame that is filled with black by default, as shown in the following screenshot:

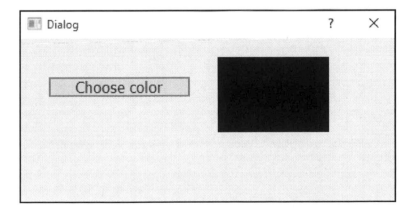

On clicking the **Choose color** button, the color dialog opens up, showing the basic colors shown in the following screenshot. The color dialog also enables you to create your own custom color too:

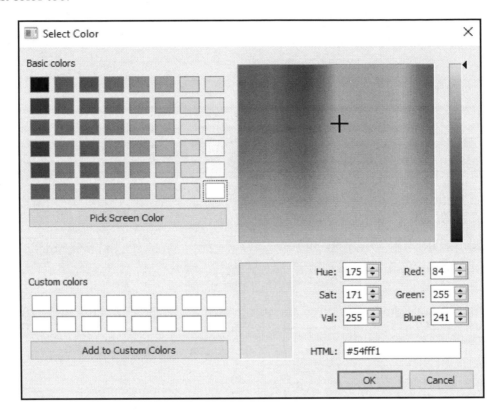

After selecting a color, when you select the **OK** button, the chosen color will be applied to the frame and the hex code of the chosen color will be displayed via the **Label** widget, as shown in the following screenshot:

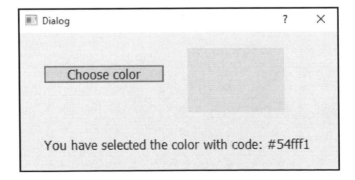

Using the font dialog

In this recipe, we will learn to use a font dialog to apply different fonts and styles to the selected text.

We will make use of a **Text Edit** widget and a **Push Button** widget in this application. The push button, when clicked, will open the font dialog. The font and style selected from the font dialog will be applied to the text written in the **Text Edit** widget.

In this recipe, we will be making use of the QFontDialog class, which displays a **Dialog** widget meant for selecting a font.

How to do it...

Let's create a new application based on the **Dialog without Buttons** template by performing the following steps:

1. Drag and drop a **Push Button** and a **Text Edit** widget onto the form.
2. Set the text property of the **Push Button** widget to Choose Font.
3. Set the **objectName** property of the **Push Button** widget to pushButtonFont.
4. Save the application with the name demoFontDialog.ui.
5. After performing the preceding steps, the application will appear as shown in the following screenshot:

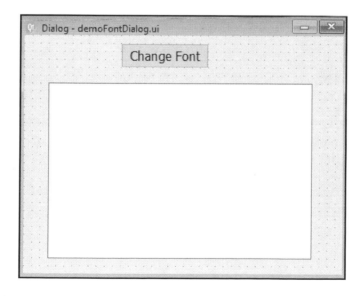

The user interface created with Qt Designer is stored in a `.ui` file, which is an XML file. Using the `pyuic5` command, you can convert the XML file into Python code. The generated Python script, `demoFontDialog.py`, can be seen in the source code bundle of this book. The `demoFontDialog.py` script will be used as a header file, and will be imported in another Python script file, which will invoke this user interface design.

6. Create another Python file with the name `callFontDialog.pyw` and import the `demoFontDialog.py` code into it:

```python
import sys
from PyQt5.QtWidgets import QDialog, QApplication, QFontDialog
from demoFontDialog import *
class MyForm(QDialog):
    def __init__(self):
        super().__init__()
        self.ui = Ui_Dialog()
        self.ui.setupUi(self)
        self.ui.pushButtonFont.clicked.connect(self.changefont)
        self.show()
    def changefont(self):
        font, ok = QFontDialog.getFont()
        if ok:
            self.ui.textEdit.setFont(font)
if __name__=="__main__":
    app = QApplication(sys.argv)
    w = MyForm()
    w.show()
    sys.exit(app.exec_())
```

How it works...

In the `callFontDialog.pyw` file, you can see that the **click()** event of the push button is connected to the `changefont()` method; that is, when the user clicks the **Choose Font** button, the `change()` method will be invoked. The `changefont()` method invokes the `getFont()` method of the `QFontDialog` class, which opens up a dialog showing different fonts, font styles, sizes, and effects. On choosing a font, font style, size, or effect, the effect of the choice on the text will be displayed in the **Sample** box. On choosing the desired font, font style, size, and effect, when user clicks the **OK** button, the selected choices will be assigned to the `font` variable. Subsequently, the `setFont()` method is invoked on the `TextEdit` class to apply the chosen font and styles to the text displayed through the **Text Edit** widget.

On running the application, you see a push button, the **Change Font** widget, and the **Text Edit** widget, as shown in the following screenshot:

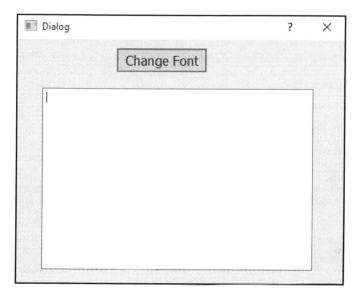

To see the impact of a chosen font from the font dialog, you need to type some text in the **Text Edit** widget, as shown in the following screenshot:

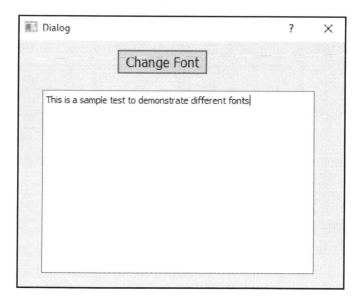

On selecting the **Change Font** button, the font dialog will open up, as shown in the following screenshot. You can see that a different font name will be displayed on the leftmost tab. The middle tab shows different font styles that enable you to make the text appear in bold, italic, bold italic, and regular. The rightmost tab shows different sizes. At the bottom, you can see different checkboxes that enable you to make text appear in underline, strikeout, and so on. Choose the options from any tab and the impact of the chosen font and style can be seen on the sample text shown in the **Sample** box. After selecting the desired font and style, click the **OK** button to close the font dialog:

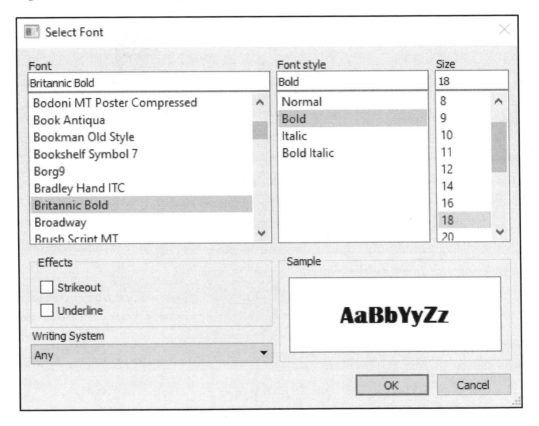

The effect of the chosen font and style will appear on the text written in the **Text Edit** widget, as shown in the following screenshot:

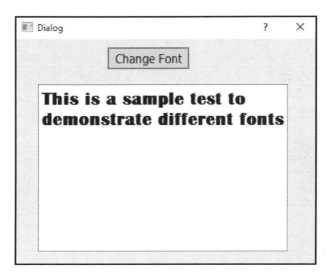

Using the file dialog

In this recipe, we will learn to use a file dialog to understand how different file operations, such as opening a file and saving a file, are done.

We will learn to create a file menu with two menu items, **Open** and **Save**. On clicking the **Open** menu item, the file open dialog box will open, which will help in browsing and choosing the file to open. The file contents of the opened file is displayed in the **Text Edit** box. The user can even update the file contents if desired. After making the desired modifications in the file, when the user clicks the **Save** option from the **File** menu, the file contents will be updated.

Getting ready

In this recipe, we will be making use of the QFileDialog class, which displays a dialog that allows users to select files or directories. The files can be selected for both opening and saving.

In this recipe, I will be using the following two methods of the QFileDialog class:

- getOpenFileName(): This method opens the file dialog, enabling the user to browse the directories and open the desired file. The syntax of the getOpenFileName() method is as follows:

```
file_name = QFileDialog.getOpenFileName(self, dialog_title, path,
filter)
```

In the preceding code, filter represents the file extensions; it determines the types of file displayed to open, for example as follows:

```
file_name = QFileDialog.getOpenFileName(self, 'Open file', '/home')
```

```
In the preceding example, file dialog is opened that shows all the
files of home directory to browse from.
```

```
file_name = QFileDialog.getOpenFileName(self, 'Open file', '/home',
"Images (*.png *.jpg);;Text files (.txt);;XML files (*.xml)")
```

In the preceding example, you can see that files from the home directory are displayed. The files with the extensions .png, .jpg, .txt, and .xml will be displayed in the dialog box.

- getSaveFileName(): This method opens the file save dialog, enabling the user to save the file with the desired name and in the desired folder. The syntax of the getSaveFileName() method is as follows:

```
file_name = QFileDialog.getSaveFileName(self, dialog_title, path,
filter, options)
```

options represents various options for how to run the dialog, for example, take a look at the following code:

```
file_name, _ =
QFileDialog.getSaveFileName(self,"QFileDialog.getSaveFileName()",""
,"All Files (*);;Text Files (*.txt)", options=options)
```

```
In the preceding example, the File Save dialog box will be opened
allowing you to save the files with the desired extension. If you
don't specify the file extension, then it will be saved with the
default extension, .txt.
```

How to do it...

Let's create a new application based on the **Main Window** template. The **Main Window** template includes a menu at the top by default:

1. We can even use two push buttons to initiate the file open dialog box and file save dialog box, but using the menu items to initiate file operations will give the feel of a real-time application.

2. The default menu bar in the **Main Window** template shows **Type Here** in place of the menu name.

3. The **Type Here** option indicates that the user can type the desired menu name, replacing the **Type Here** text. Let's type `File`, creating a menu in the menu bar.

4. On pressing the *Enter* key, the term **Type Here** will appear as a menu item under the **File** menu.

5. Let's type `Open` as the first menu item in the **File** menu.

6. On pressing the *Enter* key after creating the first menu item, **Open**, the term **Type Here** will appear below **Open**.

7. Replace **Type Here** with the menu item, **Save**.

8. After creating the **File** menu along with two menu items, **Open** and **Save**

9. The application will appear as shown in the following screenshot:

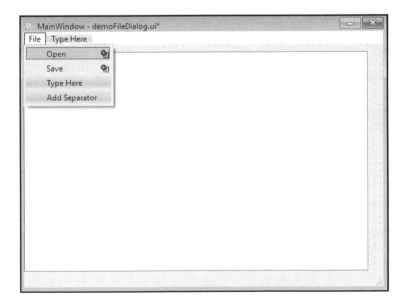

In the **Action Editor** window that is below the **Property Editor** window, you can see that the default object names of the **Open** and **Save** menu items are `actionOpen` and `actionSave`, respectively. The **Shortcut** tab in the **Action Editor** window is currently blank, as no shortcut has yet been assigned to either menu item:

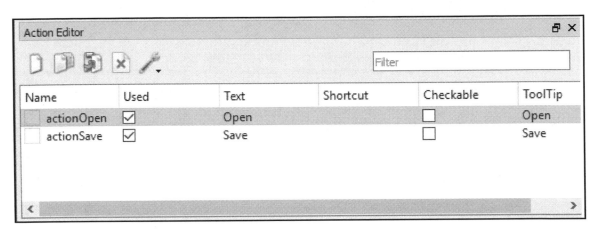

10. To assign a shortcut to the **Open** menu item, double-click on the blank space in the **Shortcut** tab of the `actionOpen` menu item. You get the dialog box, as shown in the following screenshot:

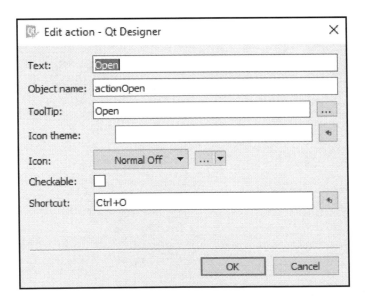

The **Text**, **Object name**, and **ToolTip** boxes are automatically filled with default text.

11. Click on the **Shortcut** box to place the cursor in that box, and press the *Ctrl* and *O* keys to assign *Ctrl + O* as a shortcut to the **Open** menu item.

12. Double-click on the blank space in the **Shortcut** tab of the `actionSave` menu item and press *Ctrl + S* in the **Shortcut** box of the dialog box that opens up.

13. After assigning the shortcut keys to both the menu items, **Open** and **Save.** The **Action Editor** window will appear as shown in the following screenshot:

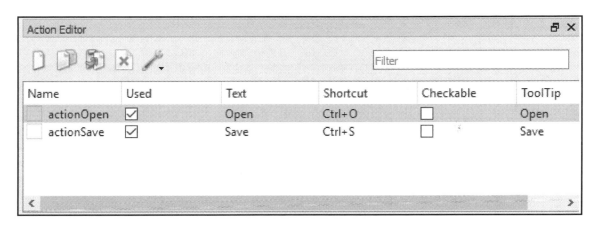

The user interface created with Qt Designer is stored in a `.ui` file, which is an XML file. On application of the `pyuic5` command, the XML file will be converted into Python code. The generated Python script, `demoFileDialog.py`, can be seen in the source code bundle of the book. The `demoFileDialog.py` script will be used as a header file, and will be imported in another Python script file, which will invoke this user interface design, the `File` menu and its respective menu items.

14. Create another Python file with the name `callFileDialog.pyw` and import the `demoFileDialog.py` code into it:

```
import sys
from PyQt5.QtWidgets import QMainWindow, QApplication, QAction,
QFileDialog
from demoFileDialog import *
class MyForm(QMainWindow):
    def __init__(self):
        super().__init__()
        self.ui = Ui_MainWindow()
```

```
            self.ui.setupUi(self)
            self.ui.actionOpen.triggered.connect(self.openFileDialog)
            self.ui.actionSave.triggered.connect(self.saveFileDialog)
            self.show()
    def openFileDialog(self):
            fname = QFileDialog.getOpenFileName(self, 'Open file',
            '/home')
            if fname[0]:
                f = open(fname[0], 'r')
            with f:
                data = f.read()
                self.ui.textEdit.setText(data)
    def saveFileDialog(self):
            options = QFileDialog.Options()
            options |= QFileDialog.DontUseNativeDialog
            fileName, _ = QFileDialog.getSaveFileName(self,
            "QFileDialog.
            getSaveFileName()","","All Files (*);;Text Files (*.txt)",
            options=options)
            f = open(fileName,'w')
            text = self.ui.textEdit.toPlainText()
            f.write(text)
            f.close()
if __name__=="__main__":
    app = QApplication(sys.argv)
    w = MyForm()
    w.show()
    sys.exit(app.exec_())
```

How it works...

In the `callFileDialog.pyw` file, you can see that the **click()** event of the **Open** menu item with `objectName`, `actionOpen`, is connected to the `openFileDialog` method; when the user clicks the **Open** menu item, the `openFileDialog` method will be invoked. Similarly, the **click()** event of the **Save** menu item with `objectName`, `actionSave`, is connected to the `saveFileDialog` method; when the user clicks the **Save** menu item, the `saveFileDialog` method will be invoked.

In the `openFileDialog` method, the open file dialog is opened by invoking the `getOpenFileName` method of the `QFileDialog` class. The open file dialog enables the user to browse the directories and choose the desired file to open. After selecting the file, when the user clicks the **OK** button, the selected filename is assigned to the `fname` variable. The file is opened in read-only mode and the file contents are read and assigned to the **Text Edit** widget; that is, the file content is displayed in the **Text Edit** widget.

After making the changes in the file contents being displayed in the **Text Edit** widget, when the user clicks the **Save** menu item from the **File** dialog, the `saveFileDialog()` method will be invoked.

In the `saveFileDialog()` method, the `getSaveFileName()` method is invoked on the `QFileDialog` class, which will open the file save dialog box. You can save the file with the same name at the same location, or with some other name. If the same filename is provided at the same location, then, on clicking the **OK** button, you get a dialog box asking whether you want to overwrite the original file with the updated content. On supplying the filename, that file is opened in write mode and the content in the **Text Edit** widget will be read and written into the file. That is, the updated file contents that are available in the **Text Edit** widget are written into the supplied filename.

On running the application, you find a **File** menu with two menu items, **Open** and **Save**, as shown in the following screenshot. You can see the shortcuts of the **Open** and **Save** menu items too:

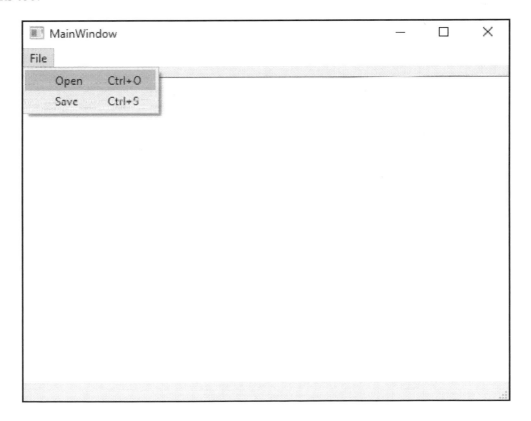

On clicking the **Open** menu item from the **File** menu, or on pressing the shortcut keys *Ctrl + O*, you get the **Open** file dialog, as shown in the following screenshot. You can browse the desired directory and select the file to open. After selecting the file, you need to click the **Open** button from the dialog:

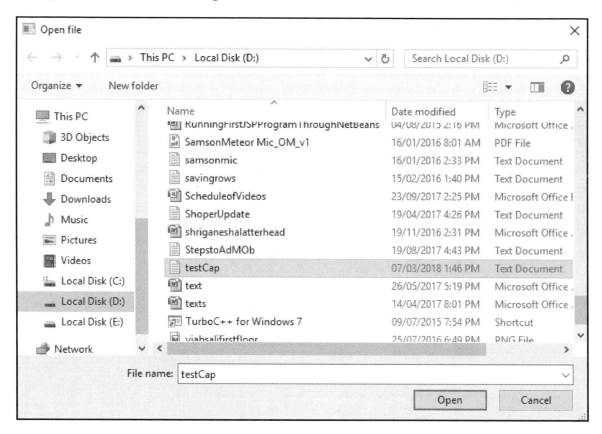

The content of the selected file will be displayed in the **Text Edit** box, as shown in the following screenshot:

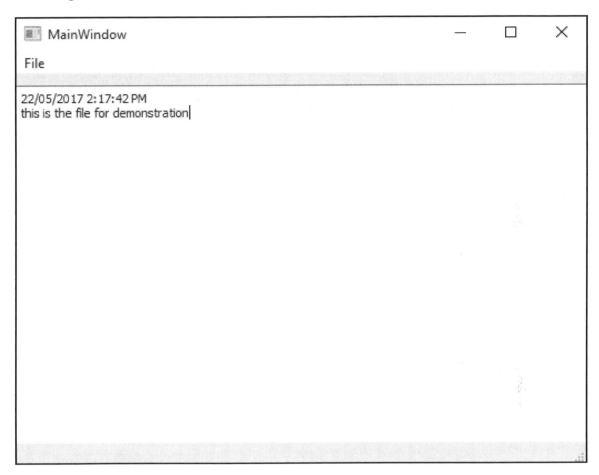

After making modifications in the file contents shown in the **Text Edit** box, when the user clicks on the **Save** menu item from the **File** menu, the `getSaveFileName` method will be invoked to display the save file dialog box. Let's save the file with the original name, followed by clicking the **Save** button, as shown in the following screenshot:

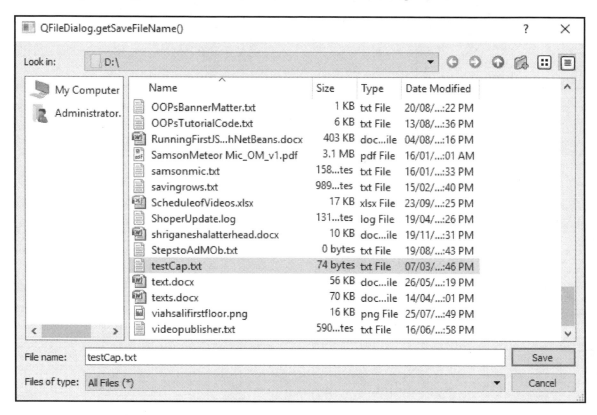

Because the file is being saved with the same name, you will get a dialog box asking for confirmation to replace the original file with the new content, as shown in the following screenshot. Click on **Yes** to update the file with the new content:

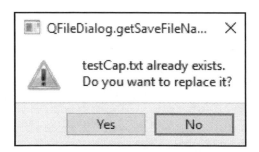

6
Understanding Layouts

In this chapter, we will focus on the following topics:

- Using Horizontal Layout
- Using Vertical Layout
- Using Grid Layout
- Using Form Layout

Understanding layouts

As the name suggest, layouts are used for arranging widgets in the desired format. On arranging certain widgets in a layout, certain size and alignment constraints are applied to the widgets automatically. For example, on increasing the size of the window, the widgets in the layout also increase in size to use up the increased space. Similarly, on reducing the size of the window, the widgets in the layout also decrease in size. The following question arises: how does the layout know what the recommended size of the widget is?

Basically, each widget has a property called **sizeHint** that contains the widget's recommended size. When the window is resized and the layout size also changes, it is through the **sizeHint** property of the widget that the layout managers know the size requirement of the widget.

In order to apply the size constraints on the widgets, you can make use of the following two properties:

- **minimumSize**: If the window size is decreased, the widget will still not become smaller than the size specified in the **minimumSize** property.
- **maximumSize**: Similarly, if the window is increased, the widget will not become larger than the size specified in the **maximumSize** property.

When the preceding properties are set, the value specified in the **sizeHint** property will be overridden.

To arrange widgets in a layout, simply select all the widgets with *Ctrl* + left-click and click **Layout Manager** on the toolbar. Another way is to right-click to open the context menu. From the context menu, you can select the **Layout** menu option, followed by selecting the desired layout from the submenu that pops up.

On selecting the desired layout, the widgets will be laid out in the selected layout, and the layout will be indicated by a red line around the widgets that is not visible at runtime. To see whether the widgets are properly laid out, you can preview the form by selecting **Form**, **Preview**, or *Ctrl* + *R*. To break the layout, select **Form**, **Break Layout**, enter *Ctrl* + *O*, or select the **Break Layout** icon from the toolbar.

The layouts can be nested.

The following are layout managers provided by Qt Designer:

- **Horizontal Layout**
- **Vertical Layout**
- **Grid Layout**
- **Form Layout**

Spacers

In order to control spacing between widgets, horizontal and vertical spacers are used. When a horizontal spacer is kept between the two widgets, the two widgets will be pushed as far left and right as possible. If the window size is increased, the widget sizes will not change and the extra space will be consumed by the spacer. Similarly, when the window size is decreased, the spacer will automatically reduce but the widget sizes will not be changed.

Spacers expand to fill empty space and shrink if the space is decreased.

Let's look at the procedure for arranging widgets in a horizontal box layout.

Using Horizontal Layout

A horizontal layout arranges widgets next to each other in a row that is, widgets are horizontally aligned using **Horizontal Layout**. Let's understand this concept by making an application.

How to do it...

In this application, we will prompt the user to enter an email address and password. The main focus of this recipe is to understand how two pairs of the **Label** and **Line Edit** widgets are horizontally aligned. Here is the step-by-step procedure to create this application:

1. Let's create an application based on the **Dialog without Buttons** template and add two QLabel, two QlineEdit, and one QPushButton widget to the form by dragging and dropping two **Label**, two **Line Edit**, and a **Push Button** widget on the form.
2. Set the **text** property of the two **Label** widgets to Name and Email Address.
3. Also, set the **text** property of the **Push Button** widget to Submit.
4. As the purpose of this application is to understand the layout and nothing else, we won't be setting the **objectName** property of any of the widgets in the application.

The form will now appear as shown in the following screenshot:

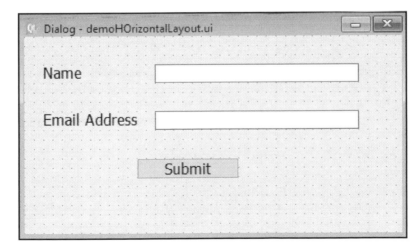

5. We will be applying **Horizontal Layout** on each pair of **Label** and **Line Edit** widgets. So, click on the **Label** widget with the text, Name, and, keeping the *Ctrl* key pressed, click on the **Line Edit** widget besides it.

 You can select more than one widget by using *Ctrl* + left-click.

6. After selecting the **Label** and **Line Edit** widgets, right-click and select the **Layout** menu option from the context menu that opens up.

7. On selecting the **Layout** menu option, several submenu options will appear on the screen; select the **Layout Horizontally** submenu option. Both the **Label** and **Line Edit** widgets will be aligned horizontally, as shown in the following screenshot:

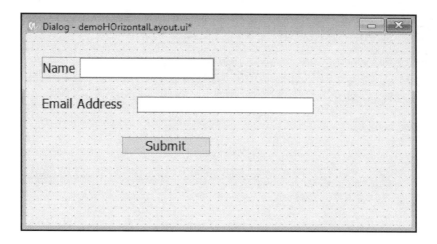

8. What if you want to break the layout? This is very simple: you can break any layout at any time by just selecting the layout and right-clicking on it. The context menu will pop up; select the **Layout** menu option from the context menu, followed by the **Break Layout** submenu option.

9. To horizontally align the second pair of **Label** widgets with the text, Email Address, and the **Line Edit** widget beside it, repeat the same procedure as mentioned in steps 6 and 7. This pair of **Label** and **Line Edit** widgets will also be horizontally aligned, as shown in the following screenshot.

You can see that a red rectangle surrounds the two widgets. This red rectangle is the horizontal layout window:

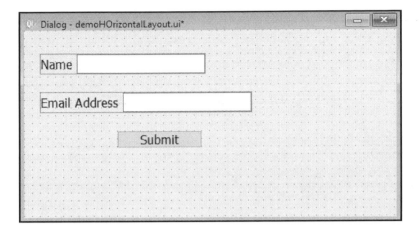

10. To create some space between the first pair of **Label** and **Line Edit** widgets, drag the **Horizontal Spacer** widget from the **Spacers** tab of **Widget Box** and drop it in between the **Label** widget with the text, Name, and the **Line Edit** widget beside it.

 The **Horizontal Spacer** widget initially takes up the default space between the two widgets. The spacers appear as blue springs on the form.

11. Adjust the size of the horizontal spacer by dragging its nodes to constrain the width of the **Line Edit** widget, as shown in the following screenshot:

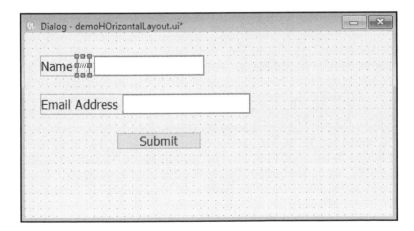

12. Select the red rectangle of the **Horizontal Layout** widget from the first pair of **Label** and **Line Edit** widgets, and drag it to the right so that its width becomes equal to the second pair.
13. On dragging the **Horizontal Layout** widget, the horizontal spacer will increase its width to consume the extra blank space between the two widgets, as shown in the following screenshot:

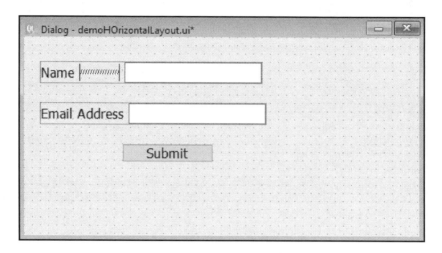

14. Save the application as demoHorizontalLayout.ui.

The user interface created with Qt Designer is stored in a .ui file, which is an XML file, and we need to convert it to Python code. To do the conversion, you need to open a Command Prompt window and navigate to the folder where the file is saved, then issue the following command line:

```
C:\Pythonbook\PyQt5>pyuic5 demoHorizontalLayout.ui -o
demoHorizontalLayout.py
```

The Python script file demoHorizontalLayout.py may have the following code:

```
from PyQt5 import QtCore, QtGui, QtWidgets
class Ui_Dialog(object):
    def setupUi(self, Dialog):
        Dialog.setObjectName("Dialog")
        Dialog.resize(483, 243)
        self.pushButton = QtWidgets.QPushButton(Dialog)
        self.pushButton.setGeometry(QtCore.QRect(120, 130, 111,
        23))
        font = QtGui.QFont()
        font.setPointSize(12)
```

```
        self.pushButton.setFont(font)
        self.pushButton.setObjectName("pushButton")
        self.widget = QtWidgets.QWidget(Dialog)
        self.widget.setGeometry(QtCore.QRect(20, 30, 271, 27))
        self.widget.setObjectName("widget")
        self.horizontalLayout = QtWidgets.QHBoxLayout(self.widget)
        self.horizontalLayout.setContentsMargins(0, 0, 0, 0)
        self.horizontalLayout.setObjectName("horizontalLayout")
        self.label = QtWidgets.QLabel(self.widget)
        font = QtGui.QFont()
        font.setPointSize(12)
        self.label.setFont(font)
        self.label.setObjectName("label")
        self.horizontalLayout.addWidget(self.label)
        spacerItem = QtWidgets.QSpacerItem(40, 20, QtWidgets.
QSizePolicy.Expanding,QtWidgets.QSizePolicy.Minimum)
        self.horizontalLayout.addItem(spacerItem)
        self.lineEdit = QtWidgets.QLineEdit(self.widget)
        font = QtGui.QFont()
        font.setPointSize(12)
        self.lineEdit.setFont(font)
        self.lineEdit.setObjectName("lineEdit")
        self.horizontalLayout.addWidget(self.lineEdit)
        self.widget1 = QtWidgets.QWidget(Dialog)
        self.widget1.setGeometry(QtCore.QRect(20, 80, 276, 27))
        self.widget1.setObjectName("widget1")
        self.horizontalLayout_2 = QtWidgets.QHBoxLayout(self.
widget1)
        self.horizontalLayout_2.setContentsMargins(0, 0, 0, 0)
        self.horizontalLayout_2.setObjectName("horizontalLayout_2")
        self.label_2 = QtWidgets.QLabel(self.widget1)
        font = QtGui.QFont()
        font.setPointSize(12)
        self.label_2.setFont(font)
        self.label_2.setObjectName("label_2")
        self.horizontalLayout_2.addWidget(self.label_2)
        self.lineEdit_2 = QtWidgets.QLineEdit(self.widget1)
        font = QtGui.QFont()
        font.setPointSize(12)
        self.lineEdit_2.setFont(font)
        self.lineEdit_2.setObjectName("lineEdit_2")
        self.horizontalLayout_2.addWidget(self.lineEdit_2)
        self.retranslateUi(Dialog)
        QtCore.QMetaObject.connectSlotsByName(Dialog)
    def retranslateUi(self, Dialog):
        _translate = QtCore.QCoreApplication.translate
        Dialog.setWindowTitle(_translate("Dialog", "Dialog"))
        self.pushButton.setText(_translate("Dialog", "Submit"))
```

```
            self.label.setText(_translate("Dialog", "Name"))
            self.label_2.setText(_translate("Dialog", "Email Address"))
if __name__ == "__main__":
    import sys
    app = QtWidgets.QApplication(sys.argv)
    Dialog = QtWidgets.QDialog()
    ui = Ui_Dialog()
    ui.setupUi(Dialog)
    Dialog.show()
    sys.exit(app.exec_())
```

How it works...

You can see in the code that a **Line Edit** widget with the default **objectName** property, `lineEdit`, and a **Label** widget with the default **objectName** property as **label** are placed on the form. Both the **Line Edit** and **Label** widgets are horizontally aligned using the Horizontal Layout widget. The **Horizontal Layout** widget has the default **objectName** property, `horizontalLayout`. On aligning the **Label** and **Line Edit** widgets, the horizontal space between the two widgets is reduced. So, a spacer is kept between the **Label** and **Line Edit** widgets. The second pair, **Label** with the default **objectName** property `label_2` and the **Line Edit** widget with the default **objectName** property `lineEdit_2`, are horizontally aligned by **Horizontal Layout** with the default **objectName** property, `horizontalLayout_2`.

On running the application, you will find that the two pairs of **Label** and **Line Edit** widgets are horizontally aligned, as shown in the following screenshot:

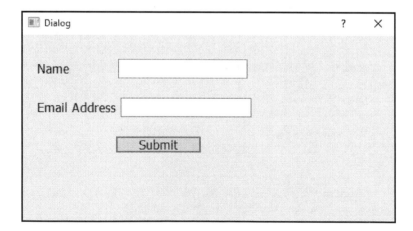

Using Vertical Layout

Vertical Layout arranges the selected widgets vertically, in a column one below the other. In the following application, you will learn the process of laying widgets in a vertical layout.

How to do it...

In this application, we will prompt the user to enter a name and email address. The labels and textboxes for entering names and email addresses, along with the submit button, will be arranged vertically one below the other via **Vertical Layout**. Here are the steps to create the application:

1. Launch Qt Designer and create an application based on the **Dialog without Buttons** template, then add two `QLabel`, two `QlineEdit`, and one `QPushButton` widget to the form by dragging and dropping two **Label**, two **Line Edit**, and one **Push Button** widget onto the form.
2. Set the **text** property of the two **Label** widgets to `Name` and `Email Address`.
3. Set the **text** property of the **Push Button** widget to `Submit`. Because the purpose of this application is to understand the layout and nothing else, we won't be setting the **objectName** property of any of the widgets in the application. The form will now appear as shown in the following screenshot:

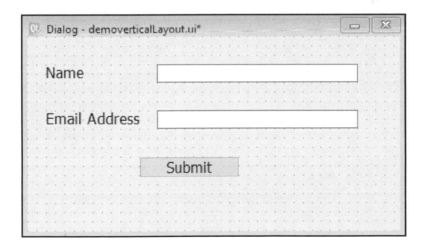

4. Before the application of **Vertical Layout** on the widgets, we need to align the widgets horizontally. So, we will apply the **Horizontal Layout** widget on each pair of **Label** and **Line Edit** widgets. So, click the **Label** widget with the text Name and, keeping the *Ctrl* key pressed, click on the **Line Edit** widget besides it.

5. After selecting the **Label** and **Line Edit** widgets, right-click the mouse button and select the **Layout** menu option from the context menu that opens up.

6. On selecting the **Layout** menu option, several submenu options will appear on the screen. Select the **Layout Horizontally** submenu option. Both the **Label** and **Line Edit** widgets will be aligned horizontally.

7. To horizontally align the second pair of **Label** with the text, Email Address, and the **Line Edit** widget beside it, repeat the same procedure as mentioned in the previous steps, 5 and 6. You can see that a red rectangle surrounds the two widgets. This red rectangle is the horizontal layout window.

8. To create some space between the first pair of **Label** and **Line Edit** widgets, drag the **Horizontal Spacer** widget from the **Spacers** tab of **Widget Box** and drop it in between the **Label** widget with the text, Name, and the **Line Edit** widget besides it. The horizontal spacer will initially take up the default space between the two widgets.

9. Select the red rectangle of the **Horizontal Layout** widget from the first pair of **Label** and **Line Edit** widgets, and drag it to the right so that its width becomes equal to the second pair.

10. On dragging the **Horizontal Layout** widget, the horizontal spacer will increase its width to consume the extra blank space between the two widgets, as shown in the following screenshot:

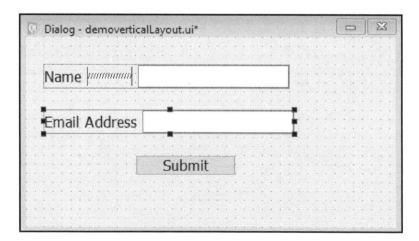

11. Now, select three things: the first **Horizontal Layout** window, the second **Horizontal Layout** window, and the **Submit** button. Keep the *Ctrl* key pressed during these multiple selections.

12. Once these three things are selected, right-click to open the context menu.

13. From the context menu, select the **Layout** menu option, followed by the **Layout Vertically** submenu option. The three items will be aligned vertically, and the width of the **Submit** button will be increased to match the width of the widest layout, as shown in the following screenshot:

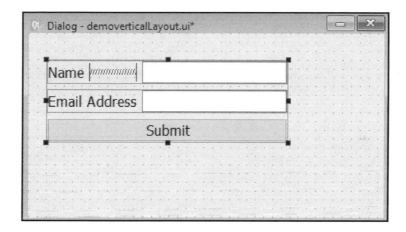

14. You can also select the **Layout Vertically** icon from the toolbar to arrange the widgets in a vertical layout.

15. If you want to control the width of the **Submit** button, you can use the **minimumSize** and **maximumSize** properties of this widget. You will notice that the vertical space between the two horizontal layouts is greatly reduced.

16. To create some space between the two horizontal layouts, drag the **Vertical Spacer** widget from the **Spacers** tab of **Widget Box** and drop it in between the two horizontal layouts.

 The vertical spacer will initially take up the default space between the two horizontal layouts

17. To create vertical space between the second horizontal layout and the **Submit** button, drag the vertical spacer and drop it between the second horizontal layout and the **Submit** button.

18. Select the red rectangle of **Vertical Layout** and drag it down to increase its height.

19. On dragging the **Vertical Layout** widget, the vertical spacer will increase its height to consume the extra blank space between the two horizontal layouts and the **Submit** button, as shown in the following screenshot:

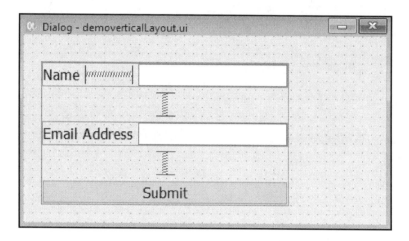

20. Save the application as demoverticalLayout.ui.

As we know that the user interface created with Qt Designer is stored in a .ui file, which is an XML file, it needs to be converted into Python code. To do the conversion, you need to open a Command Prompt window and navigate to the folder where the file is saved, then issue the following command:

```
C:PyQt5>pyuic5 demoverticalLayout.ui -o demoverticalLayout.py
```

The Python script file, demoverticalLayout.py, may have the following code:

```
from PyQt5 import QtCore, QtGui, QtWidgets
class Ui_Dialog(object):
    def setupUi(self, Dialog):
        Dialog.setObjectName("Dialog")
        Dialog.resize(407, 211)
        self.widget = QtWidgets.QWidget(Dialog)
        self.widget.setGeometry(QtCore.QRect(20, 30, 278, 161))
        self.widget.setObjectName("widget")
        self.verticalLayout = QtWidgets.QVBoxLayout(self.widget)
```

```python
self.verticalLayout.setContentsMargins(0, 0, 0, 0)
self.verticalLayout.setObjectName("verticalLayout")
self.horizontalLayout = QtWidgets.QHBoxLayout()
self.horizontalLayout.setObjectName("horizontalLayout")
self.label = QtWidgets.QLabel(self.widget)
font = QtGui.QFont()
font.setPointSize(12)
self.label.setFont(font)
self.label.setObjectName("label")
self.horizontalLayout.addWidget(self.label)
spacerItem = QtWidgets.QSpacerItem(40, 20, QtWidgets.
QSizePolicy.Expanding,QtWidgets.QSizePolicy.Minimum)
self.horizontalLayout.addItem(spacerItem)
self.lineEdit = QtWidgets.QLineEdit(self.widget)
font = QtGui.QFont()
font.setPointSize(12)
self.lineEdit.setFont(font)
self.lineEdit.setObjectName("lineEdit")
self.horizontalLayout.addWidget(self.lineEdit)
self.verticalLayout.addLayout(self.horizontalLayout)
spacerItem1 = QtWidgets.QSpacerItem(20, 40, QtWidgets.
QSizePolicy.Minimum, QtWidgets.QSizePolicy.Expanding)
self.verticalLayout.addItem(spacerItem1)
self.horizontalLayout_2 = QtWidgets.QHBoxLayout()
self.horizontalLayout_2.setObjectName("horizontalLayout_2")
self.label_2 = QtWidgets.QLabel(self.widget)
font = QtGui.QFont()
font.setPointSize(12)
self.label_2.setFont(font)
self.label_2.setObjectName("label_2")
self.horizontalLayout_2.addWidget(self.label_2)
self.lineEdit_2 = QtWidgets.QLineEdit(self.widget)
font = QtGui.QFont()
font.setPointSize(12)
self.lineEdit_2.setFont(font)
self.lineEdit_2.setObjectName("lineEdit_2")
self.horizontalLayout_2.addWidget(self.lineEdit_2)
self.verticalLayout.addLayout(self.horizontalLayout_2)
spacerItem2 = QtWidgets.QSpacerItem(20, 40, QtWidgets.
QSizePolicy.Minimum,QtWidgets.QSizePolicy.
Expanding)
self.verticalLayout.addItem(spacerItem2)
self.pushButton = QtWidgets.QPushButton(self.widget)
font = QtGui.QFont()
font.setPointSize(12)
self.pushButton.setFont(font)
self.pushButton.setObjectName("pushButton")
self.verticalLayout.addWidget(self.pushButton)
```

```
        self.retranslateUi(Dialog)
        QtCore.QMetaObject.connectSlotsByName(Dialog)
    def retranslateUi(self, Dialog):
        _translate = QtCore.QCoreApplication.translate
        Dialog.setWindowTitle(_translate("Dialog", "Dialog"))
        self.label.setText(_translate("Dialog", "Name"))
        self.label_2.setText(_translate("Dialog", "Email Address"))
        self.pushButton.setText(_translate("Dialog", "Submit"))
if __name__ == "__main__":
    import sys
    app = QtWidgets.QApplication(sys.argv)
    Dialog = QtWidgets.QDialog()
    ui = Ui_Dialog()
    ui.setupUi(Dialog)
    Dialog.show()
    sys.exit(app.exec_())
```

How it works...

You can see in the code that a **Line Edit** widget with the default **objectName** `lineEdit` property and the **Label** widget with the default **objectName** `label` property are placed on the form and are horizontally aligned using the horizontal layout with the default **objectName** property, `horizontalLayout`. On aligning the **Label** and **Line Edit** widgets, the horizontal space between the two widgets is reduced. So, a spacer is kept between the **Label** and **Line Edit** widgets. The second pair, the **Label** widget with the default **objectName** `label_2` property and the **Line Edit** widget with the default **objectName** `lineEdit_2` property, are horizontally aligned using the horizontal layout with the default **objectName** `horizontalLayout_2` property. Then, the first two horizontal layouts and the **Submit** button with the default **objectName** `pushButton` property are vertically aligned using the **Vertical Layout** widget with the default `objectName` property, `verticalLayout`. The horizontal space between the first pair of **Label** and **Line Edit** widgets is increased by placing a horizontal spacer between them. Similarly, the vertical space between the two horizontal layouts is increased by placing a vertical spacer called `spacerItem1` between them. Also, a vertical spacer called `spacerItem2` is placed between the second horizontal layout and the **Submit** button to increase the vertical space between them.

On running the application, you will find that the two pairs of **Label** and **Line Edit** widgets, and the **Submit** button, are vertically aligned, as shown in the following screenshot:

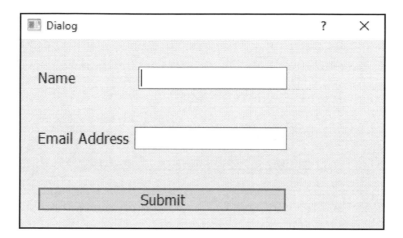

Using Grid Layout

Grid Layout arranges widgets in a stretchable grid. To understand how the **Gird Layout** widget arranges the widgets, let's create an application.

How to do it...

In this application, we will make a simple sign-in form, prompting the user to enter an email address and password, followed by clicking the **Submit** button. Below the **Submit** button, there will be two buttons, **Cancel** and **Forgot Password**. The application will help you understand how these widgets are arranged in a grid pattern. Following are the steps to create this application:

1. Launch Qt Designer and create an application based on the **Dialog without Buttons** template, then add two QLabel, two QlineEdit, and three QPushButton widgets to the form by dragging and dropping two **Label**, two **Line Edit**, and three **Push Button** widgets on the form.
2. Set the **text** property of the two **Label** widgets to Name and Email Address.

3. Set the **text** property of the three **Push Button** widgets to `Submit`, `Cancel`, and `Forgot Password`.

4. Because the purpose of this application is to understand the layout and nothing else, we won't be setting the **objectName** property of any of the widgets in the application.

5. To increase the vertical space between the two **Line Edit** widgets, drag the **Vertical Spacer** widget from the **Spacers** tab of **Widget Box** and drop it in between the two **Line Edit** widgets. The vertical spacer will initially take up the blank space between the two **Line Edit** widgets.

6. To create vertical space between the second **Line Edit** widget and the **Submit** button, drag the **Vertical Spacer** widget and drop it between them.

The application will appear as shown in the following screenshot:

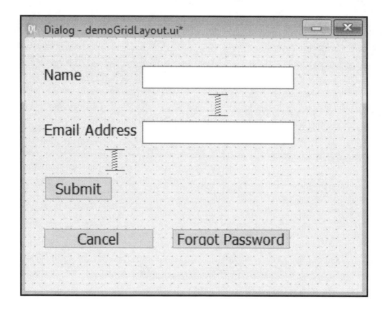

7. Select all the widgets on the form by pressing the *Ctrl* key and clicking all the widgets on the form.

8. After selecting all the widgets, right-click the mouse button to open the context menu.

9. From the context menu, select the **Layout** menu option, followed by selecting the **Layout in a Grid** submenu option.

The widgets will be aligned in the grid as shown in the following screenshot:

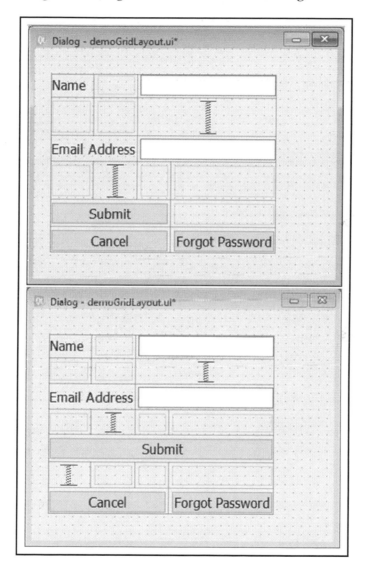

10. To increase the vertical space between the **Submit** and **Cancel** push buttons, drag the **Vertical Spacer** widget from the **Spacers** tab of **Widget Box** and drop it in between them.

11. To increase the horizontal space between the **Cancel** and **Forgot Password** push buttons, drag the **Horizontal Spacer** widget from the **Spacers** tab and drop it in between them.

The form will now appear as shown in the following screenshot:

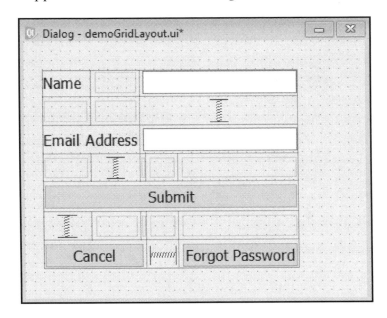

12. Save the application by name as demoGridLayout.ui.

The user interface created with Qt Designer is stored in a .ui file, which is an XML file, and needs to be converted into Python code. To do the conversion, you need to open a Command Prompt window and navigate to the folder where the file is saved, then issue the following command:

```
C:PyQt5>pyuic5 demoGridLayout.ui -o demoGridLayout.py
```

The Python script file demoGridLayout.py may have the following code:

```python
from PyQt5 import QtCore, QtGui, QtWidgets
class Ui_Dialog(object):
    def setupUi(self, Dialog):
        Dialog.setObjectName("Dialog")
        Dialog.resize(369, 279)
```

```
self.widget = QtWidgets.QWidget(Dialog)
self.widget.setGeometry(QtCore.QRect(20, 31, 276, 216))
self.widget.setObjectName("widget")
self.gridLayout = QtWidgets.QGridLayout(self.widget)
self.gridLayout.setContentsMargins(0, 0, 0, 0)
self.gridLayout.setObjectName("gridLayout")
self.pushButton = QtWidgets.QPushButton(self.widget)
font = QtGui.QFont()
font.setPointSize(12)
self.pushButton.setFont(font)
self.pushButton.setObjectName("pushButton")
self.gridLayout.addWidget(self.pushButton, 4, 0, 1, 5)
spacerItem = QtWidgets.QSpacerItem(20, 40, QtWidgets.
QSizePolicy.Minimum,QtWidgets.QSizePolicy.Expanding)
self.gridLayout.addItem(spacerItem, 5, 0, 1, 1)
self.label = QtWidgets.QLabel(self.widget)
font = QtGui.QFont()
font.setPointSize(12)
self.label.setFont(font)
self.label.setObjectName("label")
self.gridLayout.addWidget(self.label, 0, 0, 1, 1)
self.label_2 = QtWidgets.QLabel(self.widget)
font = QtGui.QFont()
font.setPointSize(12)
self.label_2.setFont(font)
self.label_2.setObjectName("label_2")
self.gridLayout.addWidget(self.label_2, 2, 0, 1, 2)
self.lineEdit_2 = QtWidgets.QLineEdit(self.widget)
font = QtGui.QFont()
font.setPointSize(12)
self.lineEdit_2.setFont(font)
self.lineEdit_2.setObjectName("lineEdit_2")
self.gridLayout.addWidget(self.lineEdit_2, 2, 2, 1, 3)
self.lineEdit = QtWidgets.QLineEdit(self.widget)
font = QtGui.QFont()
font.setPointSize(12)
self.lineEdit.setFont(font)
self.lineEdit.setObjectName("lineEdit")
self.gridLayout.addWidget(self.lineEdit, 0, 2, 1, 3)
spacerItem1 = QtWidgets.QSpacerItem(20, 40, QtWidgets.
QSizePolicy.Minimum,QtWidgets.QSizePolicy.Expanding)
self.gridLayout.addItem(spacerItem1, 3, 1, 1, 1)
spacerItem2 = QtWidgets.QSpacerItem(20, 40, QtWidgets.
QSizePolicy.Minimum,QtWidgets.QSizePolicy.Expanding)
self.gridLayout.addItem(spacerItem2, 1, 2, 1, 3)
self.pushButton_2 = QtWidgets.QPushButton(self.widget)
font = QtGui.QFont()
font.setPointSize(12)
```

```
            self.pushButton_2.setFont(font)
            self.pushButton_2.setObjectName("pushButton_2")
            self.gridLayout.addWidget(self.pushButton_2, 6, 0, 1, 3)
            self.pushButton_3 = QtWidgets.QPushButton(self.widget)
            font = QtGui.QFont()
            font.setPointSize(12)
            self.pushButton_3.setFont(font)
            self.pushButton_3.setObjectName("pushButton_3")
            self.gridLayout.addWidget(self.pushButton_3, 6, 4, 1, 1)
            spacerItem3 = QtWidgets.QSpacerItem(40, 20, QtWidgets.
            QSizePolicy.Expanding,QtWidgets.QSizePolicy.Minimum)
            self.gridLayout.addItem(spacerItem3, 6, 3, 1, 1)
            self.retranslateUi(Dialog)
            QtCore.QMetaObject.connectSlotsByName(Dialog)
        def retranslateUi(self, Dialog):
            _translate = QtCore.QCoreApplication.translate
            Dialog.setWindowTitle(_translate("Dialog", "Dialog"))
            self.pushButton.setText(_translate("Dialog", "Submit"))
            self.label.setText(_translate("Dialog", "Name"))
            self.label_2.setText(_translate("Dialog", "Email Address"))
            self.pushButton_2.setText(_translate("Dialog", "Cancel"))
            self.pushButton_3.setText(_translate("Dialog",
            "Forgot Password"))
    if __name__ == "__main__":
        import sys
        app = QtWidgets.QApplication(sys.argv)
        Dialog = QtWidgets.QDialog()
        ui = Ui_Dialog()
        ui.setupUi(Dialog)
        Dialog.show()
        sys.exit(app.exec_())
```

How it works...

You can see in the code that a **Line Edit** widget with the default **objectName** `lineEdit` property and a **Label** widget with the default **objectName** `label` property are placed on the form. Similarly, a second pair, a **Label** widget with the default **objectName** `label_2` property and a **Line Edit** widget with the default **objectName** `lineEdit_2` property are placed on the form. The vertical space between the two pairs of **Label** and **Line Edit** widgets is increased by placing a vertical spacer called `spacerItem1` between them. A **Push Button** widget with the text, `Submit`, and **objectName**, `pushButton`, is also placed on the form. Again, the vertical space between the second **Label** with **objectName** `label_2` and the **Push Button** widget with **objectName** `pushButton` is increased by placing a vertical spacer called `spacerItem2` between them. Two more push buttons with the default **objectName** properties, `pushButton_2` and `pushButton_3`, are placed on the form. All the widgets are arranged in a stretchable grid layout with the default object name, `gridLayout`. The vertical space between the two push buttons with the object names, `pushButton` and `pushButton_2`, is increased by placing a vertical spacer called `spacerItem3` between them.

On running the application, you will find that the two pairs of **Label** and **Line Edit** widgets, and the **Submit**, **Cancel**, and **Forgot Password** buttons, are arranged in a stretchable grid, as shown in the following screenshot:

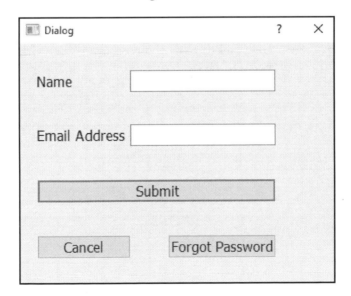

Using Form Layout

Form Layout is considered to be the most demanding layout in almost all applications. This two-column layout is required when displaying products, services, and so on, as well as in accepting feedback or other information from users or customers.

Getting ready

The form layout arranges the widgets in a two-column format. Like a sign-up form of any site or any order form, where the form is divided into two columns, the column on the left shows labels or text and the column on the right shows empty textboxes. Similarly, the form layout arranges the widgets in the left and right columns. Let's understand the concept of **Form Layout** using an application.

How to do it...

In this application, we will make two columns, one for displaying messages and the other column for accepting input from the user. Besides two pairs of **Label** and **Line Edit** widgets for taking input from the user, the application will have two buttons that will also be arranged in the form layout. Here are the steps to create an application that arranges widgets using **Form Layout**:

1. Launch Qt Designer and create an application based on the **Dialog without Buttons** template, then add two `QLabel`, two `QLineEdit`, and two `QPushButton` widgets to the form by dragging and dropping two **Label**, two **Line Edit**, and two **PushButton** widgets on the form.
2. Set the **text** property of the two **Label** widgets to `Name` and `Email Address`.
3. Set the **text** property of the two **Push Button** widgets to `Cancel` and `Submit`.
4. Because the purpose of this application is to understand the layout and nothing else, we won't be setting the **objectName** property of any of the widgets in the application.

The application will appear as shown in the following screenshot:

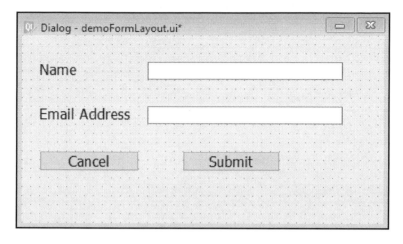

5. Select all the widgets on the form by pressing the *Ctrl* key and clicking all the widgets on the form.
6. After selecting all the widgets, right-click the mouse button to open the context menu.
7. From the context menu, select the **Layout** menu option, followed by selecting the **Layout in a Form Layout** submenu option.

The widgets will be aligned in the **Form Layout** widget, as shown in the following screenshot:

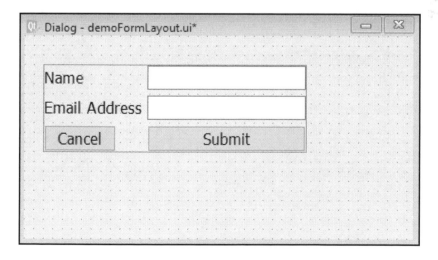

8. To increase the vertical space between the two **Line Edit** widgets, drag the **Vertical Spacer** widget from the **Spacers** tab of **Widget Box** and drop it in between them.

9. To increase the vertical space between the second **Line Edit** widget and the **Submit** button, drag the **Vertical Spacer** widget from the **Spacers** tab and drop it in between them.

10. Select the red rectangle of the **Form Layout** widget and drag it vertically to increase its height. The two vertical spacers will automatically increase in height to use the empty space in between the widgets.

The form will now appear as shown in the following screenshot:

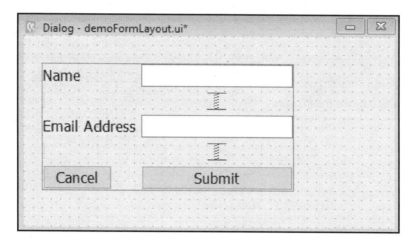

11. Save the application as demoFormLayout.ui.

The user interface created with Qt Designer is stored in a .ui file, which is an XML file, and needs to be converted into Python code. To do the conversion, you need to open a Command Prompt window and navigate to the folder where the file is saved, then issue the following command:

```
C:PyQt5>pyuic5 demoFormLayout.ui -o demoFormLayout.py
```

The Python script file, demoFormLayout.py, may have the following code:

```
from PyQt5 import QtCore, QtGui, QtWidgets
class Ui_Dialog(object):
    def setupUi(self, Dialog):
        Dialog.setObjectName("Dialog")
        Dialog.resize(407, 211)
        self.widget = QtWidgets.QWidget(Dialog)
```

```
self.widget.setGeometry(QtCore.QRect(20, 30, 276, 141))
self.widget.setObjectName("widget")
self.formLayout = QtWidgets.QFormLayout(self.widget)
self.formLayout.setContentsMargins(0, 0, 0, 0)
self.formLayout.setObjectName("formLayout")
self.label = QtWidgets.QLabel(self.widget)
font = QtGui.QFont()
font.setPointSize(12)
self.label.setFont(font)
self.label.setObjectName("label")
self.formLayout.setWidget(0, QtWidgets.QFormLayout.
LabelRole,self.label)
self.lineEdit = QtWidgets.QLineEdit(self.widget)
font = QtGui.QFont()
font.setPointSize(12)
self.lineEdit.setFont(font)
self.lineEdit.setObjectName("lineEdit")
self.formLayout.setWidget(0, QtWidgets.QFormLayout.
FieldRole,self.lineEdit)
self.label_2 = QtWidgets.QLabel(self.widget)
font = QtGui.QFont()
font.setPointSize(12)
self.label_2.setFont(font)
self.label_2.setObjectName("label_2")
self.formLayout.setWidget(2, QtWidgets.QFormLayout.
LabelRole,self.label_2)
self.lineEdit_2 = QtWidgets.QLineEdit(self.widget)
font = QtGui.QFont()
font.setPointSize(12)
self.lineEdit_2.setFont(font)
self.lineEdit_2.setObjectName("lineEdit_2")
self.formLayout.setWidget(2, QtWidgets.QFormLayout.
FieldRole, self.lineEdit_2)
self.pushButton_2 = QtWidgets.QPushButton(self.widget)
font = QtGui.QFont()
font.setPointSize(12)
self.pushButton_2.setFont(font)
self.pushButton_2.setObjectName("pushButton_2")
self.formLayout.setWidget(4, QtWidgets.QFormLayout.
LabelRole,self.pushButton_2)
self.pushButton = QtWidgets.QPushButton(self.widget)
font = QtGui.QFont()
font.setPointSize(12)
self.pushButton.setFont(font)
self.pushButton.setObjectName("pushButton")
self.formLayout.setWidget(4, QtWidgets.QFormLayout.
FieldRole,self.pushButton)
spacerItem = QtWidgets.QSpacerItem(20, 40, QtWidgets.
```

```
                    QSizePolicy.Minimum,QtWidgets.QSizePolicy.Expanding)
                    self.formLayout.setItem(1, QtWidgets.QFormLayout.FieldRole,
                    spacerItem)
                    spacerItem1 = QtWidgets.QSpacerItem(20, 40, QtWidgets.
                    QSizePolicy.Minimum,QtWidgets.QSizePolicy.Expanding)
                    self.formLayout.setItem(3, QtWidgets.QFormLayout.FieldRole,
                    spacerItem1)
                    self.retranslateUi(Dialog)
                    QtCore.QMetaObject.connectSlotsByName(Dialog)
            def retranslateUi(self, Dialog):
                    _translate = QtCore.QCoreApplication.translate
                    Dialog.setWindowTitle(_translate("Dialog", "Dialog"))
                    self.label.setText(_translate("Dialog", "Name"))
                    self.label_2.setText(_translate("Dialog", "Email Address"))
                    self.pushButton_2.setText(_translate("Dialog", "Cancel"))
                    self.pushButton.setText(_translate("Dialog", "Submit"))
        if __name__ == "__main__":
            import sys
            app = QtWidgets.QApplication(sys.argv)
            Dialog = QtWidgets.QDialog()
            ui = Ui_Dialog()
            ui.setupUi(Dialog)
            Dialog.show()
            sys.exit(app.exec_())
```

How it works...

You can see in the code that a **Line Edit** widget with the default
objectName lineEdit property and a **Label** widget with the default **objectName**
labels property is placed on the form. Similarly, a second pair, a **Label** widget with the
default **objectName** label_2 property and a **Line Edit** widget with the default
objectName lineEdit_2 property are placed on the form. The two push buttons with the
object names, pushButton and pushButton_2, are placed on the form. All six widgets are
selected and aligned in a two-column format using the **Form Layout** widget with the
default **objectName** formLayout property.

On running the application, you will find that the two pairs of **Label** and **Line Edit** widgets, and the **Cancel** and **Submit** buttons, are arranged in a **Form Layout** widget as shown in the following screenshot:

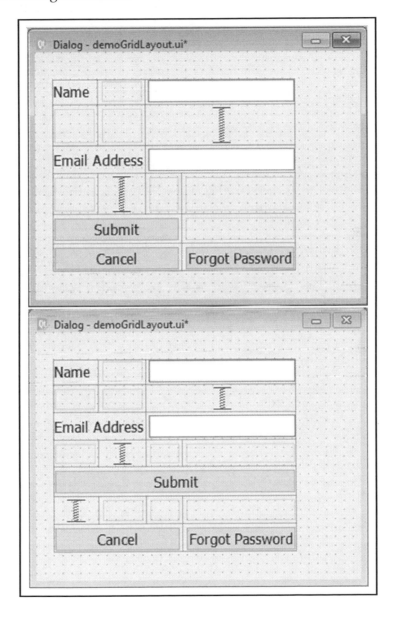

7
Networking and Managing Large Documents

In this chapter, we will learn how to use networking concepts and about how large documents can be viewed in chunks. We will cover the following topics:

- Creating a small browser
- Creating a server-side application
- Establishing client-server communication
- Creating a dockable and floatable sign-in form
- Multiple Document Interface
- Displaying information in sections using Tab Widget
- Creating a custom menu bar

Introduction

Space on a device screen is always limited, but sometimes you come across a situation in which you want to display lots of information or services on the screen. In such a situation, you can either use dockable widgets that can be floated anywhere on the screen; MDI to display multiple documents as and when desired; a **Tab Widget** box to display information in different chunks; or menus to display the required information on the click of a menu item. Also, to better understand networking concepts, you need to understand how clients and servers communicate. This chapter will help you understand all this.

Creating a small browser

Let's now learn a technique to display a web page or the content of an HTML document. We will simply be making use of the **Line Edit** and **Push Button** widgets so that the user can enter the URL of the desired site, followed by clicking on the **Push Button** widget. On clicking the push button, that site will appear in a customized widget. Let's see how.

In this recipe, we will learn how to make a small browser. Because Qt Designer does not includes any widgets specifically, the focus of this recipe is to make you understand how a custom widget can be promoted into `QWebEngineView`, which in turn can be used for displaying a web page.

The application will prompt for a URL and when the user clicks the **Go** button after entering the URL, the specified web page will open in the `QWebEngineView` object.

How to do it...

In this recipe, we will require just three widgets: one for entering the URL, a second for clicking the button, and a third for displaying the website. Here are the steps to creating a simple browser:

1. Create an application based on the **Dialog without Buttons** template.
2. Add the `QLabel`, `QLineEdit`, `QPushButton`, and `QWidget` widgets to the form by dragging and dropping **Label**, **Line Edit**, **Push Button**, and **Widget** onto the form.
3. Set the **text** property of the **Label** widget to `Enter URL`.
4. Set the **text** property of the **Push Button** widget to `Go`.
5. Set the **objectName** property of the **Line Edit** widget to `lineEditURL` and that of the **Push Button** widget to `pushButtonGo`.
6. Save the application as `demoBrowser.ui`.

The form will now appear as shown in the following screenshot:

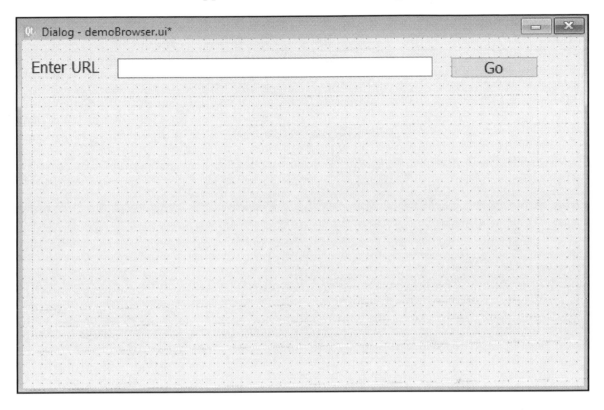

7. The next step is to promote `QWidget` to `QWebEngineView` because, to display web pages, `QWebEngineView` is required.
8. Promote the `QWidget` object by right-clicking on it and selecting the **Promote to ...** option from the menu that pops up.
9. In the dialog box that appears, leave the **Base class name** option as the default, **QWidget**.
10. In the **Promoted class name** box, enter `QWebEngineView` and in the **Header file** box type `PyQt5.QtWebEngineWidgets`.

11. Select the **Promote** button to promote **QWidget** to the `QWebEngineView` class, as shown in the following screenshot:

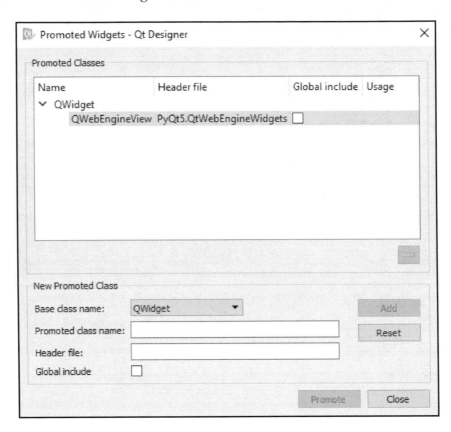

The user interface created with Qt Designer is stored in a `.ui` file, which is an XML file, and needs to be converted into Python code.

12. To do the conversion, you need to open a Command Prompt window and navigate to the folder where the file is saved, then issue the following command:

```
C:\Pythonbook\PyQt5>pyuic5 demoBrowser.ui -o demoBrowser.py
```

You can see the auto-generated Python script file `demoBrowser.py` in the source code bundle of this book.

13. Treat the preceding code as a header file, and import it into the file from which you will invoke its user interface design.

14. Let's create another Python file with the name `callBrowser.pyw` and import the `demoBrowser.py` code into it:

```python
import sys
from PyQt5.QtCore import QUrl
from PyQt5.QtWidgets import QApplication, QDialog
from PyQt5.QtWebEngineWidgets import QWebEngineView
from demoBrowser import *
class MyForm(QDialog):
    def __init__(self):
        super().__init__()
        self.ui = Ui_Dialog()
        self.ui.setupUi(self)
        self.ui.pushButtonGo.clicked.connect(self.dispSite)
        self.show()
    def dispSite(self):
        self.ui.widget.load(QUrl(self.ui.lineEditURL.text()))
if __name__=="__main__":
    app = QApplication(sys.argv)
    w = MyForm()
    w.show()
    sys.exit(app.exec_())
```

How it works...

In the `demoBrowser.py` file, a class with the name of the top-level object is created, with `Ui_` prepended. That is, for the top-level object, `Dialog`, the `Ui_Dialog` class is created and stores the interface elements of our widget. That class includes two methods, `setupUi()` and `retranslateUi()`. The `setupUi()` method creates the widgets that are used in defining the user interface in Qt Designer. Also, the properties of the widgets are set in this method. The `setupUi()` method takes a single argument, which is the top-level widget of the application, an instance of `QDialog`. The `retranslateUi()` method translates the interface.

In the `callBrowser.pyw` file, you see that the **click()** event of the **Push Button** widget is connected to the `dispSite` method; after entering a URL in the **Line Edit** widget, when the user clicks the Push Button, the `dispSite` method will be invoked.

The `dispSite()` method invokes the `load()` method of the `QWidget` class. Recall that the `QWidget` object is promoted to the `QWebEngineView` class for viewing web pages. The `load()` method of the `QWebEngineView` class is supplied with the URL entered in the `lineEditURL` object consequently, the web page of the specified URL opens up or loads in the `QWebEngine` widget.

On running the application, you get an empty **Line Edit** box and a **Push Button** widget. Enter the desired URL in the **Line Edit** widget and click on the **Go** push button, and you will find the web page opens in the QWebEngineView widget, as shown in the following screenshot:

Creating a server-side application

Networking plays a major role in modern life. We need to understand how communication is established between two machines. When two machines communicate, one is usually a server and the other is a client. The client sends requests to the server and the server responds by serving the request made by the client.

In this recipe, we will be creating a client-server application where a connection is established between client and server and each will be able to transfer text messages to the other. That is, two applications will be made and will be executed simultaneously, and the text written in one application will appear in the other.

How to do it...

Let's begin by creating a server application first, as follows:

1. Create an application based on the **Dialog without Buttons** template.
2. Add a `QLabel`, `QTextEdit`, `QLineEdit`, and `QPushButton` to the form by dragging and dropping the **Label**, a **Text Edit**, **Line Edit**, and **Push Button** widgets on the form.

2. Set the **text** property of the **Label** widget to `Server` to indicate that this is the server application.
3. Set the **text** property of the **Push Button** widget to `Send`.
4. Set the **objectName** property of the **Text Edit** widget to `textEditMessages`.
5. Set the **objectName** property of the **Line Edit** widget to `lineEditMessage`.
6. Set the **Push Button** widget to `pushButtonSend`.
7. Save the application as `demoServer.ui`. The form will now appear as shown in the following screenshot:

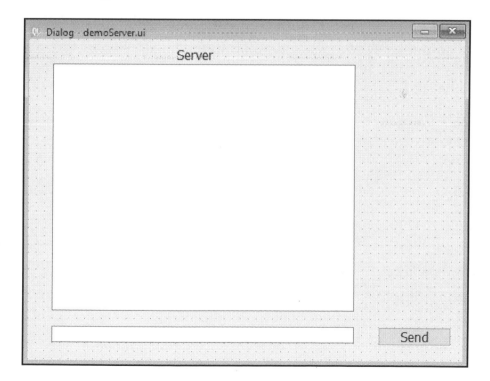

The user interface created with Qt Designer is stored in a `.ui` file, which is an XML file, and needs to be converted into Python code. The code of the generated file, `demoServer.py`, can be seen in the source code bundle of this book.

How it works...

The `demoServer.py` file will be treated as a header file and will be imported into another Python file that will use the GUI of the header file and transmit the data from the server to client and vice versa. But before that, let's create a GUI for the client application. The GUI of the client application is exactly the same as that of the server application, with the only difference that the **Label** widget at the top of this application will display the text **Client**.

The `demoServer.py` file is a generated Python script of the GUI widgets that we dragged and dropped onto the form.

To establish a connection between the server and client, we will require a socket object. To create the socket object, you need to supply the following two arguments:

- **Socket address:** The socket address is represented using certain address families. Each address family requires certain parameters to establish a connection. We will be using the `AF_INET` address family in this application. The `AF_INET` address family needs a pair of (host, port) to establish a connection where the parameter, `host` is the hostname which can either be in string format, internet domain notation, or IPv4 address format and the parameter; `port` is an integer that represents the port number used for communication.
- **Socket type:** The socket type is represented through several constants: `SOCK_STREAM`, `SOCK_DGRAM`, `SOCK_RAW`, `SOCK_RDM`, and `SOCK_SEQPACKET`. We will use the most generally used socket type, `SOCK_STREAM`, in this application.

The `setsockopt()` method is used in the application for setting the value of the given socket option. It includes the following two essential parameters:

- `SOL_SOCKET`: This parameter is the socket layer itself. It is used for protocol-independent options.
- `SO_REUSEADDR`: This parameter allows other sockets to `bind()` to this port unless there is an active listening socket bound to the port already.

You can see in the earlier code that a `ServerThread` class is created, which inherits the `Thread` class of Python's threading module. The `run()` function is overridden where the `TCP_IP` and `TCP_HOST` variables are defined and `tcpServer` is bound with these variables.

Thereafter, the server waits to see whether any client connection is made. For each new client connection, the server creates a new `ClientThread` inside the `while` loop. This is because creating a new thread for each client will not block the GUI functionality of the server. Finally, the threads are joined.

Establishing client-server communication

In this recipe, we will learn to make a client and will see how it can send messages to the server. The main idea is to understand how a message is sent, how the server listens to the port, and how communication is established between the two.

How to do it...

To send messages to the server, we will be making use of the **Line Edit** and **Push Button** widgets. The message written in the **Line Edit** widget will be passed to the server on the click of the push button. Here is the step-by-step procedure for creating a client application:

1. Create another application based on the **Dialog without Buttons** template.
2. Add `QLabel`, `QTextEdit`, `QLineEdit`, and `QPushButton` to the form by dragging and dropping the **Label**, **Text Edit**, **Line Edit**, and **Push Button** widgets on the form.
3. Set the **text** property of the **Label** widget to `Client`.
4. Set the **text** property of the **Push Button** widget to `Send`.
5. Set the **objectName** property of the **Text Edit** widget to `textEditMessages`.
6. Set the **objectName** property of the **Line Edit** widget to `lineEditMessage`.
7. Set the **Push Button** widget to `pushButtonSend`.
8. Save the application by name as `demoClient.ui`.

The form will now appear as shown in the following screenshot:

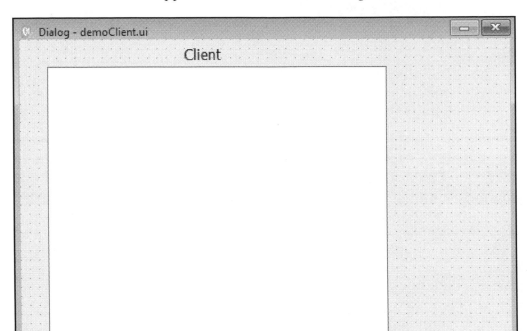

The user interface created with Qt Designer is stored in a `.ui` file, which is an XML file, and needs to be converted into Python code. The code of the autogenerated file, `demoClient.py`, can be seen in the source code bundle of this book. To use the GUI created in the `demoClient.py` file, it needs to be imported into another Python file that will use the GUI and will transmit data from the server to the client and vice versa.

9. Create another Python file with the name `callServer.pyw` and import the `demoServer.py` code into it. The code in the `callServer.pyw` script is as shown here:

```
import sys, time
from PyQt5 import QtGui
from PyQt5 import QtCore
from PyQt5.QtWidgets import QApplication, QDialog
from PyQt5.QtCore import QCoreApplication
```

```python
import socket
from threading import Thread
from socketserver import ThreadingMixIn
conn=None
from demoServer import *
class Window(QDialog):
    def __init__(self):
        super().__init__()
        self.ui = Ui_Dialog()
        self.ui.setupUi(self)
        self.textEditMessages=self.ui.textEditMessages
        self.ui.pushButtonSend.clicked.connect(self.dispMessage)
        self.show()

    def dispMessage(self):
        text=self.ui.lineEditMessage.text()
        global conn
        conn.send(text.encode("utf-8"))
        self.ui.textEditMessages.append("Server:
        "+self.ui.lineEditMessage.text())
        self.ui.lineEditMessage.setText("")
class ServerThread(Thread):
    def __init__(self,window):
        Thread.__init__(self)
        self.window=window
    def run(self):
        TCP_IP = '0.0.0.0'
        TCP_PORT = 80
        BUFFER_SIZE = 1024
        tcpServer = socket.socket(socket.AF_INET,
        socket.SOCK_STREAM)
        tcpServer.setsockopt(socket.SOL_SOCKET,
        socket.SO_REUSEADDR, 1)
        tcpServer.bind((TCP_IP, TCP_PORT))
        threads = []
        tcpServer.listen(4)
        while True:
            global conn
            (conn, (ip,port)) = tcpServer.accept()
            newthread = ClientThread(ip,port,window)
            newthread.start()
            threads.append(newthread)
        for t in threads:
            t.join()
class ClientThread(Thread):
    def __init__(self,ip,port,window):
        Thread.__init__(self)
        self.window=window
```

```
            self.ip = ip
            self.port = port
    def run(self):
        while True :
            global conn
            data = conn.recv(1024)
            window.textEditMessages.append("Client:
            "+data.decode("utf-8"))

if __name__=="__main__":
    app = QApplication(sys.argv)
    window = Window()
    serverThread=ServerThread(window)
    serverThread.start()
    window.exec()
    sys.exit(app.exec_())
```

How it works...

In the `ClientThread` class, the `run` function is overridden. In the `run` function, each client waits for data received from the server and displays that data in the **Text Edit** widget. A `window` class object is passed to the `ServerThread` class, which passes that object to `ClientThread`, which, in turn, uses it to access the content written in the **Line Edit** element.

The received data is decoded because the data received is in the form of bytes, which have to be converted into strings using UTF-8 encoding.

The `demoClient.py` file that we generated in the preceding section needs to be treated as a header file and needs to be imported into another Python file that will use the GUI of the header file and transmit data from the client to the server and vice versa. So, let's create another Python file with the name `callClient.pyw` and import the `demoClient.py` code into it:

```
import sys
from PyQt5.QtWidgets import QApplication, QDialog
import socket
from threading import Thread
from socketserver import ThreadingMixIn
from demoClient import *
tcpClientA=None
class Window(QDialog):
    def __init__(self):
        super().__init__()
        self.ui = Ui_Dialog()
```

```
            self.ui.setupUi(self)
            self.textEditMessages=self.ui.textEditMessages
            self.ui.pushButtonSend.clicked.connect(self.dispMessage)
            self.show()
        def dispMessage(self):
            text=self.ui.lineEditMessage.text()
            self.ui.textEditMessages.append("Client:
            "+self.ui.lineEditMessage.text())
            tcpClientA.send(text.encode())
            self.ui.lineEditMessage.setText("")
    class ClientThread(Thread):
        def __init__(self,window):
            Thread.__init__(self)
            self.window=window
        def run(self):
            host = socket.gethostname()
            port = 80
            BUFFER_SIZE = 1024
            global tcpClientA
            tcpClientA = socket.socket(socket.AF_INET,
            socket.SOCK_STREAM)
            tcpClientA.connect((host, port))
            while True:
                data = tcpClientA.recv(BUFFER_SIZE)
                window.textEditMessages.append("Server:
                "+data.decode("utf-8"))
                tcpClientA.close()
    if __name__=="__main__":
        app = QApplication(sys.argv)
        window = Window()
        clientThread=ClientThread(window)
        clientThread.start()
        window.exec()
        sys.exit(app.exec_())
```

A ClientThread class is a class that inherits the Thread class and overrides the run function. In the run function, you fetch the IP address of the server by invoking the hostname method on the socket class; and, using port 80, the client tries to connect to the server. Once a connection with the server is made, the client tries to receive data from the server inside the while loop.

On receiving the data from the server, the data is converted into string format from byte format and displayed in the **Text Edit** widget.

We need to run both applications to see client-server communication. On running the `callServer.pyw` file, you get the output shown on the left side of the following screenshot, and on running the `callClient.pyw` file, you get the output shown on the right side. Both are same; only the labels at the top distinguish them:

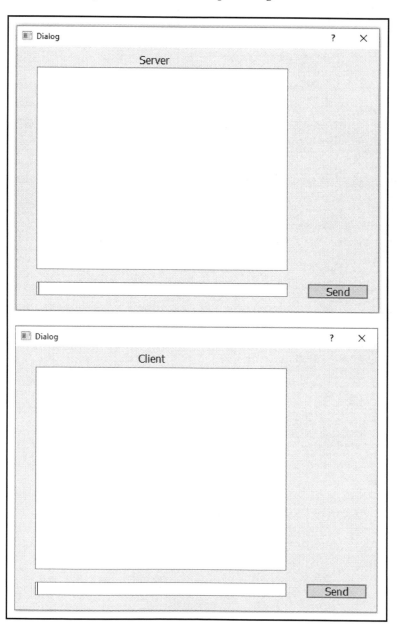

The user can type the text in the **Line Edit** box at the bottom, followed by pressing the **Send** button. On pressing the **Send** button, the text entered in the **Line Edit** widget will appear in the **Text Edit** box of both server and client applications. Text is prefixed with `Server:` to indicate that the text is sent from the server, as shown in the following screenshot:

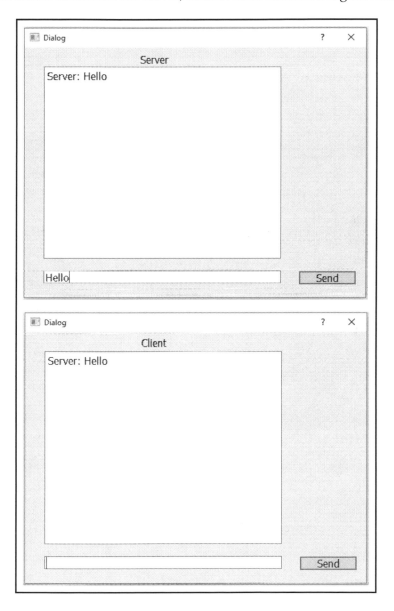

Similarly, if text is written in the **Line Edit** widget of the client application followed by pressing the **Send** button, the text will appear in the **Text Edit** widget of both applications. The text will be prefixed with `Client:` to indicate that the text has been sent from the client, as shown in the following screenshot:

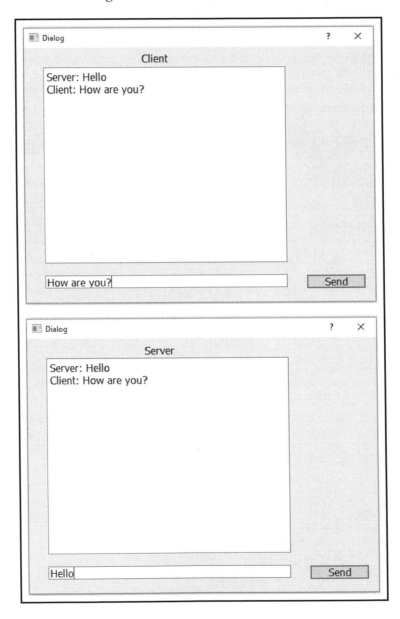

Creating a dockable and floatable sign-in form

In this recipe, we will learn to create a sign-in form that will ask for the email address and password of the user for authentication. This sign-in form is different from the usual sign-in form, in the sense that it is a dockable form. That is, you can dock this sign-in form to any of the four sides of the window—top, left, right, and bottom and can even use it as a floatable form. This dockable sign-in form will be created using the **Dock** widget, so let's get a quick idea about the **Dock** widget.

Getting ready

To create a detachable set of widgets or tools, you need a **Dock** widget. A **Dock** widget is created with the `QDockWidget` class and is a container that has a title bar and buttons at the top to size it. The **Dock** widget, which contains a collection of widgets or tools, can be closed, docked in the dock area, or floated and placed anywhere on the desktop. The **Dock** widget can be docked in different dock areas, such as `LeftDockWidgetArea`, `RightDockWidgetArea`, `TopDockWidgetArea`, and `BottomDockWidgetArea`. The `TopDockWidgetArea` dock area is below the toolbar. You can also restrict the dock areas where the **Dock** widget can be docked. When you do so, the **Dock** widget can be docked to the specified dock areas only. When a **Dock** window is dragged out of the dock area, it becomes a free-floating window.

Here are the properties that control the movement of the **Dock** widget and the appearance of its title bar and other buttons:

Property	Description
DockWidgetClosable	Makes the **Dock** widget closable.
DockWidgetMovable	Makes the **Dock** widget movable between dock areas.
DockWidgetFloatable	Makes the **Dock** widget floatable, that is, the **Dock** widget can be detached from the main window and floated on the desktop.
DockWidgetVerticalTitleBar	Displays a vertical title bar on the left side of the **Dock** widget.
AllDockWidgetFeatures	It switches on properties such as DockWidgetClosable, DockWidgetMovable, and DockWidgetFloatable, that is, the **Dock** widget can be closed, moved, or floated.
NoDockWidgetFeatures	If selected, the **Dock** widget cannot be closed, moved, or floated.

In order to make a dockable sign-in form for this recipe, we will be making use of the **Dock** widget and a few more widgets. Let's see the step-by-step procedure for doing this.

How to do it...

Let's make a small sign-in form in the **Dock** widget that will prompt the user for their email address and password. Being dockable, this sign-in form can be moved anywhere on the screen and can be made floatable. Here are the steps to create this application:

1. Launch Qt Designer and create a new **Main Window** application.
2. Drag and drop a **Dock** widget onto the form.
3. Drag and drop the widgets that you want to be available in dock areas or as floating windows in the **Dock** widget.
4. Drag and drop three **Label** widgets, two **Line Edit** widgets, and a **Push Button** widget on the **Dock** widget.
5. Set the **text** property of the three **Label** widgets to `Sign In`, `Email Address`, and `Password`.
6. Set the **text** property of the **Push Button** widget to `Sign In`.
7. We will not set the **objectName** property of the **Line Edit** and **Push Button** widgets and will not provide any code for the **Push Button** widget, because the purpose of this application is to understand how the **Dock** widget works.
8. Save the application as `demoDockWidget.ui`.

The form will appear as shown in the following screenshot:

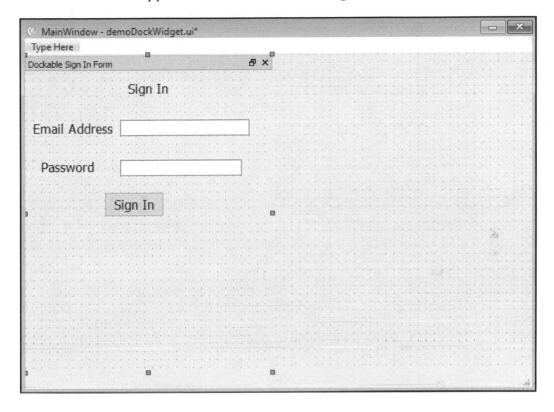

9. To enable all features in the **Dock** widget, select it and check its
   AllDockWidgetFeatures property in the **features** section of the **Property Editor**
   window, as shown in the following screenshot:

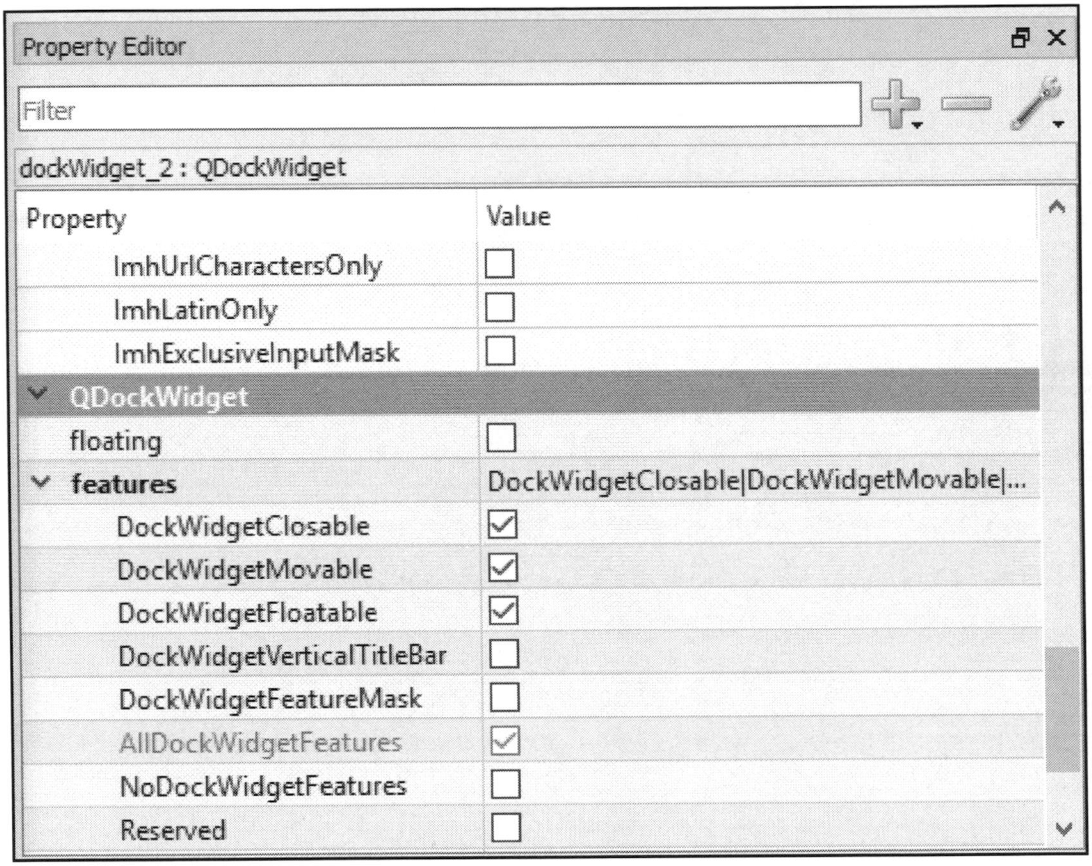

In the preceding screenshot, the **AllDockWidgetFeatures** property is to make the
Dock widget closable, movable in the dock, and floatable anywhere on the
Desktop. If the **NoDockWidgetFeatures** property is selected, then all other
properties in the **features** section are unchecked automatically. That means all
buttons will disappear from the **Dock** widget, and you will not be able to close or
move it. If you want the **Dock** widget to appear as floatable on application
startup, check the **floating** property just above the **features** section in the
Property Editor window.

Look at the following screenshot depicting various features and constraints on the **Dock** widget:

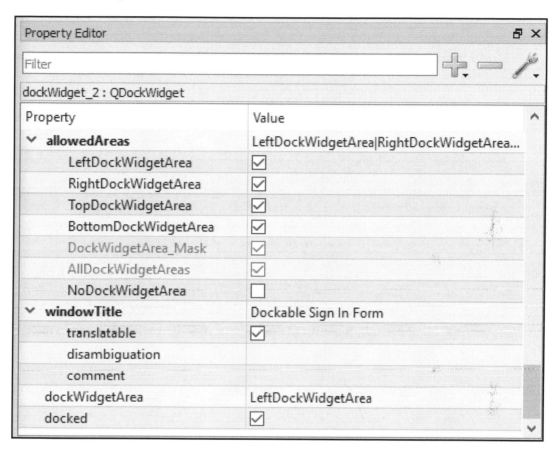

Perform the following steps to apply the desired features and constraints to the **Dock** widget:

1. Check the **AllDockWidgetAreas** option in the **allowedAreas** section to enable the **Dock** widget to be docked in all of the left, right, top, and bottom **Dock** widget areas.
2. Also, by using the **windowTitle** property in the **Property Editor** window, set the title of the dock window to **Dockable Sign In Form**, as shown in the preceding screenshot.

3. Check the **docked** property because it is an essential property to make a **Dock** widget dockable. If the **docked** property is not checked, the **Dock** widget cannot be docked to any of the allowable areas.

4. Leave the **dockWidgetArea** property with its default value, **LeftDockWidgetArea**. The **dockWidgetArea** property determines the location where you want the **Dock** widget to appear as docked when the application is launched. The **LeftDockWidgetArea** value for the **dockWidgetArea** property will make the **Dock** widget first appear as docked in the left **Dock** widget area. If the **NoDockWidgetArea** property is set in the **allowedAreas** section, then all other properties in the **allowedAreas** section are unselected automatically. Consequently, you can move the **Dock** window anywhere on the desktop, but you cannot dock it in the dock areas of the **Main Window** template. The user interface created with Qt Designer is stored in a .ui file, which is an XML file, and needs to be converted into Python code. On the application of the pyuic5 command line utility on the XML file, the generated file is a Python script file, demoDockWidget.py. You can see the code of the generated demoDockWidget.py file in the source code bundle of this book.

5. Treat the code in the demoDockWidget.py file as a header file, and import it into the file from which you will invoke its user interface design.

6. Create another Python file with the name callDockWidget.pyw and import the demoDockWidget.py code into it:

```
import sys
from PyQt5.QtWidgets import QMainWindow, QApplication
from demoDockWidget import *
class AppWindow(QMainWindow):
    def __init__(self):
        super().__init__()
        self.ui = Ui_MainWindow()
        self.ui.setupUi(self)
        self.show()
if __name__=="__main__":
    app = QApplication(sys.argv)
    w = AppWindow()
    w.show()
    sys.exit(app.exec_())
```

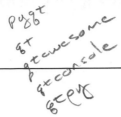
How it works...

As you can see in the preceding code, the necessary modules are imported. An `AppWindow` class is created that inherits from the base class, `QMainWindow`. The default constructor for `QMainWindow` is invoked.

Because every PyQt5 application needs an application object, in the preceding code, an application object was created with the name app by invoking the `QApplication()` method. For passing command line arguments and other external attributes to the application, the `sys.argv` parameter was passed as a parameter to the `QApplication()` method. The `sys.argv` parameter contains command line arguments and other external attributes, if there are any. In order to display the widgets defined in the interface, an instance of the `AppWindow` class was created with the name w, and the `show()` method was invoked on it. To exit the application and return the code to Python interpreter that might be used for error handling, the `sys.exit()` method was called.

When the application is executed, you get a **Dock** widget that is docked to the left dockable area by default, as shown in the following screenshot. This is because you have assigned the `LeftDockWidgetArea` value to the `dockWidgetArea` property of the **Dock** widget:

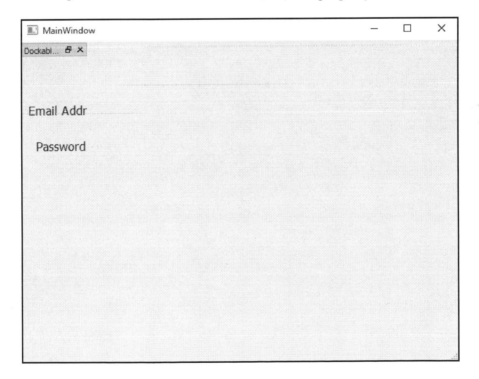

The widgets inside the **Dock** widget are not completely visible, as the default left and dockable areas are narrower than the widgets placed in the **Dock** widget. So, you can drag the right border of the **Dock** widget to make all the contained widgets visible, as shown in the following screenshot:

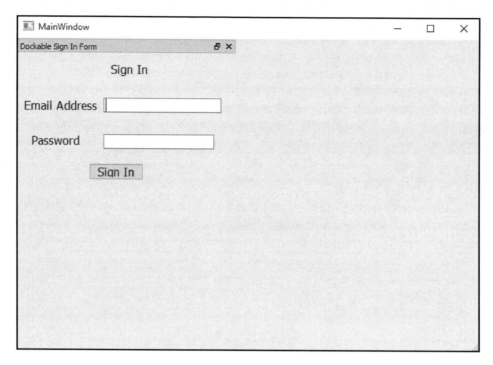

You can drag the widget to any area. If you drag it to the top, it will be docked in the TopDockWidgetArea dock area, as shown in the following screenshot:

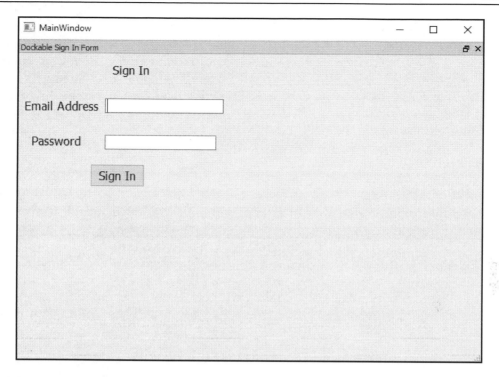

Similarly, when the **Dock** widget is dragged to the right, it will be docked in the
`RightDockWidgetArea`

You can drag the **Dock** widget outside the **Main Window** template to make it an
independent floating window. The **Dock** widget will appear as an independent floating
window and can be moved anywhere on the desktop:

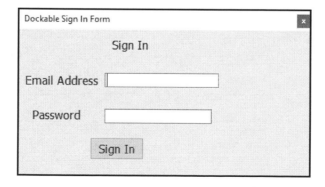

Multiple Document Interface

In this recipe, we will learn how to create an application that will display more than one document at a time. Not only will we be able to manage more than one document, but we will also learn to arrange the documents in different formats. We will be able to manage more than one document using a concept called Multiple Document Interface, so let's see a quick introduction to this.

Getting ready

Usually, an application provides one document per main window and such applications are said to be **Single Document Interface (SDI)** applications. As the name suggests, a **Multiple Document Interface (MDI)** application is able to display several documents. An MDI application consists of a main window along with a menu bar, a toolbar, and a central space. Several documents can be displayed in the central space, where each document can be managed through individual child window widgets; in MDI, several documents can be displayed and each document is displayed in its own window. These child windows are also known as subwindows.

MDI is implemented by making use of the MdiArea widget. The MdiArea widget provides an area where child windows or subwindows are displayed. A subwindow has a title and buttons to show, hide, and maximize its size. Each subwindow can display an individual document. The subwindows can be arranged in a cascade or tile pattern by setting the respective property of the MdiArea widget. The MdiArea widget is an instance of the QMdiArea class and the subwindows are instances of QMdiSubWindow.

Here are the methods provided by QMdiArea:

- subWindowList(): This method returns a list of all subwindows in the MDI area. The returned list is arranged in the order that is set through the WindowOrder() function.
- WindowOrder: This static variable sets the criteria for ordering the list of child windows. Following are the valid values that can be assigned to this static variable:
    - CreationOrder: The windows are returned in the order of their creation. This is the default order.

- StackingOrder: The windows are returned in the order in which they are stacked, with the topmost window last in the list.
- ActivationHistoryOrder: The windows are returned in the order in which they were activated.

- activateNextSubWindow(): This method sets the focus to the next window in the list of child windows. The current window order determines the next window to be activated.
- activatePreviousSubWindow(): This method sets the focus to the previous window in the list of child windows. The current window order determines the previous window to be activated.
- cascadeSubWindows(): This method arranges subwindows in cascade fashion.
- tileSubWindows(): This method arranges subwindows in tile fashion.
- closeAllSubWindows(): This method closes all subwindows.
- setViewMode(): This method sets the view mode of the MDI area. The subwindows can be viewed in two modes, **SubWindow View** and **Tabbed View**:
  - **SubWindow View**: This method displays subwindows with window frames (default). You can see the content of more than one subwindow if arranged in tile fashion. It is also represented by a constant value, 0.
  - **Tabbed View**: Displays subwindows with tabs in a tab bar. Only the content of one subwindow contents can be seen at a time. It is also represented by a constant value, 1.

How to do it...

Let's create an application that consists of two documents, and each document will be displayed via its individual subwindow. We will learn how to arrange and view these subwindows as desired:

1. Launch Qt Designer and create a new **Main Window** application.
2. Drag and drop a MdiArea widget onto the form.
3. Right-click on the widget and select **Add Subwindow** from the context menu to add a subwindow to the MdiArea widget.

When the subwindow is added to the `MdiArea` widget, the widget appears as the dark background, as shown in the following screenshot:

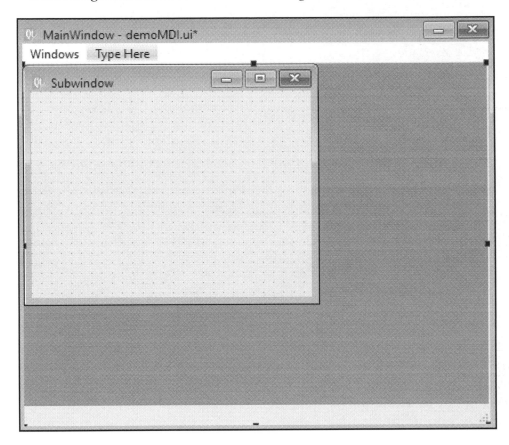

4. Let's, right-click again on the `MdiArea` widget and add one more subwindow to it.
5. To know which one is the first and which one is the second subwindow, drag and drop a **Label** widget onto each subwindow.
6. Set the **text** property of the **Label** widget placed in the first subwindow to `First subwindow`.

7. Set the **text** property of the **Label** widget placed in the second subwindow to `Second subwindow`, as shown in the following screenshot:

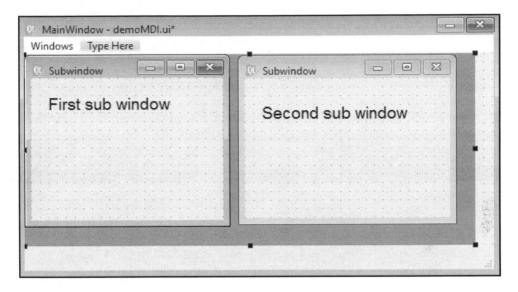

The `MdiArea` widget displays the documents placed in its subwindows in the following two modes:

- **SubWindow View**: This is the default view mode. The subwindows can be arranged in cascade or tile fashion in this view mode. When subwindows are arranged in tile fashion, you can see the content of more than one subwindow simultaneously.
- **Tabbed View**: In this mode, several tabs appear in a tab bar. When a tab is selected, the subwindow associated with it is displayed. Only the content of one subwindow can be seen at a time.

8. To activate the **SubWindow View** and **Tabbed View** modes through the menu options, double-click the **Type Here** placeholder in the menu in the menu bar and add two entries to it: **SubWindow View** and **Tabbed View**.

Also, to see how the subwindows appear when arranged in cascade and tile fashion, add two more menu items, **Cascade View** and **Tile View,** to the menu bar as shown in the following screenshot:

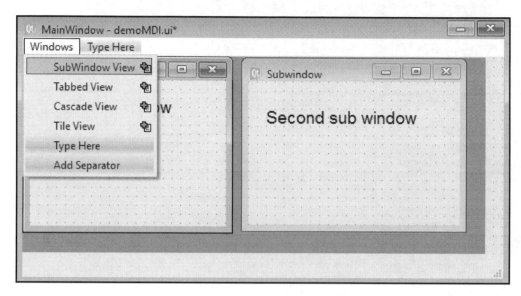

9. Save the application as demoMDI.ui. The user interface created with Qt Designer is stored in a .ui file, which is an XML file, and needs to be converted into Python code.On the application of the pyuic5 command line utility, the .ui (XML) file will be converted into Python code:

```
C:\Pythonbook\PyQt5>pyuic5 demoMDI.ui -o demoMDI.py.
```

You can see the generated Python code, demoMDI.py, in the source code bundle of this book.

10. Treat the code in the demoMDI.py file as a header file, and you will import it to the file from which you will invoke its user interface design. The user interface design in the previous code includes MdiArea to display the subwindows created in it, along with their respective widgets. The Python script that we are going to create will contain the code for the menu options to do different tasks, such as cascading and tiling the subwindows, changing the view mode from **SubWindow View** to **Tabbed View**, and vice versa. Let's name that Python script callMDI.pyw and import the demoMDI.py code into it:

```
import sys
from PyQt5.QtWidgets import QMainWindow, QApplication, QAction,
```

```
            QFileDialog
            from demoMDI import *
            class MyForm(QMainWindow):
                def __init__(self):
                    super().__init__()
                    self.ui = Ui_MainWindow()
                    self.ui.setupUi(self)
                    self.ui.mdiArea.addSubWindow(self.ui.subwindow)
                    self.ui.mdiArea.addSubWindow(self.ui.subwindow_2)
                    self.ui.actionSubWindow_View.triggered.connect
                    (self.SubWindow_View)
                    self.ui.actionTabbed_View.triggered.connect(self.
                    Tabbed_View)
                    self.ui.actionCascade_View.triggered.connect(self.
                    cascadeArrange)
                    self.ui.actionTile_View.triggered.connect(self.tileArrange)
                    self.show()
                def SubWindow_View(self):
                    self.ui.mdiArea.setViewMode(0)
                def Tabbed_View(self):
                    self.ui.mdiArea.setViewMode(1)
                def cascadeArrange(self):
                    self.ui.mdiArea.cascadeSubWindows()
                def tileArrange(self):
                    self.ui.mdiArea.tileSubWindows()
            if __name__=="__main__":
                app = QApplication(sys.argv)
                w = MyForm()
                w.show()
                sys.exit(app.exec_())
```

How it works...

In the preceding code, you can see that the two subwindows with the default **objectName** properties, subwindow and subwindow_2, are added to the MdiArea widget. After that, the four menu options with objectName properties, actionSubWindow_View, actionTabbed_View, actionCascade_View, and actionTile_View are connected to the four methods SubWindow_View, Tabbed_View, cascadeArrange, and tileArrange respectively. Hence, when the **SubWindow View** menu option is selected by the user, the SubWindow_View method will be invoked. In the SubWindow_View method, the **SubWindow View** mode is activated by passing the 0 constant value to the setViewMode method of the MdiArea widget. The **SubWindow View** displays subwindows with window frames.

Similarly, when the **Tabbed View** menu option is selected by the user, the Tabbed_View method will be invoked. In the Tabbed_View method, the **Tabbed View** mode is activated by passing the 1 constant value to the setViewMode method of the MdiArea widget. The **Tabbed View** mode displays tabs in a tab bar and on clicking a tab, the associated subwindow will be displayed.

When the **Cascade View** menu option is selected, the cascadeArrange method is invoked, which in turn invokes the cascadeSubWindows method of the MdiArea widget to arrange subwindows in cascade form.

When the **Tile View** menu option is selected, the tileArrange method is invoked, which in turn invokes the tileSubWindows method of the MdiArea widget to arrange subwindows in tile form.

On running the application, the subwindows initially appear in shrunken mode in the MdiArea widget, as shown in the following screenshot. You can see the subwindows along with their titles and minimize, maximize, and close buttons:

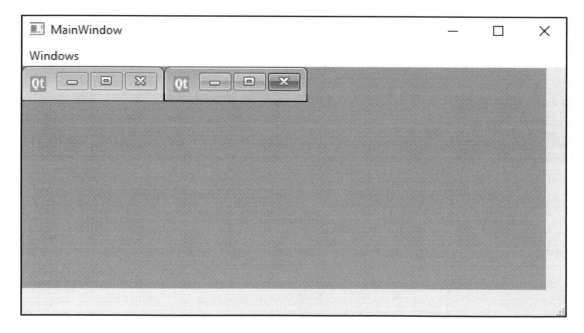

You can drag their borders to the desired size. On selecting the first window from the **Windows** menu, a subwindow becomes active; on selecting the second window, the next subwindow will become active. The active subwindow appears with the brighter title and boundary. In the following screenshot, you can notice that the second subwindow is active. You can drag the boundaries of any subwindow to increase or decrease its size. You can also minimize a subwindow and drag the boundaries of another subwindow to take up the whole width of the `MdiArea` widget. If you select maximize in any subwindow, it will take up all the space of `MdiArea`, making other subwindows invisible:

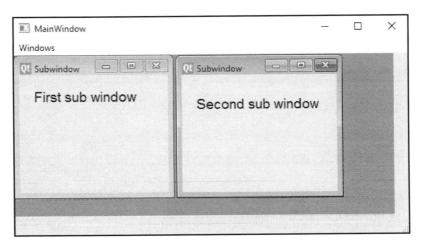

On selecting **Cascade**, the subwindows are arranged in cascade mode, as shown in the following screenshot. If windows are maximized in **Cascade** mode, the top subwindow takes up the whole `MdiArea` widget, hiding other subwindows behind it, as shown in the following screenshot:

On selecting the **Tile** button, the subwindows are expanded and tiled. Both subwindows expand equally to cover up the entire workspace, as shown in the following screenshot:

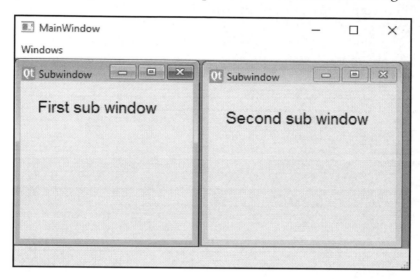

On selecting the **Tabbed View** button, the `MdiArea` widget will change from the **Subwindow** view to **Tabbed View**. You can select the tab of any subwindow to make it active, as shown in the following screenshot:

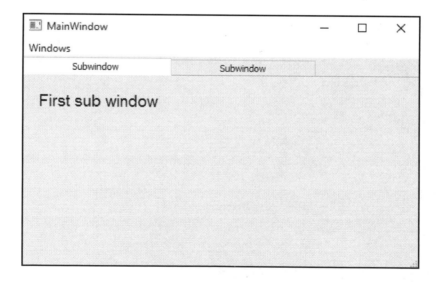

Displaying information in sections using Tab Widget

In this application, we will make a small shopping cart that will display certain products for sale in one tab; after selecting the desired products from the first tab, when the user selects the second tab, they will be prompted to enter the preferred payment option. The third tab will ask the user to enter the address for delivering the products.

We will use **Tab Widget** to enable us to select and fill in the desired information in chunks, so you must be wondering, what is a **Tab Widget**?

When certain information is divided into small sections, and you want to display the information for the section required by the user, then you need to use **Tab Widget**. In a **Tab Widget** container, there are a number of tabs and when the user selects any tab, the information assigned to that tab will be displayed.

How to do it...

Here is the step-by-step procedure to create an application that displays information in chunks using tabs:

1. Let's create a new application based on the **Dialog without Buttons** template.
2. Drag and drop **Tab Widget** onto the form. When you drag **Tab Widget** onto a dialog, it appears with two default tab buttons, labeled **Tab1** and **Tab2**, as shown in the following screenshot:

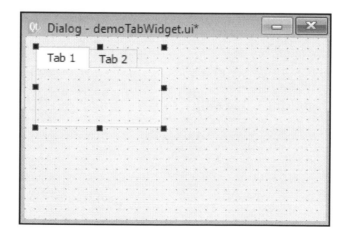

3. You can add more tab buttons to **Tab Widget** and delete existing buttons if you want by adding a new tab button; right-click on either tab button and select **Insert Page** from the menu that pops up. You will see two suboptions, **After Current Page** and **Before Current Page**.

4. Select the **After Current Page** suboption to add a new tab after the current tab. The new tab will have the default text **Page**, which you can always change. The application that we are going to make consists of the following three tabs:

   - The first tab displays certain products along with their prices. The user can select any number of products from the first tab, followed by clicking the **Add to Cart** button.
   - On selecting the second tab, all the payment options will be displayed. The user can choose to pay via **Debit Card**, **Credit Card**, **Net Banking**, or **Cash on Delivery**.
   - The third tab, when selected, will prompt the user for a delivery address: the complete address of the customer along with state, country, and contact number.

The first task that we will do is to change the default text of the tabs:

1. Using the **currentTabText** property of **Tab Widget**, change the text displayed on each tab button.
2. Set the **text** property of the first tab button to `Product Listing` and that of the second tab button to `Payment Method`.
3. To add a new tab button, right-click on the **Payment Method** tab and select **Insert Page** from the context menu that appears.
4. From the two options that appear, **After Current Page** and **Before Current Page**, select **After Current Page** to add a new tab after the **Payment Method** tab. The new tab will have the default text **Page**.
5. Using the **currentTabText** property, change its text to `Delivery Address`.
6. Expand **Tab Widget** by selecting and dragging its nodes to provide a blank space below the tab buttons, as shown in the following screenshot:

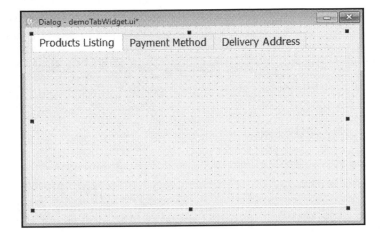

7. Select each tab button and drop the desired widgets into the blank space provided. For example, drop four **Check Box** widgets onto the first tab button, **Product Listing**, to display the items available for sale.

8. Drop a **Push Button** widget on the form.

9. Change the **text** property of the four checkboxes to `Cell Phone $150`, `Laptop $500`, `Camera $250`, and `Shoes $200`.

10. Change the **text** property of the **Push Button** widget to `Add to Cart`, as shown in the following screenshot:

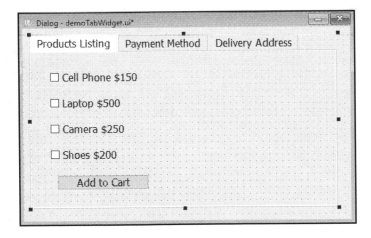

11. Similarly, to provide different payment methods, select the second tab and place four radio buttons in the available space.

12. Set the **text** property of the four radio buttons to `Debit Card`, `Credit Card`, `Net Banking`, and `Cash On Delivery`, as shown in the following screenshot:

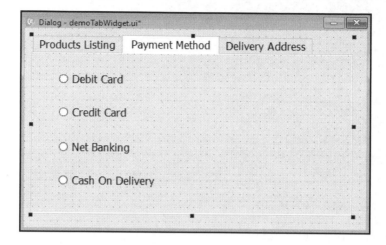

13. Select the third tab and drag and drop few **Line Edit** widgets that prompt the user to provide a delivery address.
14. Drag and drop six **Label** and six **Line Edit** widgets onto the form.
15. Set the **text** property of the **Label** widgets to `Address 1`, `Address 2`, `State`, `Country`, `Zip Code`, and `Contact Number`. The **Line Edit** widgets in front of each **Label** widget will be used to get the address for delivery, as shown in the following screenshot:

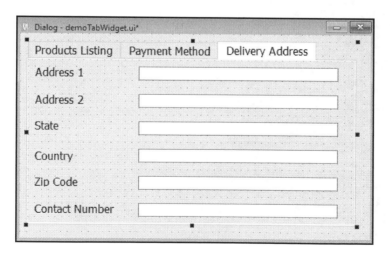

16. Save the application as demoTabWidget.ui.

17. The user interface created with Qt Designer is stored in a .ui file, which is an XML file, and needs to be converted into Python code. To do the conversion, you need to open a Command Prompt window, navigate to the folder where the file is saved, and issue this command:

    C:PythonbookPyQt5>pyuic5 demoTabWidget.ui -o demoTabWidget.py

    The code of the generated Python script file, demoTabWidget.py, can be seen in the source code bundle of this book. The user interface design created in the autogenerated code demoTablWidget.py, is used by importing it into another Python script.

18. Create another Python file with the name callTabWidget.pyw and import the demoTabWidget.py code into it:

```
import sys
from PyQt5.QtWidgets import QDialog, QApplication
from demoTabWidget import *
class MyForm(QDialog):
    def __init__(self):
        super().__init__()
        self.ui = Ui_Dialog()
        self.ui.setupUi(self)
        self.show()
if __name__=="__main__":
    app = QApplication(sys.argv)
    w = MyForm()
    w.show()
    sys.exit(app.exec_())
```

How it works...

As you can see in callTabWidget.pyw, the necessary modules are imported. The MyForm class is created and inherits from the base class, QDialog. The default constructor for QDialog is invoked.

An application object is created with the name `app` through the `QApplication()` method. Every PyQt5 application must create an application object. The `sys.argv` parameter is passed to the `QApplication()` method while creating the application object. The `sys.argv` parameter contains a list of arguments from the command line and helps in passing and controlling the startup attributes of a script. After this, an instance of the `MyForm` class is created with the name `w`. The `show()` method is invoked on the instance, which will display the widgets on the screen. The `sys.exit()` method ensures a clean exit, releasing memory resources.

When the application is executed, you will find that the first tab, **Products Listing**, is selected by default and the products available for sale specified in that tab are displayed as shown in the following screenshot:

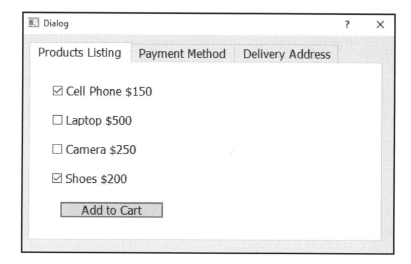

Similarly, on selecting the other tabs, **Payment Method** and **Delivery Address**, you will see the widgets prompting the user to choose the desired payment method and enter a delivery address.

Creating a custom menu bar

A big application is usually broken into small, independent, and manageable modules. These modules can be invoked either by making different toolbar buttons or menu items. That is, we can invoke a module on the click of a menu item. We have seen the **File** menu, the **Edit** menu, and so on in different packages, so let's learn to make a custom menu bar of our own.

In this recipe, we will learn to create a menu bar that shows certain menu items. We will learn to add menu items, add submenu items to a menu item, add separators between menu items, add shortcuts and tool tips to menu items, and much more. We will also learn to add actions to these menu items, so that when any menu item is clicked, a certain action will take place.

Our menu bar will consist of two menus, **Draw** and **Edit**. The **Draw** menu will consist of four menu items, **Draw Circle**, **Draw Rectangle**, **Draw Line**, and **Properties**. The **Properties** menu item will consist of two submenu items, **Page Setup** and **Set Password**. The second menu, **Edit**, will consist of three menu items, **Cut**, **Copy**, and **Paste**. Let's create a new application to understand how to create this menu bar practically.

How to do it...

We will be following a step-by-step procedure to make two menus, along with the respective menu items in each. For quick access, each menu item will be associated with a shortcut key too. Here are the steps to create our customized menu bar:

1. Launch Qt Designer and create a **Main Window** template-based application.

You get the new application with the default menu bar because the **Main Window** template of Qt Designer provides a main application window that displays a menu bar by default. The default menu bar appears as shown in the following screenshot:

2. We can always remove the default menu bar by right-clicking in the main window and selecting the **Remove Menu Bar** option from the context menu that pops up.
3. You can also add a menu bar later by selecting the **Create Menu Bar** option from the context menu.

The default menu bar contains **Type Here** placeholders. You can replace those with the menu item text.

4. Click the placeholder to highlight it and type to modify its text. When you add a menu item, **Type Here** appears below the new menu item.

5. Again, just single left-click the **Type Here** placeholder to select it and simply type the text for the next menu item.

6. You can delete any menu entry by right-clicking it and, from the context menu that pops up, select the option **Remove Action** action_name.

 The menus and menu items in the menu bar can be arranged by dragging and dropping them at the desired location.

While writing menu or menu item text, if you add an ampersand character (&) before any character, that character in the menu will appear as underlined and will be treated as a shortcut key. We will also learn how to assign a shortcut key to a menu item later.

7. When you create a new menu item by replacing the **Type Here** placeholders, that menu item will appear as an individual action in the **Action Editor** box, from where you can configure its properties.

Recall that we want to create two menus in this menu bar with text, Draw and Edit. The **Draw** menu will have three menu items, **Draw Circle**, **Draw Rectangle**, and **Draw Line**. After these three menu items, a separator will be inserted followed by a fourth menu item called **Properties**. The **Properties** menu item will have two submenu items, **Page Setup** and **Set Password**. The **Edit** menu will contain three menu items, **Cut**, **Copy**, and **Paste**.

8. Double-click the **Type Here** placeholder and enter the text for the first menu, Draw.

The down arrow key on the **Draw** menu brings up the **Type Here** and **Add Separator** options, as shown in the following screenshot:

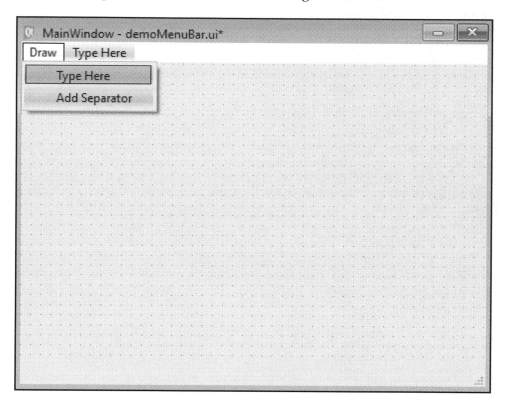

9. Double-click **Type Here** and type `Draw Circle` for the first menu item under the **Draw** menu. The down arrow key on the **Draw Circle** menu provides the **Type Here** and **Add Separator** options again.
10. Double-click **Type Here** and type `Draw Rectangle` for the menu item.
11. Press the down arrow key to get two options, **Type Here** and **Add Separator**.
12. Double-click **Type Here** and type `Draw Line` for the third menu item.
13. On pressing the down arrow key, again you get two options, **Type Here** and **Add Separator**, as shown in the following screenshot:

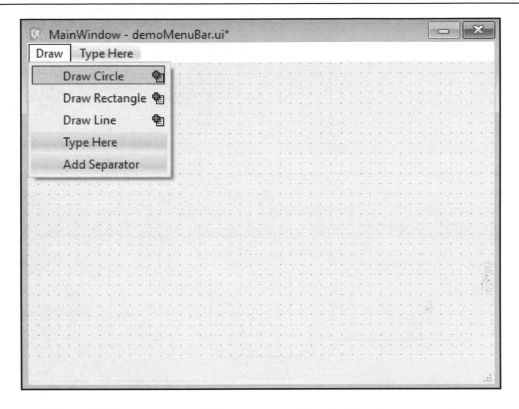

14. Select **Add Separator** to add a separator after the first three menu items.
15. Press the down arrow key after the separator and add a fourth menu item, `Properties`. This is done because we want two submenu items for the **Properties** menu item.
16. Select the right arrow to add submenu items to the **Properties** menu.
17. Press the right arrow key on any menu item to add a submenu item to it. In the submenu item, select **Type Here** and enter the first submenu, `Page Setup`.

18. Select the down arrow and enter `Set Password` below the **Page Setup** submenu item, as shown in the following screenshot:

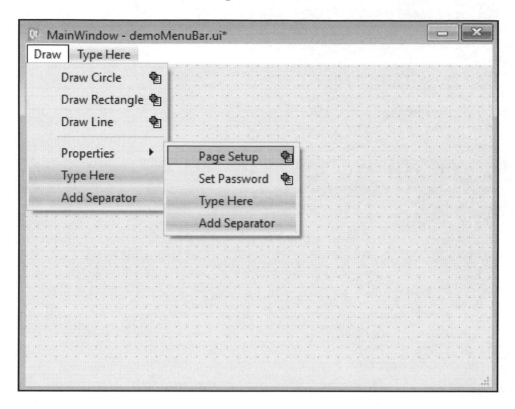

19. The first menu, **Draw**, is complete. Now, we need to add another menu, **Edit**. Select the **Draw** menu and press the right arrow key to indicate that you want to add a second menu to the menu bar.

20. Replace **Type Here** with `Edit`.

21. Press the down arrow and add three menu items, **Cut**, **Copy**, and **Paste**, as shown in the following screenshot:

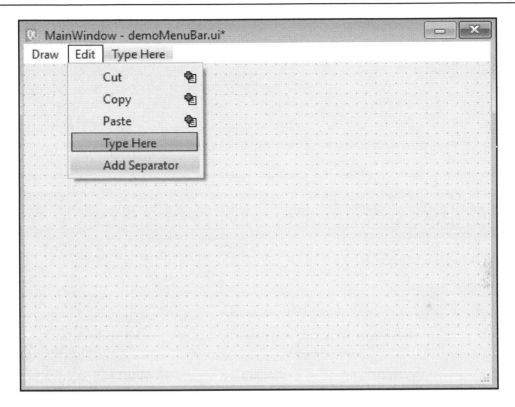

The actions for all menu items will appear in the **Action Editor** box automatically, as shown in the following screenshot:

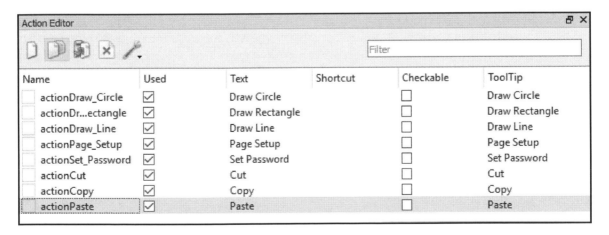

You can see that the action names are generated by prefixing the text action to every menu text and replacing the spaces with underscores. These actions can be used to configure menu items.

22. To add a tooltip message that appears when the user hovers over any menu item, you can use the **ToolTip** property.

23. To assign a tooltip message to the **Draw Circle** menu item of the **Draw** menu, select **actionDraw_Circle** in the **Action Editor** box and set the **ToolTip** property to To draw a circle. Similarly, you can assign tooltip messages to all of the menu items.

24. To assign a shortcut key to any menu item, open its action from the **Action Editor** box and click inside the **Shortcut** box.

25. In the **Shortcut** box, press the key combination that you want to assign to the selected menu item.

For example, if you press *Ctrl + C* in the **Shortcut** box, **Ctrl+C** appears in the box, as shown in the following screenshot:

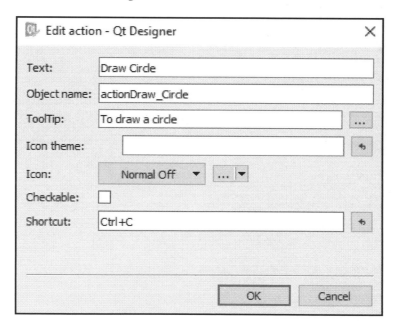

You can have any combination of shortcut keys, such as *Shift* + key, *Alt* + key, and *Ctrl* + *Shift* + key, for any menu item. The shortcut keys will appear automatically with the menu item in the menu bar. You can also make any menu item checkable, that is, you can make it a toggle menu item.

26. To do so, select the action of the desired menu item and check the **Checkable** checkbox. The actions of each menu item, along with its action name, menu text, shortcut keys, checkable status, and tooltip, appear in the **Action Editor** box. The following screenshot shows the action of the **Set Password** submenu item, which confirms that its shortcut key is *Shift* + P and it is checkable:

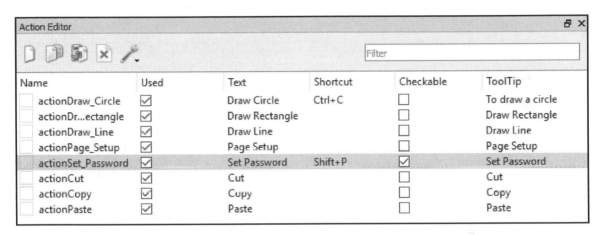

27. For the **Draw Circle**, **Draw Rectangle**, and **Draw Line** menu items, we will be adding code to draw a circle, draw a rectangle, and draw a line respectively.

28. For the rest of the menu items, we want them so that when the user selects any of them, a text message appears on the form indicating which menu item is selected.

29. To display a message, drag and drop a **Label** widget onto the form.

30. Our menu bar is complete; save the application with the name `demoMenuBar.ui`.

31. We use the `pyuic5` command line utility to convert the `.ui` (XML) file into Python code.

The generated Python code, demoMenuBar.py, can be seen in the source code bundle of this book.

32. Create a Python script with the name callMenuBar.pyw that imports the previous code, demoMenuBar.py, to invoke the menu and display the text message with a **Label** widget when a menu item is selected.

You want a message to appear that indicates which menu item is selected. Also, you want to draw a circle, rectangle, and line when the **Draw Circle**, **Draw Rectangle**, and **Draw Line** menu items are selected, respectively. The code in the Python callMenuBar.pyw script will appear as shown in the following screenshot:

```python
import sys
from PyQt5.QtWidgets import QMainWindow, QApplication
from PyQt5.QtGui import QPainter

from demoMenuBar import *

class AppWindow(QMainWindow):
    def __init__(self):
        super().__init__()
        self.ui = Ui_MainWindow()
        self.ui.setupUi(self)
        self.pos1 = [0,0]
        self.pos2 = [0,0]
        self.toDraw=""
        self.ui.actionDraw_Circle.triggered.connect(self.
        drawCircle)
        self.ui.actionDraw_Rectangle.triggered.connect(self.
        drawRectangle)
        self.ui.actionDraw_Line.triggered.connect(self.drawLine)
        self.ui.actionPage_Setup.triggered.connect(self.pageSetup)
        self.ui.actionSet_Password.triggered.connect(self.
        setPassword)
        self.ui.actionCut.triggered.connect(self.cutMethod)
        self.ui.actionCopy.triggered.connect(self.copyMethod)
        self.ui.actionPaste.triggered.connect(self.pasteMethod)
        self.show()

    def paintEvent(self, event):
        qp = QPainter()
        qp.begin(self)
        if self.toDraw=="rectangle":
            width = self.pos2[0]-self.pos1[0]
            height = self.pos2[1] - self.pos1[1]
            qp.drawRect(self.pos1[0], self.pos1[1], width, height)
```

```
        if self.toDraw=="line":
            qp.drawLine(self.pos1[0], self.pos1[1], self.pos2[0],
            self.pos2[1])
        if self.toDraw=="circle":
            width = self.pos2[0]-self.pos1[0]
            height = self.pos2[1] - self.pos1[1]
            rect = QtCore.QRect(self.pos1[0], self.pos1[1], width,
            height)
            startAngle = 0
            arcLength = 360 *16
            qp.drawArc(rect, startAngle,
            arcLength)
        qp.end()

    def mousePressEvent(self, event):
        if event.buttons() & QtCore.Qt.LeftButton:
            self.pos1[0], self.pos1[1] = event.pos().x(),
            event.pos().y()

    def mouseReleaseEvent(self, event):
        self.pos2[0], self.pos2[1] = event.pos().x(),
        event.pos().y()
        self.update()

    def drawCircle(self):
        self.ui.label.setText("")
        self.toDraw="circle"

    def drawRectangle(self):
        self.ui.label.setText("")
        self.toDraw="rectangle"

    def drawLine(self):
        self.ui.label.setText("")
        self.toDraw="line"

    def pageSetup(self):
        self.ui.label.setText("Page Setup menu item is selected")

    def setPassword(self):
        self.ui.label.setText("Set Password menu item is selected")

    def cutMethod(self):
        self.ui.label.setText("Cut menu item is selected")

    def copyMethod(self):
        self.ui.label.setText("Copy menu item is selected")
```

```
        def pasteMethod(self):
            self.ui.label.setText("Paste menu item is selected")

    app = QApplication(sys.argv)
    w = AppWindow()
    w.show()
    sys.exit(app.exec_())
```

How it works...

The **triggered()** signal of the action of each menu item is connected to its respective method. The **triggered()** signal of the **actionDraw_Circle** menu item is connected to the drawCircle() method, so that whenever the **Draw Circle** menu item is selected from the menu bar, the drawCircle() method will be invoked. Similarly, the **triggered()** signal of the **actionDraw_Rectangle** and **actionDraw_Line** menus are connected to the drawRectangle() and drawLine() methods respectively. In the drawCircle() method, the toDraw variable is assigned a string, circle. The toDraw variable will be used to determine the graphics to be drawn in the paintEvent method. The toDraw variable can be assigned any of the three strings, line, circle, or rectangle. A conditional branching is applied to the value in the toDraw variable and the methods to draw a line, rectangle, or circle will be invoked accordingly. The figures will be drawn to the size determined by the mouse, that is, the user needs to click the mouse and drag it to determine the size of the figure.

Two methods, mousePressEvent() and mouseReleaseEvent(), are automatically called when left mouse button is pressed and released respectively. To store the x and y coordinates of the location where the left mouse button was pressed and released, two arrays, pos1 and pos2, are used. The x and y coordinate values of the locations where the left mouse button was pressed and released are assigned to the pos1 and pos2 arrays via the mousePressEvent and mouseReleaseEvent methods.

In the mouseReleaseEvent method, after assigning the x and y coordinate values of the location where the mouse button was released, the self.update method is invoked to invoke the paintEvent() method. In the paintEvent() method, branching takes place on the basis of the string assigned to the toDraw variable. If the toDraw variable is assigned the line string, the drawLine() method will be invoked by the QPainter class to draw the line between the two mouse locations. Similarly, if the toDraw variable is assigned the circle string, the drawArc() method will be invoked by the QPainter class to draw a circle with the diameter supplied by mouse locations. If the toDraw variable is assigned the rectangle string, then the drawRect() method will be invoked by the QPainter class to draw the rectangle of the width and height supplied by the mouse locations.

Besides the three menu items, **Draw Circle**, **Draw Rectangle**, and **Draw Line**, if the user clicks any other menu item, a message will be displayed indicating the menu item clicked on by the user. Hence, the **triggered()** signals of the rest of the menu items are connected to the methods that display the message information for the menu item that has been selected by the user through a **Label** widget.

On running the application, you will find a menu bar with two menus, **Draw** and **Edit**. The **Draw** menu will show the four menu items **Draw Circle**, **Draw Rectangle**, **Draw Line**, and **Properties**, with a separator before the **Properties** menu item. The **Properties** menu item shows two submenu items, **Page Setup** and **Set Password**, along with their shortcut keys, as shown in the following screenshot:

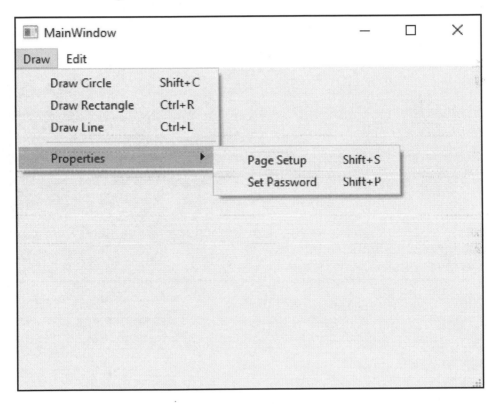

To draw a circle, click on the **Draw Circle** menu item, click the mouse button at a location on the form, and keeping the mouse button pressed, drag it to define the diameter of the circle. On releasing the mouse button, a circle will be drawn between the mouse pressed and mouse released locations, as shown in the following screenshot:

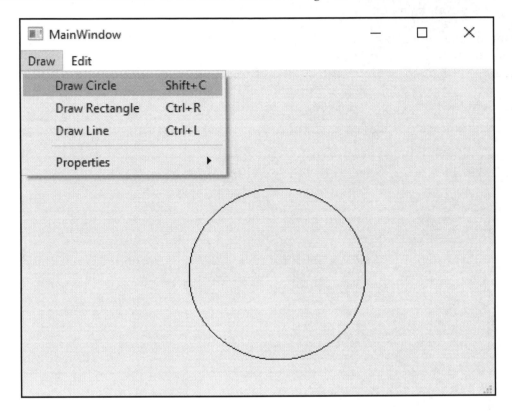

On selecting any other menu item, a message will be displayed, indicating the menu item that is pressed. For example, on selecting the **Copy** menu item, you get a message, **Copy menu item is selected**, as shown in the following screenshot:

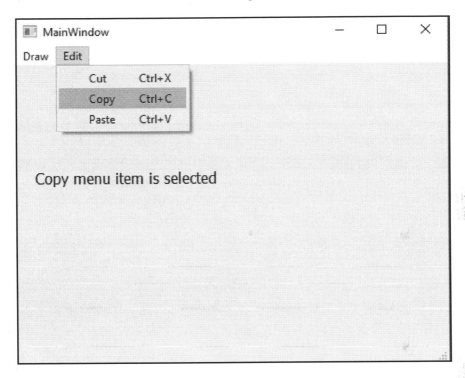

8

Doing Asynchronous Programming in Python

In this chapter, we will learn to use asynchronous programming in Python, which is how more than one task can be executed in parallel. We will be covering the following topics:

- Updating a progress bar using a thread
- Updating two progress bars using two threads
- Updating progress bars using threads bound with a locking mechanism
- Updating progress bars simultaneously using asynchronous operations
- Managing resources using context manager

Introduction

Threads are used for running several programs concurrently in a single process, so they help in implementing multitasking. Threads, once created, execute simultaneously and independently of each other. Threads are basically small processes that are created for executing certain tasks independently. Threads can be pre-empted, that is, interrupted or stopped temporarily by setting them in sleep mode and then resuming execution.

To work with threads in Python, we will be making use of its `threading` module. The `threading` module provides several methods that provide information on currently active threads. A few of the methods provided by the `threading` module are as follows:

- `threading.activeCount()`: This method returns the number of currently active thread objects
- `threading.currentThread()`: This method returns the current thread object
- `threading.enumerate()`: This method returns a list of all currently active thread objects

Besides the preceding methods, the `threading` module has the `Thread` class, which implements threading. The following are the methods provided by the `Thread` class:

- `run()`: This method begins the execution of a thread
- `start()`: This method starts a thread by calling the run method
- `join([time])`: This method waits for threads to terminate
- `isAlive()`: This method checks whether a thread is still executing
- `getName()`: This method returns the name of a thread
- `setName()`: This method sets the name of a thread

Multithreading

In multithreading, more than one thread runs simultaneously. Consequently, computation and other jobs are performed quicker. This is because the time that is usually wasted in waiting for I/O operations is used by another thread to perform its task.

 Python includes GIL too. **Global Interpreter Lock (GIL)**, a lock that allows only one thread to execute at a time. But this feature is used that often as it executes only one thread even in an architecture that has more than one CPU, hence limiting the full utilization of all CPUs.

When two or more threads run concurrently, there may be an ambiguous situation where two or more threads try to run a block of statements together. In such a situation, we need to implement a mechanism that makes a thread wait until the current thread finishes its processing on a block of statements. When the current thread finishes its processing, only then is another thread allowed to process those statements. Such a mechanism is called **synchronization** of threads. Locking is a popular technique used in synchronization of threads. When a thread wants to execute a block of shared statements, it acquires a lock. No thread can execute statements whose lock is acquired by another thread, hence such threads are asked to wait to get those statements unlocked. The thread that acquired the lock processes those statements, and when finished, releases the lock. The waiting thread can then acquire the lock on that block of statements and begin its execution.

Asynchronous programming

Asynchronous programming makes processing a lot faster as more than one task executes in parallel to the main thread. A Python library that is very commonly used in asynchronous programming is `asyncio`. For asynchronous programming, you need an event loop that schedules asynchronous tasks, that is, the event loop picks up a task that is waiting in a queue for processing. Functions that need to be run asynchronously need to be prefixed with the `async` keyword.

The functions that will be executed asynchronously are marked with the `async` keyword. The event loop recognizes the `asynchronous` function through the `async` prefix. All asynchronous functions are known as coroutine. Any asynchronous function (`coroutine`) after starting a task, continues its task until either the task is over or it is asked to wait by the await call. The asynchronous function will suspend its execution if the await call occurs. The period of suspension is determined by the await `asyncio.sleep(delay)` method. The function will go to sleep for the specified delay period.

The following are the methods that are required in asynchronous programming:

- `asyncio.get_event_loop()`: This method is used to get the default event `loop ()`. The event loop schedules and runs asynchronous tasks.
- `loop.run_until_complete()`: This method won't return until all of the asynchronous tasks are done.

Updating progress bar using thread

Progress bars are actively used in applications to indicate that a task is working in the background. Threads also do the same; threads too work in the background and do their assigned task. Let's see how the progress bar and threads can be linked.

In this recipe, we will be displaying a progress bar that is being updated using threads. The value in the progress bar will be updated through a running thread.

How to do it...

To associate a progress bar with a thread and to update the progress bar interactively via the thread, use the following steps:

1. Let's create an application based on the **Dialog without Buttons** template.

2. Add `QLabel` and `QProgressBar` widgets to the form by dragging and dropping the **Label** and **Progress Bar** widgets onto the form.

3. Set the **text** property of the **Label** widget to `Downloading the file`.

4. Let the **objectName** property of the **Progress Bar** widget be the default, **progressBar**.

5. Save the application as `demoProgressBarThread.ui`. The form will now appear as shown in the following screenshot:

The user interface created with Qt Designer is stored in a `.ui` file, which is an XML file and needs to be converted into Python code. The generated Python script, `demoProgressBarThread.py`, can be seen in the source code bundle of the book.

6. Treat the `demoProgressBarThread.py` script as a header file, and import it into the file from which you will invoke its user interface design.

7. Create another Python file with the name `callProgressBar.pyw` and import the `demoProgressBarThread.py` code into it:

```
import sys
import threading
import time
from PyQt5.QtWidgets import QDialog, QApplication
from demoProgressBarThread import *
class MyForm(QDialog):
    def __init__(self):
        super().__init__()
        self.ui = Ui_Dialog()
        self.ui.setupUi(self)
        self.show()
class myThread (threading.Thread):
        counter=0
    def __init__(self, w):
        threading.Thread.__init__(self)
```

```
            self.w=w
            self.counter=0
        def run(self):
            print ("Starting " + self.name)
            while self.counter <=100:
                time.sleep(1)
                w.ui.progressBar.setValue(self.counter)
                self.counter+=10
                print ("Exiting " + self.name)
    if __name__=="__main__":
        app = QApplication(sys.argv)
        w = MyForm()
        thread1 = myThread(w)
        thread1.start()
        w.exec()
        sys.exit(app.exec_())
```

How it works...

In the `callProgressBarThread.pyw` file, there are two classes: one is the main class, called the `MyForm` class, which basically interacts with the GUI form, and the second class is the `myThread` class, which creates and invokes the thread to update the progress bar made in the GUI form.

To use threads in Python, the first step is to import `Thread`. The `import threading` statement imports `Thread` in the current script. After importing `Thread`, the second step is to subclass our class from the `Thread` class. Hence, our class called `myThread` inherits the `Thread` class.

In the main section of the script, an object of the main class, `MyForm`, is defined by name `w`. Then, an object of the `myThread` class is defined by name, `thread1`. The progress bar which is invoked in the main class, `MyForm`, has to be updated through the thread, hence the object of the main class, `w`, is passed as a parameter while creating the thread object, `thread1`. On invoking the start method on the thread object, `thread1`, the run method defined in the `myThread` class will be invoked. In the `run` method, a counter is set to run from value `0%` to `100%` with a delay of 1 second between every increment in the counter. The value of the counter will be used to display progress in the progress bar. Hence, the progress bar will progress from `0` to `100` with a delay of 1 second in between each percentage.

On running the application, you will find the progress bar progressing from 0% to 100%, as shown in the following screenshot:

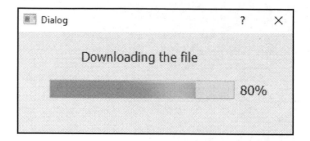

 Very few widgets in Qt natively support being edited from another thread. QProgressBar is an exception.

Updating two progress bars using two threads

For multitasking, you need more than one thread running simultaneously. The focus of this recipe is on understanding how two tasks can be performed asynchronously via two threads, that is, how CPU time is allocated to these two threads and how switching is done between them.

This recipe will help you understand how two threads run independently without interfering with each other. We will be making use of two progress bars in this recipe. One progress bar will represent progress in downloading a file, and the other progress bar will represent progress in scanning for viruses on the current drive. Both progress bars will progress independently of each other through two different threads.

How to do it...

Let's learn how two progress bars are managed by two threads. To understand how CPU time is allocated to each running thread to execute two tasks simultaneously, perform the following steps:

1. Let's create an application based on the **Dialog without Buttons** template. We need two pair of QLabel and QProgressBar widgets in this application.

2. Add a QLabel and a QProgressBar widget to the form by dragging and dropping a **Label** widget onto the form and, below the **Label** widget, drag and drop a progress bar on the form.

3. Repeat the procedure for another pair of **Label** and **Progress Bar** widgets.

4. Set the **text** property of the first **Label** widget to Downloading the file.

5. Set the **text** property of the second **Label** widget to Scanning for Virus.

6. Set the **objectName** property of the first progress bar to progressBarFileDownload.

7. Set the **objectName** property of the second progress bar to progressBarVirusScan.

8. Save the application as demoTwoProgressBars.ui. After performing the preceding steps, the form will now appear as shown in the following screenshot:

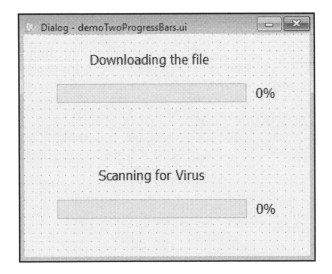

The user interface created with Qt Designer is stored in a `.ui` file, which is an XML file. By applying the `pyuic5` utility, the XML file can be converted into Python code. You can find the generated Python script, `demoTwoProgressBars.py`, in the source code bundle for the book.

9. Treat the `demoTwoProgressBars.py` script as a header file, and import it into the file from which you will invoke its user interface design.

10. Create another Python file with the name `callProgressBarTwoThreads.pyw` and import the `demoTwoProgressBars.py` code into it:

```python
import sys
import threading
import time
from PyQt5.QtWidgets import QDialog, QApplication
from demoTwoProgressBars import *
class MyForm(QDialog):
    def __init__(self):
        super().__init__()
        self.ui = Ui_Dialog()
        self.ui.setupUi(self)
        self.show()
class myThread (threading.Thread):
        counter=0
    def __init__(self, w, ProgressBar):
        threading.Thread.__init__(self)
        self.w=w
        self.counter=0
        self.progreassBar=ProgressBar
    def run(self):
        print ("Starting " + self.name+"n")
        while self.counter <=100:
            time.sleep(1)
            self.progreassBar.setValue(self.counter)
            self.counter+=10
            print ("Exiting " + self.name+"n")
if __name__=="__main__":
    app = QApplication(sys.argv)
    w = MyForm()
    thread1 = myThread(w, w.ui.progressBarFileDownload)
    thread2 = myThread(w, w.ui.progressBarVirusScan)
    thread1.start()
    thread2.start()
    w.exec()
    thread1.join()
    thread2.join()
    sys.exit(app.exec_())
```

How it works...

In the `callProgressBarTwoThreads.pyw` file, there are two classes: one is the main class, called the `MyForm` class, which basically interacts with the GUI form, and the second class is the `myThread` class, which creates and invokes two threads, which in turn update the two **Progress Bar** widgets used in the GUI. Recall, the two progress bars are defined in the GUI to represent progress in downloading a file and scanning for viruses.

When using threads in Python, the first step is to import `Thread`. The `import threading` statement imports `Thread` in the current script. After importing `Thread`, the second step is to subclass our class from the `Thread` class. Hence, our class called `myThread` inherits the `Thread` class.

In the main section of the script, an object of the main class, `MyForm`, is made, called `w`. Thereafter, two threads are created by name, `thread1` and `thread2`, by creating two instances of the `myThread` class. Because `thread1` is supposed to update the progress bar that represents progress in file downloading, while creating it two parameters are passed to it: the first is the instance of the main class, `MyForm`, and the second parameter is the progress bar with the object name `progressBarFileDownload`.

The second thread, `thread2`, will update the progress bar that represents virus scanning, so while creating the `thread2` instance, two parameters are passed: the first is the `MyForm` class instance, `w`, and the second parameter is `ProgressBar` with the object name `progressBarVirusScan`.

On invoking the `start` method on the thread object, `thread1`, the `run()` method defined in the `myThread` class will be invoked. In the `run()` method, a counter is set to run from 0% to 100% with a delay of 1 second between every increment in the counter. The value of `counter` will be used to display progress in the progress bar . Hence, the progress bar with the object name `progressBarFileDownload` will progress from 0 to 100 with a delay of 1 second in between each percentage.

Similarly, when the `start()` method is invoked on the `thread2` object, its `run()` method will be invoked. Remember, the run methods of both threads will run independently, without interfering with each other. The `run()` method of `thread2` will make the progress bar with the object name `progressBarVirusScan` progress from 0% to 100% with a delay of 1 second between each increment in value.

On running the application, you will find the two progress bars progressing from `0%` to `100%`, independently of each other. The thread will automatically stop when the associated progress bar reaches 100%, as shown in the following screenshot:

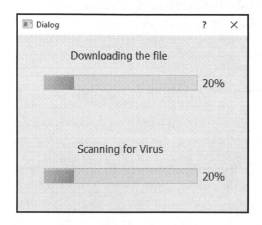

In order to control access to shared resources, a locking mechanism is applied to threads: the `Lock` object is used to prevent two threads from accessing the same resource simultaneously.

To work on any resource, a thread is compelled to acquire a lock on that resource first. Only one thread at a time can acquire a lock on a resource. If a resource is locked, that is, it is being used by some other thread, no other thread can access or perform tasks on that resource until the current thread finishes its task on that resource and unlocks the resource, that is, all other threads need to wait until the resource is unlocked. A lock can be in one of two states, "locked" or "unlocked". Initially, a lock is in the unlocked state and the moment a thread needs to access a resource, it acquires a lock and turns that lock into the "locked" state, informing the other threads that the resource is in use.

To acquire and release the locks, a thread can use the following two basic methods:

- `acquire()`: This method is invoked by a thread to inform other threads that it needs to work on a resource and needs to get a lock on it. If the resource is already in a locked state, then this method will block the invoking thread. Only when the resource becomes free will the blocked thread be unblocked, signaling that the resource that it was waiting for is free now and can be locked by it. A resource becomes free when a thread that is using it invokes the `release()` method, which indicates that the resource is now in an unlocked state and the waiting thread is welcome to lock it.

- release(): As the name suggests, this method is invoked by a thread that has locked a resource and has finished its tasks on that thread. By invoking the release() method, the resource gets unlocked and can be acquired by any waiting thread. This method should only be called when the resource is in the locked state, otherwise, this method will result in an error.

Updating progress bars using threads bound with a locking mechanism

This recipe will help you understand how two threads can avoid ambiguity by making use of locks. That is how shared resources can be accessed and manipulated by two threads simultaneously, without giving ambiguous results.

We will be making use of two progress bars in this recipe. One progress bar will represent progress in downloading a file, and the other progress bar will represent progress in scanning for viruses on the current drive. Only one progress bar will progress at a time.

How to do it...

The following steps will help you understand how two threads can run simultaneously, updating a common shareable resource, without giving ambiguous results:

1. Let's create an application based on the **Dialog without Buttons** template. We need two pair of QLabel and QProgressBar widgets in this application.
2. Add a QLabel and a QProgressBar widget to the form by dragging and dropping a **Label** widget on the form and, below the **Label** widget, drag and drop a **Progress Bar** widget on the form.
3. Repeat the procedure for another pair of **Label** and **Progress Bar** widgets.
4. Set the **text** property of the first **Label** widget to Downloading the file and the second **Label** widget to Scanning for Virus.
5. Set the **objectName** property of the first **Progress Bar** widget to progressBarFileDownload.
6. Set the **objectName** property of the second **Progress Bar** widget to progressBarVirusScan.

7. Save the application as demoTwoProgressBarsLocks.ui. The form will now appear as shown in the following screenshot:

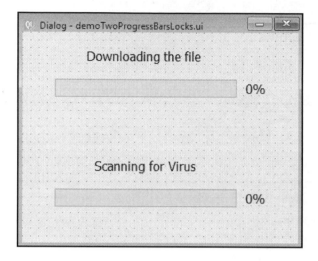

The user interface created with Qt Designer is stored in a .ui file, which is an XML file, and needs to convert into Python code. The pyuic5 command is used for converting the XML file into a Python script. You can find the generated Python script, demoTwoProgressBarsLocks.py, in the source code bundle for this book.

8. Treat the demoTwoProgressBarsLocks.py file as a header file, and import it into the file from which you will invoke its user interface design.

9. Create another Python file with the name callProgressBarTwoThreadsLocks.pyw and import the demoTwoProgressBarsLocks.py code into it:

```python
import sys
import threading
import time
from PyQt5.QtWidgets import QDialog, QApplication
from demoTwoProgressBarsLocks import *
class MyForm(QDialog):
    def __init__(self):
        super().__init__()
        self.ui = Ui_Dialog()
        self.ui.setupUi(self)
        self.show()
class myThread (threading.Thread):
    counter=0
```

```
        def __init__(self, w, ProgressBar):
            threading.Thread.__init__(self)
            self.w=w
            self.counter=0
            self.progreassBar=ProgressBar
        def run(self):
            print ("Starting " + self.name+"n")
            threadLock.acquire()
            while self.counter <=100:
                time.sleep(1)
                self.progreassBar.setValue(self.counter)
                self.counter+=10
                threadLock.release()
                print ("Exiting " + self.name+"n")
if __name__=="__main__":
    app = QApplication(sys.argv)
    w = MyForm()
    thread1 = myThread(w, w.ui.progressBarFileDownload)
    thread2 = myThread(w, w.ui.progressBarVirusScan)
    threadLock = threading.Lock()
    threads = []
    thread1.start()
    thread2.start()
    w.exec()
    threads.append(thread1)
    threads.append(thread2)
    for t in threads:
        t.join()
    sys.exit(app.exec_())
```

How it works...

In the `callProgressBarTwoThreadsLocks.pyw` file, there are two classes: one is the main class, called the `MyForm` class, which basically interacts with the GUI form, and the second class is the `myThread` class, which creates and invokes two threads, which in turn update the two **Progress Bar** widgets used in the GUI.

To use threads in Python, the first step is to import `Thread`. The `import threading` statement imports `Thread` in the current script. After importing `Thread`, the second step is to subclass our class from the `Thread` class. Hence, our class called `myThread` inherits the `Thread` class.

In the main section of the script, an object of the main class, MyForm, is made, called w. Thereafter, two threads are created by name, thread1 and thread2, by creating two instances of the myThread class. Because thread1 is supposed to update the progress bar that represents progress in file downloading, while creating it two parameters are passed to it. The first is the instance of the main class, MyForm, and the second parameter is the ProgressBar with the object name progressBarFileDownload.

The second thread, thread2, will update the progress bar that represents virus scanning, so while creating the thread2 instance, two parameters are passed. The first is the MyForm class instance, w, and the second parameter is the ProgressBar with the object name progressBarVirusScan.

On invoking the start method on the thread object thread1, the run method defined in the myThread class will be invoked.

In the run method, the thread1 object acquires the lock by invoking the acquire method. Consequently, the while block will execute completely for this thread1 object only. That is, until the release method is called by thread1, the while loop for thread2 will not run. In other words, the progress bar with the object name progressBarFileDownload, which is being updated by thread1, will progress alone from 0 to 100. Once the progress bar from thread1 reaches 100, the release method is invoked by thread1. The thread2 object will execute its run method on release of the lock by thread1.

The run method of thread2 also acquires the lock so that no other thread can run this block of code until thread2 releases the lock. The run method makes the progress bar with the object name progressBarVirusScan progress from 0 to 100 with a delay of 1 second between each increment in value.

On running the application, you will find that the first progress bar, which represents file downloading, progresses from **0%** till **100%**, whereas the other progress bar is still at **0%** (see the left side of the next screenshot). When the first progress bar reaches **100%**, meaning when the first thread releases the lock, the second thread will start its job and hence the second progress bar will begin progressing from **0%** to **100%** (see the right side of the screenshot):

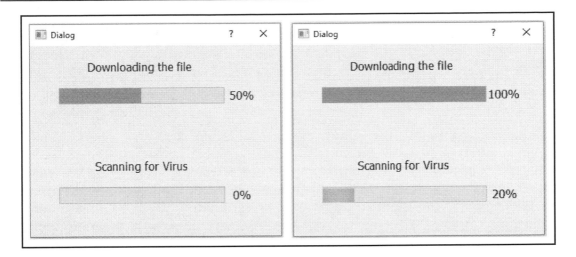

Updating progress bars simultaneously using asynchronous operations

This recipe will help you understand how asynchronous operations are performed in Python. `asyncio` is a library in Python that supports asynchronous programming. Asynchronous means, that besides the main thread, one or more tasks will also execute in parallel. While using `asyncio`, you should remember that only code written in methods flagged as `async` can call any code in an asynchronous way. Besides this, `async` code can only run inside an event loop. The event loop is the code that implements multitasking. It also means that to perform asynchronous programming in Python, we need to either create an event loop or get the current thread's default event loop object.

We will be making use of two progress bars and both will be updated simultaneously via asynchronous operations.

How to do it...

Perform the following steps to understand how asynchronous operations are performed:

1. Let's create an application based on the **Dialog without Buttons** template. We will require two pair of QLabel and QProgressBar widgets in this application.

2. Add a `QLabel` and a `QProgressBar` widget to the form by dragging and dropping a **Label** widget on the form and, below the **Label** widget, drag and drop a **Progress Bar** widget on the form.

3. Repeat the procedure for another pair of **Label** and **Progress Bar** widgets.

4. Above the **Label** and **Progress Bar** pair, drag and drop a push button on the form.

5. Set the **text** property of the push button to **Start**.

6. Set the **text** property of the first **Label** widget to `Downloading the file` and the second **Label** widget to `Scanning for Virus`.

7. Set the **objectName** property of the push button to `pushButtonStart`.

8. Set the **objectName** property of the first **Progress Bar** widget to `progressBarFileDownload` and that of the second **Progress Bar** widget to `progressBarVirusScan`.

9. Save the application as `demoTwoProgressBarsAsync.ui`. The form will appear as shown in the following screenshot:

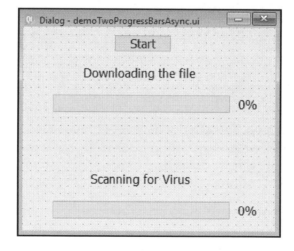

The user interface created with Qt Designer is stored in a `.ui` file, which is an XML file and needs to convert into the Python code. The `pyuic5` command is used for converting the XML file into the Python code. The generated Python script, `demoTwoProgressBarsAsync.py`, can be seen in the source code bundle for this book.

10. Treat the `demoTwoProgressBarsAsync.py` script as a header file, and import it into the file from which you will invoke its user interface design.

11. Create another Python file with the name `callProgressBarAsync1.pyw` and import the `demoTwoProgressBarsAsync.py` code into it:

```
import sys, time
import asyncio
from PyQt5.QtWidgets import QDialog, QApplication
from quamash import QEventLoop
from demoTwoProgressBarsAsync import *
class MyForm(QDialog):
    def __init__(self):
        super().__init__()
        self.ui = Ui_Dialog()
        self.ui.setupUi(self)
        self.ui.pushButtonStart.clicked.connect(self.invokeAsync)
        self.show()
    def invokeAsync(self):
        asyncio.ensure_future(self.updt(0.5, self.ui.
        progressBarFileDownload))
        asyncio.ensure_future(self.updt(1, self.ui.
        progressBarVirusScan))
    @staticmethod
    async def updt(delay, ProgressBar):
        for i in range(101):
            await asyncio.sleep(delay)
            ProgressBar.setValue(i)
        def stopper(loop):
            loop.stop()
if __name__=="__main__":
    app = QApplication(sys.argv)
    loop = QEventLoop(app)
    asyncio.set_event_loop(loop)
    w = MyForm()
    w.exec()
    with loop:
        loop.run_forever()
        loop.close()
    sys.exit(app.exec_())
```

How it works...

In the `callProgressBarAsync1.pyw` file, in the main section, an object of the `QEventLoop` class is made called **loop**. For asynchronous programming, we use event loops. Why?

In asynchronous programming, there might be more than one task in a queue waiting for the CPU's attention. The event loop picks up a task from the queue and processes it. These tasks that are picked up from the queue are also known as **coroutines**. After getting picked up, the event loop is executed forever; that is, it will see whether there are any tasks in the queue to be executed. If any are found, the task is executed. Following the current task, the next in the queue is picked up, and so on.

The **clicked()** signal of the push button is connected with the `invokeAsync()` method. Whenever the push button is clicked, it will invoke the `invokeAsync()` method.

In the `invokeAsync()` method, the `asyncio.ensure_future` method is called, scheduling the execution of a `coroutine` object in the future. The `asyncio.ensure_future` method is called twice.

When the `asyncio.ensure_future` method is called for the first time, it invokes the `updt` static method and passes two parameters: one is a time delay of 0.5 seconds and the second parameter is the progress bar with the object name `progressBarFileDownload`.

In the second call to the `asyncio.ensure_future` method, it again invokes the `updt` static method and passes two parameters: one is the time delay of 1 seconds and the second parameter is the progress bar with the object name `progressBarVirusScan`.

In the `updt` static method, the progress bar that is supplied as a parameter is updated from 0 to 100. The progress bar is updated after the supplied delay. That is, the progress bar with the object name `progressBarFileDownload` is updated from 0 to 100 with a delay of 0.5 seconds. Similarly, the progress bar with the object name `progressBarVirusScan` is updated from 0 to 100 with a delay of 1 second.

When the progress bar with the object name `progressBarFileDownload` is updated by a value of 1 and is asked to sleep for 0.5 seconds, the event loop picks up the next task; that is, it updates the progress bar with the object name `progressBarVirusScan`. After updating the progressBarVirusScan object name, a delay of 1 second is inserted. During this delay of 1 second, the progress bar with the object name `progressBarFileDownload` will be updated twice. Hence, the file download progress bar will update at double speed when compared with the progress bar with the object name `progressBarVirusScan`.

To work with event loops in Python, you need to install `quamash` on your drive. So, execute the following command:

```
Python -m pip install quamash
```

The preceding command will generate the following output:

```
Administrator: Command Prompt                                          —    □    ×
Microsoft Windows [Version 10.0.16299.371]
(c) 2017 Microsoft Corporation. All rights reserved.

C:\Users\Administrator.bintu1>python -m pip install quamash
Collecting quamash
  Downloading Quamash-0.6.0-py3-none-any.whl
Installing collected packages: quamash
Successfully installed quamash-0.6.0
You are using pip version 9.0.1, however version 10.0.0 is available.
You should consider upgrading via the 'python -m pip install --upgrade pip' command.

C:\Users\Administrator.bintu1>
```

On running the application, you will find two progress bars and a push button at the top. On clicking the **Start** button, both threads will start progressing. The file download progress bar will progress at double the speed of the virus scanning progress bar, as shown in the following screenshot:

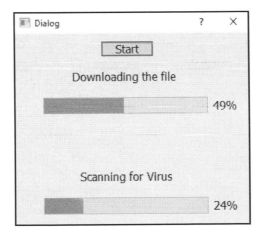

Managing resources using context manager

In this recipe, you will learn to update two progress bars simultaneously using two threads. Synchronizing between the two threads and locking them will be handled through the context manager. What is context manager? Let's have a quick look.

Context manager

Context manager enables us to allocate and release resources whenever desired. To optimize the use of resources, it is essential that, when any resources are allocated by any application or thread, they are freed or cleaned up so that they can be used by some other application or thread. But sometimes the program crashes while executing, or for some other reason the program does not terminate properly, and consequently, the allocated resources are not properly freed. Context managers help in such situations by ensuring the cleaning up of allocated resources takes place. Here is a small example of using the context manager:

```
with method_call() as variable_name:
statements that use variable_name
  .........
  .........
variable_name is automatically cleaned
```

The `with` keyword plays a major role in the context manager. Using the `with` keyword, we can call any method that returns a context manager. We assign the returned context manager to any variable by using, `as variable_name`. The variable_name will exist only within the indented block of the `with` statement, and will be automatically cleaned up when the `with` block ends.

Context managers are very useful while using multiple threads. While using multiple threads, you need to acquire locks when a thread accesses a common resource. Also, when a task on a common resource is performed, you need to release the lock. If the locks are not released because of some exception, it might lead to deadlocks. Context manager automatically releases the lock by making use of its `with` keyword. Here is a small example showing acquiring and releasing locks:

```
threadLock.acquire()
statements that use resource
.................
.................
threadLock.release()
```

You can see that once the lock is acquired, resources are used and finally the lock is released. But this code might cause a disaster if the `threadLock.release()` command does not execute because of some exception in the preceding statements. In such a situation, it is better to use context manager. Here is the syntax for automatically releasing a lock using context manager:

```
with threadLock;acquire();
statements that use resource
. . . . . . . . . . . . . . . . .
. . . . . . . . . . . . . . . . .
lock is released automatically
```

You can see in the preceding syntax that the moment the `with` block is over, the lock is automatically released without executing the `release()` method.

Let's begin with creating an application in which two progress bars are updated using two threads, and the locks in the threads are handled using context manager.

How to do it...

Let's create an application based on the **Dialog without Buttons** template with the following steps:

1. We need two pair of QLabel and QProgressBar widgets in this application. Add a `QLabel` widget to the form by dragging and dropping a **Label** widget on the form.

2. Below the **Label** widget, drag and drop a **Progress Bar** widget on the form.

3. Repeat the procedure for another pair of **Label** and **Progress Bar** widgets.

4. Set the **text** property of the first **Label** widget to `Downloading the file` and that of the second **Label** widget to `Scanning for Virus`.

5. Set the **objectName** property of the first **Progress Bar** widget to `progressBarFileDownload`.

6. Set the **objectName** property of the second **Progress Bar** widget to `progressBarVirusScan`.

7. Save the application as `demoTwoProgressBarsContextManager.ui`. The form will now appear as shown in the following screenshot:

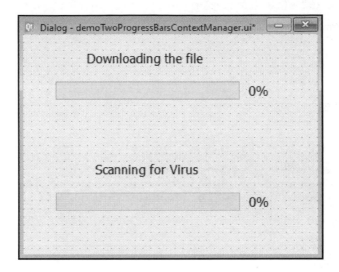

The user interface created with Qt Designer is stored in a `.ui` file, which is an XML file and needs to convert into Python code. The `pyuic5` utility is used for converting the XML file into Python code. You can see the generated Python script, `demoTwoProgressBarsContextManager.py`, in the source code bundle for this book.

8. Treat the `demoTwoProgressBarsContextManager.py` file as a header file and import it into the file from which you will invoke its user interface design.

9. Create another Python file with the name `callProgressBarContextManager.pyw` and import the `demoTwoProgressBarsContextManager.py` code into it:

```python
import sys
import threading
import time
from PyQt5.QtWidgets import QDialog, QApplication
from demoTwoProgressBarsContextManager import *
class MyForm(QDialog):
    def __init__(self):
        super().__init__()
        self.ui = Ui_Dialog()
        self.ui.setupUi(self)
        self.show()
```

```
class myThread (threading.Thread):
counter=0
    def __init__(self, w, ProgressBar):
        threading.Thread.__init__(self)
        self.w=w
        self.counter=0
        self.progreassBar=ProgressBar

    def run(self):
        print ("Starting " + self.name+"\n")
        with threadLock:
            while self.counter <=100:
                time.sleep(1)
                self.progreassBar.setValue(self.counter)
                self.counter+=10
                print ("Exiting " + self.name+"\n")
if __name__=="__main__":
    app = QApplication(sys.argv)
    w = MyForm()
    thread1 = myThread(w, w.ui.progressBarFileDownload)
    thread2 = myThread(w, w.ui.progressBarVirusScan)
    threadLock = threading.Lock()
    threads = []
    thread1.start()
    thread2.start()
    w.exec()
    threads.append(thread1)
    threads.append(thread2)
    for t in threads:
        t.join()
    sys.exit(app.exec_())
```

How it works...

You can see that there are two classes in this script: one is the main class, called the `MyForm` class, which does the task of interacting with the GUI form. The second class is the `myThread` class, which creates and invokes two threads, which in turn will update the two **Progress Bar** widgets used in the GUI.

The import threading statement imports Thread into the current script. Thereafter, your class, myThread, inherits the Thread class. An object of the main class, MyForm, is made, called w. Thereafter, two threads are created, thread1 and thread2, by creating two instances of the myThread class. Because thread1 is supposed to update the progress bar that represents progress in file downloading while creating it, two parameters are passed to it: the first is the instance of the main class, MyForm, and the second parameter is ProgressBar with the object name progressBarFileDownload.

The second thread, thread2, will update the progress bar that represents virus scanning, so while creating the thread2 instance two parameters are passed. The first is the MyForm class instance, w, and the second parameter is ProgressBar with the object name progressBarVirusScan. On, invoking the start method on the thread object, thread1, the run method defined in the myThread class will be invoked.

In the run method, the thread1 object does not acquire the lock but uses the context manager by calling the with threadLock block. In the with block, the resources automatically get locked. Also, the lock on resources automatically gets released when the with block completes. So, there is no need to execute the acquire method or the release method.

The progress bar with objectName progressBarFileDownload, which is being updated by thread1, will progress from 0 to 100. Once the progress bar from thread1 reaches 100, the with block completes and the release method is automatically invoked internally by thread1 (via the context manager). The thread2 object will execute its run() method once the with block of thread1 completes.

The run() method of thread2 also makes use of the context manager, so thread2 also does not have to execute the acquire() and release() methods; the context manager automatically locks the resource at the beginning of the with block, and releases the resources when the with block completes. The run() method makes the **Progress Bar** widget with the object name progressBarVirusScan progress from 0 to 100 with a delay of 1 second between each increment in value.

On running the application, you will find that the first progress bar that represents the file download progresses from **0%** to **100%** and executes completely, that is, it reaches 100%, then the second progress bar will begin progressing from 0% to 100%, as shown in the following screenshot:

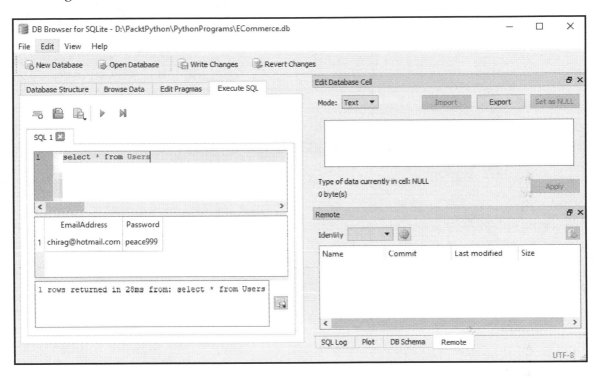

9

Database Handling

Database handling plays a major role in any application as data needs to be stored for future use. You need to store customer information, user information, product information, order information, and so on. In this chapter, you will learn every task that is related to database handling:

- Creating a database
- Creating a database table
- Inserting rows in the specified database table
- Displaying rows in the specified database table
- Navigating through the rows of the specified database table
- Searching a database table for specific information
- Creating a signin form – applying an authentication procedure
- Updating a database table – changing a user's password
- Deleting a row from a database table

We will be using SQLite for database handling. Before we move further into the chapter, let's have a quick introduction to SQLite.

Introduction

SQLite is a very easy-to-use database engine. Basically, it is a lightweight database meant to be used in small applications that can be stored in a single disk file. It is a very popular database used in phones, tablets, small appliances, and instruments. SQLite does not require a separate server process, and does not even require any configuration.

To make this database easy to use in Python scripts, the Python Standard Library includes a module called `sqlite3`. So, to use SQLite in any Python application, you need to import the `sqlite3` module using the `import` statement shown here:

```
import sqlite3
```

The first step to use any database is to create a `connect` object, by means of which you need to establish a connection with the database. The following example establishes a connection to the `ECommerce` database:

```
conn = sqlite3.connect('ECommerce.db')
```

This example will establish a connection to the `ECommerce` database if it already exists. If the database does not already exist, the database will be created first and then the connection established.

You can also create a temporary database in memory, that is, in RAM by using the `:memory:` argument in the `connect` method, as shown here:

```
conn = sqlite3.connect(':memory:')
```

You can also supply the special name `:memory:` to create a database in RAM.

Once the job associated with the database is over, you need to close the connection using the following statement:

```
conn.close()
```

Creating the cursor object

To work with database tables, you need to get a `cursor` object and pass the SQL statements to the `cursor` object to execute them. The following statement creates a `cursor` object called `cur`:

```
cur = conn.cursor()
```

Using the `cursor` object, `cur`, you can execute SQL statements. For example, the following set of statements creates a `Users` table consisting of three columns, `id`, `EmailAddress`, and `Password`:

```
# Get a cursor object
cur = conn.cursor()
cur.execute('''CREATE TABLE Users(id INTEGER PRIMARY KEY, EmailAddress
TEXT, Password TEXT)''')
conn.commit()
```

Remember, you need to commit the changes to the database by invoking the `commit()` method on the connection object, otherwise all the changes made to the database will be lost.

The following set of statements will drop the `Users` table:

```
# Get a cursor object
cur = conn.cursor()
cur.execute('''DROP TABLE Users''')
conn.commit()
```

Creating a database

In this recipe, we will be prompting the user to enter a database name, followed by clicking the push button. Upon clicking the push button, if the specified database does not exist, it is created and, if it already exists, it is connected.

How to do it...

Follow this step-by-step procedure to create a database in SQLite:

1. Let's create an application based on the **Dialog without Buttons** template.
2. Add two `QLabel` widgets, one `QLineEdit` widget, and one `QPushButton` widget to the form by dragging and dropping two **Label** widget, one **Line Edit** widget, and a **Push Button** widget on the form.
3. Set the **text** property of the first **Label** widget to `Enter database name`.
4. Delete the **text** property of the second **Label** widget because this is established.
5. Set the **objectName** property of the **Line Edit** widget to `lineEditDBName`.
6. Set the **objectName** property of the **Push Button** widget to `pushButtonCreateDB`.
7. Set the **objectName** property of the second **Label** widget to `labelResponse`.
8. Save the application by name as `demoDatabase.ui`. The form will now appear as shown in the following screenshot:

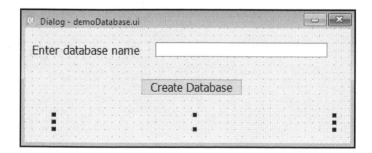

The user interface created with Qt Designer is stored in a `.ui` file, which is an XML file, and needs to be converted into Python code. By applying the `pyuic5` utility, the XML file is converted into Python code. The Python script generated, `demoDatabase.py`, can be seen in the source code bundle of the book.

9. Treat the `demoDatabase.py` script as a header file, and import it into the file from which you will invoke its user interface design.

10. Create another Python file with the name `callDatabase.pyw` and import the `demoDatabase.py` code into it:

```python
import sqlite3, sys
from PyQt5.QtWidgets import QDialog, QApplication
from sqlite3 import Error
from demoDatabase import *
class MyForm(QDialog):
    def __init__(self):
        super().__init__()
        self.ui = Ui_Dialog()
        self.ui.setupUi(self)
        self.ui.pushButtonCreateDB.clicked.connect(self.
        createDatabase)
        self.show()
    def createDatabase(self):
        try:
            conn = sqlite3.connect(self.ui.lineEditDBName.
            text()+".db")
            self.ui.labelResponse.setText("Database is created")
        except Error as e:
            self.ui.labelResponse.setText("Some error has
            occurred")
        finally:
            conn.close()
if __name__=="__main__":
    app = QApplication(sys.argv)
    w = MyForm()
    w.show()
    sys.exit(app.exec_())
```

How it works...

You can see in the script that the **click()** event of the push button with the **objectName** property `pushButtonCreateDB` is connected to the `createDatabase()` method. This means that, whenever the push button is clicked, the `createDatabase()` method is invoked. In the `createDatabase()` method, the `connect()` method is invoked on the `sqlite3` class and the database name entered by the user in the **Line Edit** widget is passed to the `connect()` method. The `connect()` method will create the database if it does not exist already. If no error occurs in creating the database, the message **Database is created** is displayed via the **Label** widget to inform the user; otherwise, a **Some error has occurred** message is displayed via the **Label** widget to indicate the occurrence of an error.

On running the application, you will be prompted to enter the database name. Suppose we enter the database name as `Ecommerce`. Upon clicking the **Create Database** button, the database will be created and you get the message **Database is created**:

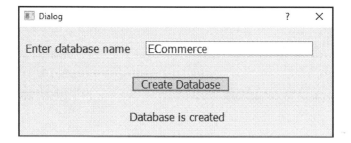

Creating a database table

In this recipe, we will be learning to create a database table. The user will be prompted to specify the database name, followed by the table name that is to be created. The recipe enables you to enter column names and their data types. Upon clicking the push button, the table with the defined columns will be created in the specified database.

How to do it...

Here are the steps to create a GUI that enables the user to enter all the information for the database table to be created. Using this GUI, the user can specify the database name, column names, and choose column types too:

1. Let's create an application based on the **Dialog without Buttons** template.
2. Add five `QLabel`, three `QLineEdit`, one `QComboBox`, and two `QPushButton` widgets to the form by dragging and dropping five **Label**, three **Line Edit**, one **Combo Box**, and two **Push Button** widgets on the form.
3. Set the **text** property of the first four **Label** widgets to `Enter database name`, `Enter table name`, `Column Name`, and `Data Type`.
4. Delete the **text** property of the fifth **Label** widget because this is established through code.
5. Set the **text** property of the two push buttons to `Add Column` and `Create Table`.
6. Set the **objectName** property of the three **Line Edit** widgets to `lineEditDBName`, `lineEditTableName`, and `lineEditColumnName`.
7. Set the **objectName** property of the **Combo Box** widget to `ComboBoxDataType`.
8. Set the **objectName** property of the two push buttons to `pushButtonAddColumn` and `pushButtonCreateTable`.
9. Set the **objectName** property of the fifth **Label** widget to `labelResponse`.
10. Save the application by name as `demoCreateTable.ui`. The form will now appear as shown in the following screenshot:

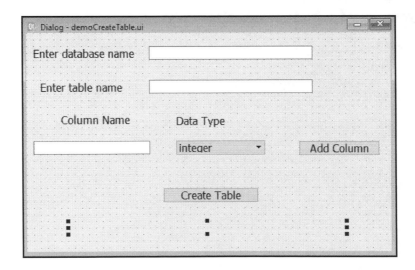

The user interface created with Qt Designer is stored in a `.ui` file, which is an XML file, and needs to be converted into Python code. The `pyuic5` command is used to convert the XML file into Python code. The Python script generated, `demoCreateTable.py`, can be seen in the source code bundle of this book.

11. Treat the `demoCreateTable.py` script as a header file, and import it into the file from which you will invoke its user interface design.

12. Create another Python file with the name `callCreateTable.pyw` and import the `demoCreateTable.py` code into it:

```python
import sqlite3, sys
from PyQt5.QtWidgets import QDialog, QApplication
from sqlite3 import Error
from demoCreateTable import *
tabledefinition=""
class MyForm(QDialog):
    def __init__(self):
        super().__init__()
        self.ui = Ui_Dialog()
        self.ui.setupUi(self)
        self.ui.pushButtonCreateTable.clicked.connect(
        self.createTable)
        self.ui.pushButtonAddColumn.clicked.connect(self.
        addColumns)
        self.show()
    def addColumns(self):
        global tabledefinition
        if tabledefinition=="":
            tabledefinition="CREATE TABLE IF NOT EXISTS "+
            self.ui.lineEditTableName.text()+" ("+
            self.ui.lineEditColumnName.text()+"  "+
            self.ui.comboBoxDataType.itemText(self.ui.
            comboBoxDataType.currentIndex())
        else:
            tabledefinition+=","+self.ui.lineEditColumnName
            .text()+"  "+ self.ui.comboBoxDataType.itemText
            (self.ui.comboBoxDataType.currentIndex())
            self.ui.lineEditColumnName.setText("")
            self.ui.lineEditColumnName.setFocus()
    def createTable(self):
        global tabledefinition
        try:
            conn = sqlite3.connect(self.ui.lineEditDBName.
            text()+".db")
            self.ui.labelResponse.setText("Database is
            connected")
```

```
        c = conn.cursor()
        tabledefinition+=");"
        c.execute(tabledefinition)
        self.ui.labelResponse.setText("Table is successfully
        created")
    except Error as e:
        self.ui.labelResponse.setText("Error in creating
        table")
    finally:
        conn.close()
if __name__=="__main__":
    app = QApplication(sys.argv)
    w = MyForm()
    w.show()
    sys.exit(app.exec_())
```

How it works...

You can see in the script that the **click()** event of the push button with the **objectName** property `pushButtonCreateTable` is connected to the `createTable()` method. This means that, whenever this push button is clicked, the `createTable()` method will be invoked. Similarly, the **click()** event of the push button with the **objectName** property `pushButtonAddColumn` is connected to the `addColumns()` method. That is, this button, when clicked, will invoke the `addColumns()` method.

In the `addColumns()` method, the `CREATE TABLE SQL` statement is defined, which consists of the column name entered in the **Line Edit** widget and the data type selected from the combo box. The user can add any number of columns to the table.

In the `createTable()` method, first the connection to the database is established, and thereafter the `CREATE TABLE SQL` statement defined in the `addColumns()` method is executed. If the table is successfully created, a message is displayed informing you of the successful creation of the table through the last **Label** widget. Finally, the connection to the database is closed.

On running the application, you will be prompted to enter the database name and table name that you want to create, followed by the columns required in that table. Let's assume you want to create a `Users` table in the `ECommerce` table consisting of two columns, `EmailAddress` and `Password`. Both the columns are assumed to be of the text type.

The first column name, `Email Address`, in the `Users` table can be defined as shown in the following screenshot:

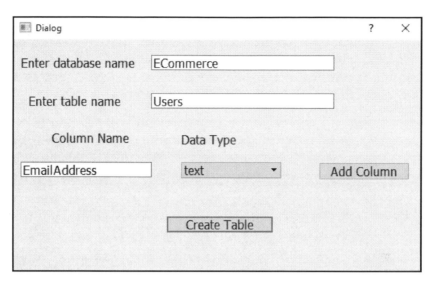

Let's define one more column, called `Password`, of the text type in the `Users` table, followed by clicking the **Create Table** button. If the table is created with the specified number of columns successfully, a message, **Table is successfully created**, is displayed via the last **Label** widget, as shown in the following screenshot:

To verify that the table was created, I will be making use of a visual tool that enables you to create, edit, and view the database tables and rows inside them. That visual tool is DB Browser for SQLite, which I downloaded from `http://sqlitebrowser.org/`. On launching DB Browser for SQLite, click the **Open Database** tab below the main menu. Browse and select the `ECommerce` database from the current folder. The `ECommerce` database shows the `Users` table consisting of two columns, `EmailAddress` and `Password`, as shown in the following screenshot, confirming that the database table was created successfully:

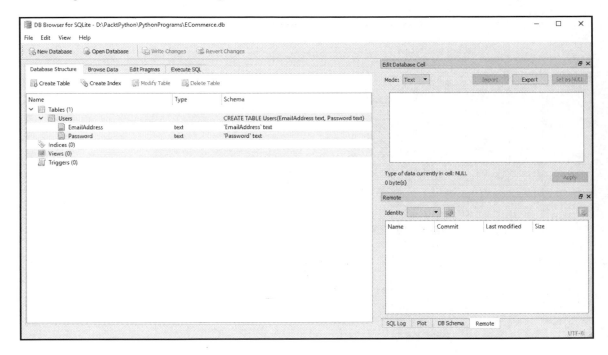

Inserting rows in the specified database table

In this recipe, we will be learning to insert rows into a table. We assume a table called `Users` consisting of two columns, `EmailAddress` and `Password`, already exists in a database called `ECommerce`.

After entering the email address and password in the respective **Line Edit** widgets, when the user clicks the **Insert Row** button, the row will be inserted into the specified database table.

How to do it...

Here are the steps to insert rows into a database table that exists in SQLite:

1. Let's create an application based on the **Dialog without Buttons** template.
2. Add five `QLabel` widgets, four `QLineEdit` widgets, and one `QPushButton` widgets to the form by dragging and dropping five **Label** widgets, four **Line Edit** widgtes, and one **Push Button** widget on the form.
3. Set the **text** property of the first four **Label** widgets to `Enter database name`, `Enter table name`, `Email Address`, and `Password`.
4. Delete the **text** property of the fifth **Label** widget this is established through code.
5. Set the **text** property of the push button to **Insert Row**.
6. Set the **objectName** property of the four **Line Edit** widgets to `lineEditDBName`, `lineEditTableName`, `lineEditEmailAddress`, and `lineEditPassword`.
7. Set the **objectName** property of the **Push Button** widget to `pushButtonInsertRow`.
8. Set the **objectName** property of the fifth **Label** widget to `labelResponse`. As we don't want the password to be displayed, we want asterisks to appear when the user enters their password.
9. To do this, select the **Line Edit** widget that is meant for entering the password and, from the **Property Editor** window, select the **echoMode** property and set it to **Password**, instead of the default **Normal**, as shown in the following screenshot:

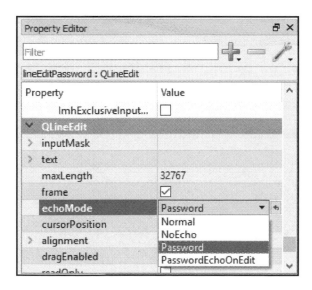

The **echoMode** property shows the following four options:

- **Normal**: It is the default property and it displays characters when typed in the **Line Edit** widget.
- **NoEcho**: It does not display anything when typed in the **Line Edit** widget, that is, you will not even know the length of the text entered.
- **Password**: It is used mostly for passwords. It displays asterisks when typed in the **Line Edit** widget.
- **PasswordEchoOnEdit**: It displays the password while being typed in the **Line Edit** widget, although the content typed is quickly replaced by asterisks.

10. Save the application by name as `demoInsertRowsInTable.ui`. The form will now appear as shown in the following screenshot:

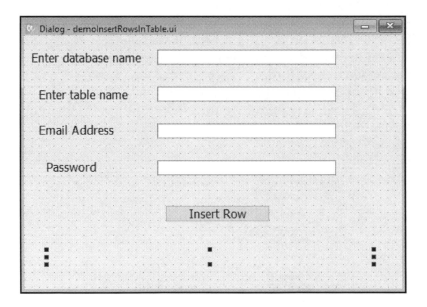

The user interface created with Qt Designer is stored in a `.ui` file, which is an XML file and needs to be converted into Python code. By applying the `pyuic5` utility, the XML file will be converted into Python code. The Python script generated, `demoInsertRowsInTable.py`, can be seen in the source code bundle of the book.

11. Create another Python file with the name `callInsertRows.pyw` and import the `demoInsertRowsInTable.py` code into it. The code in the Python script `callInsertRows.pyw` is as shown here:

```python
import sqlite3, sys
from PyQt5.QtWidgets import QDialog, QApplication
from sqlite3 import Error
from demoInsertRowsInTable import *
class MyForm(QDialog):
    def __init__(self):
        super().__init__()
        self.ui = Ui_Dialog()
        self.ui.setupUi(self)
        self.ui.pushButtonInsertRow.clicked.connect(self.
        InsertRows)
        self.show()
    def InsertRows(self):
        sqlStatement="INSERT INTO "+
        self.ui.lineEditTableName.text() +"
        VALUES('"+self.ui.lineEditEmailAddress.text()+"',
        '"+self.ui.lineEditPassword.text()+"')"
        try:
            conn = sqlite3.connect(self.ui.lineEditDBName.
            text()+ ".db")
        with conn:
            cur = conn.cursor()
            cur.execute(sqlStatement)
            self.ui.labelResponse.setText("Row successfully
            inserted")
        except Error as e:
            self.ui.labelResponse.setText("Error in inserting
            row")
        finally:
            conn.close()
if __name__=="__main__":
    app = QApplication(sys.argv)
    w = MyForm()
    w.show()
    sys.exit(app.exec_())
```

How it works...

You can see in the script that the click event of the push button with the **objectName** property `pushButtonInsertRow` is connected to the `InsertRows()` method. This means that, whenever this push button is clicked, the `InsertRows()` method will be invoked. In the `InsertRows()` method, an `INSERT SQL` statement is defined that fetches the email address and password entered in the **Line Edit** widgets. A connection is established with the database whose name is entered in the **Line Edit** widget. Thereafter, the `INSERT SQL` statement is executed, which adds a new row to the specified database table. Finally, the connection to the database is closed.

On running the application, you will be prompted to specify the database name, table name, and the data for the two columns, `Email Address` and `Password`. After entering the required information, when you click the **Insert Row** button, a new row will be added to the table and a message, **Row successfully inserted**, will be displayed, as shown in the following screenshot:

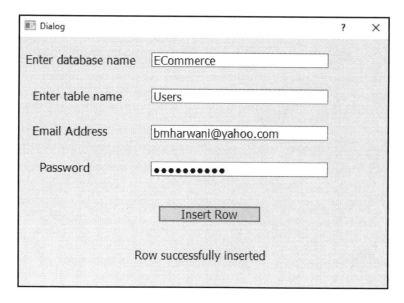

To verify that the row was inserted into the Users table, I will be making use of a visual tool called DB Browser for SQLite. It is a wonderful tool that enables you to create, edit, and view the database tables and rows inside them. You can download DB Browser for SQLite from http://sqlitebrowser.org/. On launching DB Browser for SQLite, you need to first open the database. To do so, click the **Open Database** tab below the main menu. Browse and select the Ecommerce database from the current folder. The Ecommerce database shows the Users table. Click on the **Execute SQL** button; you get a small window to type the SQL statement. Write an SQL statement, select * from Users, and click the Run icon above the window.

All the rows entered in the Users table will be displayed in tabular format, as shown in the following screenshot. It confirms that the application made in our recipe is working perfectly well:

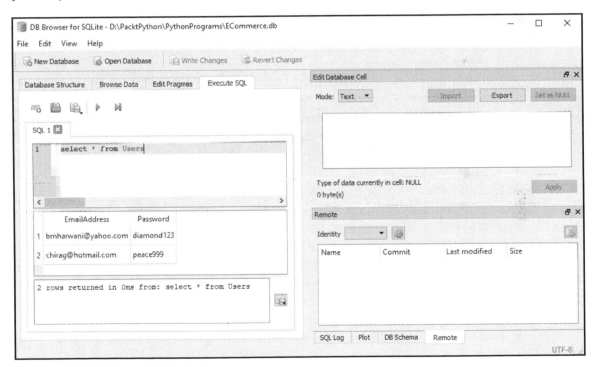

Displaying rows in the specified database table

In this recipe, we will be learning to fetch rows from a given database table and display them in tabular format via the **Table** widget. We assume a table called `Users` consisting of two columns, `EmailAddress` and `Password`, already exists in a database called `ECommerce`. Also, we assume that the `Users` table contains some rows in it.

How to do it...

Follow this step-by-step procedure to access rows from the database table in SQLite:

1. Let's create an application based on the **Dialog without Buttons** template.
2. Add three `QLabel` widgets, two `QLineEdit` widgets, one `QPushButton`, and one `QTableWidget` widget to the form by dragging and dropping three **Label** widgets, two **Line Edit** widgets, one **Push Button** widget, and a **Table** widget on the form.
3. Set the **text** property of the two **Label** widgets to `Enter database name` and `Enter table name`.
4. Delete the **text** property of the third **Label** widget because its **text** property will be set through code.
5. Set the **text** property of the push button to `Display Rows`.
6. Set the **objectName** property of the two **Line Edit** widgets to `lineEditDBName` and `lineEditTableName`.
7. Set the **objectName** property of the **Push Button** widget to `pushButtonDisplayRows`.
8. Set the `objectName` property of the third **Label** widget to `labelResponse`.

9. Save the application by name as `demoDisplayRowsOfTable.ui`. The form will now appear as shown in the following screenshot:

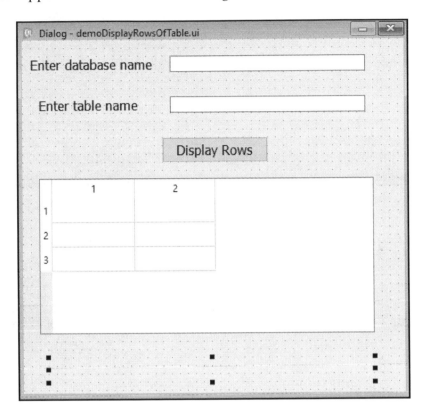

The `Users` table whose rows will be displayed through the **Table** widget consists of two columns.

10. Select the **Table** widget and select its **columnCount** property in the **Property Editor** window.

11. Set the **columnCount** property to 2 and the **rowCount** property to 3, as shown in the following screenshot:

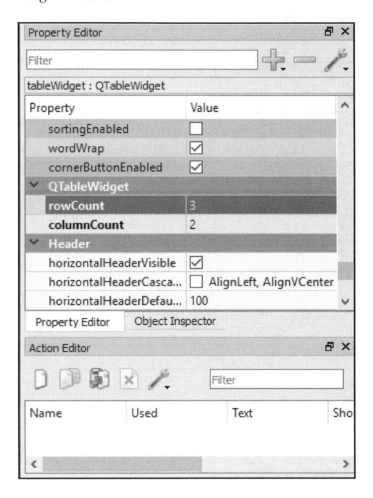

The user interface created with Qt Designer is stored in a `.ui` file, which is an XML file and needs to be converted into Python code. By applying the `pyuic5` utility, the XML file will be converted into Python code. The Python script generated, `demoInsertRowsInTable.py`, can be seen in the source code bundle of this book.

12. Treat the `demoInsertRowsInTable.py` script as a header file, and import it into the file from which you will invoke its user interface design.

13. Create another Python file with the name `callDisplayRows.pyw` and import the `demoDisplayRowsOfTable.py` code into it:

```python
import sqlite3, sys
from PyQt5.QtWidgets import QDialog, QApplication,QTableWidgetItem
from sqlite3 import Error
from demoDisplayRowsOfTable import *
class MyForm(QDialog):
    def __init__(self):
        super().__init__()
        self.ui = Ui_Dialog()
        self.ui.setupUi(self)
        self.ui.pushButtonDisplayRows.clicked.
            connect(self.DisplayRows)
        self.show()

    def DisplayRows(self):
        sqlStatement="SELECT * FROM "+
            self.ui.lineEditTableName.text()
        try:
            conn = sqlite3.connect(self.ui.lineEditDBName.
            text()+ ".db")
            cur = conn.cursor()
            cur.execute(sqlStatement)
            rows = cur.fetchall()
            rowNo=0
        for tuple in rows:
            self.ui.labelResponse.setText("")
            colNo=0
        for columns in tuple:
            oneColumn=QTableWidgetItem(columns)
            self.ui.tableWidget.setItem(rowNo, colNo, oneColumn)
            colNo+=1
            rowNo+=1
        except Error as e:
            self.ui.tableWidget.clear()
            self.ui.labelResponse.setText("Error in accessing
            table")
        finally:
            conn.close()
if __name__=="__main__":
    app = QApplication(sys.argv)
    w = MyForm()
    w.show()
    sys.exit(app.exec_())
```

How it works...

You can see in the script that the **click()** event of the push button with the **objectName** property `pushButtonDisplayRows` is connected to the `DisplayRows()` method. This means that, whenever this push button is clicked, the `DisplayRows()` method will be invoked. In the `DisplayRows()` method, an `SQL SELECT` statement is defined that fetches the rows from the table whose name is specified in the **Line Edit** widget. Also, a connection is established with the database whose name is entered in the **Line Edit** widget. Thereafter, the `SQL SELECT` statement is executed. The `fetchall()` method is executed on the cursor to keep all the rows that are accessed from the database table.

A `for` loop is executed to access one tuple at a time from the received rows, and again a `for` loop is executed on the tuple to get data in each column of that row. The data accessed in each column of the row is assigned to the **Table** widget for display. After displaying the data in the first row, the second row is picked up from the rows and the procedure is repeated to display the data in the second row in the **Table** widget. The two nested `for` loops are executed until all the rows are displayed through the **Table** widget.

Upon running the application, you will be prompted to specify the database name and table name. After entering the required information, when you click the **Display Rows** button, the content of the specified database table is displayed through the **Table** widget, as shown in the following screenshot:

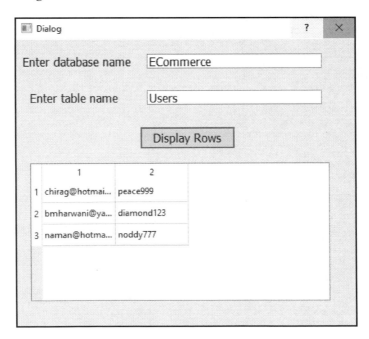

Navigating through the rows of the specified database table

In this recipe, we will be learning to fetch rows from a given database table one at a time. That is, on running the application, the first row of the database table will be displayed. You will be provided with four push buttons in the application, called **Next**, **Previous**, **First**, and **Last**. As the name suggests, upon clicking the **Next** button, the next row in the sequence will be displayed. Similarly, upon clicking the **Previous** button, the previous row in the sequence will be displayed. Upon clicking the **Last** button, the last row of the database table will be displayed and, upon clicking the **First** button, the first row of the database table will be displayed.

How to do it...

Here are the steps to understand how rows from a database table are accessed and displayed one by one:

1. Let's create an application based on the **Dialog without Buttons** template.
2. Add three QLabel widgets, two QLineEdit widgets, and four QPushButton widgets to the form by dragging and dropping three **Label** widgets, two **Line Edit** widgets, and four **Push Button** widgets on the form.
3. Set the **text** property of the two **Label** widgets to Email Address and Password.
4. Delete the **text** property of the third **Label** widget because its **text** property will be set through code.
5. Set the **text** property of the four push buttons to First Row, Previous, Next, and Last Row.
6. Set the **objectName** property of the two **Line Edit** widgets to lineEditEmailAddress and lineEditPassword.
7. Set the **objectName** property of the four push buttons to pushButtonFirst, pushButtonPrevious, pushButtonNext, and pushButtonLast.
8. Set the **objectName** property of the third **Label** widget to labelResponse. Because we don't want the password to be displayed, we want the asterisks to appear when the user enters their password.
9. Select the **Line Edit** widget that is meant for entering the password (lineEditPassword) and, from the **Property Editor** window, select the **echoMode** property and set it to **Password** instead of the default **Normal**.

10. Save the application by name as `demoShowRecords`. The form will now appear as shown in the following screenshot:

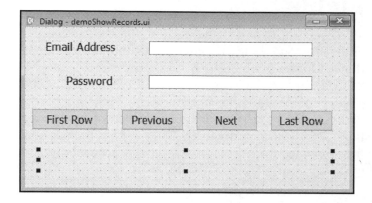

The user interface created with Qt Designer is stored in a `.ui` file, which is an XML file, and on applying the `pyuic5` command, the XML file can be converted into Python code. The Python script generated, `demoShowRecords.py`, can be seen in the source code bundle of the book.

11. Treat the `demoShowRecords.py` script as a header file, and import it into the file from which you will invoke its user interface design.

12. Create another Python file with the name `callShowRecords.pyw` and import the `demoShowRecords.py` code into it.

```
import sqlite3, sys
from PyQt5.QtWidgets import QDialog, QApplication,QTableWidgetItem
from sqlite3 import Error
from demoShowRecords import *
rowNo=1
sqlStatement="SELECT EmailAddress, Password FROM Users"
conn = sqlite3.connect("ECommerce.db")
cur = conn.cursor()
class MyForm(QDialog):
    def __init__(self):
        super().__init__()
        self.ui = Ui_Dialog()
        self.ui.setupUi(self)
        cur.execute(sqlStatement)
        self.ui.pushButtonFirst.clicked.connect(self.
        ShowFirstRow)
        self.ui.pushButtonPrevious.clicked.connect(self.
        ShowPreviousRow)
        self.ui.pushButtonNext.clicked.connect(self.ShowNextRow)
```

```
        self.ui.pushButtonLast.clicked.connect(self.ShowLastRow)
        self.show()
    def ShowFirstRow(self):
        try:
            cur.execute(sqlStatement)
            row=cur.fetchone()
        if row:
            self.ui.lineEditEmailAddress.setText(row[0])
            self.ui.lineEditPassword.setText(row[1])
        except Error as e:
            self.ui.labelResponse.setText("Error in accessing
            table")
    def ShowPreviousRow(self):
        global rowNo
        rowNo -= 1
        sqlStatement="SELECT EmailAddress, Password FROM Users
        where rowid="+str(rowNo)
        cur.execute(sqlStatement)
        row=cur.fetchone()
        if row:
            self.ui.labelResponse.setText("")
            self.ui.lineEditEmailAddress.setText(row[0])
            self.ui.lineEditPassword.setText(row[1])
        else:
            rowNo += 1
            self.ui.labelResponse.setText("This is the first
            row")
    def ShowNextRow(self):
        global rowNo
        rowNo += 1
        sqlStatement="SELECT EmailAddress, Password FROM
        Users where rowid="+str(rowNo)
        cur.execute(sqlStatement)
        row=cur.fetchone()
        if row:
            self.ui.labelResponse.setText("")
            self.ui.lineEditEmailAddress.setText(row[0])
            self.ui.lineEditPassword.setText(row[1])
        else:
            rowNo -= 1
            self.ui.labelResponse.setText("This is the last
            row")
    def ShowLastRow(self):
        cur.execute(sqlStatement)
        for row in cur.fetchall():
            self.ui.lineEditEmailAddress.setText(row[0])
            self.ui.lineEditPassword.setText(row[1])
if __name__=="__main__":
```

```
app = QApplication(sys.argv)
w = MyForm()
w.show()
sys.exit(app.exec_())
```

How it works...

You can see in the script that the **click()** event of the push button with the **objectName** property `pushButtonFirst` is connected to the `ShowFirstRow()` method, the push button with the **objectName** property `pushButtonPrevious` is connected to the `ShowPreviousRow()` method, the push button with the **objectName** property `pushButtonNext` is connected to the `ShowNextRow()` method, and the push button with the **objectName** property `pushButtonLast` is connected to the `ShowLastRow()` method.

Whenever a push button is clicked, the associated method will be invoked.

In the `ShowFirstRow()` method, an SQL SELECT statement is executed that fetches the email address and password columns of the `Users` table. The `fetchone()` method is executed on the cursor to access the first row from the rows that are received on execution of the SQL SELECT statement. The data in the `EmailAddress` and `Password` columns is displayed through two **Line Edit** widgets on the screen. If an error occurs when accessing the rows, an error message, `Error in accessing table`, will be displayed through the **Label** widget.

To fetch the previous row, we make use of a global variable, `rowNo`, which is initialized to 1. In the `ShowPreviousRow()` method, the value of the global variable, `rowNo`, is decremented by 1. Thereafter, an SQL SELECT statement is executed that fetches the `EmailAddress` and `Password` columns of the `Users` table whose `rowid=rowNo`. Because the `rowNo` variable is decremented by 1, the SQL SELECT statement will fetch the previous row in the sequence. The `fetchone()` method is executed on the cursor to access the received row, and the data in the `EmailAddress` and `Password` columns is displayed through two **Line Edit** widgets on the screen.

If the first row is already being displayed, then, upon clicking the **Previous** button, it will simply display a message, **This is the first row**, through the **Label** widget.

We make use of the global variable rowNo while accessing the next row in the sequence too. In the ShowNextRow() method, the value of the global variable rowNo is incremented by 1. Thereafter, an SQL SELECT statement is executed that fetches the EmailAddress and Password columns of the Users table whose rowid=rowNo; hence, the next row, that is, the one whose rowid is one higher than the current row, is accessed. The fetchone() method is executed on the cursor to access the received row and the data in the EmailAddress and Password columns is displayed through two **Line Edit** widgets on the screen.

If you are looking at the last row in the database table, then, upon clicking the **Next** button, it will simply display a message, **This is the last row**, through the **Label** widget.

In the ShowLastRow() method, an SQL SELECT statement is executed that fetches the EmailAddress and Password columns of the Users table. The fetchall() method is executed on the cursor to access the remainder of the rows in the database table. Using the for loop, a row variable is moved to the last row from the rows that are received upon execution of the SQL SELECT statement. The data in the EmailAddress and Password columns of the last row is displayed through two **Line Edit** widgets on the screen.

Upon running the application, you will get the first row of the database table displayed on the screen, as shown in the following screenshot. If you click the **Previous** button now, you get the message, **This is the first row**:

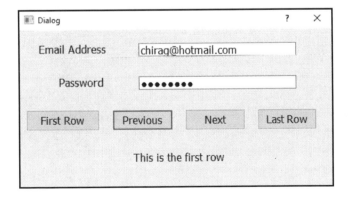

Upon clicking the **Next** button, the next row in the sequence will be displayed on the screen, as shown in the following screenshot:

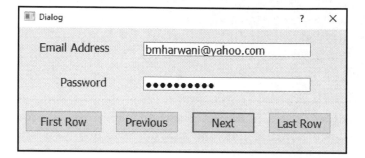

Upon clicking the **Last Row** button, the last row in the database table will be displayed, as shown in the following screenshot:

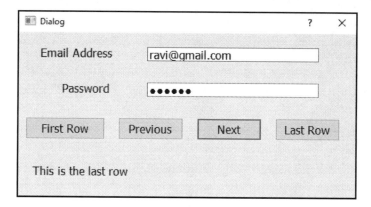

Searching a database table for specific information

In this recipe, we will be learning how searching is performed in a database table to fetch the desired information. We assume that a user has forgotten their password. So, you will be prompted to enter the database name, table name, and email address of the user whose password is required. If any user with the email address supplied exists in the database table, then the password of that user will be searched for, accessed, and displayed on the screen.

How to do it...

Follow these steps to find out how data can be searched for in a database table in SQLite:

1. Let's create an application based on the **Dialog without Buttons** template.
2. Add five `QLabel` widgets, four `QLineEdit` widgets, and one `QPushButton` widget to the form by dragging and dropping five **Label** widgets, four **Line Edit** widgets, and one **Push Button** widget on the form.
3. Set the **text** property of the first three **Label** widgets to `Enter database name`, `Enter table name`, and `Email Address`.
4. Delete the **text** property of the fourth **Label** widget this is established through code.
5. Set the **text** property of the fifth **Label** widget to `Password`.
6. Set the **text** property of the push button to `Search`.
7. Set the **objectName** property of the four **Line Edit** widgets to `lineEditDBName`, `lineEditTableName`, `lineEditEmailAddress`, and `lineEditPassword`.
8. Set the **objectName** property of the **Push Button** widget to `pushButtonSearch`.
9. Set the **objectName** property of the fourth **Label** widget to `labelResponse`.
10. Save the application by name as `demoSearchRows.ui`. The form will now appear as shown in the following screenshot:

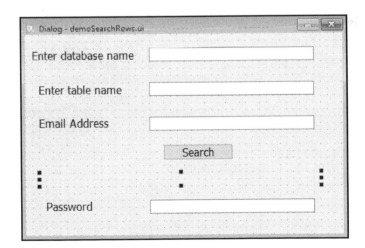

The user interface created with Qt Designer is stored in a `.ui` file, an XML file that needs to be converted into Python code through application of the `pyuic5` command. The generated Python script, `demoSearchRows.py`, can be seen in the source code bundle of the book.

11. Treat the `demoSearchRows.py` script as a header file, and import it into the file from which you will invoke its user interface design.

12. Create another Python file with the name `callSearchRows.pyw` and import the `demoSearchRows.py` code into it:

```
import sqlite3, sys
from PyQt5.QtWidgets import QDialog, QApplication
from sqlite3 import Error
from demoSearchRows import *
class MyForm(QDialog):
    def __init__(self):
        super().__init__()
        self.ui = Ui_Dialog()
        self.ui.setupUi(self)
        self.ui.pushButtonSearch.clicked.connect(self.
        SearchRows)
        self.show()
    def SearchRows(self):
        sqlStatement="SELECT Password FROM
        "+self.ui.lineEditTableName.text()+" where EmailAddress
        like'"+self.ui.lineEditEmailAddress.text()+"'"
    try:
        conn = sqlite3.connect(self.ui.lineEditDBName.text()+
        ".db")
        cur = conn.cursor()
        cur.execute(sqlStatement)
        row = cur.fetchone()
    if row==None:
        self.ui.labelResponse.setText("Sorry, No User found with
        this email address")
        self.ui.lineEditPassword.setText("")
    else:
        self.ui.labelResponse.setText("Email Address Found,
        Password of this User is :")
        self.ui.lineEditPassword.setText(row[0])
    except Error as e:
        self.ui.labelResponse.setText("Error in accessing row")
    finally:
        conn.close()
if __name__=="__main__":
    app = QApplication(sys.argv)
    w = MyForm()
    w.show()
    sys.exit(app.exec_())
```

How it works...

You can see in the script that the **click()** event of the push button with the **objectName** property `pushButtonSearch` is connected to the `SearchRows()` method. This means that, whenever the push button is clicked, the `SearchRows()` method is invoked. In the `SearchRows()` method, the `connect()` method is invoked on the `sqlite3` class and the database name entered by the user in the **Line Edit** widget is passed to the `connect()` method. The connection to the database is established. An SQL `search` statement is defined that fetches the `Password` column from the table supplied whose email address matches the email address supplied. The `search` SQL statement is executed on the given database table. The `fetchone()` method is executed on the cursor to fetch one row from the executed SQL statement. If the fetched row is not `None`, that is, there is a row in the database table that matches the given email address, the password in the row is accessed and assigned to the **Line Edit** widget with the object name `lineEditPassword` for display. Finally, the connection to the database is closed.

If an error occurs in the execution of the SQL statement, that is, if the database is not found, the table name is incorrectly entered, or the email address column does not exist in the given table, an error message, **Error in accessing row**, is displayed via the **Label** widget with the **objectName** property, `labelResponse`.

Upon running the application, we get a dialog that prompts us for the database name, table name, and column name from the table. Suppose we want to find out the password of the user whose email address is `bmharwani@yahoo.com` in the `Users` table of the `ECommerce` database. After entering the required information in the boxes, when you click on the **Search** button, the password of the user will be accessed from the table and displayed through the **Line Edit** widget, as shown in the following screenshot:

If the email address supplied is not found in the Users table, you get the message "Sorry, No User found with this email address," which is displayed through the Label widget as shown here:

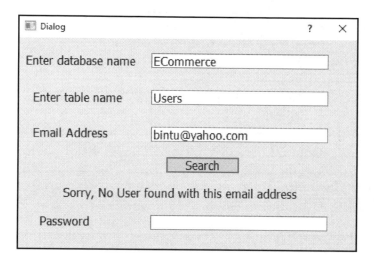

Creating a signin form – applying an authentication procedure

In this recipe, we will be learning how rows can be accessed from a specific table and compared with the information supplied.

We assume that a database called ECommerce already exists and a table called Users also exists in the ECommerce database. The Users table consists of two columns, EmailAddress and Password. Also, we assume that the Users table contains a few rows in it. The user will be prompted to enter their email address and password in the signin form. The Users table is searched for the specified email address. If the email address is found in the Users table, then the password in that row is compared with the password entered. If the two passwords match, a welcome message is displayed; otherwise, an error message indicating that the email address or password don't match is displayed.

How to do it...

Here are the steps to understand how data in a database table can be compared with data entered by the user and authenticate a user:

1. Let's create an application based on the **Dialog without Buttons** template.

2. Add three `QLabel` widgets, two `QLineEdit` widgets, and one `QPushButton` widget to the form by dragging and dropping three **Label** widgets, two **Line Edit** widgets, and one **Push Button** widget on the form.

3. Set the **text** property of the first two **Label** widgets to `Email Address` and `Password`.

4. Delete the **text** property of the third **Label** widget this is established through code.

5. Set the **text** property of the push button to `Sign In`.

6. Set the **objectName** property of the two **Line Edit** widgets to `lineEditEmailAddress` and `lineEditPassword`.

7. Set the **objectName** property of the **Push Button** widget to `pushButtonSearch`.

8. Set the **objectName** property of the third **Label** widget to `labelResponse`.

9. Save the application by name as `demoSignInForm.ui`. The form will now appear as shown in the following screenshot:

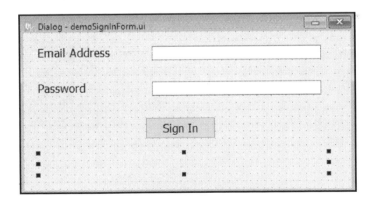

The user interface created with Qt Designer is stored in a `.ui` file, which is an XML file, and needs to be converted into Python code. By applying the `pyuic5` command, the XML file can be converted into Python code. The Python script generated, `demoSignInForm.py`, can be seen in the source code bundle of the book.

10. Treat the `demoSignInForm.py` file as a header file, and import it into the file from which you will invoke its user interface design.

11. Create another Python file with the name `callSignInForm.pyw` and import the `demoSignInForm.py` code into it:

```python
import sqlite3, sys
from PyQt5.QtWidgets import QDialog, QApplication
from sqlite3 import Error
from demoSignInForm import *
class MyForm(QDialog):
    def __init__(self):
        super().__init__()
        self.ui = Ui_Dialog()
        self.ui.setupUi(self)
        self.ui.pushButtonSearch.clicked.connect(self.
        SearchRows)
        self.show()
    def SearchRows(self):
        sqlStatement="SELECT EmailAddress, Password FROM Users
        where EmailAddress like'"+self.ui.lineEditEmailAddress.
        text()+"'and Password like '"+ self.ui.lineEditPassword.
        text()+"'"
        try:
            conn = sqlite3.connect("ECommerce.db")
            cur = conn.cursor()
            cur.execute(sqlStatement)
            row = cur.fetchone()
        if row==None:
            self.ui.labelResponse.setText("Sorry, Incorrect
            email address or password ")
        else:
            self.ui.labelResponse.setText("You are welcome ")
        except Error as e:
            self.ui.labelResponse.setText("Error in accessing
            row")
        finally:
            conn.close()
if __name__=="__main__":
    app = QApplication(sys.argv)
    w = MyForm()
    w.show()
    sys.exit(app.exec_())
```

How it works...

You can see in the script that the click event of the push button with the **objectName** property `pushButtonSearch` is connected to the `SearchRows()` method. This means that, whenever the push button is clicked, the `SearchRows()` method is invoked. In the `SearchRows()` method, the `connect()` method is invoked on the `sqlite3` class to establish a connection with the `ECommerce` database. An SQL `search` statement is defined that fetches the `EmailAddress` and `Password` columns from the `Users` table whose email address matches the email address supplied. The `search` SQL statement is executed on the `Users` table. The `fetchone()` method is executed on the cursor to fetch one row from the executed SQL statement. If the fetched row is not `None`, that is, there is a row in the database table that matches the given email address and password, a welcome message is displayed with the **Label** widget with the **objectName** property, `labelResponse`. Finally, the connection to the database is closed.

If an error occurs in the execution of the SQL statement, if the database is not found, or if the table name is incorrectly entered, or the email address or password columns do not exist in the `Users` table, an error message, **Error in accessing row**, is displayed via the **Label** widget with the **objectName** property, `labelResponse`.

Upon running the application, you will be prompted to enter an email address and password. Upon entering the correct email address and password, when you click the **Sign In** button, you receive the message, **You are welcome**, as shown in the following screenshot:

But if either email address or password is entered incorrectly, you get the message, **Sorry, Incorrect email address or password**, as shown in the following screenshot:

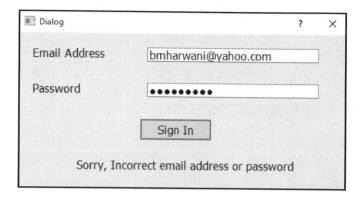

Updating a database table – changing a user's password

In this recipe, you will learn how to update any information in the database. Changing passwords is a very common requirement in almost all applications. In this recipe, we assume that a database called ECommerce already exists and a table called Users also exists in the ECommerce database. The Users table consists of two columns, EmailAddress and Password. Also, we assume that the Users table contains a few rows in it. The user will be prompted to enter their email address and password in the form. The Users table is searched for the specified email address and password. If a row is found with the specified email address and password, the user will be prompted to enter a new password. The new password will be asked for twice, that is, the user will be asked to enter their new password in both the **New Password** box and the **Re-enter New Password** box. If the passwords entered in the two boxes match, the password will be changed, that is, the old password will be replaced by the new password.

How to do it...

The procedure for deleting data from the database table is very critical, and any mistake in executing such an application can lead to disaster. Here come the steps to delete any row from the given database table:

1. Let's create an application based on the **Dialog without Buttons** template.

2. Add five `QLabel` widgets, four `QLineEdit` widgets, and one `QPushButton` widget to the form by dragging and dropping five **Label** widgets, four **Line Edit** widgets, and one **Push Button** widget on the form.

3. Set the **text** property of the first four **Label** widgets to `Email Address`, `Old Password`, `New Password`, and `Re-enter New Password`.

4. Delete the **text** property of the fifth **Label** widget this is established through code. Set the **text** property of the push button to `Change Password`.

5. Set the **objectName** property of the four **Line Edit** widgets to `lineEditEmailAddress`, `lineEditOldPassword`, `lineEditNewPassword`, and `lineEditRePassword`. Since we don't want the password to be displayed in any of the **Line Edit** widgets that are associated with the password, we want the asterisks to appear when the user enters the password.

6. Select the three **Line Edit** widgets one at a time and from the **Property Editor** window.

7. Select the **echoMode** property and set it to `Password` instead of the default **Normal**.

8. Set the **objectName** property of the **Push Button** widget to `pushButtonChangePassword`.

9. Set the **objectName** property of the fifth **Label** widget to `labelResponse`.

10. Save the application by name as `demoChangePassword.ui`. The form will now appear as shown in the following screenshot:

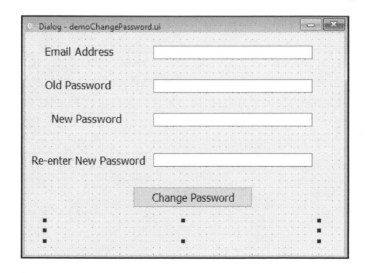

The user interface created with Qt Designer is stored in a `.ui` file, which is an XML file, and needs to be converted into Python code. The `pyuic5` command is used to convert the XML file into Python code. The Python script generated, `demoChangePassword.py`, can be seen in the source code bundle of this book.

11. Treat the `demoChangePassword.py` script as a header file, and import it into the file from which you will invoke its user interface design.

12. Create another Python file with the name `callChangePassword.pyw` and import the `demoChangePassword.py` code into it:

```python
import sqlite3, sys
from PyQt5.QtWidgets import QDialog, QApplication
from sqlite3 import Error
from demoChangePassword import *
class MyForm(QDialog):
    def __init__(self):
        super().__init__()
        self.ui = Ui_Dialog()
        self.ui.setupUi(self)
        self.ui.pushButtonChangePassword.clicked.connect(self.
        ChangePassword)
        self.show()
    def ChangePassword(self):
        selectStatement="SELECT EmailAddress, Password FROM
        Users where EmailAddress like '"+self.ui.
        lineEditEmailAddress.text()+"'and Password like '"+
        self.ui.lineEditOldPassword.text()+"'"
        try:
            conn = sqlite3.connect("ECommerce.db")
            cur = conn.cursor()
            cur.execute(selectStatement)
            row = cur.fetchone()
        if row==None:
            self.ui.labelResponse.setText("Sorry, Incorrect
            email address or password")
        else:
            if self.ui.lineEditNewPassword.text()==
              self.ui.lineEditRePassword.text():
                updateStatement="UPDATE Users set Password = '" +
                self.ui.lineEditNewPassword.text()+"' WHERE
                EmailAddress like'"+self.ui.lineEditEmailAddress.
                text()+"'"
        with conn:
            cur.execute(updateStatement)
            self.ui.labelResponse.setText("Password successfully
            changed")
```

```
            else:
                 self.ui.labelResponse.setText("The two passwords
                 don't match")
            except Error as e:
                 self.ui.labelResponse.setText("Error in accessing
                 row")
            finally:
                 conn.close()
    if __name__=="__main__":
        app = QApplication(sys.argv)
        w = MyForm()
        w.show()
        sys.exit(app.exec_())
```

How it works...

You can see in the script that the **click()** event of the push button with the **objectName** property pushButtonChangePassword is connected to the ChangePassword() method. This means that, whenever the push button is clicked, the ChangePassword() method will be invoked. In the ChangePassword() method, the connect() method is invoked on the sqlite3 class to establish a connection with the ECommerce database. An SQL SELECT statement is defined that fetches the EmailAddress and Password columns from the Users table whose email address and password matches the email address and password entered in the **Line Edit** widgets. The SQL SELECT statement is executed on the Users table. The fetchone() method is executed on the cursor to fetch one row from the executed SQL statement. If the fetched row is not None, that is, there is a row in the database table, then it is confirmed whether the new passwords entered in the two **Line Edit** widgets, lineEditNewPassword and lineEditRePassword, are exactly the same. If the two passwords are the same, then an UPDATE SQL statement is executed to update the Users table, changing the password to the new one.

If the two passwords do not match, then no updating is applied to the database table and a message, **The two passwords don't match**, is displayed through the **Label** widget.

If an error occurs in the execution of the SQL SELECT or UPDATE statement, then an error message, **Error in accessing row**, is displayed via a **Label** widget with the **objectName** property labelResponse.

Upon running the application, you will be prompted to enter the email address and password, along with the new password, too. If the email address or password does not match, an error message, **Sorry, Incorrect email address or password**, is displayed via the **Label** widget, as shown in the following screenshot:

If the email address and password entered are correct, but the new passwords entered in the **New Password** and **Re-enter New Password** boxes do not match, then the message **The two passwords don't match** is displayed on the screen, as shown in the following screenshot:

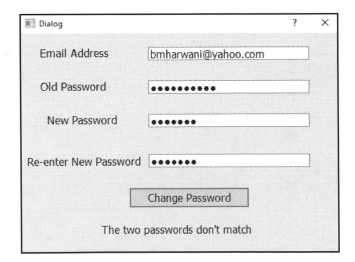

If the email address and passwords are all entered correctly, that is, if the user row is found in the database table and the new passwords entered in the **New Password** and **Re-enter New Password** boxes match, then the Users table is updated and, upon successfully updating the table, a message, **Password successfully changed**, is displayed on the screen, as shown in the following screenshot:

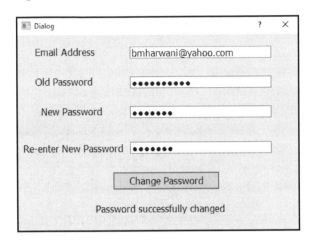

Deleting a row from a database table

In this recipe, we will be learning how to remove a row from a database table. We assume that a database called ECommerce already exists and a table called Users also exists in the ECommerce database. The Users table consists of two columns, EmailAddress and Password. Also, we assume that the User table contains a few rows in it. The user will be prompted to enter their email address and password in the form. The Users table is searched for the specified email address and password. If any row is found with the specified email address and password in the Users table, you will be prompted to confirm whether you are sure that you want to delete the row. If you click on the **Yes** button, the row will be deleted.

How to do it...

The procedure for deleting data from the database table is very critical, and any mistake in executing such an application can lead to disaster. The following are the steps for deleting any row from the given database table:

1. Let's create an application based on the **Dialog without Buttons** template.

2. Add four `QLabel` widgets, two `QLineEdit` widgets, and three `QPushButton` widgets to the form by dragging and dropping four **Label** widgets, two **LineEdit** widgets, and three **Push Button** widgets on the form.

3. Set the **text** property of the first three **Label** widgets to `Email Address`, `Password`, and `Are you Sure?`

4. Delete the **text** property of the fourth **Label** widget this is established through code.

5. Set the **text** property of the three push buttons to `Delete User`, `Yes`, and `No`.

6. Set the **objectName** property of the two **Line Edit** widgets to `lineEditEmailAddress` and `lineEditPassword`.

7. Set the **objectName** property of the three **Push Button** widgets to `pushButtonDelete`, `pushButtonYes`, and `pushButtonNo`.

8. Set the **objectName** property of the fourth **Label** widget to `labelResponse`.

9. Save the application by name as `demoDeleteUser.ui`. The form will now appear as shown in the following screenshot:

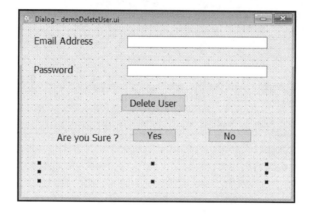

The user interface created with Qt Designer is stored in a `.ui` file, which is an XML file and needs to be converted into Python code. The `pyuic5` command is used for converting the XML file into Python code. The Python script generated, `demoDeleteUser.py`, can be seen in the source code bundle of this book.

10. Treat the `demoDeleteUser.py` script as a header file, and import it into the file from which you will invoke its user interface design.

11. Create another Python file with the name `callDeleteUser.pyw` and import the `demoDeleteUser.py` code into it:

```
import sqlite3, sys
```

```
from PyQt5.QtWidgets import QDialog, QApplication
from sqlite3 import Error
from demoDeleteUser import *
class MyForm(QDialog):
    def __init__(self):
        super().__init__()
        self.ui = Ui_Dialog()
        self.ui.setupUi(self)
        self.ui.pushButtonDelete.clicked.connect(self.
        DeleteUser)
        self.ui.pushButtonYes.clicked.connect(self.
        ConfirmDelete)
        self.ui.labelSure.hide()
        self.ui.pushButtonYes.hide()
        self.ui.pushButtonNo.hide()
        self.show()
    def DeleteUser(self):
        selectStatement="SELECT * FROM Users where EmailAddress
        like'"+self.ui.lineEditEmailAddress.text()+"'
        and Password like '"+ self.ui.lineEditPassword.
        text()+"'"
        try:
            conn = sqlite3.connect("ECommerce.db")
            cur = conn.cursor()
            cur.execute(selectStatement)
            row = cur.fetchone()
        if row==None:
            self.ui.labelSure.hide()
            self.ui.pushButtonYes.hide()
            self.ui.pushButtonNo.hide()
            self.ui.labelResponse.setText("Sorry, Incorrect
            email address or password ")
        else:
            self.ui.labelSure.show()
            self.ui.pushButtonYes.show()
            self.ui.pushButtonNo.show()
            self.ui.labelResponse.setText("")
        except Error as e:
            self.ui.labelResponse.setText("Error in accessing
            user account")
        finally:
            conn.close()
    def ConfirmDelete(self):
        deleteStatement="DELETE FROM Users where EmailAddress
        like '"+self.ui.lineEditEmailAddress.text()+"'
        and Password like '"+ self.ui.lineEditPassword.
        text()+"'"
        try:
```

```
        conn = sqlite3.connect("ECommerce.db")
        cur = conn.cursor()
    with conn:
        cur.execute(deleteStatement)
        self.ui.labelResponse.setText("User successfully
        deleted")
    except Error as e:
        self.ui.labelResponse.setText("Error in deleting
        user account")
    finally:
        conn.close()
if __name__=="__main__":
    app = QApplication(sys.argv)
    w = MyForm()
    w.show()
    sys.exit(app.exec_())
```

How it works...

In this application, the **Label** widget with the text **Are you Sure?** and the two push buttons, **Yes** and **No**, are initially hidden. These three widgets will be displayed only when the email address and password entered by the user are found in the database table. These three widgets enable the user to confirm that they really want to delete the row. So, the hide() method is invoked on these three widgets to make them initially invisible. Also, the **click()** event of the push button with the **objectName** property pushButtonDelete is connected to the DeleteUser() method. This means that whenever the **Delete** button is clicked, the DeleteUser() method is invoked. Similarly, the **click()** event of the push button with the **objectName** property pushButtonYes is connected to the ConfirmDelete() method. This means that when the user confirms deletion of the row by clicking the **Yes** button, the ConfirmDelete() method will be invoked.

In the DeleteUser() method, you first search to see whether any row exists in the Users table that matches the email address and password entered. The connect() method is invoked on the sqlite3 class to establish a connection with the ECommerce database. An SQL SELECT statement is defined that fetches the EmailAddress and Password columns from the Users table whose email address and password matches the email address and passwords supplied. The SQL SELECT statement is executed on the Users table. The fetchone() method is executed on the cursor to fetch one row from the executed SQL statement. If the fetched row is not None, that is, there is a row in the database table that matches the given email address and password, the three widgets, the **Label**, and two push buttons, will be made visible. The user will be shown the message **Are you Sure?** followed by two push buttons with the text **Yes** and **No**.

If the user clicks the **Yes** button, then the `ConfirmDelete()` method is executed. In the `ConfirmDelete()` method, an SQL `DELETE` method is defined that deletes the row that matches the entered email address and password from the `Users` table. After establishing a connection with the `ECommerce` database, the SQL `DELETE` method is executed. If the row is successfully deleted from the `Users` table, a message, **User successfully deleted**, will be displayed through the **Label** widget; otherwise, an error message, **Error in deleting user account**, will be displayed.

Before running the application, we will launch a visual tool called DB Browser for SQLite. The visual tool enables us to create, edit, and view the database tables and rows inside them. Using DB Browser for SQLite, we will first see the existing rows in the `Users` table. After that, the application will run and a row will be deleted. Again, from DB Browser for SQLite, we will confirm the row was really deleted from the `Users` table.

So, launch DB Browser for SQLite and click the **Open Database** tab below the main menu. Browse and select the `Ecommerce` database from the current folder. The `Ecommerce` database shows the `Users` table consisting of two columns, `EmailAddress` and `Password`. Click on the **Execute SQL** button to write an SQL statement. In the window, write the SQL statement `select * from Users`, followed by clicking the Run icon. All existing rows in the `Users` table will be displayed on the screen. You can see in the following screenshot that the `Users` table has two rows:

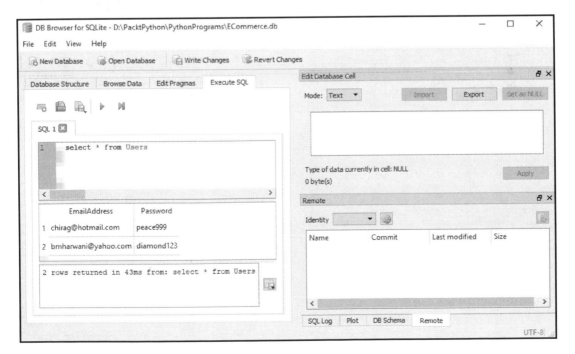

Upon running the application, you will be prompted to enter your email address and password. If you enter the wrong email address and password, you get the message **Sorry, Incorrect email address or password**, as shown in the following screenshot:

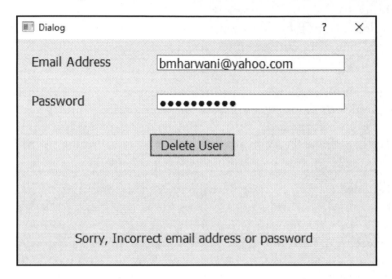

Upon entering the correct email address and password, when you click the **Delete User** button, the three widgets—the **Label** widget and two push buttons, will be made visible, and you get the message **Are you Sure?**, along with the two push buttons, **Yes** and **No**, as shown in the following screenshot:

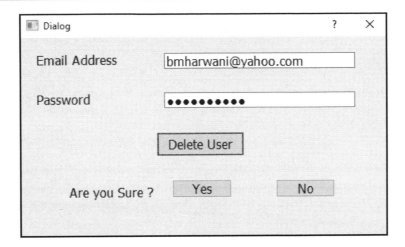

Upon clicking the **Yes** push button, the row in the `Users` table whose email address and password matches the email address and password supplied will be deleted and a confirmation message, **User successfully deleted**, will be displayed through the **Label** widget, as shown in the following screenshot:

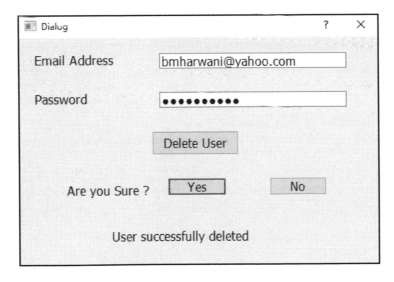

Let's check through the visual tool as to whether the row was actually deleted from the **Users** table. Therefore, launch the DB Browser for SQLite and click the **Open Database** tab below the main menu. Browse and select the `Ecommerce` database from the current folder. The `Ecommerce` database will show the `Users` table. Click on the **Execute SQL** button to write an SQL statement. In the window, write the SQL statement `select * from Users`, followed by clicking the Run icon. All existing rows in the `Users` table will be displayed on the screen. Before running the application, we saw that there were two rows in the `Users` table. This time, you see only one row in the `Users` table (see the following screenshot), confirming that a row was deleted from the `Users` table:

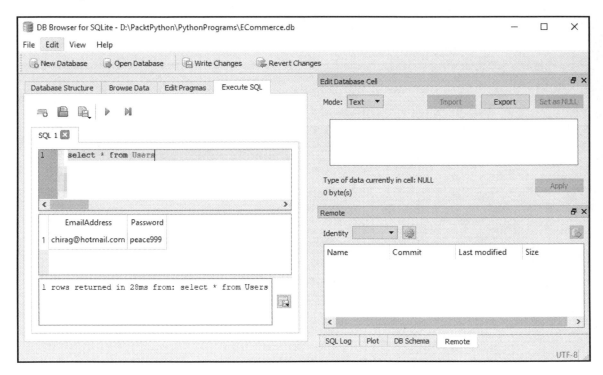

10
Using Graphics

In every application, graphics play a major role in making it more user-friendly. Graphics make concepts easier to understand. In this chapter, we will be covering the following topics:

- Displaying mouse coordinates
- Displaying coordinates where the mouse button is clicked and released
- Displaying a point where the mouse button is clicked
- Drawing a line between two mouse clicks
- Drawing lines of different types
- Drawing a circle of a desired size
- Drawing a rectangle between two mouse clicks
- Drawing text in a desired font and size
- Creating a toolbar that shows different graphics tools
- Plotting a line using Matplotlib
- Plotting a bar using Matplotlib

Introduction

For drawing and painting in Python, we will be making use of several classes. The most important of them is the `QPainter` class.

This class is used for painting. It can draw lines, rectangles, circles, and complex shapes. While drawing with `QPainter`, you can use the `QPainter` class pen to define the color of the drawing; thickness of the pen/brush; style; whether the line is drawn as solid, dotted, or dash-dot; and so on.

Several methods of the QPainter class are used in this chapter to draw different shapes. A few of them are listed here:

- QPainter::drawLine(): This method is used for drawing a line between two sets of *x* and *y* coordinates
- QPainter::drawPoints(): This method is used for drawing a point at a location specified through the supplied *x* and *y* coordinates
- QPainter::drawRect(): This method is used for drawing a rectangle between two sets of *x* and *y* coordinates
- QPainter::drawArc(): This method is used for drawing an arc from the specified center location, between two specified angles, and with a specified radius
- QPainter::drawText(): This method is used for drawing text in a specified font style, color, and size

To understand the different classes and methods required to display graphics practically, let's follow some recipes.

Displaying mouse coordinates

To draw any shape with the mouse, you need to know where the mouse button is clicked, to where the mouse is dragged, and where the mouse button is released. Only after knowing the coordinates where the mouse button is clicked can you go ahead and execute commands to draw different shapes. In this recipe, we will be learning to display the *x* and *y* coordinates to which the mouse is moved on the form.

How to do it...

In this recipe, we will be tracking mouse movement and will be displaying the *x* and *y* coordinates which the mouse is moved on the form. So, in all, we will be using two **Label** widgets in this application, one for displaying a message and the other for displaying mouse coordinates. The complete steps for creating this application are shown here:

1. Let's create an application based on the **Dialog without Buttons** template.
2. Add two QLabel widgets to the form by dragging and dropping two **Label** widgets on the form.
3. Set the **text** property of the first **Label** widget to This app will display x,y coordinates where mouse is moved on.

4. Delete the **text** property of the second **Label** widget as its **text** property will be set through code.

5. Save the application by name as `demoMousetrack.ui`.

The form will now appear as shown in the following screenshot:

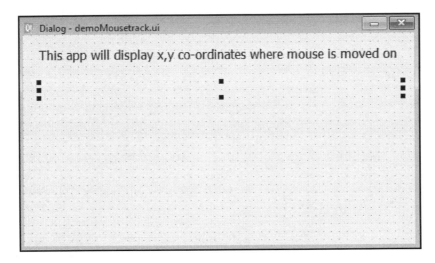

The user interface created with Qt Designer is stored in a `.ui` file, which is an XML file, and needs to be converted into Python code. The `pyuic5` utility is used for converting the XML file into Python code. The generated Python script, `demoMousetrack.py`, can be seen in the source code bundle of the book.

6. Treat the `demoMousetrack.py` script as a header file, and import it into the file from which you will invoke its user interface design.

7. Create another Python file with the name `callMouseTrack.pyw` and import the `demoMousetrack.py` code into it:

```python
import sys
from PyQt5.QtWidgets import QDialog, QApplication
from demoMousetrack import *
class MyForm(QDialog):
    def __init__(self):
        super().__init__()
        self.ui = Ui_Dialog()
        self.setMouseTracking(True)
        self.ui.setupUi(self)
        self.show()
    def mouseMoveEvent(self, event):
        x = event.x()
```

```
            y = event.y()
            text = "x: {0}, y: {1}".format(x, y)
            self.ui.label.setText(text)
    if __name__=="__main__":
        app = QApplication(sys.argv)
        w = MyForm()
        w.show()
        sys.exit(app.exec_())
```

How it works...

To enable the application to keep track of the mouse, a method, `setMouseTracking(True)`, is used. This method will sense the mouse movement and whenever the mouse is moved, it will invoke the `mouseMoveEvent()` method. In `mouseMoveEvent()`, the x and y methods are invoked on the `event` object to get the x and y coordinate values of the mouse's location. The x and y coordinates are assigned to the x and y variables respectively. The values in the x and y coordinates are displayed in the desired format via the **Label** widget.

On running the application, you will get a message that on moving the mouse, its x and y coordinate values will be displayed. When you move the mouse on the form, the x and y coordinates of the mouse location will be displayed through the second **Label** widget, as shown in the following screenshot:

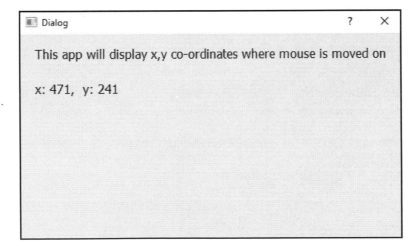

Displaying coordinates where the mouse button is clicked and released

In this recipe, we will be learning to display the x and y coordinates where the mouse button is clicked, along with the coordinates of where the mouse button is released.

How to do it...

Two methods, `mousePressEvent()` and `mouseReleaseEvent()`, will play major role in this recipe. The `mousePressEvent()` method will be automatically invoked when the mouse is pressed and will reveal the x and y coordinates when the mouse press event has occurred. Similarly, the `mouseReleaseEvent()` method will be invoked automatically whenever the mouse button is released. Two **Label** widgets will be used in this recipe to display the coordinates where the mouse button is clicked and where the mouse button is released. Here are the steps to create such an application:

1. Let's create an application based on the **Dialog without Buttons** template.
2. Add three `QLabel` widgets to the form by dragging and dropping three **Label** widgets on the form.
3. Set the **text** property of the first **Label** widget to `Displays the x,y coordinates where mouse is pressed and released`.
4. Delete the **text** property of the second and third **Label** widgets, as their **text** properties will be set through code.
5. Set the **objectName** property of the second **Label** widget to `labelPress`, as it will be used for displaying the x and y coordinates of the location where the mouse button is clicked.
6. Set the **objectName** property of the third **Label** widget to `labelRelease` because it will be used for displaying the x and y coordinates of the location where the mouse button is released.
7. Save the application by name as `demoMouseClicks.ui`.

The form will now appear as shown in the following screenshot:

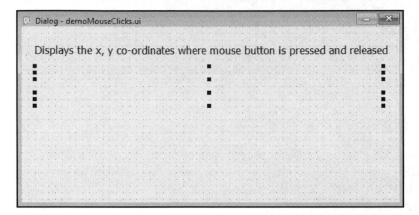

The user interface created with Qt Designer is stored in a `.ui` file, which is an XML file, and needs to be converted into Python code. The `pyuic5` utility is used for converting the XML file into Python code. The generated Python script, `demoMouseClicks.py`, can be seen in the source code bundle of the book.

8. Treat the `demoMouseClicks.py` script as a header file, and import it into the file from which you will invoke its user interface design.
9. Create another Python file with the name `callMouseClickCoordinates.pyw` and import the `demoMouseClicks.py` code into it:

```
import sys
from PyQt5.QtWidgets import QDialog, QApplication
from demoMouseClicks import *
class MyForm(QDialog):
    def __init__(self):
        super().__init__()
        self.ui = Ui_Dialog()
        self.ui.setupUi(self)
        self.show()
    def mousePressEvent(self, event):
        if event.buttons() & QtCore.Qt.LeftButton:
            x = event.x()
            y = event.y()
            text = "x: {0}, y: {1}".format(x, y)
            self.ui.labelPress.setText('Mouse button pressed at
            '+text)
    def mouseReleaseEvent(self, event):
        x = event.x()
        y = event.y()
```

```
                text = "x: {0}, y: {1}".format(x, y)
                self.ui.labelRelease.setText('Mouse button released at
                '+text)
                self.update()
    if __name__=="__main__":
        app = QApplication(sys.argv)
        w = MyForm()
        w.show()
        sys.exit(app.exec_())
```

How it works...

Two methods are automatically invoked when you click the mouse. The
`mousePressEvent()` method is invoked when you press the mouse button and the
`mouseReleaseEvent()` method is invoked when you release the mouse button. To display
the *x* and *y* coordinates of the location where the mouse button is clicked and released, we
make use of these two methods. In both the methods, we simply invoke the `x()` and `y()`
methods on the `event` object to fetch the *x* and *y* coordinate values of the mouse location.
The fetched x and y values will be assigned to the x and y variables, respectively. The
values in the x and y variables are formatted in the desired format and displayed through
the two **Label** widgets.

On running the application, you will get a message that the *x* and *y* coordinates of the
location where the mouse button is clicked and released will be displayed.

When you press the mouse button and release it, the *x* and *y* coordinates of the location
where the mouse is pressed and released will be displayed through the two **Label** widgets,
as shown in the following screenshot:

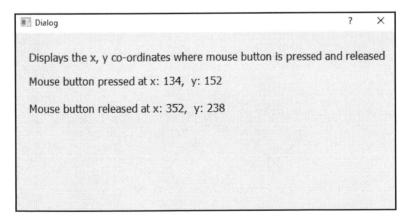

Displaying a point where the mouse button is clicked

In this recipe, we will be learning to display the point where the mouse button is clicked on the form. Point here means a dot. That is, wherever the user presses the mouse, a dot will appear at that coordinate. You will also learn to define the size of the dot too.

How to do it...

The `mousePressEvent()` method will be used in this recipe as it is the method that is automatically invoked when the mouse is pressed on the form. In the `mousePressEvent()` method, we will execute the command to display a dot or point of the desired size. Here are the steps to understand how you can display a point or dot on the form where the mouse button is clicked:

1. Let's create an application based on the **Dialog without Buttons** template.
2. Add a `QLabel` widgets to the form by dragging and dropping a **Label** widget on the form.
3. Set the **text** property of the **Label** widget to `Click the mouse where you want to display a dot`.
4. Save the application by name as `demoDrawDot.ui`.

The form will now appear as shown in the following screenshot:

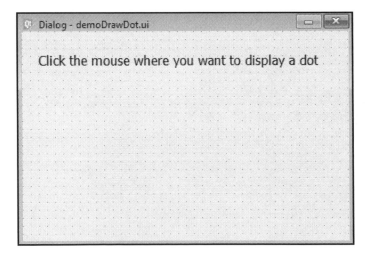

The user interface created with Qt Designer is stored in a `.ui` file, which is an XML file, and needs to be converted into Python code. The `pyuic5` utility is used for converting the XML file into Python code. The generated Python script, demoDrawDot.py, can be seen in the source code bundle of the book.

5. Treat the demoDrawDot.py script as a header file, and import it into the file from which you will invoke its user interface design.

6. Create another Python file with the name callDrawDot.pyw and import the demoDrawDot.py code into it:

```python
import sys
from PyQt5.QtWidgets import QDialog, QApplication
from PyQt5.QtGui import QPainter, QPen
from PyQt5.QtCore import Qt
from demoDrawDot import *
class MyForm(QDialog):
    def __init__(self):
        super().__init__()
        self.ui = Ui_Dialog()
        self.ui.setupUi(self)
        self.pos1 = [0,0]
        self.show()
    def paintEvent(self, event):
        qp = QPainter()
        qp.begin(self)
        pen = QPen(Qt.black, 5)
        qp.setPen(pen)
        qp.drawPoint(self.pos1[0], self.pos1[1])
        qp.end()
    def mousePressEvent(self, event):
        if event.buttons() & QtCore.Qt.LeftButton:
            self.pos1[0], self.pos1[1] = event.pos().x(),
            event.pos().y()
            self.update()
if __name__=="__main__":
    app = QApplication(sys.argv)
    w = MyForm()
    w.show()
    sys.exit(app.exec_())
```

How it works...

Because we want to display the point where the mouse button is clicked, the
`mousePressEvent()` method is used. In the `mousePressEvent()` method, the
`pos().x()` and `pos().y()` methods are invoked on the `event` object to fetch the locations
of the x and y coordinates and assign them to the 0 and 1 elements of the `pos1` array. That
is, the `pos1` array is initialized to the x and y coordinate values where the mouse button is
clicked. After initializing the `pos1` array, the `self.update()` method is called to invoke
the `paintEvent()` method.

In the `paintEvent()` method, an object of the `QPainter` class is defined by name as `qp`.
An object of the `QPen` class is defined by name as pen to set the thickness of the pen and its
color. Finally, a point is displayed by invoking the `drawPoint()` method at the location
whose value is defined in the `pos1` array, that is, where the mouse button is clicked.

On running the application, you will get a message that a dot will be displayed where the
mouse button will be clicked. When you click the mouse, a point will appear at that
location, as shown in the following screenshot:

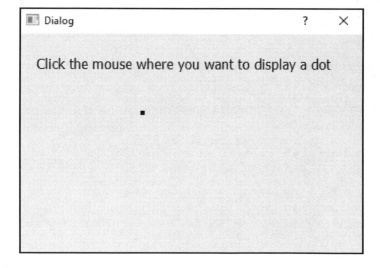

Drawing a line between two mouse clicks

In this recipe, we will learn to display a line between two points, from where the mouse button is clicked till where the mouse button is released on the form. The focus of this recipe is to understand how the mouse press and release events are handled, how the x *a* and *y* coordinates where the mouse button is clicked and released are accessed, and how a line is drawn from the location where the mouse button is clicked to the location where the mouse button is released.

How to do it...

The major players in this recipe are the mousePressEvent(), mouseReleaseEvent(), and paintEvent() methods. The mousePressEvent() and mouseReleaseEvent() methods are automatically executed whenever the mouse button is clicked or released, respectively. These two methods will be used to access the *x* and *y* coordinates where the mouse button is clicked and released. Finally, the paintEvent() method is used to draw a line between the coordinates that were supplied by the mousePressEvent() and mouseReleaseEvent() methods. Here is the step-by-step procedure to create this application:

1. Let's create an application based on the **Dialog without Buttons** template.
2. Add a QLabel widget to the form by dragging and dropping a **Label** widget on the form.
3. Set the **text** property of the **Label** widget to Click the mouse and drag it to draw the line of desired size.
4. Save the application by name as demoDrawLine.ui.

The form will now appear as shown in the following screenshot:

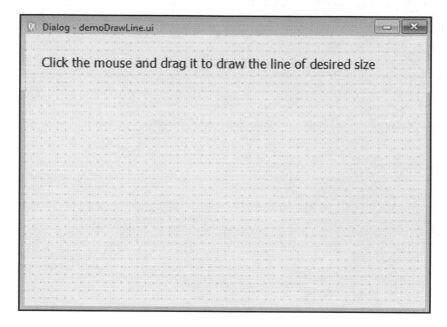

The user interface created with Qt Designer is stored in a .ui file, which is an XML file, and needs to be converted into Python code. The pyuic5 utility is used for converting the XML file into Python code. The generated Python script, demoDrawLine.py, can be seen in the source code bundle of the book.

5. Treat the demoDrawLine.py script as a header file, and import it into the file from which you will invoke its user interface design.

6. Create another Python file with the name callDrawLine.pyw and import the demoDrawLine.py code into it:

```
import sys
from PyQt5.QtWidgets import QDialog, QApplication
from PyQt5.QtGui import QPainter
from demoDrawLine import *
class MyForm(QDialog):
    def __init__(self):
        super().__init__()
        self.ui = Ui_Dialog()
        self.ui.setupUi(self)
        self.pos1 = [0,0]
        self.pos2 = [0,0]
        self.show()
```

```
    def paintEvent(self, event):
        qp = QPainter()
        qp.begin(self)
        qp.drawLine(self.pos1[0], self.pos1[1], self.pos2[0],
        self.pos2[1])
        qp.end()
    def mousePressEvent(self, event):
        if event.buttons() & QtCore.Qt.LeftButton:
            self.pos1[0], self.pos1[1] = event.pos().x(),
            event.pos().y()
    def mouseReleaseEvent(self, event):
            self.pos2[0], self.pos2[1] = event.pos().x(),
            event.pos().y()
            self.update()
if __name__=="__main__":
    app = QApplication(sys.argv)
    w = MyForm()
    w.show()
    sys.exit(app.exec_())
```

How it works...

As we want to display a line between the locations where the mouse button is clicked and released, we will be making use of two methods, mousePressEvent() and mouseReleaseEvent(). As the name suggests, the mousePressEvent() method is automatically invoked when a mouse button is pressed. Similarly, the mouseReleaseEvent() method is automatically invoked when the mouse button is released. In these two methods, we will be simply saving the values of the *x* and *y* coordinates where the mouse button is clicked and released. Two arrays are defined in this application, pos1 and pos2, where pos1 stores the *x* and *y* coordinates of the location where the mouse button is clicked, and the pos2 array stores the *x* and *y* coordinates of the location where the mouse button is released. Once the *x* and *y* coordinates of the locations where the mouse button is clicked and released are assigned to the pos1 and pos2 arrays, the self.update() method is invoked in the mouseReleaseEvent() method to invoke the paintEvent() method. In the paintEvent() method, the drawLine() method is invoked and the *x* and *y* coordinates stored in the pos1 and pos2 array are passed to it to draw a line between the mouse press and mouse release locations.

On running the application, you will get a message to click and drag the mouse button between the locations where the line is required. So, click the mouse button and keeping the mouse button pressed, drag it to the desired location and release the mouse button. A line will be drawn between the locations where the mouse button is clicked and where it is released, as shown in the following screenshot:

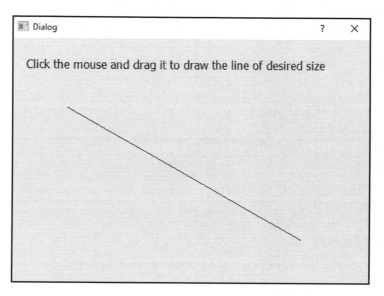

Drawing lines of different types

In this recipe, we will be learning to display lines of different types between two points, from the mouse click location to where the mouse button is released. The user will be shown different line types to choose from, such as solid, dash line, dash-dot line, and so on. The line will be draw in the selected line type.

How to do it...

It is the QPen class that is used for defining the size or thickness of the pen used for drawing shapes. The setStyle() method of the QPen class is used in this recipe to define the style of the line. Here is the step-by-step procedure to draw lines of different styles:

1. Let's create an application based on the **Dialog without Buttons** template.
2. Add a QLabel widget to the form by dragging and dropping a **Label** widget on the form.

3. Add a `QListWidget` widget by dragging and dropping a **List Widget** item on the form.

4. Set the **text** property of the **Label** widget to `Select the style from the list and then click and drag to draw a line.`

5. Save the application by name as `demoDrawDiffLine.ui`.

6. The **List Widget** item will be used for showing different types of lines, so right-click on the **List Widget** widget and select the **Edit Items** option to add a few line types to the **List Widget** item. Click the **+** (plus) button at the bottom of the dialog box that opens up and add a few line types, as shown in the following screenshot:

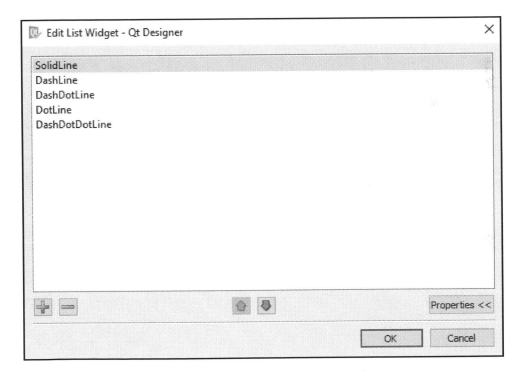

7. Set the **objectName** property of the **List Widget** item to `listWidgetLineType`.

The form will now appear as shown in the following screenshot:

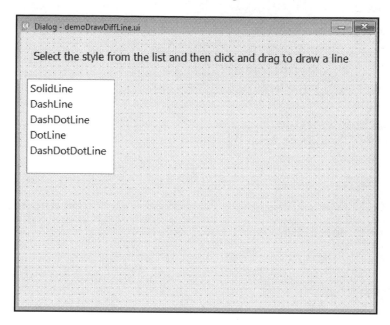

The user interface created with Qt Designer is stored in a `.ui` file, which is an XML file, and needs to be converted into Python code. The `pyuic5` utility is used for converting the XML file into Python code. The generated Python script, `demoDrawDiffLine.py`, can be seen in the source code bundle of the book.

8. Treat the `demoDrawDiffLine.py` script as a header file, and import it into the file from which you will invoke its user interface design.

9. Create another Python file with the name `callDrawDiffLine.pyw` and import the `demoDrawDiffLine.py` code into it:

```python
import sys
from PyQt5.QtWidgets import QDialog, QApplication
from PyQt5.QtGui import QPainter, QPen
from PyQt5.QtCore import Qt
from demoDrawDiffLine import *
class MyForm(QDialog):
    def __init__(self):
        super().__init__()
        self.ui = Ui_Dialog()
        self.ui.setupUi(self)
        self.lineType="SolidLine"
        self.pos1 = [0,0]
```

```
            self.pos2 = [0,0]
            self.show()
    def paintEvent(self, event):
        qp = QPainter()
        qp.begin(self)
        pen = QPen(Qt.black, 4)
        self.lineTypeFormat="Qt."+self.lineType
        if self.lineTypeFormat == "Qt.SolidLine":
            pen.setStyle(Qt.SolidLine)
            elif self.lineTypeFormat == "Qt.DashLine":
            pen.setStyle(Qt.DashLine)
            elif self.lineTypeFormat =="Qt.DashDotLine":
                pen.setStyle(Qt.DashDotLine)
            elif self.lineTypeFormat =="Qt.DotLine":
                pen.setStyle(Qt.DotLine)
            elif self.lineTypeFormat =="Qt.DashDotDotLine":
                pen.setStyle(Qt.DashDotDotLine)
                qp.setPen(pen)
                qp.drawLine(self.pos1[0], self.pos1[1],
                self.pos2[0], self.pos2[1])
                qp.end()
    def mousePressEvent(self, event):
        if event.buttons() & QtCore.Qt.LeftButton:
            self.pos1[0], self.pos1[1] = event.pos().x(),
            event.pos().y()
    def mouseReleaseEvent(self, event):
        self.lineType=self.ui.listWidgetLineType.currentItem()
        .text()
        self.pos2[0], self.pos2[1] = event.pos().x(),
        event.pos().y()
        self.update()
if __name__=="__main__":
    app = QApplication(sys.argv)
    w = MyForm()
    w.show()
    sys.exit(app.exec_())
```

How it works...

A line has to be drawn between the mouse press and mouse release locations, so we will be making use of two methods in this application, mousePressEvent() and mouseReleaseEvent(). The mousePressEvent() method is automatically invoked when the left mouse button is clicked. Similarly, the mouseReleaseEvent() method is automatically invoked when the mouse button is released.

In these two methods, we will be saving the values of the *x* and *y* coordinates where the mouse button is clicked and released respectively. Two arrays are defined in this application, `pos1` and `pos2`, where `pos1` stores the *x* and *y* coordinates of the location where the mouse button is clicked and the `pos2` array stores the *x* and *y* coordinates of the location where the mouse button is released. In the `mouseReleaseEvent()` method, we fetch the line type chosen by the user from the **List** widget and assign the chosen line type to the `lineType` variable. Also, the `self.update()` method is invoked in the `mouseReleaseEvent()` method to invoke the `paintEvent()` method. In the `paintEvent()` method, you define a pen of 4 pixels in **width** and assign it a black color. Also, you assign a style to the pen that matches the line type chosen by the user from the **List** widget. Finally, the `drawLine()` method is invoked and the *x* and *y* coordinates stored in the `pos1` and `pos2` array are passed to it to draw a line between the mouse press and mouse release locations. The line will be displayed in the style that is selected from the **List** widget.

On running the application, you will get a message to select the line type from the list and click and drag the mouse button between the locations where the line is required. So, after selecting a desired line type, click the mouse button and keeping the mouse button pressed, drag it to the desired location and release the mouse button. A line will be drawn between the locations where the mouse button is clicked and where it is released in the style that is chosen from the list. The following screenshot shows the lines of different types:

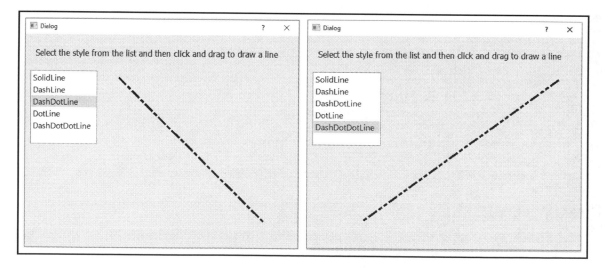

Drawing a circle of a desired size

In this recipe, we will be learning to draw a circle. The user will click and drag the mouse to define the diameter of the circle, and the circle will be drawn at the diameter specified by the user.

How to do it...

A circle is nothing but an arc that is drawn from 0 to 360 degrees. The length of the arc, or you can say the diameter of the circle, is determined by the distance of mouse press event and mouse release events. A rectangle is defined internally from mouse press event until mouse release event, and the circle is drawn within that rectangle. Here are the complete steps to create this application:

1. Let's create an application based on the **Dialog without Buttons** template.
2. Add a `QLabel` widget to the form by dragging and dropping a **Label** widget on the form.
3. Set the **text** property of the **Label** widget to `Click the mouse and drag it to draw a circle of the desired size`.
4. Save the application by name as `demoDrawCircle.ui`. The form will now appear as shown in the following screenshot:

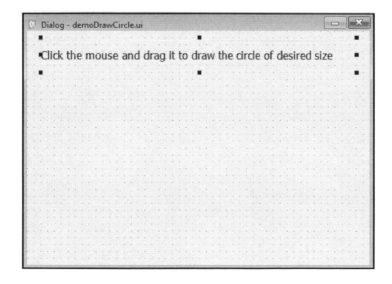

The user interface created with Qt Designer is stored in a `.ui` file and it is an XML file. The XML file is converted into Python code by applying the `pyuic5` utility. You can find the generated Python code, `demoDrawCircle.py`, in the source code bundle of the book.

5. Treat the `demoDrawCircle.py` script as a header file, and import it into the file from which you will invoke its user interface design.

6. Create another Python file with the name `callDrawCircle.pyw` and import the `demoDrawCircle.py` code into it:

```python
import sys
from PyQt5.QtWidgets import QDialog, QApplication
from PyQt5.QtGui import QPainter
from demoDrawCircle import *
class MyForm(QDialog):
    def __init__(self):
        super().__init__()
        self.ui = Ui_Dialog()
        self.ui.setupUi(self)
        self.pos1 = [0,0]
        self.pos2 = [0,0]
        self.show()
    def paintEvent(self, event):
        width = self.pos2[0]-self.pos1[0]
        height = self.pos2[1] - self.pos1[1]
        qp = QPainter()
        qp.begin(self)
        rect = QtCore.QRect(self.pos1[0], self.pos1[1], width,
        height)
        startAngle = 0
        arcLength = 360 *16
        qp.drawArc(rect, startAngle, arcLength)
        qp.end()
    def mousePressEvent(self, event):
        if event.buttons() & QtCore.Qt.LeftButton:
            self.pos1[0], self.pos1[1] = event.pos().x(),
            event.pos().y()
    def mouseReleaseEvent(self, event):
        self.pos2[0], self.pos2[1] = event.pos().x(),
        event.pos().y()
        self.update()
if __name__=="__main__":
    app = QApplication(sys.argv)
    w = MyForm()
    w.show()
    sys.exit(app.exec_())
```

How it works...

To draw a circle with the diameter defined between the mouse button pressed and released locations, we will be making use of two methods, `mousePressEvent()` and `mouseReleaseEvent()`. The `mousePressEvent()` method is automatically invoked when a mouse button is pressed and the `mouseReleaseEvent()` method is automatically invoked when the mouse button is released. In these two methods, we will be simply saving the values of the *x* and *y* coordinates where the mouse button is clicked and released. Two arrays, `pos1` and `pos2`, are defined, where the `pos1` array stores the *x* and *y* coordinates of the location where the mouse button is clicked and the `pos2` array stores the *x* and *y* coordinates of the location where the mouse button is released. The `self.update()` method that is invoked in the `mouseReleaseEvent()` method will invoke the `paintEvent()` method. In the `paintEvent()` method, the width of the rectangle is computed by finding the difference between the *x* coordinates of mouse press and mouse release locations. Similarly, the height of the rectangle is computed by finding the difference between the y coordinates of mouse press and mouse release events.

The circle will be created of a size equal to the width and height of the rectangle, that is, the circle will be created within the boundaries specified by the user with the mouse.

Also, in the `paintEvent()` method, the `drawArc()` method is invoked and the rectangle, starting angle of the arc, and length of the arc are passed to it. The starting angle is specified as `0`.

On running the application, you will get a message to click and drag the mouse button to define the diameter of the circle to be drawn. So, click the mouse button and keeping the mouse button pressed, drag it to the desired location and release the mouse button. A circle will be drawn between the locations where the mouse button is clicked and where it is released, as shown in the following screenshot:

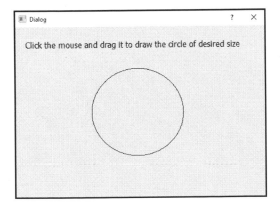

Drawing a rectangle between two mouse clicks

In this recipe, we will be learning to display a rectangle between the two points where the mouse button is clicked and released on the form.

How to do it...

It is a very simple application, where the `mousePressEvent()` and `mouseReleaseEvent()` methods are used to find the x and y coordinates of the location where the mouse is pressed and released, respectively. Thereafter, the `drawRect()` method is invoked to draw the rectangle from the coordinates where the mouse button is clicked to the coordinates where the mouse button is released. The step-by-step procedure for creating this application is as follows:

1. Let's create an application based on the **Dialog without Buttons** template.
2. Add a `QLabel` widget to the form by dragging and dropping a **Label** widget on the form.
3. Set the **text** property of the **Label** widget to `Click the mouse and drag it to draw a rectangle of the desired size`.
4. Save the application by name as `demoDrawRectangle.ui`. The form will now appear as shown in the following screenshot:

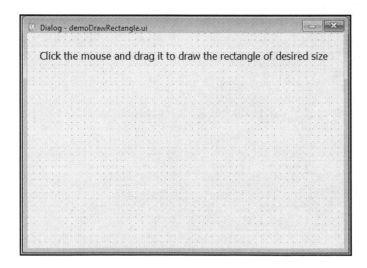

Chapter 10

The user interface created with Qt Designer is stored in a `.ui` file, which is an XML file, and needs to be converted into Python code. The `pyuic5` utility is used for converting the XML file into Python code. The generated Python script, `demoDrawRectangle.py`, can be seen in the source code bundle of the book.

5. Treat the `demoDrawRectangle.py` script as a header file, and import it into the file from which you will invoke its user interface design.

6. Create another Python file with the name `callDrawRectangle.pyw` and import the `demoDrawRectangle.py` code into it:

```python
import sys
from PyQt5.QtWidgets import QDialog, QApplication
from PyQt5.QtGui import QPainter
from demoDrawRectangle import *
class MyForm(QDialog):
    def __init__(self):
        super().__init__()
        self.ui = Ui_Dialog()
        self.ui.setupUi(self)
        self.pos1 = [0,0]
        self.pos2 = [0,0]
        self.show()
    def paintEvent(self, event):
        width = self.pos2[0]-self.pos1[0]
        height = self.pos2[1] - self.pos1[1]
        qp = QPainter()
        qp.begin(self)
        qp.drawRect(self.pos1[0], self.pos1[1], width, height)
        qp.end()
    def mousePressEvent(self, event):
        if event.buttons() & QtCore.Qt.LeftButton:
            self.pos1[0], self.pos1[1] = event.pos().x(),
            event.pos().y()
    def mouseReleaseEvent(self, event):
        self.pos2[0], self.pos2[1] = event.pos().x(),
        event.pos().y()
        self.update()
if __name__=="__main__":
    app = QApplication(sys.argv)
    w = MyForm()
    w.show()
    sys.exit(app.exec_())
```

[345]

How it works...

To draw a rectangle between the mouse button pressed and released locations, we will be making use of two methods, `mousePressEvent()` and `mouseReleaseEvent()`. The `mousePressEvent()` method is automatically invoked when a mouse button is pressed and the `mouseReleaseEvent()` method is automatically invoked when the mouse button is released. In these two methods, we will be simply saving the values of the *x* and *y* coordinates where the mouse button is clicked and released respectively. Two arrays, `pos1` and `pos2`, are defined, where the `pos1` array stores the *x* and *y* coordinates of the location where the mouse button is clicked and the `pos2` array stores the *x* and *y* coordinates of the location where the mouse button is released. The `self.update()` method that is invoked in the `mouseReleaseEvent()` method will invoke the `paintEvent()` method. In the `paintEvent()` method, the width of the rectangle is computed by finding the difference between the *x* coordinates of mouse press and mouse release locations. Similarly, the height of the rectangle is computed by finding the difference between the *y* coordinates of mouse press and mouse release events.

Also, in the `paintEvent()` method, the `drawRect()` method is invoked and the *x* and *y* coordinates stored in the `pos1` array are passed to it. Also, the width and height of the rectangle are passed to the `drawRect()` method to draw the rectangle between the mouse press and mouse release locations.

On running the application, you will get a message to click and drag the mouse button between the locations where the rectangle is required. So, click the mouse button and keeping the mouse button pressed, drag it to the desired location and release the mouse button.

A rectangle will be drawn between the locations where the mouse button is clicked and where it is released, as shown in the following screenshot:

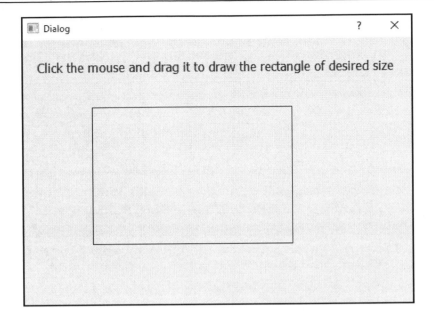

Drawing text in a desired font and size

In this recipe, we will learn to draw text in a specific font and at a specific font size. Four widgets will be required in this recipe such as **Text Edit**, **List Widget**, **Combo Box**, and **Push Button**. The **Text Edit** widget will be used to enter the text that the user wants to display in the desired font and size. The **List Widget** box will display different font names that the user can select from. The **Combo Box** widget will display font sizes that the user can select to define the size of the text. The **Push Button** widget will initiate the action, that is, the text entered in the **Text Edit** widget will be displayed in the chosen font and size on clicking the push button.

How to do it...

The QPainter class is the focus of this recipe. The setFont() and drawText() methods of the QPainter class will be used in this recipe. The setFont() method will be invoked to set the font style and font size chosen by the user and the drawText() method will draw the text written by the user in the **Text Edit** widget in the specified font style and size. Here is the step-by-step procedure to learn how these methods are used:

1. Let's create an application based on the **Dialog without Buttons** template.

2. Add the `QLabel`, `QTextEdit`, `QListWidget`, `QComboBox`, and `QPushButton` widgets to the form by dragging and dropping a **Label** widget, a **Text Edit** widget, a **List Widget** box, a **Combo Box** widget, and a **Push Button** widget on the form.

3. Set the **text** property of the **Label** widget to `Enter some text in leftmost box, select font and size, and click the Draw Text button`.

4. The **List Widget** box will be used for showing different fonts, so right-click on the **List Widget** box and select the **Edit Items** option to add a few font names to the **List Widget** box. Click the **+** (plus) button at the bottom of the dialog box that opens up and add a few font names, as shown in the following screenshot:

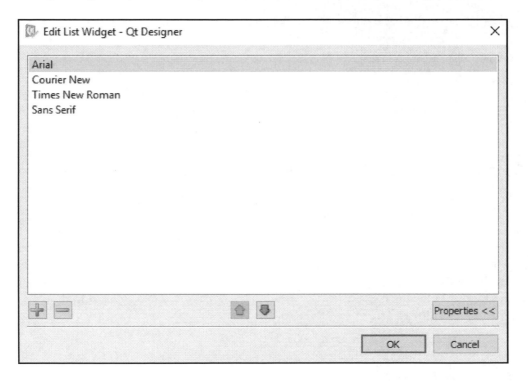

5. The **Combo Box** widget will be used for showing different font sizes, so we need to add certain font sizes to the **Combo Box** widget. Right-click on the **Combo Box** widget and select the **Edit Items** option.

6. Click the **+** (plus) button at the bottom of the dialog box that opens up and add a couple of font sizes, as shown in the following screenshot:

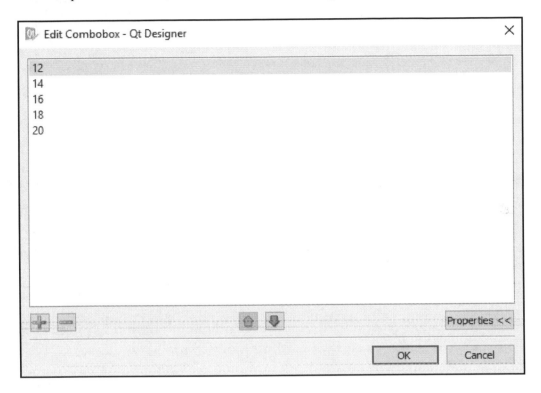

7. Set the **text** property of the **Push Button** widget to `Draw Text`.
8. Set the **objectName** property of the **List Widget** box to `listWidgetFont`.
9. Set the **objectName** property of the **Combo Box** widget to `comboBoxFontSize`.
10. Set the **objectName** property of the **Push Button** widget to pushButtonDrawText.
11. Save the application by name as `demoDrawText.ui`.

The form will now appear as shown in this screenshot:

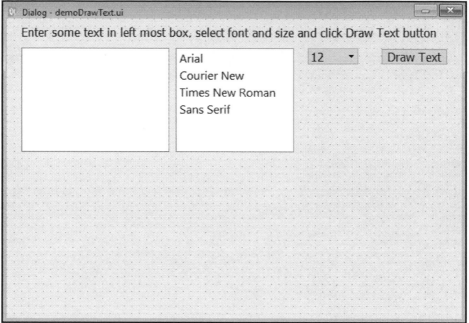

The user interface created with Qt Designer is stored in a `.ui` file and it is an XML file. The XML file is converted into Python code by applying the `pyuic5` utility. You can find the generated Python code, `demoDrawText.py`, in the source code bundle of the book.

12. Treat the `demoDrawText.py` script as a header file, and import it into the file from which you will invoke its user interface design.

13. Create another Python file with the name `callDrawText.pyw` and import the `demoDrawText.py` code into it:

```python
import sys
from PyQt5.QtWidgets import QDialog, QApplication
from PyQt5.QtGui import QPainter, QColor, QFont
from PyQt5.QtCore import Qt
from demoDrawText import *
class MyForm(QDialog):
    def __init__(self):
        super().__init__()
        self.ui = Ui_Dialog()
        self.ui.setupUi(self)
        self.ui.pushButtonDrawText.clicked.connect(self.
```

```
                    dispText)
                    self.textToDraw=""
                    self.fontName="Courier New"
                    self.fontSize=5
                    self.show()
            def paintEvent(self, event):
                    qp = QPainter()
                    qp.begin(self)
                    qp.setPen(QColor(168, 34, 3))
                    qp.setFont(QFont(self.fontName, self.fontSize))
                    qp.drawText(event.rect(), Qt.AlignCenter,
                    self.textToDraw)
                    qp.end()
            def dispText(self):
                    self.fontName=self.ui.listWidgetFont.currentItem().
                    text()
                    self.fontSize=int(self.ui.comboBoxFontSize.itemText(
                    self.ui.comboBoxFontSize.currentIndex()))
                    self.textToDraw=self.ui.textEdit.toPlainText()
                    self.update()
    if __name__=="__main__":
            app = QApplication(sys.argv)
            w = MyForm()
            w.show()
            sys.exit(app.exec_())
```

How it works...

The **click()** event of the **Push Button** widget is connected to the `dispText()` method, that is, whenever the push button is clicked, the `dispText()` method will be invoked.

In the `dispText()` method, the font name selected from the **List Widget** box is accessed and assigned to the `fontName` variable. Also, the font size selected from the combo box is accessed and assigned to the `fontSize` variable. Besides this, the text written in the **Text Edit** widget is fetched and assigned to the `textToDraw` variable. Finally, the `self.update()` method is invoked; it will invoke the `paintEvent()` method.

In the `paintEvent()` method, the `drawText()` method is called and will draw the text written in the **Text Edit** widget in the font style that is assigned to the `fontName` variable, and in the font size specified in the `fontSize` variable. On running the application, you will find a **Text Edit** widget on the extreme left, font names displayed in the **List Widget** box, and font sizes displayed via the **Combo box** widget. You need to enter some text in the **Text Edit** widget, select a font style from the **List Widget** box and font size from the **Combo Box** widget, and click on the **Draw Text** button. On clicking the **Draw Text** button, the text written in the **Text Edit** widget will be displayed in the selected font and selected font size, as shown in the following screenshot:

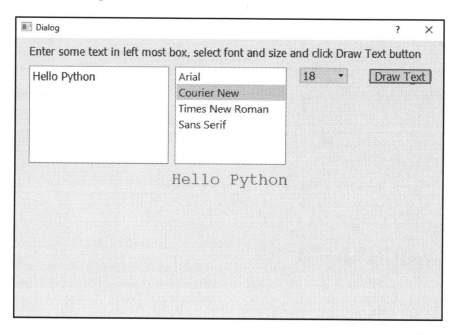

Creating a toolbar that shows different graphics tools

In this recipe, we will learn to create a toolbar that shows three toolbar buttons. These three toolbar buttons show the icons for the line, circle, and rectangle. When the user clicks the line toolbar button from the toolbar, he/she can click and drag the mouse on the form to draw a line between the two mouse locations. Similarly, by clicking on the circle toolbar button, the user can draw a circle on the form by clicking and dragging the mouse.

How to do it...

The focus of this recipe is to help you understand how frequently used commands in an application can be provided to the user via a toolbar, making them easy to access and use. You will learn to create toolbar buttons, define their shortcuts, and their icons too. To define the icons for the toolbar buttons, you will learn to create and use the resource file. The creation and execution of each toolbar button is explained very clearly step by step:

1. Let's create a new application to understand the steps involved in creating a toolbar.
2. Launch Qt Designer and create a main window-based application. You get a new application with the default menu bar.
3. You can remove the menu bar by right-clicking on it and selecting the **Remove Menu Bar** option from the shortcut menu that pops up.
4. To add a toolbar, right-click on the **Main Window** template and select **Add Tool Bar** from the context menu. A blank toolbar will be added below the menu bar, as shown in the following screenshot:

We want to create a toolbar with three toolbar buttons, line, circle, and rectangle. Since the three toolbar buttons will represent three icon images, we assume we have icon files, that is, files with an extension .ico for the line, circle, and rectangle.

5. To add tools to the toolbar, create an action in the **Action Editor** box; each toolbar button in the toolbar is represented by an action. The **Action Editor** box is usually found below the **Property Editor** window.

6. If the **Action Editor** window is not visible, select Action Editor from the View menu. The **Action Editor** window appears as shown here:

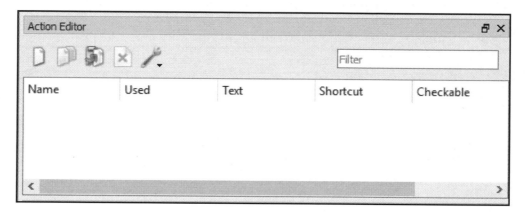

7. In the **Action Editor** window, select the New button to create an action for the first toolbar button. You get the dialog to enter detailed information for the new action.

8. In the **Text** box, specify the name of the action, Circle.

9. In the **Object name** box, the name of the action object automatically appears, prefixed with the text action.

10. In the **ToolTip** box, enter any descriptive text.

11. In the **Shortcut** box, press *Ctrl + C* character to assign `Ctrl + C` as the shortcut key for drawing a circle.

12. The **Icon** drop-down list shows two options, **Choose Resource...** and **Choose File**.

13. You can assign an icon image to the action either by clicking the **Choose File...** option or from the resource file:

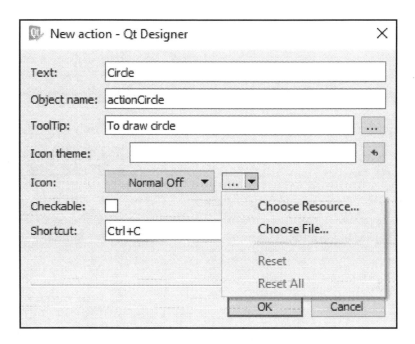

You can select several icons in a resource file and that resource file can then be used in different applications.

14. Select the **Choose Resource...** option. You get the **Select Resource** dialog, as shown in the following screenshot:

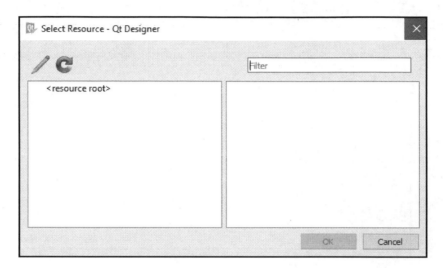

Since no resource has yet been created, the dialog box is empty. You see two icons at the top. The first icon represents Edit Resources and the second icon represents Reload. On clicking the Edit Resources icon, you get the dialog shown here:

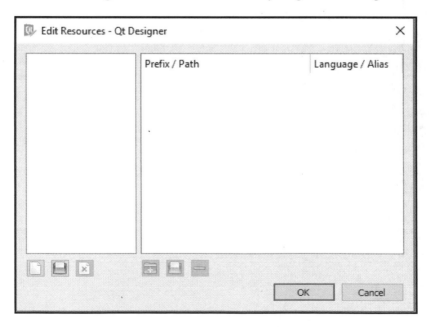

Now let's see how we can create a resource file by performing the following steps:

1. The first step is to create a resource file or load an existing resource file. The first three icons at the bottom represent New Resource File, Edit Resource File, and Remove.

2. Click on New Resource File icon. You will be prompted to specify the name of the resource file.

3. Let's name the new resource file `iconresource`. The file will be saved with the extension `.qrc`.

4. The next step is to add a prefix to the resource file. The three icons below the **Prefix / Path** pane are Add Prefix, Add Files, and Remove.

5. Click on the Add Prefix option, and you will be prompted to enter the prefix name.

6. Enter the prefix as `Graphics`. After adding the prefix, we are ready to add our three icons, circle, rectangle, and line, to the resource file. Recall that we have three icon files with the extension `.ico`.

7. Click the Add Files option to add icons. On clicking the Add Files option, you will be asked to browse to the drive/directory and select the icon files.

8. Select the three icon files one by one. After adding the three icons, the Edit Resources dialog appears as shown here:

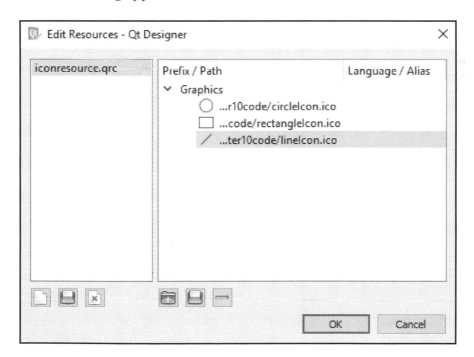

9. On clicking the **OK** button, the resource file will appear, showing the three icons to choose from.

10. Since we want to assign an icon for the circle action, click on the circle icon, followed by clicking the **OK** button:

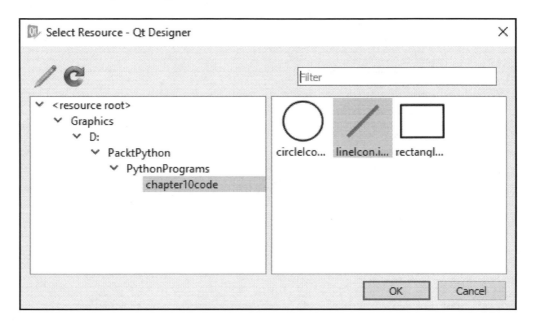

The selected circle icon will be assigned to **actionCircle**.

11. Similarly, create two more actions, `actionRectangle` and `actionLine`, for the rectangle and line toolbar buttons. After adding the three actions, the **Action Editor** window will appear as shown here:

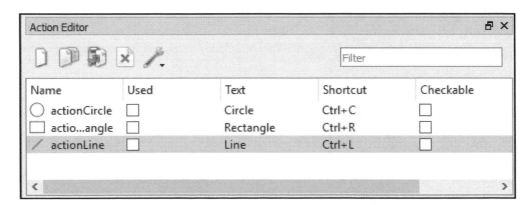

12. To display the toolbar buttons in the toolbar, click one action from the **Action Editor** window and, keeping it pressed, drag it to the toolbar.

13. Save the application with the name `demoToolBars.ui`.

After dragging the three actions to the toolbar, the toolbar will appear as shown here:

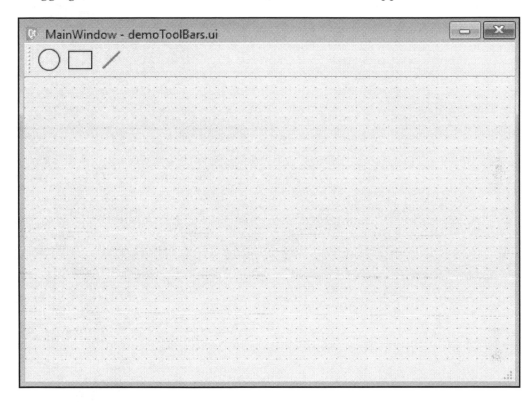

The `pyuic5` command line utility will convert the `.ui` (XML) file into Python code, and the generated code will be named `demoToolBars.py`. You can find the `demoToolBars.py` script in the source code bundle of this book. The `iconresource.qrc` file that we created must be converted into Python format before we move further. The following command line will convert the resource file into a Python script:

```
pyrcc5 iconresource.qrc -o iconresource_rc.py
```

14. Create a Python script named `callToolBars.pyw` that imports the code, `demoToolBar.py`, to invoke the toolbar and to draw the graphic whose toolbar button is selected from the toolbar. The script file will appear as follows:

```python
import sys
from PyQt5.QtWidgets import QMainWindow, QApplication
from PyQt5.QtGui import QPainter
from demoToolBars import *

class AppWindow(QMainWindow):
    def __init__(self):
        super().__init__()
        self.ui = Ui_MainWindow()
        self.ui.setupUi(self)
        self.pos1 = [0,0]
        self.pos2 = [0,0]
        self.toDraw=""
        self.ui.actionCircle.triggered.connect(self.drawCircle)
        self.ui.actionRectangle.triggered.connect(self.
        drawRectangle)
        self.ui.actionLine.triggered.connect(self.drawLine)
        self.show()

    def paintEvent(self, event):
        qp = QPainter()
        qp.begin(self)
        if self.toDraw=="rectangle":
            width = self.pos2[0]-self.pos1[0]
            height = self.pos2[1] - self.pos1[1]
            qp.drawRect(self.pos1[0], self.pos1[1], width,
            height)
        if self.toDraw=="line":
            qp.drawLine(self.pos1[0], self.pos1[1],
            self.pos2[0], self.pos2[1])
        if self.toDraw=="circle":
            width = self.pos2[0]-self.pos1[0]
            height = self.pos2[1] - self.pos1[1]
            rect = QtCore.QRect(self.pos1[0], self.pos1[1],
            width, height)
            startAngle = 0
            arcLength = 360 *16
            qp.drawArc(rect, startAngle, arcLength)
            qp.end()

    def mousePressEvent(self, event):
        if event.buttons() & QtCore.Qt.LeftButton:
            self.pos1[0], self.pos1[1] = event.pos().x(),
            event.pos().y()
```

```
    def mouseReleaseEvent(self, event):
        self.pos2[0], self.pos2[1] = event.pos().x(),
        event.pos().y()
        self.update()

    def drawCircle(self):
        self.toDraw="circle"

    def drawRectangle(self):
        self.toDraw="rectangle"

    def drawLine(self):
        self.toDraw="line"

app = QApplication(sys.argv)
w = AppWindow()
w.show()
sys.exit(app.exec_())
```

How it works...

The **triggered()** signal of the action of each toolbar button is connected to the respective method. The **triggered()** signal of the **actionCircle** toolbar button is connected to the drawCircle() method, so whenever the circle toolbar button is selected from the toolbar, the drawCircle() method will be invoked. Similarly, the **triggered()** signal of actionRectangle and actionLine are connected to the drawRectangle() and drawLine() methods, respectively. In the drawCircle() method, a variable toDraw is assigned a string, circle. The toDraw variable will be used to determine the graphics to be drawn in the paintEvent() method. The toDraw variable can be assigned any of the three strings, line, circle, or rectangle. A conditional branching is applied on the value in the toDraw variable and accordingly, methods to draw a line, rectangle, or circle will be invoked.

How big a line, circle, or rectangle will be drawn is determined by the mouse clicks; the user needs to click the mouse on the form and drag the mouse and release it at the location up to which he/she wants to draw the line, circle, or rectangle. In other words, the length of the line, width and height of the rectangle, and diameter of the circle will be determined by the mouse.

Two arrays, `pos1` and `pos2`, are used to store the *x* and *y* coordinates of the location where the mouse is clicked and the location where the mouse is released, respectively. The *x* and *y* coordinate values are assigned to the `pos1` and `pos2` array via two methods, `mousePressEvent()` and `mouseReleaseEvent()`. The `mousePressEvent()` method is automatically invoked when the mouse button is clicked and the `mouseReleaseEvent()` method is automatically invoked when the mouse button is released.

In the `mouseReleaseEvent()` method, after assigning the *x* and *y* coordinate values of the location where the mouse button is released, the `self.update()` method is invoked to invoke the `paintEvent()` method. In the `paintEvent()` method, branching takes place on the basis of the string assigned to the `toDraw` variable. If the `toDraw` variable is assigned the string `line` (by the `drawLine()` method), the `drawLine()` method will be invoked of `QPainter` class to draw the line between the two mouse locations. Similarly, if the `toDraw` variable is assigned the string `circle` (by the `drawCircle()` method), the `drawArc()` method will be invoked of the `QPainter` class to draw a circle with a diameter supplied by mouse locations. If the `toDraw` variable is assigned the string `rectangle` by the `drawRectangle()` method, then the `drawRect()` method will be invoked of the `QPainter` class to draw a rectangle of the width and height supplied by the mouse locations.

On running the application, you will find a toolbar with three toolbar buttons, circle, rectangle, and line, as shown in the following screenshot (left). Click on the circle toolbar button, then click the mouse button on the form, and, keeping the mouse button pressed, drag it to define the diameter of the circle and release the mouse button. A circle will be drawn from the location where the mouse button is clicked up to the location where the mouse button is released (right):

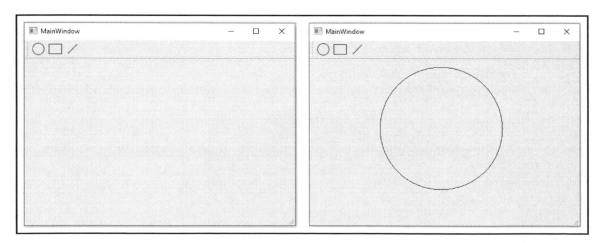

To draw a rectangle, click on the rectangle tool, click the mouse button at a location on the form, and, keeping the mouse button pressed, drag it to define the height and width of the rectangle. On releasing the mouse button, a rectangle will be drawn between the mouse pressed and mouse released locations (left). Similarly, click the line toolbar button and click the mouse button on the form. Keeping the mouse button pressed, drag it up to the location where you want the line to be drawn. On releasing the mouse button, a line will be drawn between the locations where the mouse button is clicked and released (right):

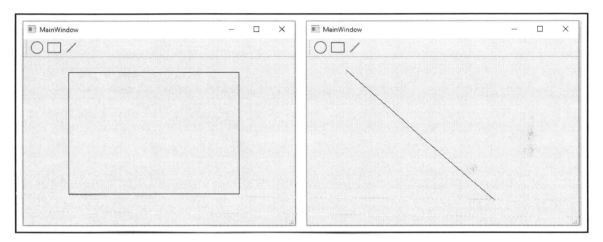

Plotting a line using Matplotlib

In this recipe, we will learn to plot a line using Matplotlib that passes through specific x and y coordinates.

Matplotlib is a Python 2D plotting library that makes the complicated task of plotting lines, histograms, bar charts, and so on quite easy. This library not only plots, but also provides an API that enables the embedding of plots in applications too.

Getting ready

You can install Matplotlib by using the following statement:

```
pip install matplotlib
```

Let's assume that we want to plot a line that uses the following sets of *x* and *y* coordinates:

```
x=10, y=20
x=20, y=40
x=30, y=60
```

On the *x* axis, the value of x begins from 0 and increases towards the right and on the *y* axis, the value of y is 0 at the bottom and increases as we move up. Because the last pair of coordinates is 30, 60, the graph will have the maximum x value of 30 and the maximum y value of 60.

The following methods of `matplotlib.pyplot` will be used in this recipe:

- `title()`: This method is used to set the title of the graph
- `xlabel()`: This method is to display the specific text along the *x* axis
- `ylabel()`: This method is to display the specific text along the *y* axis
- `plot()`: This method is used for plotting at the specified *x* and *y* coordinates

How to do it...

Create a Python script with the name `demoPlotLine.py` and write the following code in it:

```python
import matplotlib.pyplot as graph
graph.title('Plotting a Line!')
graph.xlabel('x - axis')
graph.ylabel('y - axis')
x = [10,20,30]
y = [20,40,60]
graph.plot(x, y)
graph.show()
```

How it works...

You import `matplotlib.pyplot` in the script and name it graph. Using the `title()` method, you set the title of the graph. Thereafter, the `xlabel()` and `ylabel()` methods are invoked to define the text for the *x* axis and *y* axis, respectively. Because we want to plot a line using three sets of *x* and *y* coordinates, two arrays are defined by name, *x* and *y*. The values of the *x* and *y* coordinates that we want to plot are defined in the two arrays, *x* and *y*, respectively. The `plot()` method is invoked and the two *x* and *y* arrays are passed to it to plot the line using the three *x* and *y* coordinate values defined in the two arrays. The show method is invoked to display the plotting.

On running the application, you find that a line is plotted that passes through the specified x and y coordinates. Also, the graph will show the specified title, **Plotting a Line !**. Besides this, you can see the designated text being displayed along the x axis and y axis as shown in the following screenshot:

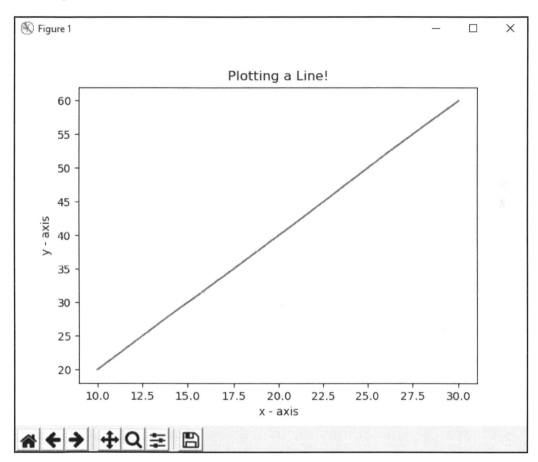

Plotting a bar using Matplotlib

In this recipe, we will learn to plot a bar using Matplotlib that compares the growth of a business over past three years. You will supply the profit percentage in 2016, 2017, and 2018 and the application will show a bar representing the profit percentage in the past three years.

Getting ready

Let's assume that the profit percentage of the organization over the last three years is as follows:

- **2016**: Profit was 70%
- **2017**: Profit was 90%
- **2018**: Profit is 80%

You want to display bars that represent profit percentages and along the *x* axis, and you want the years to be displayed: 2016, 2017, and 2018. Along the *y* axis, you want to display the bar that represent the profit percentage. The value of y on the *y* axis will begin from 0 at the bottom and increases while moving toward the top, with the maximum value, 100, at the top.

The following methods of `matplotlib.pyplot` will be used in this recipe:

- `title()`: This method is used to set the title of the graph
- `bar()`: To plot the bar from the two supplied arrays; one array will represent data for the *x* axis, and the second array will represent data for the *y* axis
- `plot()`: This method is used for plotting at the specified *x* and *y* coordinates

How to do it...

Create a Python script with the name `demoPlotBars.py` and write the following code in it:

```python
import matplotlib.pyplot as graph
years = ['2016', '2017', '2018']
profit = [70, 90, 80]
graph.bar(years, profit)
graph.title('Growth in Business')
graph.plot(100)
graph.show()
```

How it works...

You import `matplotlib.pyplot` in the script and name it graph. You define two arrays, years and profit, where the years array will contain the data for 2016, 2017, and 2018 to represent the years whose profits we want to compare. Similarly, the profit array will contain the values that represent the profit percentages for the last three years. Thereafter, the `bar()` method is invoked and the two arrays, years and profit, are passed to it to display the bar comparing profits in the last three years. The `title()` method is invoked to display the title, **Growth in Business**. The `plot()` method is invoked to indicate the maximum y value along the *y* axis. Finally, the `show()` method is invoked to display the bar.

On running the application, you find that a bar is plotted that displays the profits of the organization in the past three years. The *x* axis shows the years and the *y* axis shows the profit percentage. Also, the graph will show the specified title, **Growth in Business** as shown in the following screenshot:

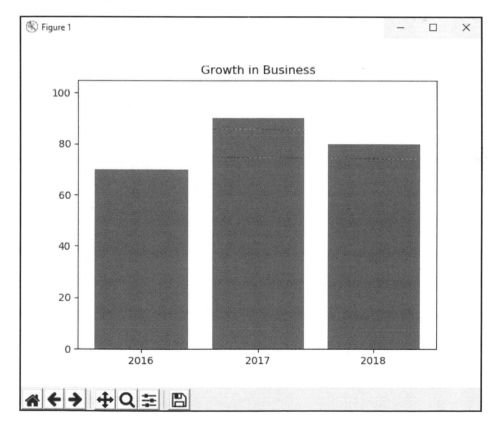

11
Implementing Animation

In this chapter, you will learn how to apply motion to a given graphic image, hence implementing animation. Animations play a major role in explaining the practical workings of any machine, process, or system. In this chapter, we will be covering the following topics:

- Displaying a 2D graphical picture
- Making a ball move down on the click of a button
- Making a bouncing ball
- Making a ball animate as per the specified curve

Introduction

To view and manage 2D graphical items in Python, we need to make use of a class called `QGraphicsScene`. In order to display the contents of `QGraphicsScene`, we need the help of another class, called `QGraphicsView`. Basically, `QGraphicsView` provides a scrollable viewport to display the contents of `QGraphicsScene`. `QGraphicsScene` acts as a container for several graphical items. It also provides several standard shapes, such as rectangles and ellipses, including text items. One more thing: the QGraphicsScene uses OpenGL for rendering the graphics. The OpenGL is very efficient for displaying images and performing multimedia processing tasks. The `QGraphicsScene` class provides several methods that help in adding or removing graphical items from the scene. That is, you can add any graphical item to the scene by calling the `addItem` function. Similarly, to remove an item from the graphics scene, you can call the `removeItem` function.

Implementing animation

To apply animation in Python, we will be making use of the QPropertyAnimation class. The QPropertyAnimation class in PyQt helps in creating and executing animations in PyQt. The QPropertyAnimation class implements animation by manipulating Qt properties such as a widget's geometry, position, and so on. The following are a few of the QPropertyAnimation methods:

- start(): This method begins the animation
- stop(): This method ends the animation
- setStartValue(): This method is used to assign the starting value of the animation
- setEndValue(): This method is used to assign the ending value of the animation
- setDuration(): This method is used to set the duration of the animation in milliseconds
- setKeyValueAt(): This method creates a keyframe at the given value
- setLoopCount(): This method sets the count of the repetitions desired in the animation

Displaying a 2D graphical image

In this recipe, you will learn to display a 2D graphical image. We assume that you have a graphical image by the name scene.jpg on your machine, and you will learn how it is displayed on the form. The focus of this recipe is to understand how the **Graphics View** widget is used to display an image.

How to do it...

The procedure for displaying graphics is very simple. You first need to create an object of QGraphicsScene, which in turn makes use of the QGraphicsView class to show its contents. Graphical items, including images, are then added to the QGraphicsScene class by invoking the addItem method of the QGraphicsScene class. Here are the steps to display a 2D graphical image on the screen:

1. Create a new application based on the **Dialog without Buttons** template.
2. Drag and drop a **Graphics View** widget onto it.

3. Save the application with the name `demoGraphicsView.ui`. The form will appear as shown in the following screenshot:

The `pyuic5` command utility converts the `.ui` (XML) file into Python code. The generated Python script, `demoGraphicsView.py`, can be seen in the source code bundle of this book.

4. Create a Python script named `callGraphicsView.pyw` that imports the code, `demoGraphicsView.py`, to invoke the user interface design, loads an image from the disk, and displays it through **Graphics View**. The Python script file, `callGraphicsView.pyw`, will include the following code:

```python
import sys
from PyQt5.QtWidgets import QDialog, QApplication, QGraphicsScene,
QGraphicsPixmapItem
from PyQt5.QtGui import QPixmap
from demoGraphicsView import *
class MyForm(QDialog):
    def __init__(self):
        super().__init__()
        self.ui = Ui_Dialog()
        self.ui.setupUi(self)
        self.scene = QGraphicsScene(self)
        pixmap= QtGui.QPixmap()
        pixmap.load("scene.jpg")
        item=QGraphicsPixmapItem(pixmap)
        self.scene.addItem(item)
        self.ui.graphicsView.setScene(self.scene)
if __name__=="__main__":
    app = QApplication(sys.argv)
    myapp = MyForm()
    myapp.show()
    sys.exit(app.exec_())
```

How it works...

In this application, you are using **Graphics View** to display an image. You add a graphics scene to the **Graphics View** widget, and you add QGraphicsPixmapItem. If you want to add an image to the graphics scene, you need to provide it in the form of a pixmap item. First, you need to represent the image as pixmap, and then you make it appear as a pixmap item before adding it to the graphics scene. You need to create an instance of QPixmap and specify the image that you want to display through its load() method. Then, you tag the pixmap item as pixmapitem by passing pixmap to the constructor of QGraphicsPixmapItem. pixmapitem is then added to the scene via addItem. If pixmapitem is bigger than QGraphicsView, scrolling is enabled automatically.

In the previous code, I used an image with the filename scene.jpg. Please replace the filename with an image filename that is available on your disk, or nothing will be displayed on the screen.

The following methods are used:

- QGraphicsView.setScene: This method (self, QGraphicsScene scene) assigns the scene that is supplied as a parameter to the GraphicView instance for display. If the scene is already being viewed, this function does nothing. When a scene is set on a view, the QGraphicsScene.changed signal is generated, and the view's scrollbars are adjusted to fit the size of the scene.
- addItem: This method adds the specified item to the scene. If an item is already in a different scene, it will first be removed from its old scene and then added to the current scene. On running the application, the scene.jpg image will be displayed via the GrahicsView widget, as shown in the following screenshot:

Making a ball move down on the click of a button

In this recipe, you will understand how a basic animation is applied on an object. This recipe will consist of a push button and a ball, and when the push button is pressed, the ball will start animating towards the ground.

How to do it...

To make this recipe, we will be making use of the QPropertyAnimation class. The setStartValue() and setEndValue() methods of the QPropertyAnimation class will be used to define the coordinates where the animation needs to start and end, respectively. The setDuration() method will be invoked to specify the delay in milliseconds between every animation move. The following is the step-by-step procedure to apply an animation:

1. Create a new application based on the **Dialog without Buttons** template.
2. Drag and drop a **Label** widget and one **Push Button** widget onto the form.
3. Set the **text** property of the **Push Button** widget to Move Down. We assume that you have a ball image on your computer with the filename coloredball.jpg.
4. Select its **pixmap** property to assign the ball image to the **Label** widget.
5. In the **pixmap** property, out of the two options, **Choose Resource** and **Choose File**, select the **Choose File** option, browse your disk, and select the coloredball.jpg file. The image of the ball will appear in place of the **Label** widget.
6. Set the **objectName** property of the **Push Button** widget to pushButtonPushDown and that of the **Label** widget to labelPic.
7. Save the application with the name demoAnimation1.ui. The application will appear as shown in the following screenshot:

The user interface created with Qt Designer is stored in a `.ui` file, which is an XML file that needs to be converted into Python code. On application of the `pyuic5` command utility, the `.ui` file is converted into a Python script. The generated Python script, `demoAnimation1.py`, can be seen in the source code bundle of this book.

8. Treat the `demoAnimation1.py` script as a header file, and import it into the file from which you will invoke its user interface design.

9. Create another Python file with the name `callAnimation1.pyw` and import the `demoAnimation1.py` code into it:

```python
import sys
from PyQt5.QtWidgets import QDialog, QApplication
from PyQt5.QtCore import QRect, QPropertyAnimation
from demoAnimation1 import *
class MyForm(QDialog):
    def __init__(self):
        super().__init__()
        self.ui = Ui_Dialog()
        self.ui.setupUi(self)
        self.ui.pushButtonMoveDown.clicked.connect(self.
        startAnimation)
        self.show()
    def startAnimation(self):
        self.anim = QPropertyAnimation(self.ui.labelPic,
        b"geometry")
        self.anim.setDuration(10000)
        self.anim.setStartValue(QRect(160, 70, 80, 80))
        self.anim.setEndValue(QRect(160, 70, 220, 220))
        self.anim.start()
if __name__=="__main__":
    app = QApplication(sys.argv)
    w = MyForm()
    w.show()
    sys.exit(app.exec_())
```

How it works...

You can see that the **click()** event of the **Push Button** widget with the **objectName** property pushButtonMoveDown is connected to the startAnimation method; when the push button is clicked, the startAnimation method is invoked. In the startAnimation method, you create an object of the QPropertyAnimation class and name it anim. While creating the QPropertyAnimation instance, you pass two arguments; the first is the **Label** widget to which you want to apply the animation and the second is the property that defines the object's attribute to which you want to apply the animation to the object's attribute. Because you want to apply an animation to the ball's geometry, you pass b"geometry" as the second attribute while defining the QPropertyAnimation object. After that, you specify the duration of the animation as 10000 milliseconds, meaning you want to change the geometry of the object after every 10,000 milliseconds. Through the setStartValue method, you specify the region that is the rectangular area where you want the animation to start, and by invoking the setEndValue method, you specify the rectangular region where you want to stop the animation. By invoking the start method, you initiate the animation; consequently, the ball moves down from the rectangular region specified through the setStartValue method until it reaches the rectangular region specified through the setEndValue method.

On running the application, you will find a push button and a **Label** widget representing the ball image on the screen, as shown in the following screenshot (left). On clicking the **Move Down** push button, the ball starts animating towards the ground and stop its animation at the region specified through the setEndValue method, as shown in the following screenshot (right):

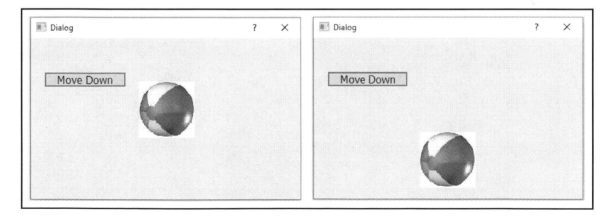

Making a bouncing ball

In this recipe, you will make a bouncing ball; when clicking a button, a ball falls towards the ground and on touching the ground, it bounces back to the top. In this recipe, you will understand how a basic animation is applied on an object. This recipe will consist of a push button and a ball, and when the push button is pressed, the ball will start animating towards the ground.

How to do it...

To make a ball appear to be bouncing, we need to make it first animate towards the ground, and then from the ground up to the sky. To do so, we will be invoking the `setKeyValueAt` method of the `QPropertyAnimation` class three times. The first and second calls to the `setKeyValueAt` method will make the ball animate from the top to the bottom. The third call to the `setKeyValueAt` method will make the ball animate from bottom to top. The coordinates in the three `setKeyValueAt` methods are provided so that the ball bounces in the opposite direction, and not where it came from. The following are the steps to understand how a ball can be animated to appear to be bouncing:

1. Create a new application based on the **Dialog without Buttons** template.
2. Drag and drop a **Label** widget and one **Push Button** widget onto the form.
3. Set the **text** property of the **Push Button** widget to `Bounce`. We assume that you have a ball image on your computer with the filename `coloredball.jpg`.
4. To assign the ball image to the **Label** widget, select its **pixmap** property.
5. In the **pixmap** property, out of the two options, `Choose Resource` and `Choose File`, select the **Choose File** option, browse your disk, and select the `coloredball.jpg` file. The image of the ball will appear in place of the **Label** widget.
6. Set the **objectName** property of the **Push Button** widget to `pushButtonBounce` and that of the **Label** widget to `labelPic`.
7. Save the application with the name `demoAnimation3.ui`.

The application will appear as shown in the following screenshot:

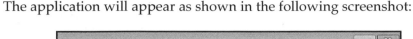

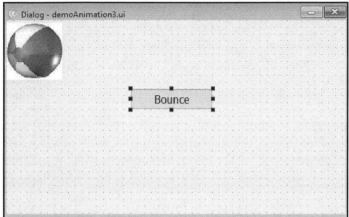

The user interface created with Qt Designer is stored in a `.ui` file, which is an XML file and needs to be converted into Python code. On application of the `pyuic5` command utility, the `.ui` file is converted into a Python script. The generated Python script, `demoAnimation3.py`, can be seen in the source code bundle of this book.

8. Treat the `demoAnimation3.py` script as a header file, and import it into the file from which you will invoke its user interface design.

9. Create another Python file with the name `callAnimation3.pyw` and import the `demoAnimation3.py` code into it:

```python
import sys
from PyQt5.QtWidgets import QDialog, QApplication
from PyQt5.QtCore import QRect, QPropertyAnimation
from demoAnimation3 import *
class MyForm(QDialog):
    def __init__(self):
        super().__init__()
        self.ui = Ui_Dialog()
        self.ui.setupUi(self)
        self.ui.pushButtonBounce.clicked.connect(self.
        startAnimation)
        self.show()
    def startAnimation(self):
        self.anim = QPropertyAnimation(self.ui.labelPic,
        b"geometry")
        self.anim.setDuration(10000)
        self.anim.setKeyValueAt(0, QRect(0, 0, 100, 80));
```

```
            self.anim.setKeyValueAt(0.5, QRect(160, 160, 200, 180));
            self.anim.setKeyValueAt(1, QRect(400, 0, 100, 80));
            self.anim.start()
    if __name__=="__main__":
        app = QApplication(sys.argv)
        w = MyForm()
        w.show()
        sys.exit(app.exec_())
```

How it works...

You can see that the **click()** event of the **Push Button** widget with the **objectName** property, pushButtonMoveDown, is connected to the startAnimation method; when the push button is clicked, the startAnimation method will be invoked. In the startAnimation method, you create an object of the QPropertyAnimation class and name it anim. While creating the QPropertyAnimation instance, you pass two arguments: the first is the **Label** widget to which you want to apply the animation, and the second is the property that defines the object's attribute to which you want to apply the animation to the object's attribute. Because you want to apply an animation to the ball's geometry, you pass b"geometry" as the second attribute while defining the QPropertyAnimation object. After that, you specify the duration of the animation as 10000 milliseconds, meaning you want to change the geometry of the object after every 10,000 milliseconds. Through the setKeyValue method, you specify the region that is the rectangular area where you want the animation to start. You mention the top-left region through this method because you want the ball to fall from the top-left corner towards the ground. Through the second call to the setKeyValue method, you supply the region in which you want the ball to fall to the ground. You also specify the angle of the fall. The ball will fall diagonally down towards the ground. By invoking the third setValue method, you specify the end value where you want the animation to stop, which in this case is in the top-right corner. Through these three calls to the setKeyValue method, you make the ball fall diagonally down towards the ground and then bounce back to the top-right corner. By invoking the start method, you initiate the animation.

On running the application, you will find the **Push Button** and **Label** widgets representing the ball image at the top-left corner of the screen, as shown in the following screenshot (left).

On clicking the **Bounce** push button, the ball starts animating diagonally down towards the ground, as shown in the middle screenshot, and after touching the ground, the ball bounces back towards the top-right corner of the screen, as shown on the right:

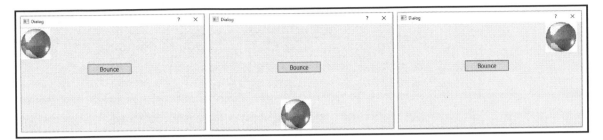

Making a ball animate as per the specified curve

A curve with the desired shape and size is created and a ball is set to move along the shape of the curve on the click of a push button. In this recipe, you will understand how to implement a guided animation.

How to do it...

The `setKeyValueAt` method of the `QPropertyAnimation` class determines the direction of an animation. For guided animation, you invoke the `setKeyValueAt` method in a loop. The coordinates of the curve are passed to the `setKeyValueAt` method in the loop to make the ball animate along the curve. Here are the steps to make an object animate as desired:

1. Create a new application based on the **Dialog without Buttons** template.
2. Drag and drop a **Label** widget and one **Push Button** widget onto the form.
3. Set the **text** property of the **Push Button** widget to Move With Curve.
4. Assuming you have a ball image on your computer with the filename `coloredball.jpg`, you can assign this ball image to the **Label** widget by using its **pixmap** property.
5. In the **pixmap** property, you will find two options, **Choose Resource** and **Choose File**; select the **Choose File** option, browse your disk, and select the `coloredball.jpg` file. The image of the ball will appear in place of the **Label** widget.

6. Set the **objectName** property of the **Push Button** widget to `pushButtonMoveCurve` and that of the **Label** widget to `labelPic`.

7. Save the application with the name `demoAnimation4.ui`. The application will appear as shown in the following screenshot:

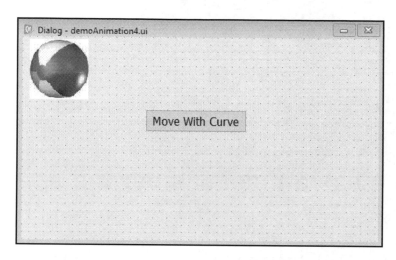

The user interface created with Qt Designer is stored in a `.ui` file and is an XML file. The XML file is converted into Python code by applying the `pyuic5` utility. You can find the generated Python code, `demoAnimation4.py`, in the source code bundle of this book.

8. Treat the `demoAnimation4.py` script as a header file, and import it into the file from which you will invoke its user interface design.

9. Create another Python file with the name `callAnimation4.pyw` and import the `demoAnimation4.py` code into it:

```
import sys
from PyQt5.QtWidgets import QDialog, QApplication
from PyQt5.QtCore import QRect, QPointF, QPropertyAnimation,
pyqtProperty
from PyQt5.QtGui import QPainter, QPainterPath
from demoAnimation4 import *
class MyForm(QDialog):
    def __init__(self):
        super().__init__()
        self.ui = Ui_Dialog()
        self.ui.setupUi(self)
        self.ui.pushButtonMoveCurve.clicked.connect(self.
        startAnimation)
```

```
            self.path = QPainterPath()
            self.path.moveTo(30, 30)
            self.path.cubicTo(30, 30, 80, 180, 180, 170)
            self.ui.labelPic.pos = QPointF(20, 20)
            self.show()
        def paintEvent(self, e):
            qp = QPainter()
            qp.begin(self)
            qp.drawPath(self.path)
            qp.end()
        def startAnimation(self):
            self.anim = QPropertyAnimation(self.ui.labelPic, b'pos')
            self.anim.setDuration(4000)
            self.anim.setStartValue(QPointF(20, 20))
            positionValues = [n/80 for n in range(0, 50)]
            for i in positionValues:
                self.anim.setKeyValueAt(i,
                self.path.pointAtPercent(i))
                self.anim.setEndValue(QPointF(160, 150))
                self.anim.start()
if __name__=="__main__":
    app = QApplication(sys.argv)
    w = MyForm()
    w.show()
    sys.exit(app.exec_())
```

How it works...

First of all, you make the curve appear on the screen. This is the curve that will guide the
ball's animation; that is, it will act as a path for the animation. You define an instance of the
QPainterPath class and name it **path**. You invoke the moveTo method of the
QPainterPath class to specify the starting location of the path or curve. The
cubicTo method is invoked to specify the curved path for the ball's animation.

You can see that the **click** event of the **Push Button** widget with the **objectName** property pushButtonMoveCurve is connected to the startAnimation method; when the **Push Button** widget is clicked, the startAnimation() method will be invoked. In the startAnimation method, you create an object of the QPropertyAnimation class and name it anim. While creating the QPropertyAnimation instance, you pass two arguments: the first is the **Label** widget to which you want to apply the animation, and the second is the property that defines the object's attribute to which you want to apply the animation to the object's attribute. Because you want to apply the animation to the ball's position, you pass b'pos" as the second attribute while defining the QPropertyAnimation object. After that, you specify the duration of the animation as 4000 milliseconds, meaning you want to change the position of the ball after every 4000 milliseconds. Using the setStartValue() method of the QPropertyAnimation class, you specify the coordinates from where you want the ball to animate. You set the for loop that specifies the values that the ball needs to move along. You specify the path of the ball's animation by invoking the setKeyValue method inside the for loop. Because the ball needs to be drawn at every point specified in the path, you set the point where the ball needs to be drawn by invoking the pointAtPercent() method and passing it to the setKeyValueAt() method. You also need to set the location where the animation needs to stop by invoking the setEndValue() method.

Shortly after, you specify the start and end locations of the animation, you specify the path of animation, and the paintEvent() method is called to redraw the ball at every point of the path.

On running the application, you find the **Push Button** widget and a **Label** widget representing the ball image in the top-left corner of the screen (left side of the screenshot) and on clicking the **Move With Curve** push button, the ball starts animating along the drawn curve and stops where the curve ends (right side of the screenshot):

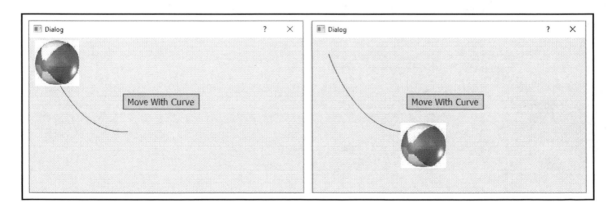

12

Using Google Maps

In this chapter, you will learn to use Google Maps in Python applications and explore the different advantages provided by Google. You will learn to do the following tasks:

- Find out details of a location or landmark
- Get complete information from latitude and longitude values
- Find out the distance between a two locations
- Display a location on Google Maps

Introduction

The Google Maps API is a set of methods and tools that can be used to find out complete information, including longitude and latitude values, for any location. You can use the Google Maps API methods to find distances between two locations or directions to any location; you can even display Google Maps, marking that location, and much more.

More precisely, there is a Python `client` library for Google Maps Services. There are several Google Maps APIs, including the Directions API, Distance Matrix API, Geocoding API, Geolocation API, and many more. To use any Google Maps web services, your Python script sends a request to Google; to serve that request, you need an API key. You need to follow these steps to get an API key:

1. Visit `https://console.developers.google.com`
2. Log in to the console using your Google account
3. Select one of your existing projects or create a new project
4. Enable the API(s) you want to use
5. Copy the API key and use it in your Python script

You need to visit the Google API Console, `https://console.developers.google.com`, and get API keys so that your application is authenticated to work with Google Maps API web services.

API keys help in several ways; first of all, they help identify your application. The API key is included with every request, hence it helps Google monitor your application's API usage, know if your application has consumed its free daily quota, and consequently bill your application too

So, in order to use Google Maps API web services in your Python application, you just need to enable the desired API and get a API key for use in your Python application.

Finding out details of a location or a landmark

In this recipe, you will be prompted to enter a location or landmark whose details you want to know. For example, if you enter `Buckingham Palace`, the recipe will display the city and postal code of the location where the palace is situated, along with its longitude and latitude values.

How to do it...

The search method of the `GoogleMaps` class is the key player in this recipe. The landmark or location entered by the user is passed to the search method. The `city`, `postal_code`, `lat`, and `lng` properties of the object returned from the search method are used to display the city, postal code, latitude, and longitude of the location, respectively. Let's see how it is done through the following step-by-step procedure:

1. Create an application based on the **Dialog without Buttons** template.
2. Add six `QLabel`, a `QLineEdit`, and a `QPushButton` widget to the form by dragging and dropping six **Label**, one **Line Edit**, and a **Push Button** widget onto the form.
3. Set the **text** property of the first **Label** widget to `Find out the City, Postal Code, Longitude and Latitude` and that of the second **Label** widget to `Enter location`.
4. Delete the **text** property of the third, fourth, fifth, and sixth **Label** widgets, because their **text** properties will be set through code; that is, the city, postal code, longitude, and latitude of the entered location will be fetched through code and will be displayed through these four **Label** widgets.
5. Set the **text** property of the **Push Button** widget to `Search`.
6. Set the **objectName** property of the **Line Edit** widget to `lineEditLocation`.

7. Set the **objectName** property of the **Push Button** widget to `pushButtonSearch`.

8. Set the **objectName** property of the rest of the four **Label** widgets to `labelCity`, `labelPostalCode`, `labelLongitude`, and `labelLatitude`.

9. Save the application by name as `demoGoogleMap1.ui`. The form will now appear as shown in the following screenshot:

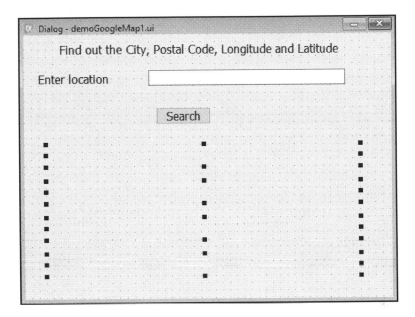

The user interface created with Qt Designer is stored in a `.ui` file and it is an XML file. The XML file is converted into Python code by applying the `pyuic5` utility. You can find the generated Python code, `demoGoogleMap1.py`, in the source code bundle for the book.

10. Treat the `demoGoogleMap1.py` script as a header file, and import it into the file from which you will invoke its user interface design.

11. Create another Python file with the name `callGoogleMap1.pyw` and import the `demoGoogleMap1.py` code into it:

```
import sys
from PyQt5.QtWidgets import QDialog, QApplication
from geolocation.main import GoogleMaps
from demoGoogleMap1 import *
class MyForm(QDialog):
    def __init__(self):
        super().__init__()
```

```
                self.ui = Ui_Dialog()
                self.ui.setupUi(self)
                self.ui.pushButtonSearch.clicked.connect(self.
                displayDetails)
                self.show()
            def displayDetails(self):
                address = str(self.ui.lineEditLocation.text())
                google_maps = GoogleMaps(api_key=
                'xxxxxxxxxxxxxxxxxxxxxxxxxxxx')
                location = google_maps.search(location=address)
                my_location = location.first()
                self.ui.labelCity.setText("City:
                "+str(my_location.city))
                self.ui.labelPostalCode.setText("Postal Code: "
                +str(my_location.postal_code))
                self.ui.labelLongitude.setText("Longitude:
                "+str(my_location.lng))
                self.ui.labelLatitude.setText("Latitude:
                "+str(my_location.lat))
    if __name__=="__main__":
        app = QApplication(sys.argv)
        w = MyForm()
        w.show()
        sys.exit(app.exec_())
```

How it works...

You can see in the script that the **click** event of the push button with the **objectName** property pushButtonSearch s connected to the displayDetails method. This means that, whenever the push button is clicked, the displayDetails method will be invoked. In the displayDetails method, you access the location entered by the user in the **Line Edit** widget and assign that location to the address variable. You define a Google Maps instance by passing the API key that you got on registering with Google. Invoke the search method on the Google Maps instance, passing the location entered by the user in this method. The result of the search method is assigned to the my_location structure. The city member of the my_location structure contains the city entered by the user. Similarly, the postal_code, lng, and lat members of the my_location structure contain the postal code, longitude, and latitude information of the location entered by the user, respectively. The city, postal code, longitude, and latitude information are displayed via the last four **Label** widgets.

On running the application, you will be prompted to enter a location you want to find information about. Suppose you enter `Taj Mahal` in the location, followed by clicking the **Search** button. The city, postal code, longitude, and latitude information of the Taj Mahal landmark will be displayed on the screen, as shown in the following screenshot:

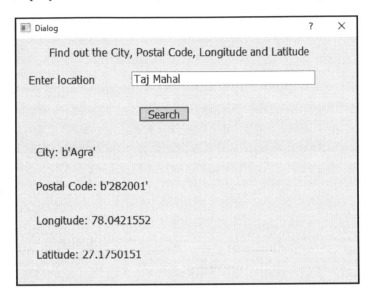

Getting complete information from latitude and longitude values

In this recipe, you will learn how to find out the complete details of a location whose longitude and latitude values you know. This process of converting a point location, that is, latitude and longitude values, into a readable address (the place name, city, country name, and so on) is known as **reverse geocoding**.

The application will prompt you to enter longitude and latitude values, and then it will display the matching location name, city, country, and postal code for that location.

How to do it...

Let's create an application based on the **Dialog without Buttons** template by performing the following steps:

1. Add seven QLabel, two QLineEdit, and a QPushButton widget to the form by dragging and dropping seven **Label**, two **Line Edit**, and a **Push Button** widget onto the form.

2. Set the **text** property of the first **Label** widget to Find out the Location, City, Country and Postal Code, that of the second **Label** widget to Enter Longitude, and that of the third **Label** widget to Enter Latitude.

3. Delete the **text** properties of the fourth, fifth, sixth, and seventh **Label** widgets because their **text** properties will be set through code; that is, the location, city, country, and postal code of the location whose longitude and latitude are entered by the user will be accessed through code and will be displayed through these four **Label** widgets.

4. Set the **text** property of the **Push Button** widget to Search.

5. Set the **objectName** property of the two **Line Edit** widgets to lineEditLongitude and lineEditLatitude.

6. Set the **objectName** property of the **Push Button** widget to pushButtonSearch.

7. Set the **objectName** property of the other four **Label** widgets to labelLocation, labelCity, labelCountry, and labelPostalCode.

8. Save the application by name as demoGoogleMap2.ui. The form will now appear as shown in the following screenshot:

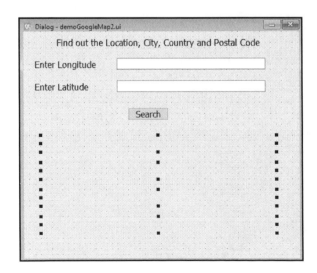

The user interface created with Qt Designer is stored in a `.ui` file, which is an XML file and needs to be converted into Python code. The `pyuic5` utility is used to convert the XML file into Python code. The generated Python script, `demoGoogleMap2.py`, can be seen in the source code bundle for the book.

9. Treat the `demoGoogleMap2.py` script as a header file, and import it into the file from which you will invoke its user interface design.

10. Create another Python file with the name `callGoogleMap2.pyw` and import the `demoGoogleMap2.py` code into it:

```python
import sys
from PyQt5.QtWidgets import QDialog, QApplication
from geolocation.main import GoogleMaps
from demoGoogleMap2 import *
class MyForm(QDialog):
    def __init__(self):
        super().__init__()
        self.ui = Ui_Dialog()
        self.ui.setupUi(self)
        self.ui.pushButtonSearch.clicked.connect(self.
        displayLocation)
        self.show()
    def displayLocation(self):
        lng = float(self.ui.lineEditLongitude.text())
        lat = float(self.ui.lineEditLatitude.text())
        google_maps = GoogleMaps(api_key=
        'AIzaSyDzCMD-JTg-IbJZZ9fKGE1lipbBiFRiGHA')
        my_location = google_maps.search(lat=lat, lng=lng).
        first()
        self.ui.labelLocation.setText("Location:
        "+str(my_location))
        self.ui.labelCity.setText("City:
        "+str(my_location.city))
        self.ui.labelCountry.setText("Country:
        "+str(my_location.country))
        self.ui.labelPostalCode.setText("Postal Code:
        "+str(my_location.postal_code))
if __name__=="__main__":
    app = QApplication(sys.argv)
    w = MyForm()
    w.show()
    sys.exit(app.exec_())
```

How it works...

In the script, you can see that the **click()** event of the push button with the **objectName** property `pushButtonSearch` is connected to the `displayLocation` method. This means that, whenever the push button is clicked, the `displayLocation` method will be invoked. In the `displayLocation` method, you access the longitude and latitude entered by the user through the two **Line Edit** widgets and assign them to two variables, `lng` and `lat`, respectively. A Google Maps instance is defined by passing the API key that you got on registering with Google. Invoke the `search` method on the Google Maps instance, passing the longitude and latitude values that were supplied by the user. The `first` method is invoked on the retrieved search and the first location that matches the supplied longitude and latitude values is assigned to the `my_location` structure. The location name is displayed through the **Label** widget. To display the city, country, and postal code of the location, the `city`, `country`, and `postal_code` members of the `my_location` structure are used.

On running the application, you will be prompted to enter longitude and latitude values. The location name, city, country, and postal code related to the supplied longitude and latitude will be displayed on the screen through the four **Label** widgets, as shown in the following screenshot:

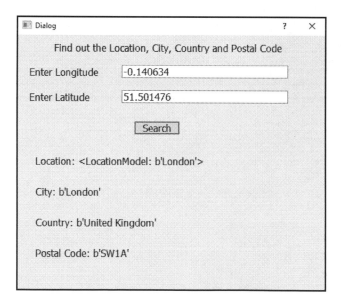

Finding out the distance between two locations

In this recipe, you will learn how to find out the distance in kilometers between the two locations entered by the user. The recipe will simply prompt the user to enter two locations, followed by clicking the **Find Distance** button, and the distance between the two will be displayed.

How to do it...

Let's create an application based on the Dialog without Buttons template by performing the following steps:

1. Add four `QLabel`, two `QLineEdit`, and a `QPushButton` widget to the form by dragging and dropping four **Label**, two **Line Edit**, and a **Push Button** widget onto the form.
2. Set the **text** property of the first **Label** widget to `Find out the distance between two locations`, that of the second **Label** widget to `Enter first location`, and that of the third **Label** widget to `Enter second location`.
3. Delete the **text** property of the fourth **Label** widget because its **text** property will be set through code; that is, the distance between the two entered locations will be computed through code and displayed in the fourth **Label** widget.
4. Set the **text** property of the **Push Button** widget to `Find Distance`.
5. Set the **objectName** properties of the two **Line Edit** widgets to `lineEditFirstLocation` and `lineEditSecondLocation`.
6. Set the **objectName** property of the **Push Button** widget to `pushButtonFindDistance`.
7. Set the **objectName** property of the fourth **Label** widget to `labelDistance`.

8. Save the application by name as `demoGoogleMap3.ui`. The form will now appear as shown in the following screenshot:

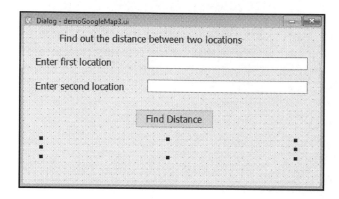

The user interface created with Qt Designer is stored in a `.ui` file and it is an XML file. The XML file is converted into Python code by applying the `pyuic5` utility. You can find the generated Python code, `demoGoogleMap3.py`, in the source code bundle for the book.

9. To use the GUI created in the `demoGoogleMap3.py` file, we need to create another Python script and import `demoGoogleMap3.py` file in that script.

10. Create another Python file with the name `callGoogleMap3.pyw` and import the `demoGoogleMap3.py` code into it:

```python
import sys
from PyQt5.QtWidgets import QDialog, QApplication
from googlemaps.client import Client
from googlemaps.distance_matrix import distance_matrix
from demoGoogleMap3 import *
class MyForm(QDialog):
    def __init__(self):
        super().__init__()
        self.ui = Ui_Dialog()
        self.ui.setupUi(self)
        self.ui.pushButtonFindDistance.clicked.connect(self.
        displayDistance)
        self.show()
    def displayDistance(self):
        api_key = 'xxxxxxxxxxxxxxxxxxxxxxxxxxxxxxxxxxxxxxxxx'
        gmaps = Client(api_key)
        data = distance_matrix(gmaps,
        self.ui.lineEditFirstLocation.text(),
        self.ui.lineEditSecondLocation.text())
```

```
                    distance = data['rows'][0]['elements'][0]['distance']
                    ['text']
                    self.ui.labelDistance.setText("Distance between
                    "+self.ui.lineEditFirstLocation.text()+"
                    and "+self.ui.lineEditSecondLocation.text()+" is
                    "+str(distance))
        if __name__=="__main__":
            app = QApplication(sys.argv)
            w = MyForm()
            w.show()
            sys.exit(app.exec_())
```

How it works...

You create an instance of the `Client` class and name it `gmaps`. While creating the `Client` instance, you need to pass the API key that you got on registering with Google. The **click()** event of the push button with **objectName**, `pushButtonFindDistance`, is connected to the `displayDistance` method. This means that, whenever the push button is clicked, the `displayDistance` method will be invoked. In the `displayDistance` method, you invoke the `distance_matrix` method, passing the `Client` instance and the two locations entered by the user, to find out the distance between them. The `distance_matrix` method returns a multidimensional array that is assigned to the data array. From the data array, the distance between the two locations is accessed and assigned to the `distance` variable. The value in the `distance` variable is finally displayed through the **Label** widget.

On running the application, you will be prompted to enter the two locations whose intervening distance you want to know. After entering the two locations, when you click the **Find Distance** button, the distance between the two locations will be displayed on the screen, as shown in the following screenshot:

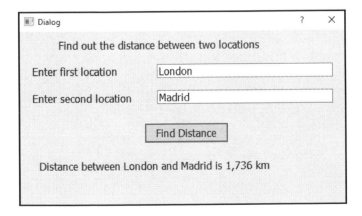

Displaying location on Google Maps

In this recipe, you will learn how to display a location on Google Maps if you know the longitude and latitude values of that location. You will be prompted to simply enter longitude and latitude values and, when you click the **Show Map** button, that location will appear on Google Maps.

How to do it...

Let's create an application based on the **Dialog without Buttons** template by performing the following steps:

1. Add two `QLabel`, two `QLineEdit`, a `QPushButton`, and a `QWidget` widget to the form by dragging and dropping two **Label**, two **Line Edit**, a **Push Button**, and a **Widget** container onto the form.

2. Set the text property of the two **Label** widgets to `Longitude` and `Latitude`.

3. Set the **text** property of the **Push Button** widget to `Show Map`.

4. Set the **objectName** property of the two **Line Edit** widgets to `lineEditLongitude` and `lineEditLatitude`.

5. Set the **objectName** property of the **Push Button** widget to `pushButtonShowMap`.

6. Save the application by name as `showGoogleMap.ui`. The form will now appear as shown in the following screenshot:

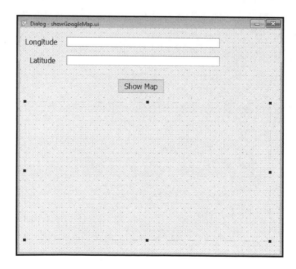

7. The next step is to promote the `QWidget` widget to `QWebEngineView` because, to display Google Maps, `QWebEngineView` is required. Because Google maps is a web application, we need a QWebEngineView to display and interact with Google maps.

8. Promote the `QWidget` widget by right-clicking on it and selecting the **Promote to ...** option from the menu that pops up. In the dialog box that appears, leave the **Base class name** option as the default, **QWidget**.

9. In the **Promoted class name** box, enter `QWebEngineView` and, in the header file box, type `PyQT5.QtWebEngineWidgets`.

10. Click on the **Promote** button to promote the `QWidget` widget to the `QWebEngineView` class, as shown in the following screenshot:

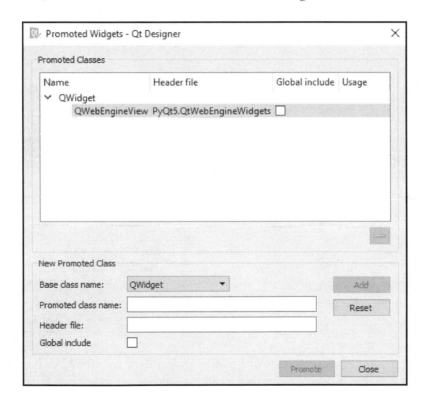

11. Click on the **Close** button to close the **Promoted Widgets** dialog box. The user interface created with Qt Designer is stored in a `.ui` file, which is an XML file and needs to be converted into Python code. The `pyuic5` utility is used to convert the XML file into Python code. The generated Python script, `showGoogleMap.py`, can be seen in the source code bundle for the book.

12. Treat the `showGoogleMap.py` script as a header file, and import it into the file from which you will invoke its user interface design.

13. Create another Python file with the name `callGoogleMap.pyw` and import the `showGoogleMap.py` code into it:

```python
import sys
from PyQt5.QtCore import QUrl
from PyQt5.QtWidgets import QApplication, QDialog
from PyQt5.QtWebEngineWidgets import QWebEngineView
from showGoogleMap import *
class MyForm(QDialog):
    def __init__(self):
        super().__init__()
        self.ui = Ui_Dialog()
        self.ui.setupUi(self)
        self.ui.pushButtonShowMap.clicked.connect(self.dispSite)
        self.show()
    def dispSite(self):
        lng = float(self.ui.lineEditLongitude.text())
        lat = float(self.ui.lineEditLatitude.text())
        URL="https://www.google.com/maps/@"+self.ui.
        lineEditLatitude.text()+","
        +self.ui.lineEditLongitude.text()+",9z"
        self.ui.widget.load(QUrl(URL))
if __name__=="__main__":
    app = QApplication(sys.argv)
    w = MyForm()
    w.show()
    sys.exit(app.exec_())
```

How it works...

In the script, you can see that the **click** event of the push button with the **objectName** property `pushButtonShowMap` is connected to the `dispSite ()` method. This means that, whenever the push button is clicked, the `dispSite()` method will be invoked. In the `dispSite ()` method, you access the longitude and latitude entered by the user through the two **Line Edit** widgets, and assign them to two variables, `lng` and `lat`, respectively. Thereafter, you create a URL that invokes Google Maps from `google.com` and passes the latitude and longitude values entered by the user. The URL is initially in text form and is typecast to a `QUrl` instance and passed to the widget that is promoted to `QWebEngineView` to display the website. The `QUrl` is a class from Qt that provides several methods and properties to manage URLs. Google Maps, with the specified latitude and longitude values, is then displayed via the `QWebEngineView` widget.

On running the application, you will be prompted to enter the longitude and latitude values of the location you want to see on Google Maps. After entering the longitude and latitude values, when you click on the **Show Map** button, Google Maps will display that location, as shown in the following screenshot:

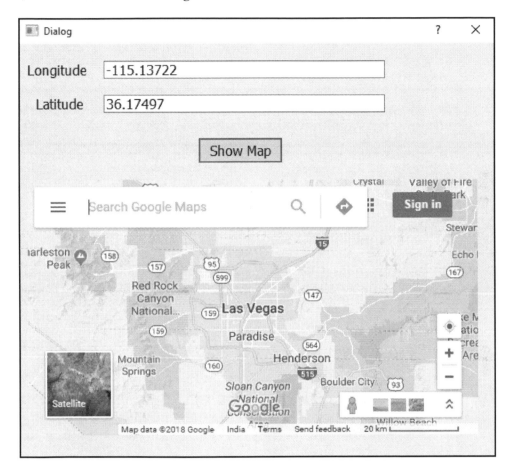

13
Running Python Scripts on Android and iOS

In this chapter, you will learn to run Python scripts on Android devices as well as on iOS. You will learn about the following topics:

- Copying scripts from PC to Android devices
- Prompting for a username and displaying a welcome message
- Understanding different buttons in a Dialog box
- Performing single selection from a list
- Performing multiple selections from a list
- Displaying a Date Picker dialog
- Capturing images using a camera
- Making an Android device speak a text input
- Creating a cross-platform Python script using Kivy
- Packaging a Python script into the Android APK using Buildozer
- Packaging Python script for iOS

In order to run Python scripts on Android devices, we will be making use of QPython3.

Introduction

What is QPython3? QPython3 is a script engine that enables you to run Python scripts on Android devices. Basically, it provides you with Python on Android as it contains the Python interpreter, console, editor, and the `SL4A` library, making it possible for you to type, edit, debug, and run Python scripts on Android devices. Not only can you run Python scripts on Android devices, but you can access device sensors too. You can even access Android APIs, such as SMS, GPS, NFC, and Bluetooth.

So, let's download QPython3 from the Google Play store and install it. When QPython3 is launched on your Android device, it will appear as shown in the following screenshot:

The first screen shows following several tools:

- **Console**: This opens the Python interpreter, allowing us to type Python commands and execute them directly
- **Editor**: This opens up a text editor where you can write, save, debug, and run code
- **Programs**: This is used to find your scripts and projects on your device
- **QPYPI**: This opens the QPYPI page in the browser, allowing you to install the packages listed there
- **course**: This opens the page showing links for courses and tutorials on Kivy, Kivy on QPython, QSL4A Android Script Library, and much more
- **Community**: This opens the **Community** page, where you can ask QPython questions and find answers

Editor is the place where you will be spending most of your time. On clicking the **Editor** icon, the **Editor** window will open, as shown in the following screenshot. The **Editor** window has several icons at the top as well as at the bottom. At the top are the following two icons:

- **QEdit - Open File**: This opens the existing folder on the device, enabling you to open any existing Python script.
- **New ...**: When you click this icon, you will be asked what kind of file you want to open, that is, whether it is **Blank file**, **Script**, **WebApp (Project)**, **ConsoleApp (Project)**, or **KivyApp (Project)**. Select the desired option and create the file. After creating the file, you will be sent back to the **Editor** screen to type the content for the newly created file.

The icons at the bottom of the **Editor** screen are used for saving the file, searching in the file, running the file, undoing any action, running the Save as ... command to save the current file by another name, and so on:

Copying scripts from PC to Android devices

To run QPython scripts on an Android device, either you can type them directly into QPython's editor on the device, or you can type on your PC and then copy them to the Android device for execution. We'll walk through the process of copying from PC to Android.

How to do it

Here is the step-by-step procedure to connect an Android device with a PC and copy the QPython script to it:

1. Connect your Android phone with your PC using a USB cable.
2. When you connect your Android phone to the PC, several USB options will appear; select the **Turn ON the USB debugging** option.
3. By turning USB debugging on, you can execute different commands on the Android device and run different tools as well.
4. To confirm that the Android device is connected properly and is recognized by your PC, use the `adb devices` command, as shown here:

   ```
   C:\Users\Bintu>adb devices
   ```

   The following output confirms that my Android device is recognized by my PC:

   ```
   List of devices attached
   d56ab82e device
   ```

   Android Debug Bridge (**ADB**) is a command-line utility that is bundled with the Android SDK. Using ADB, you can interact with your device through your PC. You can install and run apps, run shell commands, copy and delete files, and much more.

5. In order to see all the existing files in your Android device, run the `adb shell` command. The `adb shell` command will open the interactive Linux command-line shell on your Android device and you will get the $ prompt as follows:

   ```
   C:\Users\Bintu>adb shell
   shell@kenzo:/ $
   ```

The preceding $ prompt shows that you are no more on your PC but there are on your Android device. On installing QPython on your device, a directory will be created named qpython on the SD card of your device. You can change directory to SD card and list the files in it, as shown here:

```
shell@kenzo:/ $ cd sdcardshell@kenzo:/sdcard $ cd qpython
shell@kenzo:/sdcard/qpython $ ls -l
drwxrwx--x root sdcard_rw 2018-06-04 12:08 cache
drwxrwx--x root sdcard_rw 2018-06-04 12:09 lib
drwxrwx--x root sdcard_rw 2018-06-04 12:11 projects3
drwxrwx--x root sdcard_rw 2018-06-07 20:43 scripts3
drwxrwx--x root sdcard_rw 2018-06-04 12:08 snippets3
```

6. To keep our Python scripts in a separate folder, we will create a new directory named bintuscripts in the qpython folder, as shown here:

```
shell@kenzo:/sdcard/qpython $ mkdir bintuscripts
```

7. To exit from the interactive Linux command-line shell on your Android device, write the exit command followed by hitting the *Enter* key:

```
shell@kenzo:/sdcard/qpython $ exit
```

With the preceding command line, you will be back to the Command Prompt of your PC.

8. We're assuming that you have a folder on your PC called QPythonScripts that contains certain Python scripts and you want to copy or push a Python script from your PC into your Android device.
9. The following is the command line to be used in order to copy a Python script called WelcomeMessage.py from the current folder of your PC into the folder called bintuscripts in the SD card of your Android device:

```
C:\Users\Bintu\QPythonScripts>adb push WelcomeMessage.py
/sdcard/qpython/bintuscripts
```

If the preceding command line is executed successfully, you get the following message:

```
WelcomeMessage.py: 1 file pushed. 0.0 MB/s (333 bytes in 0.016s)
```

10. Once copied to the Android device, you can launch QPython3 on your Android device; open the **Editor** page, followed by opening the script that you copied to the device.

11. You can run the script to see the output.

12. In order to take a screenshot of the script run on your Android device and copy the screenshot to your PC, execute the following command line:

```
C:\Users\Bintu\QPythonScripts>adb shell screencap -p
/sdcard/screencap.png && adb pull /sdcard/screencap.png
```

The preceding command will save the screenshot of the Android screen to the SD card with the name `screencap.png` (you can give it any name), and this pulls that PNG file from the SD card to your current folder of your PC and saves it with the same name.

If this command is executed successfully, you get the following message confirming that the screenshot was successfully copied onto your PC:

```
/sdcard/screencap.png: 1 file pulled. 0.8 MB/s (12491 bytes in
0.016s)
```

Prompting for a username and displaying a welcome message

This recipe will prompt the user to enter a name, and when the user clicks the **OK** button after entering a name, they are greeted with an alert box with the text **Hello**, followed by the name entered by the user.

How to do it...

In this recipe, we will be making use of the following methods:

- `dialogGetInput()`: This method is used to take input from the user
- `app.dialogCreateAlert()`: This method is used to greet the user
- `app.dialogSetPositiveButtonText()`: This method is used to display positive button text and to keep the dialog box visible until the user presses the **OK** button

Let's take a look at the following steps:

1. Type the following code in the Python script `WelcomeMessage.py` in the current folder:

```
import android
app = android.Android()
name = app.dialogGetInput("Enter Your Information", "Name:
").result
app.dialogDismiss()
app.dialogCreateAlert("Welcome", "Hello %s" % name)
app.dialogSetPositiveButtonText('OK')
app.dialogShow()
```

2. Copy or push this Python script into the Android device by using the following command line:

```
C:\Users\Bintu\QPythonScripts>adb push WelcomeMessage.py
/sdcard/qpython/bintuscripts
```

How it works...

You invoke the `Android()` method of the `android` module to create an object called `app`. It is through this `app` object that you will communicate with Android. You show a dialog box prompting the user to enter his/her name. The name entered by the user is assigned to the `name` variable. You invoke the `dialogDismiss()` method to dismiss the dialog or make it invisible once the user presses the *Enter* key after entering a name, or presses the **OK** button.

Thereafter, you welcome the user by displaying an alert box that shows **Hello**, followed by the name of the user. To keep the alert box visible until the user sees it, a dialog box is displayed with the **OK** button in it. The welcome message will be visible until the user presses the **OK** button to close the dialog box.

A dialog is displayed using the **dialogShow()** method and is dismissed using the `dialogDismiss()` method.

On running the application, you will find a dialog box asking you to enter your name, as shown in the following left screenshot. After entering a name, when you click the **OK** button, you will be greeted with the **Hello** message, followed by the name entered by you (in the right screenshot). The dialog box displaying the greeting message will remain there until you close the dialog by clicking the **OK** button, as shown in the following screenshot:

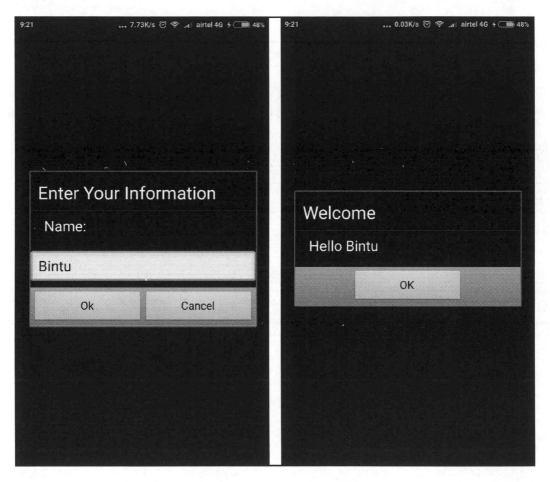

You can even display a welcome message through the Toast() method, as shown in the following statement:

```
app.makeToast("Welcome", "Hello %s" % name)
```

The only drawback is that the `Toast` output vanishes automatically after a specified duration. It doesn't wait for the user to press any key.

Understanding different buttons in a dialog box

This recipe will display a dialog box with three buttons: **Yes**, **Cancel**, and **No**. When the user clicks a button, the respective message will be displayed, informing you of which button was pressed by the user. The idea is to understand the response generated when any button is pressed and take action accordingly.

How to do it...

In this recipe, we will be making use of the following methods:

- `dialogCreateAlert()`: This method is used to display a message via a dialog box
- `dialogSetPositiveButtonText()`: This method is used to display the **Yes** button in a dialog box
- `dialogSetNegativeButtonText()`: This method is used to display the **No** button in a dialog box
- `dialogSetNeutralButtonText()`: This method is used to display the **Cancel** button in a dialog box
- `dialogGetResponse()`: This method is used to take the response from the user via a dialog box

Take a look at the following steps:

1. Type the following code in the Python script `demoDialog.py` in the current folder of your computer:

```
import android
app = android.Android()
title = 'Understanding Dialog Buttons'
message = ('Do you want to Place the Order?')
app.dialogCreateAlert(title, message)
app.dialogSetPositiveButtonText('Yes')
app.dialogSetNegativeButtonText('No')
app.dialogSetNeutralButtonText('Cancel')
```

The only drawback is that the `Toast` output vanishes automatically after a specified duration. It doesn't wait for the user to press any key.

Understanding different buttons in a dialog box

This recipe will display a dialog box with three buttons: **Yes**, **Cancel**, and **No**. When the user clicks a button, the respective message will be displayed, informing you of which button was pressed by the user. The idea is to understand the response generated when any button is pressed and take action accordingly.

How to do it...

In this recipe, we will be making use of the following methods:

- `dialogCreateAlert()`: This method is used to display a message via a dialog box
- `dialogSetPositiveButtonText()`: This method is used to display the **Yes** button in a dialog box
- `dialogSetNegativeButtonText()`: This method is used to display the **No** button in a dialog box
- `dialogSetNeutralButtonText()`: This method is used to display the **Cancel** button in a dialog box
- `dialogGetResponse()`: This method is used to take the response from the user via a dialog box

Take a look at the following steps:

1. Type the following code in the Python script `demoDialog.py` in the current folder of your computer:

```
import android
app = android.Android()
title = 'Understanding Dialog Buttons'
message = ('Do you want to Place the Order?')
app.dialogCreateAlert(title, message)
app.dialogSetPositiveButtonText('Yes')
app.dialogSetNegativeButtonText('No')
app.dialogSetNeutralButtonText('Cancel')
```

```
app.dialogShow()
response = app.dialogGetResponse().result
print(response)
app.dialogDismiss()
result=response["which"]
if result=="positive":
    print ("You have selected Yes button")elif result=="negative":
    print ("You have selected No button")elif result=="neutral":
    print ("You have selected Cancel button")
else:
    print ("Invalid response",response)
```

2. Copy or push this Python script into the Android device by using the following command line:

```
C:\Users\Bintu\QPythonScripts>adb push demoDialog.py
/sdcard/qpython/bintuscripts
```

How it works...

An instance or object called `app` is created by executing the `Android()` method of the `android` module. A dialog box is displayed with the title **Understanding Dialog Buttons**. The dialog box will display a message, **Do you want to Place the Order?** Below the message will be three buttons: **Yes**, **No**, and **Cancel**. The **Yes** button will be displayed by invoking the `dialogSetPositiveButtonText()` method. Similarly, the **No** and **Cancel** buttons will be created by invoking the `dialogSetNegativeButtonText()` and `dialogSetNeutralButtonText()` methods, respectively. By invoking the `dialogGetResponse()` method, you determine the response of the dialog box, that is, you know which button is pressed by the user. The information on the button pressed by the user is assigned to the response array. That is, the `which` element of the `response` array stores the information of the button pressed by the user. The `which` element of the `response` array will have a `positive` value if the **Yes** button is pressed, it will have a `negative` value if the **No** button is pressed, and it will have a `Neutral` value if the **Cancel** button is pressed. By observing the value assigned to the `which` element of the `response` array, the respective message is displayed on the screen.

The `dialogGetResponse()` method is used for taking input from the user, and it blocks until the user responds to the dialog.

On running the application, you will get a dialog asking whether you want to place an order. Depending on your choice, you can press the **Yes**, **Cancel**, or **No** button (see the following screenshot, on the left). Assuming you press the **Cancel** button, the `which` element of the `response` array will be assigned a `neutral` value. The `which` element is set to pass through the `if elif` ladder to display a message on the basis of the value assigned to it. The message, **You have selected Cancel button**, will be displayed (see the following screenshot, on the right):

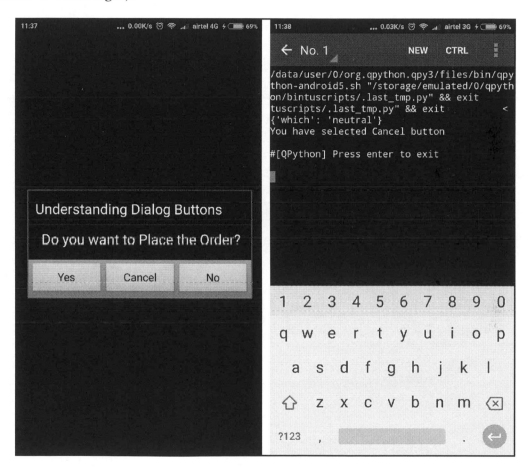

Performing single selection from a list

This recipe will display a dialog box, showing a list of items, allowing the user to select one of them. The name of the selected item will be displayed via another dialog box.

How to do it...

In this recipe, we will be making use of the following methods:

- dialogCreateAlert(): This method is used to display a message via the dialog box
- dialogSetItems(): This method is used to define the array of items to be displayed in the list
- dialogGetResponse(): This method is used to get a response from the user

Take a look at the following steps:

1. First type the following code in the Python script demoSingleSelection.py, in the current folder of your computer:

```python
import android
app = android.Android()
app.dialogCreateAlert("Select your food item")
app.dialogSetItems(['Pizza', 'Burger', 'Hot Dog'])
app.dialogShow()
response = app.dialogGetResponse().result
selectedResult=response["item"]
if selectedResult==0:
    app.dialogCreateAlert("You have selected Pizza")
elif selectedResult==1:
    app.dialogCreateAlert("You have selected Burger")
elif selectedResult==2:
    app.dialogCreateAlert("You have selected Hot Dog")
    app.dialogSetPositiveButtonText('OK')
    app.dialogShow()
```

2. Copy or push this Python script into the Android device by using the following command:

```
C:\Users\Bintu\QPythonScripts>adb push demoSingleSelection.py
/sdcard/qpython/bintuscripts
```

How it works...

An object of the `Android` class is created by the name `app`. Using the `dialogSetItems()` method, three food items, **Pizza**, **Burger**, and **Hot Dog**, are displayed in the form of a list in the dialog box. The `dialogGetResponse()` method is invoked to find the item selected by the user. The user's selection is assigned to the `response` array and the index value of the food item selected by the user will be assigned to the `item` element of the `response` array. The index value in the `item` element of the `response` array is accessed and assigned to the `selectedResult` variable. The value in the `selectedResult` variable will be 0 if the first food item in the list is selected, 1 if the second food item in the list is selected, and so on. Using the `if elif` ladder, the value in the `selectedResult` variable is branched to display the food item selected by the user. The selected food item is displayed via another dialog box. To keep the dialog box visible until the user presses the **OK** button, the dialog box is accompanied by an **OK** button. After looking at the selected food item, when the user clicks the **OK** button, the dialog box goes away.

On running the application, you get a dialog box showing three food items, **Pizza**, **Burger**, and **Hot Dog**, as shown in the following screenshot on the left. On selecting any food item, the selected food item will be displayed via another dialog box, as shown in the following screenshot on the right:

Performing multiple selections from a list

This recipe will show a list of items on an Android device, allowing you to select more than one item from the list, hence enabling multiple selections from the list.

How to do it...

In this recipe, we will be making use of the following methods:

- `dialogCreateAlert()`: To display a message via the dialog box
- `dialogSetMultiChoiceItems()`: To define the array of items to be displayed in list format in the dialog for multiple selections
- `dialogSetPositiveButtonText()`: To display a button in the dialog box to indicate that all selections are complete
- `dialogGetSelectedItems()`: To get the array of selected items

Take a look at the following steps:

1. Type the following code in the Python script `demoMultipleSelection.py` in the current folder of your computer:

```
import android
app = android.Android()
app.dialogCreateAlert("Select your food items")
app.dialogSetMultiChoiceItems(['Pizza', 'Burger', 'Hot Dog'])
app.dialogSetPositiveButtonText('Done')
app.dialogShow()
app.dialogGetResponse()
response = app.dialogGetSelectedItems()
print(response)
selectedResult=response[1]
n=len(selectedResult)
print("You have selected following food items: ")
for i in range(0, n):
    if selectedResult[i]==0:
        print("Pizza")elif selectedResult[i]==1:
        print("Burger")elif selectedResult[i]==2:
        print("Hot Dog")
```

2. Copy or push this Python script into the Android device by using the following command:

```
C:\Users\Bintu\QPythonScripts>adb push demoMultipleSelection.py
/sdcard/qpython/bintuscripts
```

How it works...

An object `Android` class is created by the `name` app. A dialog box is created with a message stating **select your food items**. The `dialogSetMultiChoiceItems()` method is invoked to display a list of food items, allowing the user to select more than one item. To indicate that the user is done selecting food items, the `dialogSetPositiveButtonText()` method is invoked to display the **Done** button that the user can click to state that he/she is done with selecting food items. The user can select any number of food items. The `dialogGetSelectedItems()` method is invoked to get the list of selected food items and the chosen list is assigned to the response array. The `response` array is a multidimensional array and at its index location, `1`, is a single dimensional array which contains the list of chosen food items. So, the array at the index 1 location from `response` is accessed and assigned to `selectedResult` single dimensional array. The length of the `selectedResult` array determines the number of food items selected by the user. If the user selects two items, their index locations will be stored in the `selectedResult` array. For example, if the user selects the first and third food items, then the `selectedResult` array will contain the values 0 and 2 because the array is zero-based. A `for` loop is used and every element of the `selectedResult` array is accessed; depending on its value, the name of the food item is displayed.

On running the application, you get a dialog box showing a list of food items, allowing the user to select more than one food item. Let's assume that the user selects the first and third food item followed by clicking the **Done** button (see the below figure on left). The list of selected food items will be displayed, as shown in the following screenshot on the right:

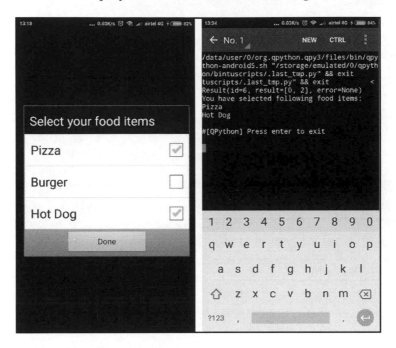

Displaying a Date Picker dialog

In this recipe, you will learn to display a date picker dialog, allowing the user to scroll through days, months, and years to select the desired date.

How to do it...

In this recipe, we will be making use of the following methods:

- `dialogCreateDatePicker()`: This method is used to display the date with the specified initial date
- `dialogGetResponse()`: This method is used to get the response, that is, the selection made by the user

- `dialogDismiss()`: This method is used to make the dialog box invisible after a selection been made by the user
- `get("day")`: This method is used to access the day in the `Date` type object
- `get("month")`: This method is used to access the month in the `Date` type object
- `get("year")`: This method is used to access the year in the `Date` type object

Let's take a look at the following steps:

1. Type the following code in the Python script `demoDateSelection.py` in the current folder of your computer:

```
import android
app = android.Android()
app.dialogCreateDatePicker(2018,7,10)
app.dialogShow()
response = app.dialogGetResponse().result
app.dialogDismiss()
print ("You have selected following date: ")
print("Day: "+ str(response.get("day")))
print("Month: " + str(response.get("month")))
print("Year: " + str(response.get("year")))
```

2. Copy or push this Python script into the Android device by using the following command line:

```
C:\Users\Bintu\QPythonScripts>adb push demoDateSelection.py
/sdcard/qpython/bintuscripts
```

How it works...

An instance of the `Android` class is created by `name` app. By invoking the `dialogCreateDatePicker()` method, the date picker is displayed; the initial date being displayed is `10 July 2018`. You can scroll to any day, month, and year by selecting the **+** (plus) or **-** (negative) symbols. The **Date Picker** dialog is dismissed or made invisible when the user clicks the **OK** button. Using the `dialogGetResponse()` method, the date selected by the user is accessed and assigned to the response object. The day in the response object is accessed by invoking the `get()` method on it and passing the `day` parameter to it. Similarly, the month and year selected in the `response` object are accessed by invoking the `get()` method on them and passing the `month` and `year` parameters to them. That is, the day, month, and year are accessed from the `response` object and displayed on the screen after being converted into string type.

On running the application, you get a date picker with initial date being displayed as **10 July 2018**. You can scroll to any day, month, and year using the **+** and **-** symbols associated with each of them. Let's select **15 Oct 2018** and click the **OK** button (see the following screenshot on the left). You get the output showing the day, month, and year selected by the user, as shown in the following screenshot on the right:

Capturing images using a camera

In this recipe, you will learn to capture a picture on your device camera. You will learn to access the Camera app on your Android device and click the pictures.

How to do it...

In this recipe, we will be making use of the following method `cameraInteractiveCapturePicture()`, which activates the picture capturing app on an Android device and the clicked picture is saved to the SD card with the specified name.

Let's take a look at the following steps:

1. Type the following code in the Python script `demoCamera.py` in the current folder of your computer:

```
import android
app =
android.Android() app.cameraInteractiveCapturePicture("/sdcard/camer
aPic.jpg")
```

2. Copy or push this Python script into the Android device by using the following command line:

```
C:\Users\Bintu\QPythonScripts>adb push demoCamera.py
/sdcard/qpython/bintuscripts
```

How it works...

This recipe starts the picture capturing app on your Android device. That is, the Camera app on your device will be invoked enabling you to click the pictures if required.

An object called `app` is defined by invoking `Android()` method of the `android` module. The `cameraInteractiveCapturePicture()` method is invoked to start the camera and take a picture. The clicked picture will be stored in the specified path in the `sdcard` folder of your Android device with the `cameraPic.jpg` filename.

On running the application, the picture capturing app will automatically start, ready to take a picture. The screenshot on the left shows the picture that is visible through the Camera app. You focus the camera of your device on the object to be photographed and click the **Take picture** button. The **Take picture** button appears as a big filled circle. On clicking the **Take picture** button, the picture will be taken and you will be shown two options to select: right or wrong.

The right option if selected will save the taken picture and wrong option if selected will discard the picture as shown in the following screenshot:

Making an Android device speak a text input

In this recipe, we will see how an Android device generates sound from the supplied text. That is, the device will speak the specified text.

How to do it...

In this recipe, we will be making use of the `ttsSpeak()` method, which activates the speech synthesis application on an Android device and the device will generate sound for the supplied text.

Let's take a look at the following steps:

1. Type the following code in the Python script `demoTextToSpeach.py` in the current folder of your computer:

```
import androidapp = android.Android()
message = "Let us count from 1 to 10"
app.ttsSpeak(message)
for i in range(1,11):
    app.ttsSpeak(str(i))
```

2. Copy or push this Python script into the Android device by using the following command line:

```
C:\Users\Bintu\QPython\Scripts>adb push demoTextToSpeach.py
/sdcard/qpython/bintuscripts
```

How it works...

An object called `app` is created by invoking the `Android()` method of the `android` module. A message, `Let us count from 1 to 10` is passed to the `ttsSpeak()` method. The `ttsSpeak()` method will invoke the speech synthesis application in the phone, which generates the spoken version of the supplied text. So, you get to hear "let us count from 1 to 10". After that, a loop is run from integer value `1` to `10` and each value in the loop is sent to the `ttsSpeak()` method. Consequently, your mobile will speak the numbers from 1 to 10.

Creating a cross-platform Python script using Kivy

Kivy is a Python library that supports multitouch devices, including smartphones. You can create cross-platform Python applications using Kivy as Kivy runs on Android, iOS, Linux, and Windows. With Kivy, you can also access mobile APIs, like the Android API to use the camera of your phone, compass sensor, and so on.

Kivy is an open source, cross-platform that is written in Python and Cython. Because Kivy has several modules that are written in C, it requires Cython for its working. Cython is a compiler that gives you the power of Python as well as C programming. You can write C functions and use C libraries in Cython for writing efficient code.

Getting started

Let's create a very simple application that consists of a single button with the caption **Python On Android Device**. The Kivy application needs to be made in a separate folder and its main program has to be named main.py.

So, let's create a folder named `helloworld`. Write the following code and save it with the name `main.py` in the `helloworld` folder:

```
from kivy.app import Appfrom kivy.uix.button import Button
class demoAndroidApp(App):
    def build(self):
        return Button(text='Python On Android Device')
if __name__ in ('__main__', '__android__'):
    demoAndroidApp().run()
```

The `App` class is imported from the `kivy` library because this class includes the properties required to make a fully featured application. A class is made, named `demoAndroidApp`, which inherits the `App` class, so the `demoAndroidApp` class gets the right to access the methods and members of the `App` class. Thereafter, you check whether this Python script is an independent script to be run individually, or is supposed to be imported into another script. Being an independent script, the `run()` method is invoked to execute the application.

To run this Kivy application, you need to install Kivy and it requires several steps. Let's learn how to do it. But before that, let us understand one keyword `pip` that we will frequently come across.

The `pip` command is a tool for installing and managing Python packages. PIP already comes installed in the Linux platforms. Also, `pip` comes installed on Python version 3.4 and later. You give the following command line on your Command Prompt to know whether `pip` is installed on your PC:

```
C:\>pip --version
```

If `pip` is installed on your PC, you get the folder location where it is installed and will show its version number too. If you do not have P installed, you can download and install it from the `https://pypi.org/project/pip/` URL.

Now, let us move ahead and learn the steps to install Kivy.

How to do it...

1. Before you install Kivy, you need to install Cython first as Kivy needs Cython. The following statement installs Cython:

   `C:\helloworld>python -m pip install Cython`

   You may get the following output while installing Cython on your machine:

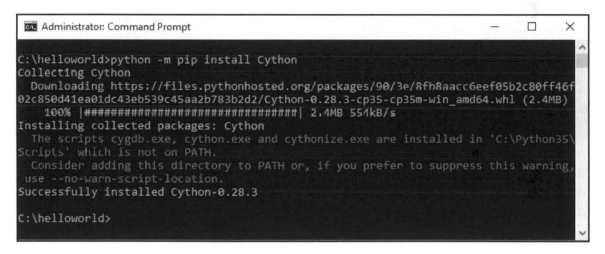

2. Once Cython is installed, you can go ahead and install Kivy by executing the following command line:

   `C:\helloworld>python -m pip install kivy`

While installing Kivy, you may get the following output on the screen:

3. You need to install Kivy dependencies, the modules that Kivy is dependent on. The following statement installs the Kivy dependencies:

```
C:\helloworld>pip install docutils pygments pypiwin32
kivy.deps.sdl2 kivy.deps.glew
```

On executing the preceding command, you may get the following output on the screen:

```
Requirement already satisfied: docutils in
c:usersBintuappdatalocalprogramspythonpython35-32libsite-packages
(0.14)
Requirement already satisfied: pygments in
c:usersBintuappdatalocalprogramspythonpython35-32libsite-packages
(2.2.0)
Collecting pypiwin32
Downloading
https://files.pythonhosted.org/packages/d0/1b/2f292bbd742e369a100c9
1faa0483172cd91a1a422a6692055ac920946c5/pypiwin32-223-py3-none-
any.whl
```

```
Collecting kivy.deps.sdl2
Downloading
https://files.pythonhosted.org/packages/d5/5a/1f8ca6e6e5343ffc4d145
fab0644e051cf52ee97bca9313307af0c8b5129/kivy.deps.sdl2-0.1.17-cp35-
cp35m-win32.whl (2.1MB)
100% |#############################| 2.1MB 369kB/s
Collecting kivy.deps.glew
Downloading
https://files.pythonhosted.org/packages/32/0f/16419ffd63c60b0c19761
4c430eab35360a94154ac1b846b3ee69f8c8061/pywin32-223-cp35-cp35m-
win32.whl (8.3MB)
100% |#############################| 8.3MB 310kB/s
Installing collected packages: pywin32, pypiwin32, kivy.deps.sdl2,
kivy.deps.glew
Successfully installed kivy.deps.glew-0.1.9 kivy.deps.sdl2-0.1.17
pypiwin32-223 pywin32-223
```

4. The Kivy platform needs OpenGL. So, you need to run the following command to support a graphics card and other graphics hardware:

```
C:\helloworld>pip install kivy.deps.angle && set
KIVY_GL_BACKEND=angle_sdl2
```

Now, Kivy is completely installed, along with its dependencies, and you are ready to run your Kivy application.

5. Run your application by running the following command line:

```
C: helloworld>python main.py
```

The application will execute, showing you a big button with the caption **Python On Android Device**, as shown in the following screenshot:

Packaging a Python Script into the Android APK using Buildozer

In this recipe, we will be learning to package a Python script into the Android APK file using Buildozer. Buildozer is a tool that packages mobile applications quite easily. Basically, it auto-creates a `buildozer.spec` file, which stores configuration and other settings of the application including its name, package, domain name, icon, and so on. It also automatically downloads the prerequisites, such as python-for-android, the Android SDK, NDK, and so on, and presents the Android APK file ready to distribute and install. Not only for Android; Buildozer makes the Python script run on iOS too. The focus of this recipe is to create a package for Android. First of all, we will be creating a Kivy Python script that consists of a button and a label. When the button is clicked, the application simply displays the message **Welcome to Python on Smartphones**.

Getting ready

This Kivy Python script is made in a folder. So, create a folder named `dispmessage()` and write the following code in a file named `main.py`:

```
from kivy.app import App
from kivy.uix.button import Button
from kivy.uix.label import Label
from kivy.uix.boxlayout import BoxLayout
class MessageApp(App):
    def build(self):
        layout = BoxLayout(orientation='horizontal')
        pushButton = Button(text='Click Me')
        pushButton.bind(on_press=self.dispMessage)
        self.labelMessage = Label(text="")
        layout.add_widget(pushButton)
        layout.add_widget(self.labelMessage)
        return layout
def dispMessage(self, event):
    self.labelMessage.text = "Welcome to Python on Smartphones"
    MessageApp().run()
```

The `App` class is imported from the `kivy` library because this class includes the properties required to make a fully featured application. Besides the `App` class, the `Button` class, the `Label` class, and the `BoxLayout` class are also imported into the application.

A `MessageApp` class is created, that inherits from the `App` class, so the `MessageApp` class gets the right to access methods and members of the `App` class. Thereafter, an object of the `Button` class is created by name, `pushButton`, and the button text supplied is `Click Me`. Also, a **Label** widget's instance is created, named `labelMessage`, with no text. The text for the **Label** widget will be supplied through the code. An object of `BoxLayout` is created called `layout` and its orientation specified as horizontal. The `pushButton` and `labelMessage` objects are added to the layout horizontally, beside each other. You also bind the `on_press` event of the `pushButton` object with the `dispMessage()` method, so that whenever the push button is pressed, the `dispMessage()` will be invoked. In the `dispMessage()` method, you set the text for the `labelMessage` object as `Welcome to Python on Smartphones`. Hence, whenever, the **Click Me** button is pressed, the `labelMessage` object will display the text **Welcome to Python on Smartphones**. The `run()` method is invoked at the end to execute the application.

To package this Python script into the Android APK, you need to install Buildozer and this requires several steps. Let's learn how to do it step by step.

How to do it...

Because the Buildozer tool runs on the Linux operating system and I am using a Windows operating system, we need to take the help of a virtual box to install Buildozer. Here are the steps:

1. First, install Oracle VM VirtualBox.
2. Once VirtualBox is loaded, click on the **New** button to create a new Virtual Machine.
3. Name the new Virtual Machine as `BuildozerAndroidVM`.

4. Set the type of this Virtual Machine as **Linux** and version as **Ubuntu (64 bit)**, as shown in the following screenshot:

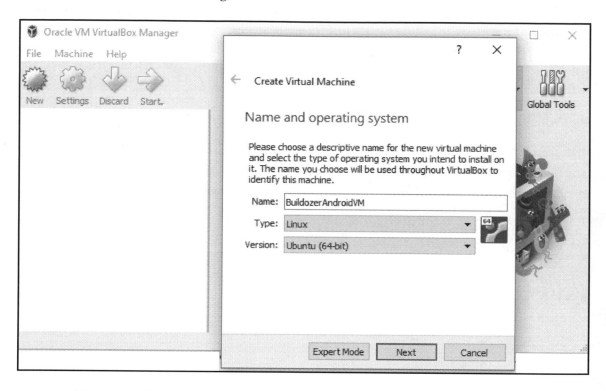

Kivy provides you a Kivy Buildozer VM that you can download from the `https:/ /kivy.org/#download` URL.

5. Click on the **Next** button, and you will be prompted to enter information for the virtual hard disk.

6. Select the **Use an existing virtual hard disk file** option, select the downloaded Kivy Virtual VM file, and then click on the **Create** button as shown in the following screenshot:

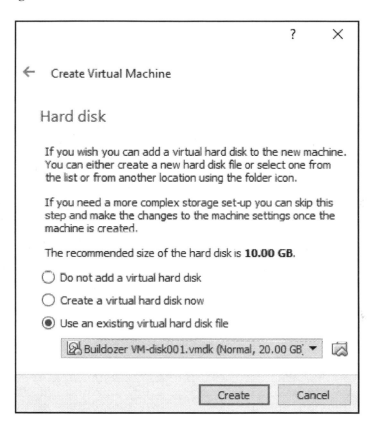

A virtual machine named `BuildozerAndroidVM` will be created.

7. Click on the **Start** icon at the top to run the virtual machine as shown in the following screenshot:

You will be asked to enter the password. The ID is `kivy`, and the password too is `kivy`.

8. Enter the password and click on the **Log In** button.
9. Once you are logged in, from the **Menu** at the top, select the **Terminal** option from the **Menu** option to open the Terminal window. By default, you will be in the `kivy` folder. Change directory to the `Downloads` folder.
10. In the **Downloads** folder, create a folder named `dispmessage()` and in that folder, create a file, `main.py`, with the code shown before.
11. Before packaging this Python script into the Android APK file, create a `buildozer.spec` file (see the following screenshot). The `buildozer.spec` file is automatically created by running the following command line in the `dispmessage` folder:

```
buildozer init
```

12. Recall that the `buildozer.spec` file is a configuration file that stores information such as the application's name, package name, domain name, icon, and other details. The `buildozer.spec` file contains certain default information. You can change the application's name, package, and other information as shown in the following screenshot:

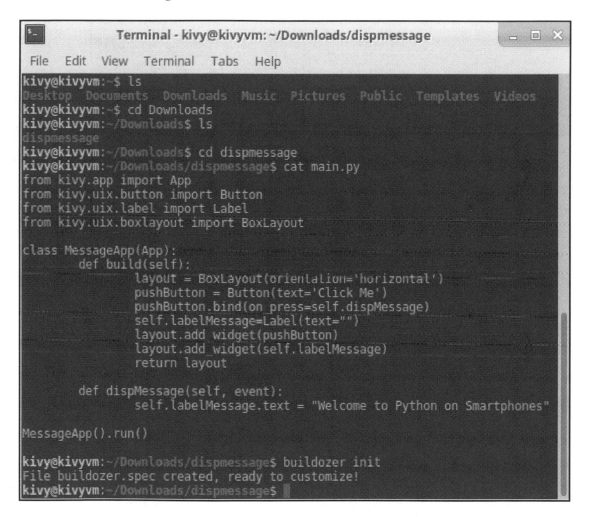

```
kivy@kivyvm:~$ ls
Desktop  Documents  Downloads  Music  Pictures  Public  Templates  Videos
kivy@kivyvm:~$ cd Downloads
kivy@kivyvm:~/Downloads$ ls
dispmessage
kivy@kivyvm:~/Downloads$ cd dispmessage
kivy@kivyvm:~/Downloads/dispmessage$ cat main.py
from kivy.app import App
from kivy.uix.button import Button
from kivy.uix.label import Label
from kivy.uix.boxlayout import BoxLayout

class MessageApp(App):
        def build(self):
                layout = BoxLayout(orientation='horizontal')
                pushButton = Button(text='Click Me')
                pushButton.bind(on_press=self.dispMessage)
                self.labelMessage=Label(text="")
                layout.add_widget(pushButton)
                layout.add_widget(self.labelMessage)
                return layout

        def dispMessage(self, event):
                self.labelMessage.text = "Welcome to Python on Smartphones"

MessageApp().run()

kivy@kivyvm:~/Downloads/dispmessage$ buildozer init
File buildozer.spec created, ready to customize!
kivy@kivyvm:~/Downloads/dispmessage$ 
```

13. To create Android's APK file, run the following command line:

```
buildozer Android debug
```

The preceding command line will download and install Android ANT, Android SDK, Android NDK, and other essential modules if they are missing, and finally packages the Python script into an APK file, which can be found in the `bin` folder that is automatically created (see the following screenshot):

14. Copy the APK file into any Android device, install it, and run it.

How it works

On running the Android application, you will find a push button, **Click Me**, on the left, as shown in the following screenshot. The label on the right does not show any text at the moment:

On clicking the push button, the label on the right shows the text **Welcome to Python on Smartphones**, as shown in the following screenshot:

Packaging Python script for iOS

In this recipe, we will be learning to package a Python script for iOS. iOS is a mobile operating system developed by Apple Inc for its devices, including the iPhone, iPad, and iPod Touch. To write, test and run this application, we will be requiring a Macintosh computer.

First of all, we will be creating a Kivy Python script that comprises a button and a label. When a button is clicked, the application simply displays the message **Welcome to Python on Smartphones**. This Kivy Python script is made in a folder. So, create a folder named `helloworld` and write the following code in a file named `main.py`:

```
from kivy.app import Appfrom kivy.uix.button import Button
from kivy.uix.label import Label
from kivy.uix.boxlayout import BoxLayout
class WelcomeApp(App):
    def build(self):
        layout = BoxLayout(orientation='horizontal')
        pushButton =  Button(text='Click Me')
        pushButton.bind(on_press=self.showMessage)
        self.labelMessage = Label(text="")
        layout.add_widget(pushButton)
        layout.add_widget(self.labelMessage)
        return layout
    def showMessage(self, event):
        self.labelMessage.text = "Python is compatible to Smartphones"
        WelcomeApp().run()
```

How to do it...

1. The first step is to install Xcode and related SDK on your computer. Give the following command line if the Xcode is not installed on your machine

   ```
   xcode-select -install
   ```

   You might be prompted to install command-line developer tools as shown in the folowing screenshot:

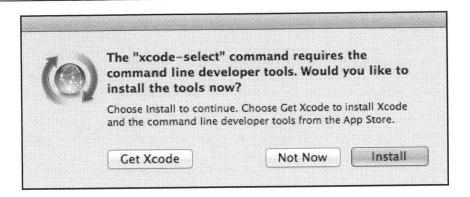

2. Click on the **Install** button to install the tools. Next, you need to install libraries for building. Give the following two command lines to install libraries:

```
brew install autoconf automake libtool pkg-config
```

On executing the preceding command line you get the output as shown in the following screenshot:

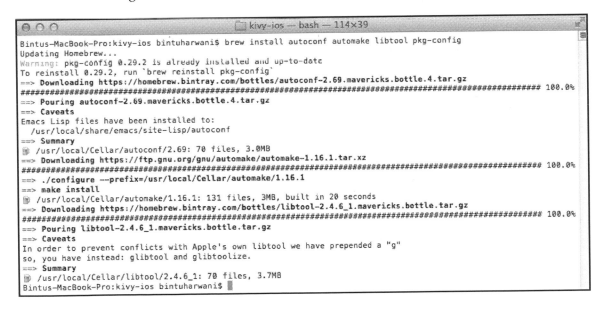

The following command is also required to install libraries:

```
brew link libtool
```

Because Kivy requires Cython, execute the following command line to install Cython:

```
sudo pip install Cython==0.28.3
```

While installing Cython, you get the output as shown in the following screenshot:

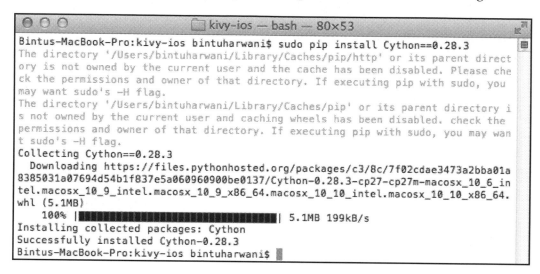

3. Next step is to download `kivy-ios` and install. To do so, execute the following command line:

```
$ git clone git://github.com/kivy/kivy-ios
```

A folder called `kivy-ios` will be created and `kivy-ios` files are downloaded and copied in it. You get the output as shown in the following screenshot:

4. Next step is to change directory to the `kivy-ios` folder and execute the `toolchain.py` file. The toolchain is used in compiling the necessary libraries for iOS to run our application. It is also very helpful in creating the Xcode project.

```
$ cd kivy-ios$ ./toolchain.py build kivy
```

5. Now, we can create an Xcode project. Execute the following command line specifying the location of our `helloworld` folder where `kivy` python script is written:

```
$ ./toolchain.py create ioskivyapp
/Users/bintuharwani/Desktop/helloworld
```

The preceding command line will create a folder `ioskivyapp-ios` and will create the Xcode project in that folder by name, `ioskivyapp.xcodeproj`. On executing the preceding command, you will get the output as shown in the following screenshot:

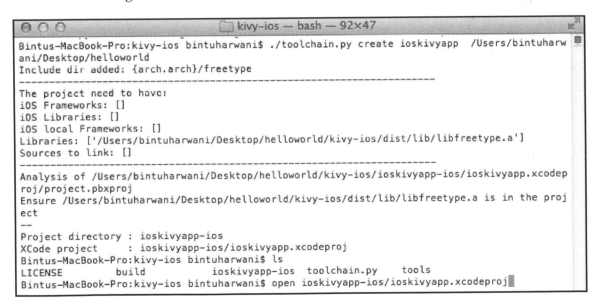

Following is the list of files that are created in the `ioskivyapp-ios` folder :

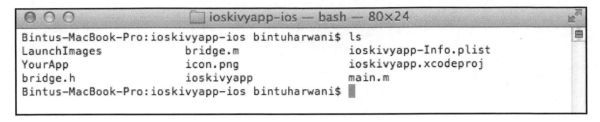

6. You can execute the Xcode project by running the following command line:

   open ioskivyapp.xcodeproj

   Xcode will open up as shown in the following screenshot:

7. You need to register as a developer in Apple developer center for running this Xcode project.

How it works...

For making a fully featured application, you need the App class which is imported from the kivy library. For creating interface elements like button, label, and so on and for arranging them, several more classes like, the Button class, Label class and BoxLayout too are imported in the application.

To access methods and members of the App class, a class is created by name WelcomeApp that inherits the App class. To create a button in the application, an object of the Button class is created by name, pushButton. The text for the button is set as Click Me. Also, a Label class's instance is created by name labelMessage without any default text. The text for the **Label** widget will be displayed through the code. An object of BoxLayout is created by name layout and its orientation specified as horizontal. The pushButton and labelMessage objects are added to the layout horizontally that is one besides the other. You also bind the on_press event of the pushButton object with the showMessage() method that is whenever the push button will be pressed, the showMessage() method will be invoked. In the showMessage() method, you set the text for the labelMessage object as, Python is compatible to Smartphones. Hence, whenever, the **Click Me** button is pressed, the labelMessage object will display the text, **Python is compatible to Smartphones**. The run() method is invoked at the end to execute the application.

Other Books You May Enjoy

If you enjoyed this book, you may be interested in these other books by Packt:

Computer Vision with OpenCV 3 and Qt5
: https://www.amazon.com/Computer-Vision-OpenCV-multithreaded-cross-platform/dp/
178847239X/ref=sr_1_1?ie=UTF8&qid=1532586055&sr=8-1&keywords=Computer+Vision+
with+OpenCV+3+and+Qt5&dpID=51Z4u1hLAzL&preST=_SX218_BO1,204,203,200_QL40
_&dpSrc=srch

Frank Kane

ISBN: 978-1-78728-074-8

- Learn how to clean your data and ready it for analysis
- Implement the popular clustering and regression methods in Python
- Train efficient machine learning models using decision trees and random forests
- Visualize the results of your analysis using Python's Matplotlib library
- Use Apache Spark's MLlib package to perform machine learning on large datasets

**Qt 5
Projects: https://www.amazon.com/Qt-Projects-cross-platform-applications-fr
amework/dp/1788293886/ref=sr_1_2_sspa?s=books&ie=UTF8&qid=1532586126
&sr=1-2-spons&keywords=Qt+5+Projects&psc=1**
Corey P. Schultz, Bob Perciaccante

ISBN: 978-1-78439-030-3

- Acquire the key skills of ethical hacking to perform penetration testing
- Learn how to perform network reconnaissance
- Discover vulnerabilities in hosts
- Attack vulnerabilities to take control of workstations and servers
- Understand password cracking to bypass security
- Learn how to hack into wireless networks
- Attack web and database servers to exfiltrate data
- Obfuscate your command and control connections to avoid firewall and IPS detection

Leave a review - let other readers know what you think

Please share your thoughts on this book with others by leaving a review on the site that you bought it from. If you purchased the book from Amazon, please leave us an honest review on this book's Amazon page. This is vital so that other potential readers can see and use your unbiased opinion to make purchasing decisions, we can understand what our customers think about our products, and our authors can see your feedback on the title that they have worked with Packt to create. It will only take a few minutes of your time, but is valuable to other potential customers, our authors, and Packt. Thank you!

Index

W

welcome message
  displaying 12, 404, 407

Label widget 12
Line Edit widget, using 13
Push Button widget 14

Made in the USA
Columbia, SC
19 August 2018